March 2013
Compliments of
Ryan

ITALIAN

ITALIAN

**The definitive professional guide to Italian ingredients and
cooking techniques, including 300 step-by-step recipes**

Kate Whiteman, Jeni Wright, Angela Boggiano

METRO BOOKS
New York

An Imprint of Sterling Publishing
387 Park Avenue South
New York, NY 10016

METRO BOOKS and the distinctive Metro Books logo are trademarks of Sterling Publishing Co., Inc.

© 2012 by Anness Publishing Ltd
Illustrations © 2012 by Anness Publishing Ltd

This 2003 edition published by Metro Books by arrangement with Anness Publishing Ltd

Publisher: Joanna Lorenz
Senior Editor: Linda Fraser
Designers: Siân Keogh, Patrick McLeavey and Ian Sandom
Photographers: William Adams-Lingwood, Amanda Heywood
and Janine Hosegood (cut-outs)
Home Economists: Carla Capalbo and Lucy McKelvie
Stylists: Carla Capalbo, Amanda Heywood and Marian Price

ISBN 978-0-7607-4950-0

For information about special sales, and premium and corporate purchases, please contact Sterling Special Sales
at 800-805-5489 or specialsales@sterlingpublishing.com.

Manufactured in Egypt

7 9 10 8 6

www.sterlingpublishing.com

Previously published as The Italian Cooking Encyclopedia

NOTES
Standard spoon and cup measures are level.
Large eggs are used unless otherwise stated.
Electric oven temperatures in this book are for conventional ovens. When using a fan oven, the temperature will probably need to be reduced by about 20–40°F. Since ovens vary, you should check with your manufacturer's instruction book for guidance.

Contents

Introduction

Italian cooking reflects the fact that the country was unified only in 1861. Until then, each region produced its own characteristic cuisine, relying exclusively on ingredients that could be gathered, cultivated or reared locally. Nowadays, of course, regional produce can be easily transported all over the country, but Italians still prefer to base their cooking on local ingredients, because they regard quality and freshness as more important than diversity and innovation. So the most flavorful sun–ripened tomatoes, eggplants and bell peppers are still found in the south, the freshest seafood is available along the coast, the finest hams come from the area where the pigs are raised, and so on. *La cucina italiana* remains distinctly regional; northern Italian cooking, for example, incorporates ingredients that are simply never found in the recipes of Sicily and Naples, and vice-versa. In the dairy-farming north, butter is used in place of the olive oil so prevalent in the south; bread and polenta are eaten instead of pasta. The only unifying feature is the insistence on high quality ingredients. Good food has always been essential to the Italian way of life. *La cucina italiana* is one of the oldest cooking cultures in the world, dating back to the Ancient Greeks and perhaps even earlier. The Romans adored food and

THIS ITALIAN BUTCHER'S SHOP (BELOW) NOT ONLY SELLS THE LOCAL *CINGHIALE* (WILD BOAR), BUT ALSO CURED MEATS, CHEESES AND OTHER ESSENTIAL COOKING INGREDIENTS.

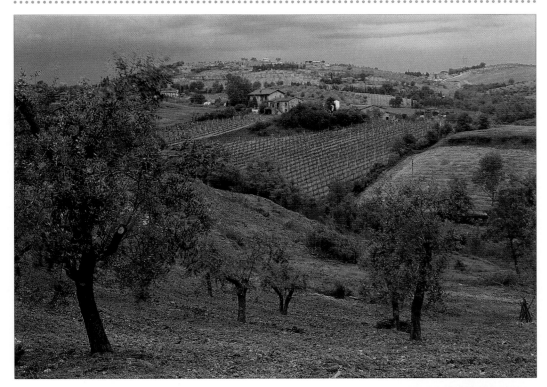

often ate and drank to excess; it was they who really laid the foundations of Italian and European cuisine. The early Romans were peasant farmers who ate only the simple, rustic foods they could produce, such as grain, cheeses and olives. For them, meat was an unheard-of luxury; animals were bred to work in the fields and were too precious to eat. Trading links with other parts of the world, however, encouraged Roman farmers to cultivate new vegetables and fruits and, of course, grapes, while their trade in salt and exotic spices enabled them to preserve and pickle all kinds of meat, game and fish. Food became a near-obsession and ever more elaborate dishes were devised to be served at the decadent and orgiastic banquets for which the Romans were famed. The decline and fall of the Roman Empire led inevitably to a deterioration in the quality of cooking and a return to simple, basic foods. For centuries, regional cuisine reverted to its original uncomplicated style. With the Renaissance, however, came great wealth and a new interest in elaborate food. Once again, rich families strove to outdo each other with lavish banquets where courses of rich, extravagant foods were served—truffles, song–birds, game, desserts dripping with honey and spices—all washed down with vast quantities of wine. The poor, of course, continued to subsist on the simple foods they

OLIVES (TOP) GROWING IN GROVES ALONGSIDE GRAPE VINES ON AN UMBRIAN HILLSIDE, AND A SELECTION OF CURED SAUSAGES AND AIR-DRIED PROSCIUTTO (ABOVE) ARE JUST TWO OF THE VAST ARRAY OF TRADITIONAL ITALIAN INGREDIENTS THAT ARE NOW EXPORTED AROUND THE WORLD.

ITALIAN COOKS INSIST ON HIGH-QUALITY
COOKING INGREDIENTS, AND EVEN LOCAL
DELICATESSENS (RIGHT) ARE PACKED FULL OF
FRESH AND PRESERVED INGREDIENTS AND
OTHER FOODS—FRUITY CAKES AND CRISP
COOKIES, SUCH AS *PANFORTE* AND *CANTUCCI*,
DRIED *FAGIOLI* (BEANS), FLAVORFUL OLIVE
OILS AND VINEGARS, *PROSCIUTTO CRUDO*
(CURED HAMS), TRADITIONAL CHEESES, SUCH
AS PARMIGIANO REGGIANO, PICKLES AND
PRESERVES, MARINATED OLIVES, CANNED
TOMATOES AND BOTTLED SAUCES.

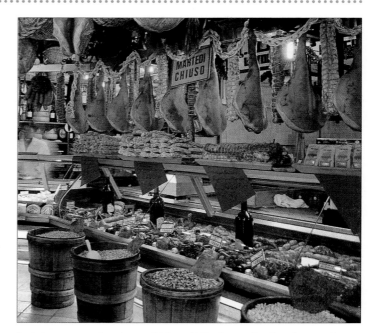

THE SUN-DRENCHED SOUTHERN REGIONS
OF ITALY PROVIDE ESSENTIAL PANTRY
INGREDIENTS, SUCH AS FULL-FLAVORED
GREEN AND BLACK OLIVES AND DELICIOUS
SUN-DRIED TOMATOES.

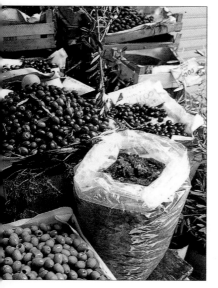

had always eaten, but the wealthier middle classes developed a taste for
fine foods and created their own bourgeois dishes. The finer features of
Italian cooking even reached the French, when Catherine de' Medici went
to Paris to marry the future Henri II, taking fifty of her own cooks with her.
They introduced new ingredients and cooking techniques to France and in
return learned the art of French cuisine. In those regions of Italy that
border France, you can still find reciprocal influences of French classical
cooking but, generally speaking, Italians do not like elaborately sauced
dishes, preferring to let the natural flavors of their raw ingredients speak
for themselves.

The essence of Italian cooking today is simplicity. The Italian way of
cooking fish is a good example of this. In coastal areas, freshly caught fish
is most often simply grilled over hot coals, then served with nothing more
than a splash of extra virgin olive oil, a wedge of lemon and freshly ground
black pepper. Recipes such as *carpaccio di tonno*, in which the fish is so
delicious raw that cooking seems unnecessary, and *branzino al forno*,
where the delicate flavor of fennel is used to complement rather than
obscure the fresh taste of the fish, are typically simple, as is *grigliata di
calamari*, squid grilled with chilies to reflect its robust character.

Italians learn to appreciate good food when they are young children,
and eating is one of the major pleasures of the day, no matter what the day
of the week or time of the year. Witness an Italian family gathered around
the Sunday lunch table in a local restaurant, and consider how the Italian

menu of *antipasto* followed by pasta, rice or gnocchi, then fish, meat and vegetables served in sequence is devised so that each can be savored separately—both the food and the occasion are to be enjoyed as long as possible. The first course, or *antipasto*, is a unique feature. In restaurants, this can be a vast array of different dishes, both hot and cold, from which diners can choose as few or as many as they wish. At home with the family, it is more likely to be a slice or two of *salame* or *prosciutto crudo* with fresh figs or melon, if these are in season. But no matter how humble or grand the setting or the occasion, the *antipasto* is always visually tempting. Colorful dishes such as *bruschetta casalinga* and *peperoni arrostiti con pesto*, are typical in this way.

The variety and diversity of the Italian ingredients available at supermarkets and delicatessens will surely inspire you to concoct any number of delicious meals, from a simple dish of pasta to a full-blown four-course dinner. A plate of *antipasto* followed by pasta or risotto flavored with seasonal ingredients, then simply-cooked meat or fish and finally a local cheese and fruit makes a veritable feast. You could prepare a different meal along these lines every day of the year and almost never repeat the same combination. If you visit Italy, avail yourself of the wonderful local ingredients to prepare a menu full of the flavors of the region. Every area has its own special delights that make cooking a real pleasure.

FRESH INGREDIENTS ARE HIGHLY PRIZED BY ITALIAN COOKS AND ARE OFTEN SOLD AT THE LOCAL OUTDOOR MARKETS: DOZENS OF *CARCIOFI* (ARTICHOKES) ARE TIED READY FOR TRANSPORT TO A LOCAL MARKET (BELOW), AND AN OUTDOOR STALL IS PILED HIGH WITH A TYPICALLY WIDE SELECTION OF HIGH-QUALITY FRESH HERBS AND SALAD GREENS, VEGETABLES AND FRUITS (BOTTOM).

The Ingredients

Italian cooks have traditionally relied on local ingredients—whatever could be gathered, cultivated or reared locally. Today, our supermarkets and delicatessens are full of these flavorful, good-quality ingredients. This comprehensive guide provides essential information on the huge range of Italian foods and shows you how to prepare and cook them.

Pasta

If there is one ingredient that sums up the essence of Italian cooking, it must surely be pasta, that wonderfully simple and nutritious staple that can be formed into an almost infinite variety of shapes and sizes. In Italy, pasta is an essential part of every full meal and does not constitute a meal on its own. Il primo, *as the pasta course is called, is eaten between the* antipasto (appetizer) *and* il secondo (the main course). *Sometimes small pasta shapes are served in soup as* pasta in brodo. *There are two basic types of pasta,* pastasciutta (dried) *and* pasta fresca (fresh).

Today pasta is almost always factory-made. The dough is made from hard durum wheat, which produces an elastic dough, ideal for shaping into literally hundreds of different forms, from long, thin spaghetti to elaborate spirals and frilly, bow-shaped *farfalle*. Basic pasta dough is made only from durum wheat and water,

although it is sometimes enriched with eggs (*pasta all'uovo*), which add an attractive yellow tinge, or colored and flavored with ingredients such as spinach (*pasta verde*) or squid ink (*pasta nera*). These traditional flavorings are more successful than modern gimmicky creations such as chocolate-flavored pasta. (Most Italians would throw up their hands in horror at this unauthentic folly.) Dried pasta has a nutty flavor and should always retain a firm texture when cooked. It is generally used for thinner-textured, more robust sauces.

Fresh pasta is usually made by hand, using superfine plain white flour enriched with eggs. Unlike dried pasta dough, it can be easily kneaded and is very malleable. Fresh pasta is often wrapped around a stuffing of meat, fish, vegetables or cheese to make ravioli, tortelli or cappelletti, or layered with sauce and meat or vegetables, as in lasagne.

Commercially made fresh pasta is made with durum wheat, water and eggs. The dough is harder than that used for handmade pasta, but it can be easily kneaded by machine. The flavor and texture of all fresh pasta is very delicate, so it is best suited to more creamy sauces.

HISTORY

The argument about the origins of pasta will probably rage on forever; the Chinese claim that they were the first to discover the art of noodle-making and that pasta was brought to Italy by Marco Polo. The Italians, of course, claim it as their own invention. Historians tell us that the Romans and probably even the Ancient Greeks used to eat pasta. Certainly the climate of southern Italy was ideally suited to growing durum wheat, so this theory is quite likely, but the popularity of pasta really spread in the fourteenth century, when bakeries in southern Italy started to sell pasta as an alternative to bread.

Then, as now, pasta was the traditional *primo* of the south, although in the poorest areas it constituted a complete meal. Its popularity filtered up to the north of Italy, and by the nineteenth century huge factories had been set up to mass-produce vast quantities of pasta, which quickly became an integral part of all Italian cooking.

BUYING AND STORING

Always buy dried pasta made from Italian durum wheat. Even after the package has been opened, dried pasta will keep for weeks in an airtight container. Handmade fresh pasta will keep only for a couple of days, but it can be successfully frozen. Machine-made fresh pasta is pasteurized and vacuum-packed, so it will keep in the refrigerator for up to two weeks and can be frozen for up to six months. When buying colored and flavored pasta, make sure that it has been made with natural ingredients.

COOKING PASTA

Allow about 3 oz pasta per serving as a first course. All pasta must be cooked in a large saucepan filled with plenty of salted, fast-boiling water.

For long shapes like spaghetti, drop one end of the pasta into the water and, as it softens, push it down gently until it bends in the middle and is completely immersed.

Cooking times vary according to the type, size and shape of the pasta, but, as a general rule, filled pasta takes about 12 minutes, dried pasta needs 8–10 minutes and fresh pasta only 2–3 minutes. All pasta should be cooked al dente, so that it is still resistant to the bite. Always test pasta for doneness just before you think it should be ready; it can easily overcook. To stop the cooking, take the pan off the heat and run a little cold water into it, then drain the pasta.

Preparing Fresh Pasta

1 Allow 1 egg to 3½ oz superfine plain flour. Sift the flour and a pinch of salt into a mound on a clean work surface and make a well. Break the eggs into the well and gradually work in the flour until completely combined.

2 Knead the dough with floured hands for at least 15 minutes, until it is very smooth, firm and elastic. (If you are short on time or energy, you can do this in a food processor.)

3 Chill the dough for 20 minutes, then roll it to the required thickness and cut it into your desired shape. (You can buy a specially shaped rolling-pin to make the squares for filled pasta.) A pasta machine will make this process much easier. Let the pasta dry for at least 1 hour before cooking it.

Pasta Varieties

Pasta shapes can be divided roughly into four categories: long strands and ribbons, flat, short and filled.

The best-known long variety is spaghetti, which comes in a thinner version, spaghettini, and the flatter *linguine*, which means "little tongues." *Bucatini* are thicker and hollow—perfect for trapping sauces in the cavity. Ribbon pasta is wider than the strands: Fettuccine, *trenette* and tagliatelle all fall into this category. Dried tagliatelle is usually sold folded into nests, which unravel during cooking. A mixture of white and green noodles is known as *paglia e fieno* (straw and hay). Pappardelle are the widest ribbon pasta; they are often served with *sugo alla lepre* (hare sauce). The thinnest pasta strands are vermicelli (little worms) and ultra-fine *capelli d'angelo* (angel's hair).

In Italy, flat fresh pasta is often called *maccheroni*, not to be confused with the short tubes with which we are familiar. Lasagne and cannelloni are larger flat rectangles, used for layering or rolling around a filling; dried cannelloni are already formed into wide tubes. Layered pasta dishes such as this are cooked *al forno* (baked). Fillings for fresh pasta squares include meat, pumpkin, artichokes, ricotta and spinach, seafood, chicken and rabbit. There are dozens of names for filled pasta, but the only difference lies in the shape and size. Ravioli are square, tortelli are usually round, while tortellini and *anolini* are ring-shaped.

As for pasta shapes, the list is almost endless and the names wonderfully descriptive. There are *maltagliati* (badly cut), *orecchiette* (little ears) and *cappellacci* (bad hats), while from the natural world come penne (quills), *conchiglie* (little shells), *farfalle* (butterflies) and *lumache* (snails).

When choosing the appropriate pasta shape for the sauce, there are no hard and fast rules, but long, thin pasta is best for olive-oil-based and delicate seafood sauces. Short pasta shapes with wide openings (such as *conchiglie* and penne) will trap meaty or spicy sauces, as will spirals and curls. Almost any pasta is suitable for tomato sauce.

Tonnarelli al nero
Flavored and colored with squid ink

Spinach fettuccine

Plain fettuccine

Bavette
Flavored with porcini *(ceps)*

Paglia e fieno

Long Pasta

*Fresh tomato,
spinach and plain
tagliatelle*

*Fresh
tagliatelle*
*Flavored
with squid
ink*

Fresh spaghetti

Fresh paglia e fieno

Fresh tagliolini

Long Pasta

Farro spaghetti

**Long, plain
spaghetti**
*In Italy, still sold in
the traditional blue
paper roll*

Spaghetti tricolori
*Mixed plain, spinach
and tomato spaghetti*

Long, plain spaghetti

Linguine

Plain tagliatelle

Tagliatelle
Flavored with
squid ink

Fettuccelle

Mushroom-flavored
tagliatelle

Linguinette

Spinach tagliatelle

Long Pasta

Bucatini

Lasagnette

Ziti

Vermicelli

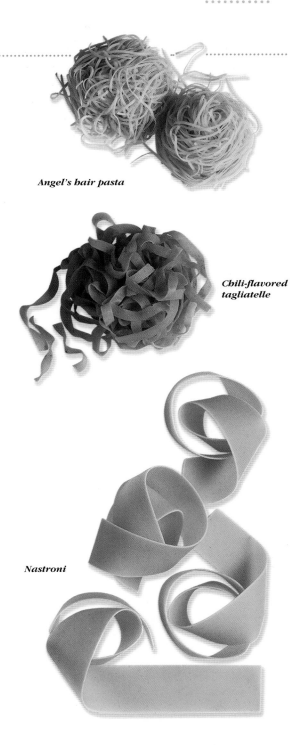

Angel's hair pasta

*Chili-flavored
tagliatelle*

Nastroni

Pappardelle

Short Pasta

Tomato and spinach orecchiette

Farfalle

Pipe rigate

Chili-flavored fusilli

Gigli del Gargano

Plain and spinach farfalle

Pepper- and spinach-flavored fusilli

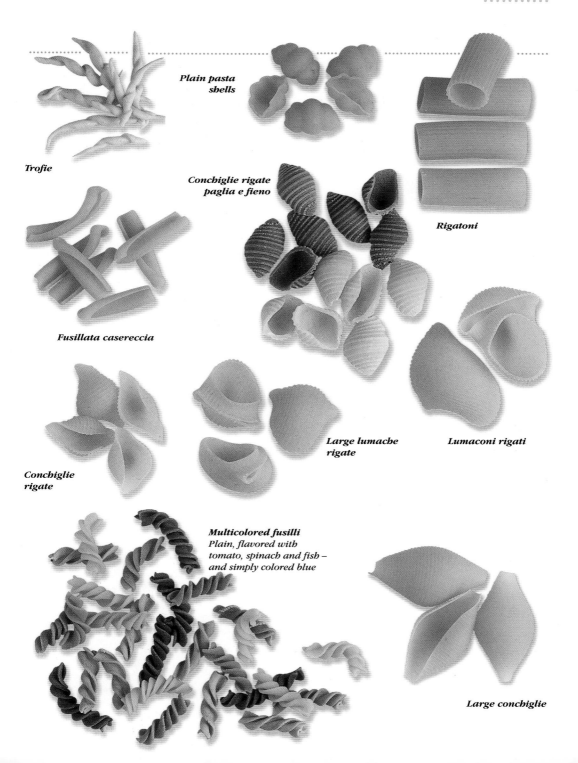

Trofie

Plain pasta
shells

Conchiglie rigate
paglia e fieno

Rigatoni

Fusillata casereccia

Large lumache
rigate

Lumaconi rigati

Conchiglie
rigate

Multicolored fusilli
Plain, flavored with
tomato, spinach and fish –
and simply colored blue

Large conchiglie

Short Pasta

Anellini

Ditalini rigati

Stellette

Pennette rigate

Anellini rigati

Fresh macheroni rigati

Gremiti

Penne

Penne rigate
Flavored with squid ink

Penne rigate
Flavored with chili

Penne rigate

Rotelle

Cappelletti tricolori

Penne rigate
Flavored with spinach

Flat Pasta

Lasagne

Spinach lasagne

Fresh lasagne

Tacconi

Filled Pasta

Tortellini

Dried cannelloni

Fresh ravioli

Fresh tortelli

Cappelletti
*Filled with sun-dried
tomatoes*

Cappelletti fantasia
*These multicolored
cappelletti are bought
ready for filling and
cooking*

**Fresh filled
cannelloni**

Tortelli
*Plain and flavored
with spinach*

Gnocchi

Gnocchi fall into a different category from other pasta, being more like small dumplings. They can be made with semolina (milled durum wheat), flour, potatoes or ricotta and spinach and may be shaped like elongated shells, ovals, cylinders or flat discs, or roughly shredded into *strozzapreti* (priest-stranglers); store-bought gnocchi are usually ridged ovals. However they are made, gnocchi should be extremely light and almost melt in the mouth.

CULINARY USES
Gnocchi can be served like any pasta, as a first course, in clear soup or occasionally as an accompaniment to the main course. Almost any pasta sauce is suitable for serving with gnocchi; they are particularly good with a creamy Gorgonzola sauce, or they can be served simply, drizzled with olive oil and dredged with freshly grated Parmesan.

BUYING AND STORING
Gnocchi are usually sold loose at better supermarkets. They are quite filling, so a small portion is enough for a first course; allow 4 oz per serving. They will keep in a ziplock bag in the refrigerator for two or three days. Homemade gnocchi dough will also keep for a couple of days before cooking.

COOKING GNOCCHI

With the exception of oven-baked gnocchi alla romana, all other types of gnocchi should be poached in a saucepan of lightly salted, barely simmering water.

Drop the gnocchi into the water in batches and cook for about 5 minutes; they will rise to the surface when they are done. Scoop out the cooked gnocchi with a slotted spoon and transfer to a plate: keep them warm while you cook the rest.

Fresh plain gnocchi

Fresh potato gnocchi

Gnocchi di patate

The best-known type of gnocchi are those from northern Italy made with potatoes and a little flour. To make 4 servings, peel 1¼ lb floury potatoes and boil until very tender. Drain and mash until smooth, then mix in 1 large egg and season with salt and pepper. Add 3½–4 oz flour, a little at a time, stirring well with a wooden spoon until you have a smooth, sticky dough that forms a ball on the spoon (you may not need all the flour). Turn out the dough onto a floured surface and knead for about 3 minutes, until soft and smooth. Cut the dough into 6 equal pieces and, with floured hands, roll these into sausage shapes about ¾ in in diameter. Slice the dough into ¾-in discs. Hold a fork in your left hand and press the discs against the tines just hard enough to make ridges, then flip them downward off the fork so that they curl up into elongated shell shapes. Poach them as above.

*Fresh spinach and
ricotta gnocchi*

*Fresh gnocchi made
with semolina*

Spinach and Parmesan gnocchi

Spinach and ricotta gnocchi

These attractive green gnocchi
originated in Tuscany where,
confusingly, they were known as
ravioli. For 4 servings, you need:
12 oz cooked spinach, well
   drained and finely chopped
1 container (8 oz) ricotta, mashed
   until smooth
2 eggs
1 cup freshly grated
   Parmesan
3 tbsp flour
5 tbsp butter, melted
salt, pepper and nutmeg

1 Put the spinach, ricotta and
seasoning in a saucepan and cook
gently, stirring continuously, for
5 minutes. Off the heat, beat in the
eggs, 3 tbsp of the Parmesan and
the flour. Chill the mixture for at
least 4 hours. Lightly shape into
small rounds and roll them in a
very little flour. Poach them as
described, left.

2 Preheat the oven to 350°F. Pour
a little melted butter into a serving
dish and put in the cooked
gnocchi. Sprinkle with some of
the remaining Parmesan and place
in the oven.

3 Add the rest of the gnocchi as
they are cooked and cover them
with melted butter and Parmesan.
Put the dish in the oven for
another 5 minutes before serving.

Gnocchi alla romana

These substantial gnocchi from
Lazio are made with semolina
milled from durum wheat.
For 4–6 servings, you need:
4 cups milk
8 oz semolina
1 cup freshly grated Parmesan
2 eggs, plus an extra yolk,
   lightly beaten
5 tbsp butter
salt, pepper and nutmeg

1 Bring the milk to a boil,
season with salt, pepper and
nutmeg, then add the semolina in
a steady stream, whisking for
about 15 minutes, until the
mixture is very thick. Off the heat,
stir in half the Parmesan and the
beaten eggs.

2 Pour the mixture into a greased
baking tray to a thickness of
about ½ in, or spread it over a
dampened work surface. Let
cool completely, then cut out
1¼ in discs with a plain or fluted
cookie cutter.

3 Preheat the oven to 350°F.
Layer the semolina discs in a
buttered baking dish, dotting each
layer with flakes of butter and a
sprinkling of grated Parmesan,
finishing with the cheese. Bake
the gnocchi for about 15 minutes,
until browned on top.

Rice, Grains & Beans

Almost as important as pasta in Italian cooking are rice, polenta and beans, which all appear as primi piatti *(first courses) in various guises. Like all basically agricultural countries, Italy relied heavily on these protein-rich ingredients when luxuries such as meat were in short supply, and a host of wholesome and delicious recipes were developed using these modest ingredients.*

Riso (Rice)

Italy produces more rice and a greater variety of rice than any other country in Europe. Most of it is grown in the Po Valley in Piedmont, where conditions are perfect for cultivating the short-grain Carnaroli, Arborio and *Vialone Nano* rice, which make the best risotto. Italian rice is classified by size, ranging from the shortest, roundest *ordinario* (used for puddings) to *semifino* (for soups and salads),

then *fino* and finally the longer grains of the finest risotto rice, *superfino*. *Superfino* rice swells to at least three times its original size during cooking, enabling it to absorb all the cooking liquid while still retaining its shape and firm *al dente* texture combined with a creamy smoothness.

HISTORY
The Saracens first introduced rice to Italy as long ago as the eleventh century (some believe even earlier), but it only became popular in the sixteenth century, when it began to be cultivated on a large scale in the Po Valley. Traditionally, rice has played a much greater part in the cooking of northern Italy than in the south, particularly in the Veneto, where the famous dish of *risi e bisi* (Venetian dialect for "rice and peas") opened the banquet served every year by the Doges to honor their patron Saint Mark.

Superfino Carnaroli rice (left and above)
This short-grained variety is one of the finest Italian rices. Its ability to absorb liquid and cook to a creamy smoothness while still retaining its shape makes it perfect for risotto

Arborio rice

Superfino Arborio rice

Vialone Nano rice

PREPARING RISOTTO

The most famous of all Italian rice dishes is risotto, which was invented in Milan in the sixteenth century. A good risotto can be made only with superfine rice. All risotti are basically prepared in the same way, although they can be flavored with an almost endless variety of ingredients. The rice is coated in butter or oil, then simmering stock is added, one ladleful at a time, and the rice is stirred over low heat until all the liquid has been completely absorbed.

Only then is more stock added, and the risotto is cooked in this way for about 20 minutes, until the rice is tender and creamy. The final touch is called mantecatura; *off the heat, a pat of butter or a couple of spoons of olive oil and some freshly grated Parmesan are stirred into the risotto to make it more creamy.*

Leftover risotto can be rolled into balls enclosing a piece of mozzarella, coated in fine bread crumbs and deep-fried to make supplì al telefono *or the Sicilian equivalent,* arancini.

Riso (Rice)

Rice is often used in Italian soups; it combines well with almost all vegetables and makes a substantial addition to minestrone. Baked rice dishes are also popular. Cooked rice is layered in a buttered ovenproof dish with meatballs, vegetables or poultry and cheese, then topped with bread crumbs and baked until the top is crispy and brown. The Italians never serve main dishes on a bed of rice, but prefer to serve plain boiled rice on its own with plenty of butter and cheese stirred in.

BUYING AND STORING
Buy only special superfine risotto rice for use in Italian cooking. Shorter grain *semifino* is best for soups, and *ordinario* for puddings (try *riso nero*, a rice pudding topped with melted chocolate). Once you have opened the package, reseal it tightly; you can then keep the rice in a dry place for several months.

Semifino rice

Brown semifino rice

Supplì al telefono

These rice croquettes contain mozzarella, which, when cooked, melts into strings that resemble "telephone wires." For 4 servings, you will need:
2 eggs, lightly beaten
8 oz cold, cooked risotto
6 oz prosciutto, cut into
 ½-in dice
4 oz mozzarella, cut into ½-in dice
fine dried bread crumbs,
 for coating
oil, for deep-frying
salt and freshly ground
 black pepper

1 Mix the eggs into the cold risotto and season to taste with plenty of salt and pepper.

2 Form the rice mixture into balls about the size of a small orange and make a hollow in each one. Fill this with a cube of ham and one of cheese, then roll each ball in your hand to enclose the ham and cheese completely, adding a little more rice if necessary.

3 Spread out the bread crumbs on a shallow tray or plate and roll the rice balls in the bread crumbs to coat them lightly.

4 Heat the oil in a deep, heavy pan and deep-fry the rice balls in batches for 3–5 minutes, until golden brown. Drain on paper towels and keep warm while you cook the remainder. Serve piping hot.

Farro

This is the Tuscan name for spelt, a hard brown wheat with pointed grains, which is rarely used in other parts of Italy. *Farro* is much harder than other wheat and therefore takes longer to process and cook, but it will grow even in poor soil. In Tuscany it is used to make *gran farro*, a delicious and nourishing soup, which is served as a first course instead of pasta.

CULINARY USES
Farro is used mainly as an ingredient for soups, but in remoter country areas of Italy it is sometimes used to make bread.

Farro

Ordinario rice

Gran farro

This Tuscan soup is often served as a first course instead of pasta. For 4 servings, you will need:
8 oz dried borlotti or
  cannellini beans,
  soaked overnight, then drained
1 onion, chopped
2 garlic cloves, chopped
4 oz finely chopped *pancetta*
4 sage leaves
a pinch of chopped fresh
  oregano
3 tbsp olive oil
8 oz chopped fresh tomatoes
5 oz prepared *farro*
salt, freshly ground black pepper
  and grated nutmeg

1 Cook the beans in fresh water until tender (reserve the cooking water). Put the beans through a vegetable mill. Gently cook the onion, garlic, *pancetta* and herbs in the olive oil until pale golden brown. Add the tomatoes, season with salt, pepper and nutmeg, then simmer for 10 minutes.

2 Add the bean purée and enough of the cooking water to make a thick soup. Stir in the *farro* and simmer for 45 minutes, adding more water if the soup becomes too thick. Serve with some extra virgin olive oil to trickle into it.

Polenta

For centuries, polenta has been a staple food of the north of Italy, particularly around Friuli and the Veneto. This grainy yellow flour is a type of cornmeal made from ground maize, which is cooked into a kind of porridge with a wide variety of uses. Polenta is sometimes branded according to the type of maize from which it is made. *Granturco* and *Fioretto* are the two most common types.

In Italy, polenta is available ground to various degrees of coarseness to suit different dishes, but there are two main types—coarse and fine. Coarse polenta has a more interesting texture but takes longer to cook.

HISTORY

The Romans made a savory porridge they called *puls* using *farro*, a kind of spelt, and the tradition continued in northern Italy, where gruels were prepared from local cereals such as buckwheat, barley and oats. Maize or corn was only introduced into Italy from the New World in the seventeenth century; soon it was being grown in all the northeastern regions, where cornmeal overtook all other types of grain in popularity, because it combined so well with the local dairy products. Traditionally, polenta was cooked in a *paiolo*, a special copper pot which hung in the fireplace; here, it was stirred for at least an hour, to be served for breakfast, lunch or dinner (sometimes all three).

CULINARY USES

Polenta is extraordinarily versatile and can be used for any number of recipes, ranging from rustic to highly sophisticated. Although it is most often served as a first course, it can also be used as a vegetable dish or main course and even made into cookies and cakes. Plain boiled polenta can be served on its own, or enriched with butter and cheese to make a very satisfying dish. It goes wonderfully well with all meats, sausages and game, helping to cut the richness and mop up the sauce. It can be cooled and cut into squares, then fried, grilled or baked and served with a topping or filling of mushrooms, meat, vegetables or cheese. Fried or grilled squares of polenta form the basis of *crostini,* which are served as an *antipasto*.

GRILLED OR FRIED POLENTA

Pour the cooked polenta onto a wooden board and spread it to a thickness of about 1 in. Let cool and harden, then cut into squares.

Fry in hot vegetable oil until crunchy and golden, then drain on paper towels or grill until golden brown on both sides.

To make a pasticciata *(layered baked dish) of polenta, cut the cold polenta horizontally into ¹/₂-in slices and layer it in a buttered baking dish with your chosen sauce, mushrooms, cheeses, etc. Bake for about 15 minutes, until the top is lightly browned.*

Fine polenta

BUYING AND STORING

It is possible to buy quick-cooking polenta, which can be prepared in only 5 minutes. However, if you can spare the 20 minutes or so that it takes to cook traditional polenta, it is best to buy this for its superior texture and flavor. Whether you choose coarse or fine meal is a matter of personal preference; for soft polenta or sweet dishes, fine-ground is better, while coarse-ground meal is better for frying. Once you have opened the bag, put the remaining polenta in an airtight container; it will keep for at least a month.

Coarse polenta

COOK'S TIP

Polenta can be cooked in water, stock or a mixture of water and milk. Whichever liquid you use, cook the polenta very slowly and steadily so that it does not become lumpy. Allow ¹/₂ cup polenta meal per person.

Recipe for Basic Polenta

To make a basic polenta for 4–6 people, bring 6 cups salted water or stock to a boil.

Gradually add 2 cups polenta in a steady stream, stirring continuously with a wooden spoon. Continue cooking, stirring constantly, until the polenta comes away from the sides of the saucepan. This will take 20–30 minutes (5 minutes for quick-cooking polenta).

One alternative, foolproof (though unauthentic) method is to put the polenta meal into a saucepan, add salt, then stir in the cold water, bring the mixture slowly to a boil and simmer gently for about 20 minutes, stirring occasionally.

Another is to cook the polenta on the stove for 5 minutes, then finish cooking it in the oven for an hour.

Pour the cooked polenta into a serving dish, season with pepper and stir in abundant quantities of butter and a strong-flavored cheese—Parmesan, Fontina, Bel Paese and Gorgonzola are all delicious with piping hot polenta.

Beans

Fagioli (beans)

Beans are another staple of Tuscan cooking; indeed, the Tuscans are sometimes nicknamed "the bean-eaters," although beans are eaten all over Italy. The most popular varieties include the pretty red-and-cream speckled borlotti, the small white cannellini (a kind of kidney bean), the larger *toscanelli* and *fagioli coll'occhio* (black-eyed beans). All these are eaten as hearty stews, with pasta and in soups, and cannellini are often served as a side dish simply anointed with extra virgin olive oil. *Ceci* (chickpeas) and *fave* (fava beans) are also popular.

HISTORY

Beans were a staple of the Roman and Greek diet, and several recipes for bean stews survive from that period. Many of the beans were brought to Italy from the Middle East, but some, such as *fave*, were indigenous and were used as ritual offerings to the dead at Roman funerals. Beans have always been a popular peasant food, but, during the Renaissance, Catherine de Medici attempted to refine Italian cuisine, and beans fell out of favor with the nobility and sophisticated urban dwellers. Thanks to their highly nutritious and economical qualities, however, beans and legumes have once again become an important element in Italian cooking.

CULINARY USES

Beans can be made into any number of nutritious soups and stews, or served as the basis of a substantial salad such as *tonno e fagioli* (tuna and beans). One popular Tuscan dish is *fagioli all'uccelletto* (beans cooked like little birds). Cooked cannellini beans are combined with chopped garlic, fresh sage leaves and tomatoes and simmered for about 15 minutes, until tender and fragrant. This dish is delicious served with coarse country sausages.

Dried red borlotti beans

Dried cannellini beans

Dried borlotti beans

Dried cannellini beans

BUYING AND STORING

During the summer and early autumn in Italy, you may find fresh beans, sometimes still in the pod. Borlotti beans come in an attractive speckled pod, cannellini in a slim yellowish pod. The pods represent a high proportion of the weight, so allow at least 12 oz per serving. Most beans, however, are sold dried. Try to buy these at a store with a quick turnover, or they may become shriveled and very hard. Prepackaged beans will have a "best before" date on the package. Loose beans will keep for several weeks in a cool, dry place, but are at their best soon after purchase.

If you don't have the time to prepare dried beans, canned varieties make an acceptable substitute, but you cannot control the texture and they are sometimes too mushy. They are, however, fine for recipes that call for puréed beans. Bear in mind, though, that they are an expensive alternative to dried beans.

Canned borlotti beans

Canned beans

COOKING BEANS

All dried beans should be soaked for about 8 hours in cold water or 4 hours in boiling water before cooking (this is not necessary for fresh beans). Discard the soaking water before cooking the beans.

Cook the beans in plenty of unsalted boiling water. Boil briskly for 10 minutes (this is essential to kill off the toxins, which may cause severe stomachaches), then simmer for 1–2 hours, depending on the size and freshness of the beans.

You can add whatever flavorings you wish to the cooking liquid, but never add salt or any acidic ingredients, such as tomatoes or vinegar, until the beans are cooked, or they will never become tender however long you cook them. To make a hearty stew, after the initial boiling, the beans can be mixed with pancetta, *garlic and herbs and cooked very slowly in the oven.*

Canned cannellini beans

Canned black-eyed peas

Beans

Fave (fava beans)

Fava beans are best eaten fresh from the fat green pod in late spring and early summer when they are very small and tender with a bittersweet flavor. They are particularly popular in the area around Rome, where they are eaten raw with prosciutto, salami or Pecorino. Later in the season, they should be cooked and skinned (hold the hot beans under cold running water; the skin will slip off quite easily). Cooked *fave* have a milder flavor than raw and are excellent with ham and *pancetta*. When buying fresh *fave* in the pod, allow about 12 oz per person; it may seem a lot, but the

pods themselves are comparatively heavy, so a lot goes only a little way. Dried *fave* should be soaked, and the skins removed before cooking. They are used for soups and stews and need about 45 minutes' cooking.

Fava beans
Dried fave *need to be soaked overnight before cooking*

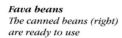

Fava beans
The canned beans (right) are ready to use

Chickpeas
These round golden legumes can be bought dried (above), or canned and ready to use (left)

Ceci (chickpeas)

These round golden legumes are shaped rather like hazelnuts and have a distinctive, nutty flavor. They are the oldest of all known legumes and, though not indigenous to Italy, have become very popular in Italian country cooking.

CULINARY USES

Chickpeas are cooked and used in the same way as beans and are an essential ingredient of *tuoni e lampi* (thunder and lightning), a sustaining dish of pasta and chickpeas served with tomato sauce and Parmesan. They can also be served cold, dressed with lemon juice, chopped fresh herbs and olive oil, to make a substantial salad.

COOK'S TIP
Chickpeas can be very hard, so it is best to soak them for at least 12 hours, then cook them in plenty of boiling water for up to 2 hours.

Lenticchie *(lentils)*

Although lentils grow in pods, they
are always sold podded and dried.
Italian lentils are the small brown
variety, which are grown in the area
around Umbria; they do not break
up during cooking and are often
mixed with small pasta shapes or rice
for a contrast of flavors and textures.
They make the perfect bed for
cooked sausage, such as zampone or
cotechino, and are delicious served
cold dressed with olive oil. The
ultimate Italian legume feast must
surely be *imbrecciata*, a nutritious
and sustaining soup from Umbria
made with chickpeas,
beans and lentils.

Brown lentils
*These are available in
different sizes, large
(below) and small
(above)*

COOK'S TIP
*Lentils will absorb the flavors
of whatever herbs they are
cooked with, so add any
appropriate herbs or spices to
the cooking liquid.*

Cheeses

Italy has an even greater variety of cheeses than France, ranging from fresh, mild creations, such as mozzarella, to aged, hard cheeses with a very mature flavor, such as Parmesan. All types of milk are used, including sheep's, goat's and buffalo's, which produces the best mozzarella, and some cheeses are made from a mixture of milks. As in France, the Italians eat their cheese after the main course, either accompanied or followed by fresh fruit. You will not, however, find the large selection of cheeses offered on a French menu; Italian restaurants serve only one or two types of cheese and rarely have a cheeseboard.

Many of the cheeses made in Italy are suitable for cooking. What would a pizza be without its delicious, stringy topping of melted mozzarella, or a pasta dish without a grating of fresh Parmesan?

HISTORY

Fresh, rindless cheeses were first introduced to Italy by the ancient Greeks, who taught the Etruscans their cheese-making skills. They in turn refined the craft, developing the first long-matured cheeses with hard rinds, which could last for many months and would travel well. Today's Parmesan and Pecorino cheeses are probably very similar to those produced 2,500 years ago.

In ancient days, the milk was left to curdle naturally before being made into cheese. The Romans discovered that rennet would speed up this process. Originally, they probably used rennet made from wild artichokes (this is still used in remoter parts of Italy), but later they began to use animal rennet. The process used to make farmhouse cheeses today has changed very little since Roman times.

Italian cheeses can be divided into four categories: hard, semi-soft, soft and fresh. Some cheeses have an enormously high fat content; others are low in fat and suitable for dieters. Many Italian cheeses are eaten at different stages of maturity; a cheese that has been matured for about a year is known as *vecchio*; after 18 months, it becomes *stravecchio* and tends to have a very powerful flavor. Almost all Italian cheeses can be eaten on their own and also used for cooking.

Hard Cheeses

Asiago

This cheese from the Veneto region develops different characteristics as it ages. The large round cheeses with reddish-brown rinds each weigh 22–55 lb. They are made from partially skimmed cow's milk and have a fat content of only 30 percent. Asiago starts life as a pale straw-colored dessert cheese, pitted with tiny holes, with a mild, almost bland flavor. After six months, the semi-matured cheese (*asiago da taglio*) develops a more piquant, saltier flavor, but can still be eaten on its own. Once it has matured for 12 to 18 months, the *stravecchio* cheese becomes grainy and sharp-tasting, resembling an inferior Grana Padano, and is really only suitable for grating and cooking.

Asiago

Parmesan

Parmesan is by far the best-known and most important of the Italian hard cheeses. There are two basic types—Parmigiano Reggiano and Grana Padano—but the former is infinitely superior.

PARMIGIANO REGGIANO

Parmigiano Reggiano can be made only in a strictly defined zone, which lies between Parma, Modena, Reggio-Emilia, Bologna and Mantua. The farmers of this area claim that the cheese has been made there for over 2,000 years; certainly it appears to be almost identical to that produced by the Etruscans and the methods of production have scarcely changed. The milk comes only from local cows, which graze on the area's rich pastureland.

It takes about 132 gallons of milk to make one 70–80 lb wheel of Parmigiano Reggiano. The milk is partially skimmed and some of the whey from the previous day's cheese-making is added, then the mixture is carefully heated before rennet is added to encourage curdling. (The rest of the whey is fed to local pigs destined to become prosciutto) The curds are poured into wheel-shaped forms and the cheese is then aged for a minimum of two years; a really fine Parmesan may be aged for up to seven years. During this time, it is nurtured like fine wine, until it becomes pale golden with a slightly granular flaky texture and a nutty, mildly salty flavor. Authentic Parmigiano Reggiano has the word "Reggiano" stamped on the rind.

GRANA PADANO

This cheese is similar to Parmigiano Reggiano, but is inferior in flavor and texture. Although it is made in the same way, the milk used comes from other regions and the cheese is matured for no more than 18 months, so it does not have the crumbly texture of Reggiano and its flavor is sharper and saltier. Its grainy texture (hence the name "grana") makes it fine for grating and it can be used for cooking in the same way as Reggiano.

CULINARY USES

A really good Parmigiano Reggiano can be eaten on its own, cut into chunks or slivers; it is delicious served with ripe pears and a good red wine. But Parmesan, both Reggiano and grana, really comes into its own when used for cooking. Unlike other cheeses, it does not become stringy or rubbery when exposed to heat, so it can be grated over any number of hot dishes, from pasta, polenta and risotto to minestrone, or layered with eggplant slices or truffles and baked in the oven. Slivers of fresh Parmesan are also excellent with asparagus or in a crisp salad. Don't throw away the rind from Parmesan; use it to add extra flavor to soups and vegetable stocks.

Parmigiano Reggiano

Grana Padano

BUYING AND STORING

If possible, buy Parmigiano Reggiano, which is easily recognizable by the imprint "Reggiano" in pinpricks on the rind. Whether you buy Reggiano or grana, always buy it in a piece cut from a whole wheel and grate it freshly when you need it; if possible, avoid pre-packed pieces and never buy ready-grated Parmesan, which is tasteless. Tightly wrapped in foil, a hunk of Parmesan will keep in the refrigerator for at least a month.

Hard Cheeses

Pecorino

All Italian cheeses made from sheep's milk are known as Pecorino, but they vary enormously in texture and flavor, from soft and mild to dry and strong. The best-known hard Pecorino cheeses are *romano* from Lazio and *sardo* from Sardinia; both are medium-fat, salty-tasting cheeses with a sharp flavor, which becomes sharper the longer the cheeses are matured. The milder *sardo* is usually aged for only a few weeks; the *romano* for up to 18 months. Hard Pecorino is a pale, creamy color with a firm granular texture with tiny holes like Parmesan. Sicilian *pecorino pepato* is studded with whole black peppercorns, which add a very piquant note.

Fresh Pecorino comes from Tuscany and is sometimes known as *caciotta*. This semi-hard cheese has a delicious mild, creamy flavor, but is not easy to find outside Italy, as it keeps for a very short time.

Pecorino pepato
This cheese is studded with whole black peppercorns

HISTORY

Pecorino romano is probably the oldest Italian cheese, dating back to Roman times. Then, as now, the cheeses were shaped and laid on *canestri* (rush mats, rather like hammocks) to be air-dried. Sicilian Pecorino is still called *canestro* after these rush mats.

Pecorino sardo
A milder version that is aged for only a few weeks

CULINARY USES

Hard Pecorino can be grated and used exactly like Parmesan. It has a more pungent flavor, which is well suited to spicy pasta dishes, such as *penne all'arrabbiata*, but it is too strong for more delicate dishes such as risotto or creamy chicken dishes. *Caciotta* can be cubed and marinated in olive oil for about 2 hours, then served with a grinding of black pepper to make a delicious and unusual *antipasto*.

BUYING AND STORING

Fresh or semi-hard Pecorino should be eaten the day you buy it, but well-matured Pecorino will keep in the refrigerator for several weeks wrapped tightly in foil.

Caciotta
A semi-hard cheese with a mild, creamy flavor

Provolone

A southern Italian cheese, straw-white in color with a smooth, supple texture and an oval or cylindrical shape, Provolone comes in many different sizes (some enormous) and can often be found hanging from the ceiling in Italian delicatessens. Provolone can be made from different types of milk and rennet; the strongest versions use goat rennet, which gives them a distinctively spicy flavor. In the south of Italy, buffalo milk is often used, and the cheeses are sometimes smoked to make *provolone affumicato*. The cheese is made by the *pasta filata* (layering) process, which gives it a smooth, silky texture; the curds are left to solidify, then they are cut into strips before being pressed together into a sausage shape. This is salted in brine for 6 to 12 hours, then the cheese is shaped and left to mature.

Variations on Provolone include *caciocavallo*, a smooth smoky cheese made from a mixture of cow's and goat's or sheep's milk, which develops a sharp flavor that becomes sharper as it matures. It gets its name from the way the oval cheeses are tied up in pairs and hung up to dry over a wooden pole, as though on horseback. (One false theory is that the cheese was originally made from mare's milk; another is that the cheeses were stamped with a horse, which is the symbol of Naples.) In Calabria, a version called *burrino* is made enclosing a lump of unsalted butter in the center of the cheese, so that when it is sliced, it resembles a hard-cooked egg.

Provolone burrino
There is a lump of butter buried in the center of this cheese, so that when cut it resembles a hard-cooked egg yolk

CULINARY USES

Milder fresh Provolone can be eaten on its own or in a sandwich with mortadella or ham. Once it becomes strong, it should only be used for cooking; its stringy texture when melted makes it ideal for pizzas and pasta dishes.

BUYING AND STORING

Enclosed in their wax rinds, Provolone and similar cheeses will keep for months. Once they have been opened, they should be eaten within a week. Provolone can be used for cooking in the same way as Parmigiano Reggiano.

Provolone affumicato

Provolone
Its stringy texture when melted makes this cheese particularly good for pizzas

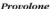

Provolone

Semi-hard Cheeses

Bel Paese

This cheese, poetically named "beautiful country," is a baby among Italian cheeses, having been created by the Galbani family from Lombardy early this century. Made from cow's milk, it contains over 50 percent fat, which makes it very creamy. It is the color of buttermilk, with a very mild flavor, and is wrapped in pale yellow wax to preserve its freshness. A whole Bel Paese weighs about 4¼ lb, but it is often sold pre-packaged in wedges.

CULINARY USES

Bel Paese can be eaten on its own; its mild creaminess makes it popular with almost everyone. It is also excellent for cooking, with a good melting quality, and can be used as a substitute for mozzarella, but because it is rather bland it will not add much flavor to a dish.

BUYING AND STORING

Like most cheeses, it is best to buy a wedge of Bel Paese cut from a whole cheese; pre-packaged pieces tend to be soggy and tasteless, although they are fine to use in cooking. Use freshly cut cheese as soon as possible after purchase, although wrapped in foil or plastic wrap it will keep in the refrigerator for two or three days.

Fontina

The only genuine Fontina comes from the Val d'Aosta in the Italian Alps, although there are plenty of poor imitations. True Fontina is made from the rich unpasteurized milk of Valdostana cows and has a fat content of 45 percent. Although today Fontina is produced on a large scale, the methods are strictly controlled and the cows are grazed only on alpine grass and herbs. Because it is matured for only about four months, the cheese has a mild, almost sweet, nutty flavor and a creamy texture, with tiny holes. Longer-matured Fontina develops a much fuller flavor and is best used for cooking. A whole Fontina weighs about 33–44 lb; the cheese is pale golden and the soft rind is orangey-brown. The rind of authentic Fontina has the words "Fontina dalla Val d'Aosta" inscribed in white writing.

HISTORY

Fontina has been made for at least 500 years; it is mentioned in the "dairy bible" *La Summa Lacticiniorum* of 1477. Its name probably comes from the mountain peak Fontin.

CULINARY USES

Fontina is delicious eaten on its own, and because it melts beautifully and does not become stringy, it can be used instead of mozzarella in a wide variety of dishes. It is also perfect for making a *fonduta*, the Italian equivalent of a Swiss cheese fondue.

Fontina
The sweet nutty flavor and creamy texture of this cheese makes it delicious to eat on its own

Bel Paese
This creamy, mild-flavored cheese can also be eaten on its own, and it is excellent for cooking, too

Soft Cheeses

Taleggio

A square creamy cheese from Lombardy with a fat content of almost 50 percent, Taleggio has a mild, salty-sweet flavor, which can become pungent if it is left to age for too long (it reaches maturity after only six weeks). The cheeses are dipped in brine for about 14 hours before maturing, which gives them a slightly salty tang. Each cheese with its soft edible rind weighs about 4¼ lb. If you intend to eat the rind, remove the paper from the top.

CULINARY USES

Taleggio is perfect eaten on its own as a cheese course. Like Fontina, it melts into a velvety smoothness when cooked and does not become stringy, so it can be used in any cooked dish that requires a good melting consistency.

BUYING AND STORING

Both Fontina and Taleggio should be eaten as soon as possible after purchase. If necessary, they can be tightly wrapped in waxed paper or plastic wrap and kept in the refrigerator for a day or two.

Stracchino

Stracchino is made from very creamy milk and matured for only about ten days, and never longer than two months. The smooth rindless cheese with a fat content of about 50 percent is reminiscent of Taleggio, but softer-textured and with a sweeter flavor. Robiola is a small, square Stracchino weighing about 3½ oz. Because these cheeses are so delicate, they are wrapped in plasticized paper to preserve their freshness.

HISTORY

The name Stracchino comes from the Lombardian dialect word meaning "tired." It does not reflect on the quality of the cheeses, but merely indicates that they were traditionally made in the winter months when the cows were tired from their long trek down from the mountains to their winter quarters on the plain of Lombardy. Some farmhouse-produced Stracchini are still made only in winter, but most are now produced all year round.

CULINARY USES

Stracchino should only be eaten as a dessert cheese; it is not suitable for cooking. On Christmas Eve in Lombardy, Robiola is served as a special delicacy with the spicy candied fruit relish, *mostarda di Cremona*.

Stracchino
A soft-textured cheese with a sweet flavor

Robiola
This is a small square stracchino and is always wrapped in paper to preserve its freshness

Taleggio
Perfect to eat on its own, Taleggio has a mild, sweet flavor

Soft Cheeses

Gorgonzola

The proper name for this famous blue-veined cheese is Stracchino Gorgonzola, because it is made from the curds of Stracchino. Originally made only in the town of Gorgonzola, the cheese is now produced all over Lombardy.

Gorgonzola is prepared by making alternate layers of hot and cold curds. The difference in temperature causes the layers to separate, leaving air pockets in which the mold (*penicillium glaucum*) will grow. The best Gorgonzola cheeses are left until the mold forms naturally, but more commonly copper wires are inserted into the cheese to encourage the growth. The cheeses are matured from three to five months; the longer the aging, the stronger the flavor.

Gorgonzola is a very creamy cheese, the color of buttermilk, with greenish-blue veining and a fat content of 48 percent. Its flavor can range from very mild (*dolce*) to extremely powerful (*piccante*). The best-known mild version outside Italy is Dolcelatte (sweet milk), which is exceptionally creamy and delicately flavored. Another version, *torta*, consists of Gorgonzola and mascarpone arranged in alternate layers like a cake.

HISTORY

Gorgonzola has been made in the village of the same name since the 1st century AD, when the cheeses were matured in the chilly caves of the Valsassina.

CULINARY USES

Although it is usually eaten as a cheese course, Gorgonzola is also used in cooking, particularly in creamy sauces for vegetables or pasta or as a filling for pancakes and ravioli. It is delicious stirred into soft polenta, or spread on deep-fried polenta *crostini*. Surprisingly, cooking diminishes the flavor of Gorgonzola, so that it does not dominate a delicate dish.

BUYING AND STORING

Supermarkets sell vacuum-packed portions of Gorgonzola, which are acceptable but not nearly as good as a wedge cut from a whole, foil-wrapped cheese. If you don't like a very strong flavor, be sure to buy *gorgonzola dolce* or Dolcelatte. Wrapped in plastic wrap, the cheese will keep for several days in the refrigerator.

Dolcelatte
An exceptionally creamy, delicately flavored Gorgonzola

Torta
This striped cheese consists of layers of Gorgonzola and mascarpone

Gorgonzola
The greenish-blue veining is typical of this classic cheese

Fresh Cheeses

Caprini

These little disc-shaped goat cheeses come from southern Italy. They have a pungent flavor, which becomes even stronger as the cheeses mature. Fresh Caprini do not travel well, so you will rarely find them outside Italy, but they are available bottled in olive oil flavored with herbs and chilies.

CULINARY USES

Fresh goat's cheeses can be fried and served warm with salad leaves as an appetizer, or crumbled over pizzas to make an unusual topping. Bottled Caprini should be drained and eaten as a cheese course. If you like a spicy kick, trickle on some of the oil from the jar, but beware— it will be very piquant.

Mascarpone

This delicately flavored triple cream cheese from Lombardy is too rich to be eaten on its own (it contains 90 percent fat), but can be used in much the same way as whipped cream and has a similar texture. Mascarpone is made from the cream of curdled cow's milk. It is mildly acidulated and adds a distinctive richness to risottos and creamy pasta sauces. It takes only 24 hours to produce, so it tastes very fresh, with a unique sweetness that makes it ideal for making desserts. A new lighter version called *fiorello light* is now being produced for the health-conscious. While it is useful for those on a diet, it is nothing like the real thing.

CULINARY USES

In Italy, mascarpone is used for savory dishes as well as desserts. It makes wonderfully creamy sauces for pasta and combines well with walnuts and artichokes. Mascarpone can also enhance the texture and flavor of risottos or a white bean soup. It is most commonly used in desserts, either served with fresh berries, or as a filling for pastries. It is an essential ingredient of tiramisù and can be churned into a rich, velvety ice cream.

BUYING AND STORING

Delicatessens in Italy serve fresh mascarpone by the *etto* (about 3¹⁄₂-oz) from large earthenware bowls, but outside Italy it is sold in 9 oz or 1¹⁄₄ lb plastic tubs. Although the flavor is not as good, pre-packaged cheese will keep for a week in the refrigerator; fresh mascarpone should be eaten immediately.

COOK'S TIP
To lighten the texture of mascarpone and make it less rich, fold in some beaten egg white.

Mascarpone (above and below)
A triple cream cheese that is too rich to eat on its own, but is ideal for dessert; it is an essential ingredient in tiramisù

Caprini
Rarely found fresh outside Italy, these cheeses are usually found bottled in flavored olive oil

Fresh Cheeses

Cow's milk mozzarella
Known as fior di latte—*"flower of the milk"*

Smoked mozzarella
This cheese has a very smooth texture, a rich golden color and an interesting smoky flavor

Mozzarella
The best is made from buffalo milk

Mozzarella

Italian cooking could hardly exist without mozzarella, the pure white, egg-shaped fresh cheese whose melting quality makes it perfect for so many dishes. The best mozzarella is made in the area around Naples, using water buffalo's milk. It has a moist, springy texture and a deliciously milky flavor. The cheeses are made by the *pasta filata* (layering) method, where the curds are cut into strips, then covered with boiling water. As they rise to the surface, they are torn into shreds and scrunched into egg-shaped balls each weighing about 7 oz. These are placed in light brine for 12 hours, then packed in their own whey inside a paper or plastic wrapping to keep them fresh.

Other types of mozzarella include a cow's milk version called *fior di latte* (flower of the milk) and tiny balls of cheese called *bocconcini* (little mouthfuls). Sometimes, the cheese is wound into braids called *trecce*. All these are fresh cheeses, but mozzarella can also be smoked, which gives it a golden-brown color and an interesting flavor. You will also find in supermarkets a pale yellow semi-hard mozzarella, which is sometimes sold ready-grated. This is the type used in cheap pizzas; it resembles mozzarella only in name and should be avoided.

HISTORY

No one is quite sure when water buffaloes were brought to Italy from India. They may have been introduced by the Greeks or the early Christians; certainly by the sixteenth century they had become a feature of southern Italian agricultural life. At this time, farmers began to use the buffalo milk to make mozzarella. Its popularity soon spread to the northern regions, where cheese-makers started to produce inferior versions made from cow's milk.

CULINARY USES

Fresh mozzarella is delicious served in an *insalata tricolore*, a salad in the colors of Italy, with white mozzarella, red tomatoes and fresh green basil. Smoked mozzarella is good in sandwiches or as part of an *antipasto*. When cooked, mozzarella becomes uniquely stringy, so it is perfect for topping pizzas or filling *mozzarella in carrozza* (mozzarella in a carriage), sandwiches dipped in beaten egg and deep-fried. A favorite Roman dish is *suppli al telefono*: mozzarella wrapped inside balls of cooked rice and fried until it melts to resemble telephone wires.

BUYING AND STORING

Cow's milk mozzarella is perfectly adequate for cooking, but for a really fine cheese buy *mozzarella di bufala*. Unopened, mozzarella will keep in the refrigerator for several days, but once the wrapping has been pierced it should be eaten as soon as possible. Opened mozzarella can be kept for a brief time in a covered bowl containing the whey from the bag or, failing that, skim milk or lightly salted water.

Mozzarella bocconcini
The name means "little mouthfuls"

Ricotta
Widely used in Italian cooking, ricotta can be combined with spinach for a ravioli filling, or used in desserts, such as cheesecake

Ricotta salata
This hard, salted version of the cheese has a compact, flaky texture and can be used as a substitute for Parmesan or Pecorino

Ricotta

Ricotta derives its name (literally "recooked") from the process of reheating the leftover whey from hard cheeses and adding a little fresh milk to make a soft white curd cheese with a rather solid yet granular consistency and a fat content of only about 20 percent. The freshly made cheeses are traditionally put into baskets to drain and take their hemispherical shape and markings from these *cestelli* (little baskets).

Commercially produced ricotta is made from cow's milk, but in rural areas sheep's or goat's milk is sometimes used.

Ricotta salata is a hard, salted version of the cheese, made from the whey of Pecorino. It has a compact, flaky texture and looks rather like a hard Pecorino.

CULINARY USES

Ricotta is widely used in Italian cooking for both savory and sweet dishes. It has an excellent texture but very little intrinsic flavor, so it makes a perfect vehicle for seasonings such as black pepper and nutmeg or chopped fresh herbs. In its best-known form, it is puréed with cooked spinach to make a classic filling for ravioli, cannelloni or lasagne, or delicious light gnocchi.

It is often used in desserts, such as baked cheesecakes, or it can be sweetened and served with fruit.

Hard *ricotta salata* can be grated and used as a lower-fat substitute for Parmesan or Pecorino.

BUYING AND STORING

Fresh ricotta should always be eaten the day it is bought, as it quickly develops a sour taste. Most supermarkets sell a pre-packaged version of the cheese, which stays fresh longer.

Ricotta salata is sometimes sold in pre-packaged wedges, but for a good flavor and texture you should buy it freshly cut from a whole cheese. Tightly wrapped in foil, it will keep in the refrigerator for up to a month.

Cured Meats & Sausages

Every region of Italy has its own special cured meats and sausages, each differing as widely as the regions themselves. Prosciutto crudo *and* salame *appear in every guise and often constitute an* antipasto *(appetizer) on their own.*

HISTORY

Italy was traditionally an agricultural country, so almost every rural family kept a pig and cured every part of it, from snout to tail, to provide food for the family throughout the year. In any Italian larder, a range of home-cured hams, sausages and bacon would be found hanging from the ceiling. Nowadays hundreds of different types of hams, cured meats and sausages are commercially produced, many still using the old artisanal methods. Wherever you travel in Italy, you will find regional variations on the same theme.

Most of these cured meats are served as an *antipasto* before a meal. A Tuscan *antipasto* will consist of a selection of thinly sliced *affettati* (sliced ham and *salame*), and it is sometimes served with pickled vegetables, which are designed to whet the appetite.

Prosciutto

Italy is famous for its *prosciutto crudo*, salted and air-dried ham that requires no cooking. The most famous of these hams, *prosciutto di Parma*, comes from the area around Parma, where Parmesan cheese is also made. The pigs in this region are fed partly on the whey from the cheese-making process, which makes their flesh very mild and sweet. Because they are always reared and kept in sheds and never allowed to roam outdoors, they tend to be rather fatty. Parma hams are made from the pig's hindquarters, which are lightly salted and air-dried for at least one year (and sometimes up to two). The zone of production of Parma ham is restricted by law to the area between the Taro and Baganza rivers, where the air and humidity levels are ideal for drying and curing the hams. In fact, every year thousands of ready-salted hams are sent here from neighboring regions to be dried and cured in the unique air around Parma.

Prosciutto di Parma
The most famous Italian ham comes from the area around Parma, where Parmesan is also made

Prosciutto cotto

Italy also produces a range of cooked hams, usually boiled. They can be flavored with all sorts of herbs and spices. Cooked ham is sometimes served as an *antipasto* together with raw ham, but it is more often eaten in sandwiches and snacks.

San Daniele

Some people regard these hams from the Friuli region as superior even to Parma ham. San Daniele pigs are kept outside, so their flesh is leaner, and their diet of acorns gives it a distinctive flavor. San Daniele is produced in much smaller quantities than Parma ham, which makes it even more expensive.

Prosciutto cotto
*This cooked ham is sometimes
served with sliced cured hams as
an* antipasto

CULINARY USES

Wafer-thin slices of *prosciutto crudo* are delicious served with melon or fresh figs or, when these are out of season, with little cubes of unsalted butter. If you serve bread with this ham, that too should be unsalted to counterbalance the salty-sweetness of the ham. *Prosciutto crudo* can be rolled up with thin slices of veal and sage leaves and pan-fried in butter and white wine or Marsala to make *saltimbocca alla romana*, finely chopped and added to risotti and pasta sauces, or used as a filling for ravioli.

BUYING AND STORING

The best part of the ham comes from the center. Avoid buying the end pieces, which are very salty and rather chewy. Because *prosciutto crudo* should be very thinly sliced, buy only what you need at any one time or it may dry out. Ideally you should eat it on the day it is bought, although it will keep in the refrigerator for up to three days.

San Daniele
*This expensive cured ham
is considered by some to be
even finer than Parma ham*

Cured Meats

Pancetta and Lardo

Pancetta resembles unsmoked bacon, except that it is not sold sliced, but rolled up into a sausage shape. It is made from pork belly, which is cured in salt and spices to give it a mild flavor. *Lardo* is very similar (but flat) and less readily available.

CULINARY USES

Pancetta can be eaten raw as an *antipasto* (although it is very fatty), but it is usually cut into strips and cooked like bacon. It is an essential ingredient for *spaghetti alla carbonara*.

Pancetta
These round rolled slices of cured pork belly are the Italian equivalent of unsmoked bacon

Smoked pancetta
The smoked version of pancetta *is sold in thin strips rather than being rolled*

Speck

This fatty bacon is made from pork belly, which is smoke-cured over beechwood with herbs and spices, then air-dried. Sometimes it is covered with peppercorns or dried herbs, which add a distinctive flavor. It comes from the Tyrol, near the Swiss border, which explains its German-sounding name.

CULINARY USES

Speck is too fatty to be eaten raw, but it is used to add flavor to soups, stews and sauces. It is excellent cooked with fresh peas or lentils.

BUYING AND STORING

Italian bacon is sold by sections, not sliced. Wrapped in plastic wrap, *pancetta*, *lardo* and *speck* will keep in the refrigerator for up to one month.

Speck
A fatty ham, smoke-cured over beechwood with herbs and spices, then air-dried

Lardo
An extremely fatty Italian bacon that is always used for cooking

Cured Meats

Bresaola

This cured raw beef is a specialty of Valtellina in Lombardy, but it is eaten and enjoyed all over Italy. It can be made from any cut of beef, but prime fillet produces the best bresaola. It is first cured in salt, then air-dried for many months before being pressed to produce an intensely dark red meat, which resembles *prosciutto crudo* in flavor, but is more delicate and less salty. Like *prosciutto crudo*, it is always sliced wafer-thin and served in small quantities, so you don't need to buy very much. Each bresaola weighs 4¼–6¼ lb, depending on the size of the original cut of beef.

CULINARY USES

Bresaola is often served as an *antipasto*, sliced very thinly and simply dressed with a drizzle of extra virgin olive oil and a sprinkling of fresh lemon juice. In Lombardy, bresaola is sometimes wrapped around a filling of soft goat cheese and then rolled up like cannelloni.

BUYING AND STORING

Only buy bresaola made from beef fillet. You can tell the type from the shape; that made from fillet is long with rounded edges, like the original cut of beef, while the cheaper bresaola made from other leg cuts is pressed into an oblong shape. Use it as soon as possible after slicing, preferably the same day, or it will dry out and develop an unpleasantly sharp flavor.

Bresaola
The delicate flavor of this salt-cured beef makes it perfect to serve, thinly sliced, as an antipasto

Sausages

Italy boasts almost as many different sausages as there are towns. Practically all are made with pork, although venison and wild boar sausages are popular in country areas. Most sausages and salami are factory-produced today, but many towns in Italy still have *salumerie* (sausage shops) selling homemade sausages flavored with local produce, such as wild mushrooms or herbs and spices. The most famous sausage-producing town is Bologna. Fresh sausages are made from coarsely chopped pork and contain a high proportion of fat for extra flavor. They are usually sold in links, tied together with string. Most Italian sausages, however, are cured and ready to eat.

Luganega

A specialty of northern Italy, luganega is a mild, spiced country sausage made from pork, which often contains Parmesan cheese. Sometimes known as *salsiccia a metro*, because it is sold in a long continuous rope, coiled up like a snake, and is sold by the foot or whatever length you require. It can be grilled or pan-fried with white wine and is often served on a bed of lentils or mashed potatoes. Luganega can also be cut into short lengths and stirred into a hearty risotto.

Cotechino

A large fresh pork sausage weighing about 2¹/₄ lb, which has been lightly spiced and salted for only a few days. Cotechino is a specialty of Emilia Romagna, Lombardy and the Veneto. It takes its name from *coteca,* meaning "skin."

COOKING COTECHINO

Cotechino is boiled and served hot, often as part of a bollito misto *(mixed boiled meats). Pierce the skin in several places and place the sausage in a large saucepan. Cover with cold water and bring slowly to a boil, then simmer slowly for 2–3 hours.*

Slice the cotechino thickly and serve on a bed of cooked lentils, mashed potatoes or cannellini beans.

Luganega
This mildly spiced sausage, which is coiled up like a snake, is sold by the foot, or whatever length you require

Sausages

Coppa

This salted and dried
sausage is made from neck
or shoulder of pork, and
the casing is made from
natural skin. *Coppa* has a
roughly rectangular shape
and a rich deep red color. It
comes from Lombardy and Emilia
Romagna, although, confusingly, in
Rome you will find a *coppa* that is a
sort of pig's head brawn (this variety
is never exported).

Zampone

This speciality sausage from Modena
is a pig's leg stuffed with minced
pork shoulder and other cuts,
including some skin. The stuffing has
a creamy texture and the skin of the
leg encloses it to retain its original
shape, complete with feet. Each
zampone weighs up to 4¼ lb.

Coppa
*Roughly rectangular in shape,
this sausage has a rich, deep
red color*

COOKING ZAMPONE

*A raw zampone needs to be
boiled for 2–3 hours, depending
on the size, although some
vacuum-packed varieties are
already partially-cooked and
need only to be heated through.
For a fresh zampone, make a
couple of slits in the skin and
cook in the same way as
cotechino. Zampone is
traditionally sliced into rings
and served with lentils or
mashed potatoes. A bollito misto
often contains a zampone.*

Zampone
*A partially-cooked zampone needs
only to be heated through*

Mortadella

The most famous of all the sausages from Bologna, mortadella is also the largest, often having a diameter of up to 18 in. Today it is cooked in hot-air ovens to a core temperature of 140°F, which means that it will keep for several weeks. It is considered to be the finest Italian pork sausage, with its wonderfully smooth texture, although it has a rather bland flavor. Apart from its huge size, mortadella is distinctive for its delicate, pale pink color studded with cubes of creamy white fat and sometimes pale green pistachios. It is the original bologna.

BUYING

Authentic Bolognese mortadella is made only from pure pork, but cheaper varieties may contain all sorts of other ingredients, such as beef, tripe, pig's head, soy flour and artificial colorings.

Beware of mortadella that looks too violently pink and, if you are buying it sliced and pre-packaged, check the ingredients on the package before you buy.

CULINARY USES

Mortadella is usually thinly sliced and eaten cold, either in a sandwich or as part of a plate of assorted cold meats as an *antipasto*. It can also be cubed and stirred into risotto or pasta sauces just before the end of cooking, or finely chopped to make an excellent stuffing for poultry or filled pasta.

Mortadella
Considered to be the finest Italian cooked sausage, mortadella has a wonderfully smooth texture, but a rather bland flavor. It is studded with cubes of creamy fat, and often has pale green pistachios peppered through the meat

Salame

Salame

There are dozens of types of *salame*, whose texture and flavor reflect the character and traditions of the different regions of Italy. Essentially, all *salami* are made from pure pork, but the finished product varies according to the kind of meat used, the proportion of lean meat to fat, how finely it is minced, the seasonings and the period of drying and seasoning.

Salame di Felino

This soft, coarse-cut sausage comes from Felino near Parma and is regarded as one of the finest Italian *salami*. It has a very high proportion of lean pork to fat

and is flavored with peppercorns, a small amount of garlic and the local white wine. Because it is only very lightly cured, it has a very delicate flavor but does not keep well. You may find it at good Italian delicatessens, where it is easily recognizable by its uneven truncheon shape, which makes it look handmade. Like its neighbor, Parma ham, *salame di Felino* is very expensive, but well worth the cost.

Salame fiorentino

This large, coarse-cut pork sausage from Tuscany is often flavored with fennel seeds and pepper, when it is known as *finocchiona*. The fennel gives it a very distinctive flavor.

Salame di Felino
One of the finest Italian salami—*this lightly cured sausage is flavored with peppercorns, garlic and white wine*

Salame fiorentino
This coarse-cut pork sausage from Tuscany is often flavored with fennel seeds and pepper

Salame milano

Probably the most commonly found of all *salami*, this Milanese sausage is made from equal quantities of finely minced pork, fat and beef, seasoned with pepper, garlic and white wine. It is deep red in color and speckled with grains of fat resembling rice. Also known as *crespone*, it is mass-produced and regarded as inferior to most other *salami*. There is also a small whole *salame milanese*, weighing about 1¼ lb, called *cacciatoro*, which is cured and matured for a much shorter time and has a more delicate flavor and softer texture.

Salame sardo

This fiery red *salame* from Sardinia is a rustic sausage flavored with red pepper. A similar sausage is *salame napoletano* from Naples, which uses a mixture of black and red pepper for a powerful kick.

Salame ungherese

Despite its name, this *salame* is manufactured in Italy, using a Hungarian recipe. It is made from very finely minced pure pork or pork and beef, and flavored with paprika, pepper, garlic and white wine. The fat is evenly spread throughout the sausage, giving it a mottled appearance.

BUYING AND STORING
With the exception of *salame di Felino*, almost all *salami* can be bought ready-sliced and vacuum-packed, but taste much better if they are freshly cut from a whole *salame*. A good delicatessen will slice the *salame* to the thickness you require. Ideally, it should be eaten the same day, but it will keep for three or four days in the refrigerator.

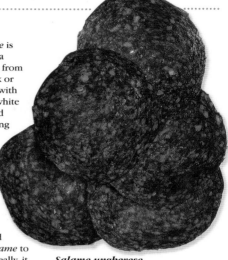

Salame ungherese
Made in Italy from a Hungarian recipe

Salame sardo
A fiery salame *flavored with red pepper*

Salame napoletano
Similar to salame sardo, *this* salame *uses a mix of black and red pepper*

Salame milano

Cacciatoro
This small whole salame milanese *is cured and matured for only a short time*

Meat & Poultry

Until recently, meat did not figure largely in Italian cooking, which relied much more heavily on the peasant staples of pasta, bread, vegetables and, in coastal areas, fish. As the country became more prosperous, however, more people added meat to their daily diet, and now animals are farmed all over Italy to provide veal, pork, beef, lamb and goat.

Veal is a favorite meat in Italy and appears in innumerable recipes from every region. The best comes from milk-fed calves that are reared in Piedmont. The area around Rome is famous for its lamb, and spit-roasted suckling lamb and goat are popular specialties of the region. Superb beef cattle are bred in Tuscany, but the beef from other regions comes from working cattle that have reached the end of their useful lives, and is best used for stews and dishes that require long, slow cooking.

Many peasant families in Italy still own a pig, which provides pork as well as a huge variety of hams, sausages and other cured meats. Every part of the pig is eaten in one form or another, from snout to tail. Indeed, Italians never waste any edible part of their meat, so offal of all kinds is used in many dishes. A Tuscan *fritto misto* is composed of a variety of offal ranging from brains to sweetbreads and lungs, while the Milanese version also includes cockscombs—so, unless you are an offal lover, be warned if you see these dishes on a menu!

Poultry is another popular food. Factory farming does exist in Italy, but many flavorful free-range birds are still available. Chicken, guinea fowl and turkey appear in a huge variety of simple and delicious dishes and are usually filleted for quick cooking. Duck and goose make their appearance, too, often cooked with sharp fruits to counteract the richness of the meat. Many recipes use wild duck, shot by the enthusiastic (some say over-enthusiastic) hunters who abound in every region. Mercifully, the Italian habit of shooting every type of wild bird,

whether edible or not, is less prevalent than it was, but hunters are lax about observing a close season for shooting, so game, both feathered and furred, seems to be available almost all year round.

Abbacchio and agnello (lamb)

Lambs are bred mainly in southern Italy, particularly in the area around Rome. They are slaughtered at different ages, resulting in distinctive flavors and textures. The youngest lamb is *abbacchio*, month-old milk-fed lamb from Lazio, whose pale

pinkish flesh is meltingly tender. *Abbacchio* is usually spit-roasted whole. Spring lamb, about four months old, is often sold as *abbacchio*. It has darker flesh, which is also very tender and can be used for roasting or grilling. A leg of spring lamb weighs about 2¼–3½ lb. Older lamb (*agnello*) has a slightly stronger flavor and is suitable for roasting or stewing.

Lamb cutlets
Allow at least three small, succulent lamb cutlets like these per serving.

Leg of lamb
*A leg of darker-colored
spring lamb is perfect
for roasting whole*

> ### COOK'S TIP
> *A leg of baby* abbacchio *is only
> enough for two people. Roast in a
> medium oven for about
> 30 minutes, basting occasionally.*

CHOOSING
Italian lamb tends to be
seasonal, so your choice
may be restricted according
to the time of year. *Abbacchio*
should have very pale flesh,
almost like veal. A milk-fed
lamb will be not much
bigger than a rabbit. Spring
lamb should have more
pinkish flesh and very little
fat. Mature lamb should
have dark red flesh with
a layer of creamy fat on
the outside.

CULINARY USES
Lamb is cooked in a variety of ways,
from *al forno* (roast) to *costolette
alla milanese* (fried breaded cutlets).
Roast lamb is the traditional Easter
dish. It is not cut into thin slices, but
served in large chunks, which should
be so tender that they fall off the
bone. A favorite recipe for spring
lamb is *agnello alla giudea* (Jewish-
style lamb), braised in a delicate egg
and lemon sauce.

Maiale (pork)
Most Italian pork is transformed
into sausages, *salami* and hams, but
fresh meat is enjoyed all over Italy,
often combined with local herbs
such as rosemary, fennel or sage.
Different regions eat different parts
of the pig; Tuscany is famous for its
arista di maiale alla fiorentina,
(loin of pork roasted with rosemary),
while in Naples *il musso* (the snout)
is considered a great delicacy.

Pork cutlets
*Tender chops or cutlets can be
grilled or braised with herbs*

CULINARY USES
Pork chops or cutlets can be grilled
or braised with herbs or artichokes.
Loin of pork is deliciously tender
braised in milk (*arrosto di maiale al
latte*), or it can be roasted with
rosemary or sage.

Meat & Poultry

Manzo (beef)

Italian beef has an unjustifiably poor reputation. It is true that in agricultural areas, particularly the south, beef can be stringy and tough. This is because the cattle are working animals, not bred for the table, and are only eaten toward the end of their hard-working life. This type of beef is only suitable for long, slow-cooked country stews. In Tuscany, however, superb beef cattle from Val di Chiana produce meat that can rival any other world-renowned beef and provide the magnificent *bistecche alla fiorentina* (T-bone steaks).

CULINARY USES

Thick-cut T-bone steaks (*bistecche alla fiorentina*) from Val di Chiana cattle are grilled over wood fires until well-browned on the outside and very rare inside. Rump or fillet steaks are also cooked very rare and sliced on the bias as a *tagliata*. A modern creation is *carpaccio*, wafer-thin slices of raw beef marinated in olive oil and herbs and served as an *antipasto*. Thinly sliced topside is rolled around a stuffing to make *involtini* (beef olives). A favorite Italian family dish is *bollito misto*, a mixture of boiled meats and offal including beef. Leftover boiled beef can be sliced and made into a salad.

Less tender cuts of meat are usually braised, stewed or ground to be used in *ragù* (meat sauce) or *polpettone* (meat loaf).

T-bone steak
Italian cooks like to grill these large steaks over wood fires

Beef olives
Thinly sliced topside rolled around a flavorful stuffing

Minced beef
Less tender cuts of beef are ground and used for ragù *(meat sauce) or* polpettone *(meat loaf)*

Carpaccio
These wafer-thin slices of raw beef are simply marinated in olive oil and served as an antipasto

Frattaglie (offal)

Nothing is wasted by Italian butchers, so a huge variety of offal is available. Liver is a great favorite; the finest is *fegato di vitello*, tender calf's liver, which is regarded as a luxury. Chicken livers are popular for topping *crostini* or for pasta sauces, and pork liver is a specialty of Tuscany. Butchers often sell pig's liver ready-wrapped in natural caul (*rete*), which keeps the liver tender as it cooks. Lamb's and calf's kidneys (*rognoni* or *rognoncini*), brains (*cervello*) and sweetbreads (*animelle*) are specialties of northern Italy. The latter two are similar in texture and flavor, but sweetbreads are creamier and more delicate. Every region has its own recipes for tripe (*trippa*); this almost always comes from veal calves rather than other cattle, whose tripe has a coarser texture and flavor. All parts of a veal calf are considered great delicacies. The head is used in *bollito misto* (mixed boiled meats), and the legs give substance to soups and stews. Oxtail (*coda di bue*) comes from older beef cattle.

Oxtail

Nothing is wasted by Italian butchers—the oxtail is used for wonderful slow-cooked stews and soups

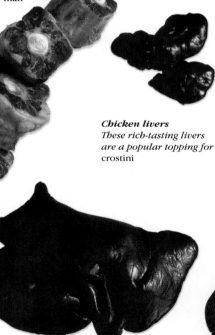

Chicken livers

These rich-tasting livers are a popular topping for crostini

Pig's liver

This is a specialty of Tuscany

Calf's liver

Thinly sliced, this is often simply pan-fried with onions

COOKING OFFAL

Most offal will benefit from being soaked in milk before cooking to remove any coarseness of flavor. Some types, such as liver and brains, require very little cooking in order to preserve their delicate texture. In Venice, thinly sliced calf's liver is cooked with onions to make *fegato alla veneziana*; this is often served with grilled polenta. The Milanese version is coated in egg and bread crumbs and fried in butter. The simplest and one of the most delicious ways with liver is to sauté it quickly in butter with fresh sage. Brains and sweetbreads can be blanched, then quickly fried in butter, or pounded to a paste and made into croquettes (*crocchette*). Kidneys should be sautéed in butter, or braised with wine and onions or Marsala (*trifolati*). Pre-prepared (dressed) tripe will have been scrubbed, soaked and boiled by the butcher, but it should still be blanched for 30 minutes before cooking. Tripe can be prepared *alla fiorentina* in tomato sauce flavored with oregano or marjoram; the version from Parma (*alla parmigiana*) is fried in butter and topped with Parmesan cheese, while in Bologna, eggs are added to the mixture.

Meat & Poultry

Vitello (veal)

Veal is the most popular meat in Italy and appears in hundreds of different recipes. Like lamb, calves are slaughtered at different ages to produce different qualities of meat. The best and most expensive veal is *vitello di latte* from Piedmont and Lombardy. The calves are fed only on milk and are slaughtered at just a few weeks old, producing extremely tender, very pale meat with no fat. Older calves, up to nine months old, are known as *vitello*. Their flesh is still tender, but darker in color than milk-fed veal. *Vitellone* is somewhere between veal and beef. It comes from bullocks aged between one and three years, who have never worked in the fields and whose flesh is therefore still quite tender and lighter in color than beef.

CULINARY USES

Young, milk-fed veal is ideal for *scaloppine* (scallops) and *piccate* (thin scallops), which need very little cooking. *Vitello* can be served as chops, cutlets or a rolled roast. The shin is cut into *osso buco* (literally "bone with a hole"), complete with bone marrow, or *stinco* (the whole shin), and braised until meltingly tender. An unusual combination that works wonderfully well is *vitello tonnato*, cold roast veal thinly sliced and coated in a rich tuna sauce. *Vitellone* should be treated like tender beef. It can be grilled, roasted or casseroled, but it is not suitable for scallops or similar cuts.

CHOOSING

Young veal should have very pale, slightly rosy fine-grained flesh with no trace of fat. *Vitellone* should be pinker and paler than beef, with only a faint marbling of fat, and should feel firm, not flabby. Scallops and *piccate* must be cut only from very young veal. They should be sliced across the grain so that they keep their shape and do not shrivel during cooking. If you are buying boned veal, ask the butcher to give you the bones, which make wonderful stock.

Veal scallops
These are always sliced very thinly across the grain

Cinghiale (wild boar)

Wild boar are the ancestors of domestic pigs, which used to roam in large numbers in the forests of Tuscany and Sardinia, but which are becoming increasingly rare because of widespread hunting. Baby wild boar are an enchanting sight, with light brown fur striped with horizontal black bands. The adults have coarse, brown coats and fierce-looking tusks. The flesh of a young *cinghiale* is as pale and tender as pork; older animals have very dark flesh, which is tougher but full of flavor.

CULINARY USES

Haunches of wild boar are made into hams, which are displayed in butchers' shops. Young animals can be cooked in the same way as pork. Older boar must be marinated for at least 24 hours to tenderize the meat before roasting or casseroling. The classic sweet and sour sauce, (*agrodolce*), sharpened with red wine vinegar, complements the gamey flavor of the meat.

Loin of veal
Usually boned, then roasted with herbs—the bones make the most wonderful stock

Coniglio (rabbit) and lepre (hare)

Farmed and wild rabbits often replace chicken or veal in Italian cooking. The meat is very pale and lean and the taste is somewhere between that of good-quality farmhouse chicken and veal. Wild rabbit has a stronger flavor, which combines well with robust flavors; farmed rabbit is very tender and much more delicate.

Hare cannot be farmed, so the only animals available come from the wild. Despite the popularity of hunting in Italy, the hare population has not been totally decimated. The wily creatures, who mange to escape the gun, continue to breed. A hare weighs about twice as much as a rabbit (4¼ lb is about average). The flesh is a rich, dark brown and has a strong gamey flavor similar to that of wild rabbit.

Hare
This is always wild—the rich brown flesh has a strong gamey flavor

Rabbit
This can be bought either farmed or wild—wild rabbit has a stronger flavor

Wild boar
Chops like these can be cooked in the same way as pork

Culinary Uses

Farmed rabbit can replace chicken or turkey in almost any recipe. Wild rabbit can be stewed or braised in white wine or Marsala, or with eggplants, bacon and tomatoes. It can be roasted with root vegetables or fresh herbs. In Sicily, rabbit is often cooked with raisins and pine nuts in an *agrodolce* (sweet and sour) sauce.

Hare is generally casseroled in red wine or Marsala, cooked *in agrodolce* or made into a rich sauce for pappardelle or other wide noodles. Both rabbit and hare are often served with polenta or fried bread.

Cooking Rabbit and Hare

Wild rabbit and hare must be cut into six or eight pieces and marinated in red wine and herbs for 24 hours before cooking. If you like a sweet and sour flavor (game in agrodolce is very popular in Italy), add plenty of red wine vinegar to the marinade. A rabbit weighing about 2¼ lb when cleaned will need about 1½ hour's braising or stewing; a hare needs about 2 hours.

Meat & Poultry

Fagiano (pheasant)

Occasionally, in the Italian countryside, you may still catch a glimpse of a pheasant with its beautiful plumage and long tail feathers. Cock pheasants have bright, iridescent blue and green feathers, while hens are browner and less dramatic-looking. Pheasant farming is still unknown in Italy, and wild pheasants are something of a rarity, so they are regarded as a luxury. They are not hung, but are eaten almost as soon as they are shot, so their flavor is less gamey than in some other countries. Although pheasants are expensive, they are meaty birds for their size, so a cock pheasant will feed three to four people and a hen pheasant two to three.

CULINARY USES

Hen pheasants are smaller than cocks, but their meat is juicier and the flavor is finer. Young hen pheasants can be roasted with or without a stuffing, but cock birds are more suitable for casseroling. Pheasant breast can tend to be dry, so it should be well wrapped with bacon or thickly smeared with butter before roasting. A big pat of butter placed inside the cavity will help to keep the flesh moist. For special occasions, pheasants can be stuffed with candied fruits or pomegranate seeds and nuts. Pheasant breasts can be sautéed and served with a wine or balsamic vinegar sauce, but they can sometimes be rather dry.

Pheasant
Usually eaten as soon as they are shot, Italian pheasants are less gamey than in some other countries. Remember that pheasants contain lead-shot pellets, so take care not to bite down on these!

COOKING QUAIL

Quail should be browned in butter until golden all over, then roasted in a hot oven for about 15 minutes. Their flavor is well complemented by the fruit of the vine, so they are often served with a light sauce containing grapes or raisins soaked in grappa. They can also be wrapped in vine leaves before roasting, which keeps them moist and adds a delicious flavor.

Quaglie (quail)

These small migratory birds are found in Italy throughout the summer months. Wild quails have the reputation of being so stupid that they never run away from hunters, but stay rooted to the spot as sitting targets. As a result, they have become very rare, and most of the birds now available are farmed. They are very small (you need two to serve one person) and have a delicate, subtly gamey flavor. Farmed quails have less flavor than the wild birds and benefit from added flavorings, such as grapes.

COOKING PHEASANTS

Unless you know for sure that a pheasant is very young, it is best to wrap the breast in fatty bacon before roasting to prevent dryness. To roast a pheasant, put a pat of butter inside the cavity, or make a stuffing, drape bacon rashers over the breast and roast at 400°F for about 40 minutes, until tender. Plain roast pheasant is often served with a risotto. Pheasant can also be pot-roasted or casseroled with wine and herbs. If you are serving cock birds, it is worth removing the lower part of the legs after cooking, as they contain hard sinews that are not pleasant to eat.

Quail
These birds have a very delicate, gamey flavor. They are very small, and so you will need to serve two per person.

Faraona (guinea fowl)

Guinea fowl are extremely decorative birds with luxuriant gray-and-white spotted plumage. They originated in West Africa, but are now farmed all over Europe, so that although they are technically game, they are classified as poultry. They taste similar to chicken, but have a firmer texture and a more robust flavor.

COOKING GUINEA FOWL

Although their abundant plumage makes them seem larger, guinea fowl are only about the size of a small spring chicken, so one bird will not feed more than three people. To roast guinea fowl, wrap the breasts with bacon slices and roast like chicken, basting frequently. A vegetable stuffing will keep the flesh moist. Guinea fowl can be substituted for chicken or turkey in any recipe.

CULINARY USES

Guinea fowl are hugely popular in Italy, where they are served in much the same ways as chicken. The flesh of an adult guinea fowl is firmer than that of a chicken, so it is best to wrap it or cover the breasts with bacon slices before roasting. The breasts are sometimes sautéed and served with the pan juices mixed with balsamic vinegar, or with a sauce of cream and Marsala. The birds can be roasted or pot-roasted whole, or cut into serving pieces and casseroled with mushrooms (wild mushrooms are especially delicious) or herbs. A favorite autumn dish in Tuscany is guinea fowl braised with chestnuts.

Guinea fowl
These popular birds can be pot-roasted, roasted or casseroled with wild mushrooms

Piccione (pigeon)

Wood pigeons have dark, gamey flesh and a robust flavor, which the Italians love. They are generally too tough to roast, but they make the most delicious casseroles. Domestic pigeons are also reared for food and you will often see large dovecotes in farmyards. Domestic birds are less likely to be tough than wild ones, but their flavor is less robust.

Wild pigeon
Italians love the rich, robust flavor of these small birds; however, they can be very tough, so cook them very slowly, either by braising or casseroling

COOKING PIGEONS

Wild pigeons can be tough, so, unless you are sure that they are young, it is best to casserole them. In Tuscany, they are braised with tomatoes and olives; the classic Venetian way is to stew them with pancetta, ox tongue and fresh green peas. If you really want to roast wild pigeons, marinate them in a red wine marinade for three days before cooking, then stuff them with a moist vegetable stuffing. Cover the breasts with fatty bacon and roast for about 20 minutes, basting with the marinade every few minutes.

Fish & Shellfish

Italy's extensive coastal waters once teemed with a huge variety of fish and shellfish, many unique to that part of the Adriatic and Mediterranean. Sadly, pollution and over-fishing have taken their toll, and there is no longer the abundance of seafood there once was, but what remains is of excellent quality. A visit to an Italian fish market will reveal fish and shellfish of every description, some beautiful, some hideous, many unknown outside Italy. Italians like their seafood very fresh and tend to cook it simply, without elaborate sauces. Large fish are usually plainly grilled or baked and dressed with olive oil, or baked in cartoccio *(enclosed in a paper bag). Small shellfish are deep-fried for a crisp* fritto misto di mare. *Every coastal area has its own version of fish soup, which uses a mixture of local fish and constitutes a meal in itself—*cacciucco *from Livorno, cold* burrida *from Sardinia,* brodetto *from the Adriatic coast— each region claims that its version is the best.*

It is impossible to give a complete list of all the fish that you will find in Italy. Popular favorites include *coda di rospo* (monkfish), *dentice* (dentex—a white-fleshed fish found only in Italy), *sogliola* (sole) and even non-indigenous fish such as salmon.

Freshwater fish—trout, perch, carp and eels—abound in the lakes and rivers and are eaten with gusto. Eels are regarded as a particular delicacy and are cooked in many different ways, from grilling to baking, stewing and frying.

Some fish are dried, salted or preserved in oil. The most popular is tuna, which is packed in olive oil and sold by weight from huge cans. *Baccalà* is salted dried cod, which is creamed to a rich paste or made into soups and stews. Anchovies are salted, or packed in olive oil, or preserved in a sweet and sour marinade. Sardines are also very popular and are used to make a Sicilian pasta sauce.

Anchovies
Canned in olive oil (above) or salted (left)—these tiny, strong-tasting fish are used to add flavor to pasta sauces and salads

Salt cod *(baccalà)*
This dried fish is creamed to a paste or made into soups and stews

Choosing Fresh Fish

You can almost guarantee that any fish you buy in an Italian early morning market will be ultra-fresh, but at fishmongers and restaurants you should look for pointers. Fish should have bright, slightly bulging eyes and shiny, faintly slimy skin. Open up the gills to check that they are clear red or dark pink and prod the fish lightly to check that the flesh is springy. All fish should have only a faint, pleasant smell; you can tell a stale fish a mile off by its unpleasant odor.

Orata (gilt-head sea bream)

This Mediterranean fish takes its name from the crescent-shaped golden mark on its domed head and the gold spots on each cheek. It has beautiful silvery scales and slightly coarse but delicious flaky white flesh. Orate usually weigh between 1 lb 6 oz and 2¼ lb; a larger fish will serve two greedy people. Orata is best simply broiled, baked *in cartoccio* or barbecued.

Pesce spada (swordfish)

In Italy, you will occasionally find a whole swordfish on the fishmonger's slab. These huge Mediterranean fish, up to 15 feet long and weighing 220–1200 lb, are immediately recognizable by their long sword-like upper jaw. Because of their size, they are more usually sold cut into steaks. Their firm, close-grained, almost meaty flesh has given them a nickname of "steak of the sea."

Cooking Swordfish

Swordfish tends to be dry, so it should be marinated in oil and lemon juice or wine and herbs before cooking. It is excellent grilled or barbecued, or part-cooked in butter or olive oil, then baked in a sauce. Its firm texture makes it ideal for kebabs. It is plentiful in the waters around Sicily, where it is cooked with traditional Mediterranean ingredients such as tomatoes, olives, capers, raisins and pine nuts. Another popular Sicilian dish is braciole di pesce spada, thin slices of swordfish rolled around a stuffing of bread crumbs, mozzarella and herbs and grilled. It is also delicious sliced wafer-thin, marinated in olive oil, lemon juice and herbs and served raw.

Swordfish
Often either baked or grilled, this firm-fleshed fish needs to be marinated to keep it moist during cooking

Tuna
Immensely popular throughout Italy, canned tuna in oil is either sold by weight from huge cans or bought in small cans like these

TONNO ALL'OLIO D'OLIVA

NOSTROMO

TONNO
DI PRIMA SCELTA

300 g

Fish

Sarde or sardelle
(sardines)

Fresh sardines probably take their name from Sardinia, where they were once abundant. These small, silvery fish are still found in Mediterranean waters, where they grow to about 5 in. They are at their best in spring. Allow about four larger sardines or six smaller fish per serving. Sardines have very oily flesh and should only be eaten when extremely fresh. They can also be bought preserved in oil or salt.

> **Sardines**
> *These fish are at their best in the spring*

PREPARING
AND COOKING SARDINES

Sardines should be gutted before cooking. If the fishmonger has not already done this, cut the head almost through to the backbone and pull it off; the gut will come away with the head.

Sardines can be barbecued, broiled or baked alla genovese with fresh potatoes, garlic and parsley. Their oily flesh combines well with spices and tart ingredients such as capers and olives. In Sicily they are stuffed with bread crumbs, pine nuts, raisins and anchovies and fried, then finished in the oven (a beccaficcu). Sardines can also be deep-fried, either plain or stuffed with mushrooms, herbs and cheese (alla ligure) or with chopped spinach and cream (alla romana).

Spigola or branzino
(sea bass)

The silvery sea bass, which come from Mediterranean waters, are as beautiful to look at as to eat, although their rapacious nature has earned them the nickname of "sea wolf." These slim, elegant fish are almost always sold whole and rarely weigh much more than 2¼ lb, so one fish will feed no more than two or three people. Sea bass is prized for its delicate white flesh and lack of irritating small bones. As a result, it is never cheap.

One way of bringing the price down is to farm sea bass, but the flavor of the farmed fish is not as fine as that of wild sea bass, whose predatory habits ensure that their flesh develops a full flavor. So far, farming of these wonderful fish does not seem to have caught on in Italy, where flavor is rarely compromised for cost.

PREPARING AND COOKING SEA BASS

Sea bass should be gutted before cooking. They have quite hard scales, which should be removed before grilling or pan-frying. Scale the fish with a de-scaler or blunt knife, working from the tail toward the head. If you are going to poach or bake sea bass, leave the scales on, as they will hold the fragile flesh together.

Sea bass has rather soft flesh, so it is best broiled, barbecued or pan-fried and dressed with a trickle of olive oil. It can be stuffed with sprigs of fresh herbs (fennel is particularly good) and baked for 20–30 minutes, depending on the size of the fish. For spigola alla livornese, lay the fish in an ovenproof dish on a layer of rich tomato sauce, sprinkle with seasoned bread crumbs and olive oil and bake.

Triglia (red mullet)

These small Mediterranean fish rarely weigh more than 2¼ lb. They have bright rose-colored skin and a faint golden streak along their sides. Their flesh is succulent with a distinctive, almost shrimp-like flavor, quite unlike any other fish. The liver of red mullet is regarded as a great delicacy and is not removed during cooking, which gives the mullet its nickname of "sea woodcock." Red mullet are extremely perishable and should be eaten the day they are bought. The skin should always look very bright; dullness is a sure indication that the fish is not fresh.

PREPARING AND COOKING RED MULLET

Larger fish should be scaled before cooking, but be warned—this is a delicate operation, as the skin is very fragile. Scaling is worth the effort, however, as it reveals the wonderful red skin in all its glory. Red mullet combines well with traditional Mediterranean flavors of olive oil, black olives, herbs, garlic, saffron and tomatoes. It can be baked, grilled or cooked in cartoccio with powerful herbs such as rosemary or fennel. For triglia all'italiana, place whole red mullet on a bed of finely chopped mushrooms and onions that have been sweated until soft and mixed with fresh bread crumbs, and bake for 20–30 minutes.

Red mullet
The flesh of these pretty fish has a distinctive almost shrimp-like flavor

Sea bass
Prized for their delicate white flesh, these slim, elegant fish are almost always sold whole

Shellfish

Italian coastal waters are host to a
huge variety of shellfish and
crustaceans, many with wonderfully
exotic names such as *datteri di mare*
(sea dates; a kind of mussel), *tartufi
di mare* (sea truffles; a type of
clam) and *fragolino di mare* (sea
strawberry; a tiny octopus that
turns bright pink when cooked).
Almost all seafood is considered
edible, from clams to *cannolicchi*
(razor-shells), *lumache di mare* (sea
snails) and *canestrelli* (small
scallops). Shrimps come in all
sizes and colors, from vibrant red
to pale gray, while crustaceans range
from bright orange crawfish to
blue-black lobsters.

Squid
Large specimens such as this one
need long, slow cooking to make
them tender—conversely, small baby
squid should be cooked very quickly
or they will become tough

COOKING SQUID AND CUTTLEFISH

*Small squid and cuttlefish
should be cooked only briefly—
just until they turn opaque—or
they will become rubbery
and tough.
Larger specimens need long,
slow cooking to make them
tender. They can be stuffed with
ground fish or meat, anchovies
and seasoned bread crumbs or
rice, baked with tomatoes and
wine sauce until tender, or cut
into rings and fried in a light
batter or simply dusted with
seasoned flour and deep-fried.
Squid and cuttlefish are also
delicious stewed in their own
ink; seal the mollusks in hot oil
with some chopped onions and
garlic, add finely chopped fresh
parsley and seasoning, then
cover with dry white wine and a
little water and simmer gently
for 15 minutes. Crush the ink
sacs, mix the inky liquid with a
little cold water and 2–3 tbsp
flour and work into a smooth
paste. Add the flour mixture to
the pan and cook for another
5–10 minutes.*

Calamari or totani (squid) *and seppie* (cuttlefish)

Despite their appearance, squid
and cuttlefish are actually mollusks
whose shell is located inside the
body. They are indistinguishable in
taste, but cuttlefish have a larger
head and a wider body with
stubbier tentacles. The cuttlebone,
much loved by parrots, is the bone
of the cuttlefish inside the body.
Once this has been removed,
cuttlefish are very tender. The "shell"
of a squid is nothing more than a
long, thin, transparent quill. Both
seppie and *calamari* have ten
tentacles.

Squid and cuttlefish are immensely
popular in Italy, cut into rings and
served as part of either an *insalata
di mare* (seafood salad) or *fritto
misto* (mixed fried fish). Their black
ink is used to flavor and color risotto
and fresh pasta.

PREPARING AND COOKING MUSSELS

*Scrub the shells under cold
running water. Pull off the
"beard" protruding from the
shell. Give any open mussels a
sharp tap; they should close
immediately. Discard any
that do not, as they are
probably dead.
The simplest way to cook
mussels is alla marinara. For
4 people, finely chop 1 large
onion, 2 garlic cloves and
1 tbsp chopped parsley,
put in a large pan with
2¼ cups white wine and simmer
for 5 minutes. Add the scrubbed
mussels, cover and steam,
shaking the pan occasionally, for
5 minutes, or until the shells
have opened. Discard any
unopened mussels, sprinkle the
rest with extra parsley and serve.
For a richer sauce, transfer the
mussels to a bowl and reduce
the sauce over high heat. Pour it
over the shellfish and serve.*

Polipi (octopus)

These are much larger than squid and have only eight tentacles. Their ink sac is not located in the head but in their liver, and the ink has a strong, pungent taste. Octopus look and taste similar to squid, but need a good deal of preparation. They must be pounded (99 times, some say) to tenderize them before they are subjected to very long, slow cooking.

If you can find very small octopus, they can be cooked in the same way as squid, but otherwise it is less trouble to substitute squid or cuttlefish.

Octopus
When small, these can be cooked like squid

Cozze (mussels)

Mussels, with their smooth texture and sweet flavor, make an attractive addition to many pasta and fish dishes. Pollution in the Mediterranean has threatened the indigenous mussel population, so nowadays most Italian mussels are farmed by the *bouchot* method, on ropes attached to long

stakes set in pure seawater, which keeps the mollusks clean and healthy and free from grit and sand. In Italian fish markets on the Adriatic coast, you may find small sweet local mussels with different names like *peoci* or *datteri di mare*. These can be prepared in the same way as other mussels.

CHOOSING

Mussels, sold by the litre in Italy, are very inexpensive. Because the shells constitute so much of the weight, allow at least a generous 2½ cups mussels per serving. Choose those that feel heavy for their size and discard any with broken shells. Use mussels the day they are gathered or bought.

Mussels
Steamed mussels combine well with black fettuccine or tagliatelle

CULINARY USES

Once mussels have been steamed open, they can be served with a garlicky tomato sauce, or baked on the half shell with garlic butter or a bread crumb topping. For *cozze gratinate al forno*, lay the mussels on the bottom shells in an ovenproof dish, sprinkle lavishly with bread crumbs seasoned with garlic and parsley and drizzle with olive oil. Bake for 10 minutes.

Shelled cooked mussels are combined with shrimp and squid for an *insalata di mare* (seafood salad), or used as a pizza topping, while mussels in the shell are often mixed with other seafood and pasta for dishes like *spaghetti allo scoglio* ("spaghetti of the rock").

Shellfish

Gamberetti, gamberelli and gamberoni (shrimp)

There are so many different varieties of shrimp in Italian coastal waters that it is almost impossible to recognize them all. The smallest are the *gamberetti*, small pink or brown shrimps that are usually boiled and served simply dressed with olive oil and lemon juice as part of an *antipasto*. Next in size come the *gamberelli*, pink shrimp with a delicate flavor. These are the shrimp that are most commonly used in a *fritto misto di mare* (mixed fried seafood). *Gamberi rossi* are the larger variety of shrimp, which turn bright red when they are cooked. They are highly prized for their fine, strong flavor, and are eaten plainly cooked and dipped into a bowl of *maionese* (mayonnaise). Best (and most expensive) of all are *gamberoni*, large succulent shrimp from the Adriatic, which have a superb flavor and texture. Similar to these is the *cicala*, which resembles a small flattish lobster.

Gamberoni
Large shrimp with a superb flavor

COOKING SHRIMP AND SCAMPI

Whatever the size, all types of shrimp can be cooked briefly in boiling salted water (sea water, if possible) until they turn pink. Medium shrimp will take only 1–2 minutes, large shrimp up to 5 minutes. The robust flavor of shrimp makes them ideal for serving in a rich tomato or cream sauce or with rice. Shell them after cooking. To grill gamberoni, *rub the shells with olive oil and coarse salt and grill over charcoal or on a grilling pan, turning them frequently. When they turn opaque, slit them through the underside and open them out flat like a butterfly. Brush the underside with oil and grill until just cooked. Peeled shrimp can be pan-fried in olive oil flavored with garlic and/or chili, parsley and capers or coated in batter or egg and bread crumbs and deep-fried.*

Gamberi rossi
These large shrimp turn bright red when cooked

PREPARING SHRIMP AND SCAMPI

Shrimp should be deveined before or after cooking. Pull off the heads, shell the tails and pick out the black thread-like intestine with a knife tip.

CHOOSING

Almost all the shrimp you buy in Italy are sold uncooked. They should have bright shells that feel firm; if they look limp or smell of ammonia, do not buy them.

CULINARY USES

Shrimp are extremely versatile and can be used in a wide variety of dishes. Small shrimps are served as *antipasti*, either on their own, or as a stuffing for tomatoes. They can be added to risotto and pasta dishes or seafood sauces.

Larger shrimp combine well with almost any other seafood. They are usually included in an *insalata di mare* (seafood salad) or *fritto misto di mare* (mixed fried seafood). They make a fine *antipasto* added to an *insalata russa* (Russian salad) or served with green beans dressed with extra virgin olive oil. They combine well with a spicy tomato sauce or mushrooms, and can be used for seafood casseroles. Large shrimp can be skewered or split and grilled, or boiled and served with mayonnaise or lemon.

Gamberetti
These small pink shrimps are delicious simply dressed with olive oil and lemon juice

Vongole *(clams)*

There are almost as many different types of clam as there are regions in Italy, ranging from tiny smooth-shelled *arselle* or *vongole* to long thin razor shells and the large Venus clams with beautiful ridged shells called *tartufi di mare* ("sea truffles"). All have a sweet flavor and a slightly chewy texture. Because they vary so much in size, it is best to ask the fishmonger how many clams you will need for a particular dish.

Clams
These smooth-shelled vongole *are often steamed and served as part of a seafood salad*

PREPARING AND COOKING CLAMS

Their habit of burying themselves in the sand makes clams rather gritty, so they should be left in fresh water for an hour or so to open up and disgorge the sand inside the shells. To open large clams, either use an oyster knife, or put them in a medium oven for a few minutes until they gape open.
Clams can be served raw like oysters, or cooked in exactly the same way as mussels (see page 70). The cooking time depends on the size of the clams; tiny specimens take only a minute or two. Steamed shelled clams are often served as part of an insalata di mare *or in a risotto. Miniature clams in their shells are stewed with olive oil, garlic and parsley and served with their juices (in bianco) or used in a tomato sauce (in rosso) for spaghetti alle vongole, or served on fried bread as* crostini. *Large varieties can be pan-fried with lemon and parsley, or stuffed with seasoned bread crumbs and grilled or baked.*

Vegetables

Vegetables have always played a very important role in Italian cooking, particularly in the south of the country, where meat was a luxury that few could afford. They are most often served as dishes in their own right, rather than accompaniments, and the range of imaginative vegetable recipes from all over Italy seems infinite.

One of the great joys of Italy is shopping at the markets, where an astonishing range of seasonal vegetables is on display, from asparagus, beans and *cavolo nero* from the north to eggplants, peppers and zucchini from Calabria and Sicily. In spring and summer, you will find at least ten different varieties of lettuce, and you will be overwhelmed by the aroma of freshly picked local tomatoes still on the vine. Italians almost never buy imported or out-of-season vegetables, but prefer to purchase fresh seasonal produce bursting with flavor.

Asparagi (asparagus)

Asparagus has been grown commercially in northeastern Italy for over 300 years and is still highly prized as a luxury vegetable. It has a short growing season from April to early June and is really only worth eating during this period. Both green and white asparagus are cultivated in Italy; the green variety is grown above ground so that the entire spear is bright green. They are harvested when they are about 6 in high. The fat white spears with their pale yellow tips are grown under mounds of soil to protect them from the light, and harvested almost as soon as the tips appear above the soil to retain their pale color. Both varieties have a delicious fresh grassy flavor.

CULINARY USES

In spring, Italians enjoy young asparagus spears simply boiled, steamed or roasted in olive oil and served as a *primo* (first course) with butter and freshly grated Parmesan. For an extra treat, they add a fried egg and dip the asparagus tips into

White asparagus
This variety is grown under mounds of earth to retain the pale color

Green asparagus
Enjoyed by Italians, simply boiled or roasted in olive oil

the creamy yolk. When served as a vegetable accompaniment, asparagus can be crisply fried in egg and bread crumbs. The tips also make a luxury addition to risotto.

BUYING AND STORING

Asparagus starts to lose its flavor as soon as it has been cut, so be sure to buy only the freshest spears. The best guide is the tips, which should be

firm and tight. If they are drooping and open, the asparagus is past its best. The stalks should be straight and fresh-looking, not yellowed and shriveled or very woody at the base. Allow about eight medium spears per serving as a first course and always buy spears of uniform thickness so that they cook evenly. Asparagus will keep in the vegetable compartment of the refrigerator for two or three days.

PREPARING AND COOKING ASPARAGUS

Freshly cut garden asparagus needs no trimming, but cut off at least ¾ in from the bottom of the stalks of bought spears until the exposed end looks fresh and moist. Peel the lower half with a potato peeler. (You need not do this for very thin stalks.)

Boiling asparagus can be problematic, since the stalks take longer to cook than the tips. The ideal solution is to use a special asparagus kettle, so as to immerse the stalks in boiling water while steaming the tips.

Asparagus can also be stood upright in a deep pan of boiling water, tented with foil and cooked for 5–8 minutes, until tender but still al dente. Alternatively, steam the spears in a vegetable steamer. Serve with a drizzle of extra virgin olive oil or melted butter.

Asparagus can also be successfully microwaved. Wash the spears and lay them in an oval dish in a single layer with the tips all pointing the same way. You need not add water. Cover tightly with plastic wrap and cook on full power for 5 minutes per 1¼ lb. If the spears are not quite done, turn them over and cook for a little longer.

To roast asparagus, heat some olive oil in a roasting pan, turn the spears in the oil, then roast in a hot oven for 5–10 minutes.

To fry, roll the spears in beaten egg and fine dried bread crumbs, then fry them a few at a time in very hot olive oil until crusty and golden. Drain on paper towel and sprinkle with sea salt.

Cardi (cardoons)

Cardoons are related to artichokes, but only the leaf-stalks are eaten. They are commercially grown in mounds of soil to keep them creamy white, but in the wild, the stalks are pale green and hairy and can grow to an enormous size. The tough outer stalks are always discarded, and only the inner stalks and hearts are eaten. Cardoons are a popular winter vegetable in Italy and can be found in the markets ready-trimmed.

CULINARY USES

Cardoons can be eaten raw as a salad, or cooked in a variety of ways—fried, puréed or boiled and served with melted butter or a rich cream and Parmesan sauce. They are traditionally used as a vegetable to dip into the hot anchovy and garlic fondue known as *bagna cauda*.

BUYING AND STORING

Cardoons bought at the market will have been trimmed of their outer stalks and are sold with a crown of leaves, like large heads of celery. The stalks should be plump and creamy-white and not too hairy. Wrapped in a plastic bag, they will keep in the vegetable compartment of the refrigerator for two or three days.

PREPARING AND COOKING CARDOONS

Cut off the roots and peel the stalks with a potato peeler to remove the stringy fibers. Cut the stalks into 2½ in lengths and the hearts into wedges, and drop into acidulated water to prevent discoloration.

Blanch in boiling salted water, then simmer or fry gently in butter until tender. To serve in a sauce, put the blanched cardoons in an ovenproof dish, cover with sauce, sprinkle with grated Parmesan and broil until browned.

Cardoons
Related to artichokes, the tough outer stalks of this vegetable are always discarded

Vegetables

Carciofi (artichokes)

As their appearance suggests, artichokes are a type of thistle. Originating from Sicily, where they grow almost wild, they are cultivated throughout Italy and are a particular specialty of Roman cooking. The artichoke itself is actually the flower bud of the large, silvery-leaved plant. There are many different varieties, from tiny purple plants with tapered leaves, which are so tender that they can be eaten raw, to large bright or pale green globes, whose leaves are pulled off one by one and the succulent flesh at the base stripped off with your teeth.

HISTORY

Although artichokes have always grown like weeds in Sicily, they were first cultivated near Naples in the fifteenth century. Their popularity spread to Florence, where they became a favorite dish of the Medici family. They were believed to have powerful properties as an aphrodisiac and women were often forbidden to eat them!

CULINARY USES

Tiny tender artichokes can be quartered and eaten raw or braised *alla romana* with olive oil, parsley and garlic. Large specimens can be served boiled with a dressing to dip the leaves into, or stuffed with savory fillings. They can be cut into wedges, dipped in batter and deep-fried. A favorite Italian dish is the ancient Jewish recipe *carciofi alla giudea*, where the artichokes are flattened out and deep-fried twice, so that the outside is very crisp while the inside remains meltingly moist.

BUYING AND STORING

Artichokes are available almost all year round, but they are at their best in summer. Whichever variety you are buying, look for tightly packed leaves (open leaves indicate that they are too mature) and a very fresh color. When an artichoke is old, the tips of the leaves will turn brown. If possible, buy artichokes still attached to their stems; they will stay fresher and the

PREPARING AND COOKING ARTICHOKES

Tiny tender artichokes can be quartered and eaten raw.

For large artichokes, snap off the stalk and pull off the tough outer leaves. Rub the cut surfaces with lemon juice to prevent discoloration and keep the prepared artichokes in a bowl of acidulated water until ready to cook.

Boil large whole artichokes for about 30 minutes, until the outer leaves can be pulled off easily.

Drain them upside-down, then pull out the center leaves and scoop out the inedible hairy choke with a spoon before serving. For stuffed artichokes, remove the choke before cooking and fill the cavity with your chosen stuffing. Braise them in olive oil and water, or invert them onto an ovenproof dish, pour on a mixture of olive oil and water, cover with foil and bake at 375°F for about 1 hour.

Very small artichokes should be quartered and boiled, braised or stewed until tender. The chokes are so soft that the artichokes can be eaten whole.

peeled, cooked stems are often as delicious as the artichoke itself.

Artichokes will stay fresh for several days if you place the stalks in water like a bunch of flowers. If they have no stalks, wrap them in plastic wrap and keep in the vegetable compartment of the refrigerator for a day or two.

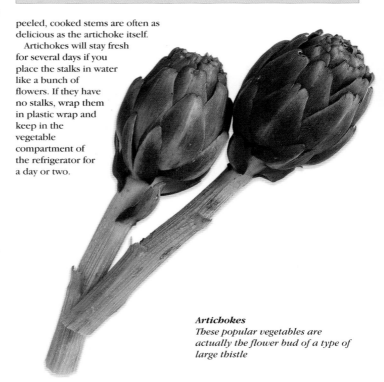

Artichokes
These popular vegetables are actually the flower bud of a type of large thistle

Cavolo (cabbage)

Cabbage is an essential ingredient of many Italian hearty winter soups. Three main types are used: *cavolo verza* (curly-leaved savoy cabbage), which is used in Milanese dishes, *cavolo cappuccio* (round white or red cabbage) and the specialty of Tuscany, *cavolo nero*, a tall leafy cabbage whose name means "black cabbage," but which is actually dark purplish green.

CULINARY USES

Italians rarely eat cabbage as a vegetable side dish, but prefer to include it in hearty soups, such as *ribollita* or minestrone, or to stuff and braise the outer leaves and serve them as a main course.

BUYING AND STORING

Cabbage heads should be solid and firm, with fresh, unyellowed leaves. It is best to buy them complete with their outer leaves; not only are these tasty for cooking, but they protect the hearts and give a good indication of the freshness of the cabbage. A cabbage will keep in the vegetable compartment of the refrigerator for up to a week.

Cavolo nero
The name of this tall leafy cabbage means "black cabbage"

Red and white cabbage
The red variety is often cooked gently with apples and spices to serve with rich meats, while the white variety is added to soups and stews

Savoy cabbage
This curly-leaved cabbage is used in Milanese dishes

PREPARING AND COOKING CABBAGE

Cut off the outer leaves and stalk, cutting out a cone-shaped section of the stalk from the inside of the cabbage. To use the leaves for stuffing, blanch them in boiling water for about 3 minutes, until malleable. For soups and braised dishes, coarsely shred the cabbage and wash it well.

Cabbage can be cooked in a variety of ways. The simplest cooking method is to toss shredded cabbage in butter or olive oil until just tender. Never overcook cabbage; it should still retain some crunch.

Winter cabbages are good shredded and braised with pancetta *and garlic, while* cavolo rosso *(red cabbage) can be spiced with apples, cinnamon and cloves and stewed in a little white wine to cut the richness of pork, duck or roast goose.*

Vegetables

Cipolle *(onions)*

Onions are an essential part of Italian cooking. Many varieties are grown, including mild yellow onions, the stronger-flavored white onions and their baby version, which is used for pickling and sweet-and-sour onions. The best-known Italian onions are the vibrant deep red variety, which are delicious raw (in a tuna and bean salad, for example), or cooked.

CULINARY USES

The best Italian onions are grown in Piedmont, so many classic Piedmontese recipes include these versatile bulbs. Large onions can be stuffed with Fontina or ground meat and herbs, and baked. Baby white onions are traditionally cooked *in agrodolce,* a sweet-and-sour sauce of sugar and wine vinegar, and served cold as an *antipasto* or hot as a vegetable accompaniment.

BUYING AND STORING

You will often find young fresh onions in Italian markets. These are sold in bunches like large, bulbous scallions, complete with their leaves. They have a mild flavor and can be used for pickling or in salads. They will keep in the refrigerator for three or four days; wrap them to prevent their smell from pervading everything else in the refrigerator. Older onions have thin, almost

papery skins that should be unblemished. The onions should feel firm and not be sprouting green leaves. They quickly deteriorate once cut, so it is best to buy assorted sizes, then you can use a small onion when the recipe calls for only a small amount. Stored in a dry, airy place, onions will keep for many weeks.

White onion
This variety is very strongly flavored

Red onion
This vibrant red variety is now widely available— they are delicious raw

Baby white onions
Traditionally cooked in agrodolce, *a classic Italian sweet-and-sour sauce, and served cold as an* antipasto

Yellow onions
These mild onions are best cooked gently in olive oil

PREPARING AND COOKING ONIONS

Some onions are easier to peel than others. The skins of red and yellow onions can be removed without much difficulty, but white onions may need to be plunged into boiling water for about 30 seconds to make peeling easier. There are all sorts of old wives' remedies to prevent your eyes from watering when peeling onions. The most effective method is to hold them as far away from you as possible while you peel. For most cooked dishes, onions should be sliced or chopped, but for salads they are sliced into very thin rings.
The flavor of onions will develop in different ways, according to how you cook them. In Italian cooking, they are rarely browned, which gives them a bitter taste, but are generally sweated gently in olive oil to add a mellow flavor to a multitude of dishes.

Finocchio *(fennel)*

Originally a medicinal remedy for such disagreeable conditions as flatulence, fennel has become one of the most important of all Italian vegetables. Bulb or Florence fennel (so-called to distinguish it from the feathery green herb) resembles a fat white celery root and has a delicate but distinctive flavor of aniseed and a very crisp, refreshing texture.

CULINARY USES

Fennel is delicious eaten raw, dressed with a vinaigrette or as part of a mixed salad. In southern Italy, raw fennel is served with cheese as a dessert instead of fruit—an excellent aid to digesting a meal.

When cooked, the aniseed flavor becomes more subtle and the texture resembles cooked celery. Braised fennel is particularly good with white fish. Fennel can be cooked in all the same ways as celery or cardoons.

BUYING AND STORING

Fennel is available all year round. If possible, buy it with its topknot of feathery green fronds, which you can chop and use as an herb or garnish in any dish where you would use dill. The bulbs should feel firm and the outer layers should be crisp and white, not shriveled and yellowish. It should have a delicate, very fresh scent of aniseed and the crisp texture of green celery. Whole fennel bulbs will keep in the refrigerator for up to a week. Once cut, however, use them immediately, or the cut surfaces will discolor and the texture will soften. Allow a whole bulb per serving.

PREPARING AND COOKING FENNEL

If the outer layer of the fennel bulb seems stringy, peel it with a sharp knife. Cut off the round greenish stalks protruding from the top. For salads, cut the bulb vertically into thin slices. For cooked dishes, quarter the bulb. Any trimmings can be chopped and used for soups or sauces for fish.

Fennel can be sautéed, baked or braised. For all cooked fennel recipes, blanch the quartered bulbs in a large saucepan of salted boiling water until it is just tender.

To sauté, heat about 2 tbsp butter per bulb with some chopped garlic, drain the fennel and fry it gently in the butter until very tender. To enhance the flavor, add a teaspoon of Pernod or other aniseed-flavored alcohol.

Braised fennel should be cooked in a little olive oil using a covered frying pan.

To bake fennel, lay the blanched bulbs in a buttered ovenproof dish, season, dot with butter and sprinkle a generous quantity of freshly grated Parmesan over the top. Bake at 400°F for 20–30 minutes or until the top is bubbling and golden brown.

Fennel
The distinctive aniseed flavor makes this vegetable a perfect partner for white fish

Vegetables

Melanzane (eggplants)

The versatile eggplant plays an important role in the cooking of southern Italy and Sicily, possibly because its dense, satisfying texture makes a good substitute for meat. You will find many different eggplants in Italian markets, the two main types being the familiar deep purple elongated variety and the rotund paler mauve type, which has a thinner skin. Some are small, some huge, but they all taste similar and can be used in the same way for any recipe.

PREPARING EGGPLANTS

Some people believe that eggplants should always be sliced and salted for about 30 minutes before cooking to draw out the bitter juices; others deem this unnecessary. Salting does prevent eggplant from soaking up large quantities of oil during cooking, so it is probably worth doing.

Slice or dice the eggplants, place them in a colander, sprinkle with 1 tbsp salt per 2¼ lb. Place a dish on the eggplants and weight it down. Set aside for 30 minutes. Rinse the eggplants and dry with paper towels.

If eggplants have a very tough skin, it is best to peel them (unless you are stuffing them and need the skin as a container). Otherwise, leave the skin on, as its color will enhance the appearance of the finished dish.

BUYING AND STORING

Shape and size are not important when choosing eggplants; the essentials are tight, glossy skins and a fairly firm texture. Do not buy eggplants with wrinkled or damaged skins. They should feel heavy for their size; a light eggplant will probably be spongy inside and contain a lot of seeds. They will keep in the refrigerator for up to a week.

Eggplants
The familiar deep purple variety plays an important role in the cooking of southern Italy

HISTORY

Eggplant originated in Asia. They were cultivated in Europe in the Middle Ages, but only very rarely featured in Italian cooking at the time, since they were regarded with suspicion; indeed, the name *melanzane* comes from the Latin *melum insanum* (unhealthy apple). This mistrust had been overcome by the Renaissance, and eggplants began to be grown and used extensively in the south of Italy.

CULINARY USES

Eggplants are extremely versatile vegetables and add a wonderful depth of flavor to any dish in which they appear. They can be broiled, baked, stuffed, stewed and sautéed, on their own or with other ingredients, and the rich color of their skins enhances the appearance of many different Italian dishes.

COOKING EGGPLANTS

The simplest way of cooking eggplants is to slice and fry them in a generous quantity of very hot olive oil.
For a more substantial dish, coat them in light batter, then fine bread crumbs, and fry until golden brown.
To bake them, halve the eggplants lengthwise, removing the calyx and stalk. Make slashes in the flesh and rub it with a cut garlic clove. Drizzle some olive oil over the top, cover with foil and bake for about 1 hour, until very soft. Season with salt and pepper and add lemon juice to taste. Probably the most famous Italian eggplant dish is melanzane alla parmigiana, *where the eggplants are layered with rich tomato sauce and Parmesan and baked. A favorite Sicilian dish,* caponata, *combines them with celery and a piquant sweet-and-sour sauce enlivened with olives and sometimes capers.*

Peperoni *(bell peppers)*

Generically known as capsicums, the shape of these peppers gives them the alternative name of "bell peppers." Although they come in a range of colors—green (these are unripe red peppers), red, yellow, orange and even purplish-black—all peppers have much the same sweetish flavor and crunchy texture, and are interchangeable in recipes. They are a very healthy food, being rich in Vitamin C. The locally grown peppers you will see in the markets in Italy are much larger and more misshapen than the uniformly perfect, hydroponically grown specimens but their flavor is sweet and delicious.

CULINARY USES

Each region of Italy has its own specialties using peppers. They can be used raw or lightly roasted in salads or as an *antipasto* and can be cooked in a variety of ways—roasted and dressed with olive oil or vinaigrette dressing and capers, stewed (as in *peperonata*), or stuffed and baked. Peppers have a great affinity with other Mediterranean ingredients, such as olives, capers, eggplants, tomatoes and anchovies.

BUYING AND STORING

Choose firm peppers with unwrinkled, shiny skins. Size does not matter unless you plan to stuff the peppers, in which case choose roundish shapes of uniform size. The skin of green peppers may be mottled with patches of orange or red; this indicates that the pepper is ripening, and as long as the pepper is unblemished, there is no reason not to buy it. Peppers can be stored in the fridge for up to two weeks.

COOKING PEPPERS

To make a classic Italian peperonata, *sweat sliced onions and garlic in olive oil, add sliced peppers, cover the pan and cook gently until just tender. Add an equal quantity of peeled, deseeded and chopped tomatoes, a splash of wine vinegar and seasoning and cook, uncovered, until meltingly tender. For* peperonata alla romana, *stir in some capers at the end.*

Peppers
Locally grown Italian peppers are often larger and more misshapen than the uniformly perfect varieties grown in hot-houses

Vegetables

Pomodori (tomatoes)

It is impossible to imagine Italian cooking without tomatoes, which seem to be a vital ingredient in almost every recipe. But these "golden apples" were unknown in Italy until the sixteenth century, when they were brought over from Mexico. At first they were grown only in the south, but as their popularity spread, tomatoes were cultivated all over Italy and were incorporated into the cooking of every region. Italians grow an enormous variety of tomatoes, from plum tomatoes (San Marzano are the best) to ridged, pumpkin-shaped, green-tinged salad tomatoes, bright red fruits bursting with aroma and flavor, and tiny *pomodorini* (cherry tomatoes).

CULINARY USES

Tomatoes are used in so many different ways that it is hard to know where to begin. They can be eaten raw, sliced and served with a trickle of extra virgin olive oil and some torn basil leaves (basil and tomatoes have an extraordinary affinity). They are the red component of an *insalata tricolore*, partnering white mozzarella and green basil to make

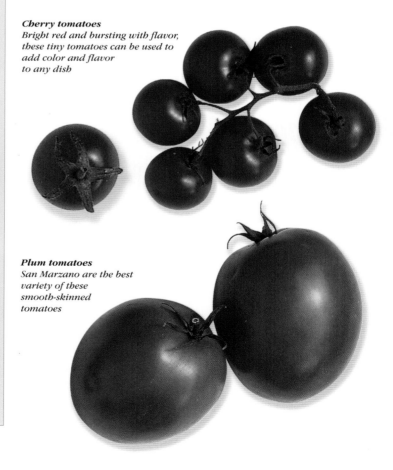

Cherry tomatoes
Bright red and bursting with flavor, these tiny tomatoes can be used to add color and flavor to any dish

Plum tomatoes
San Marzano are the best variety of these smooth-skinned tomatoes

up the colors of the Italian flag. Raw ripe tomatoes can be chopped with herbs and garlic to make a fresh-tasting pasta sauce, or made into a topping for *bruschetta*.

Tomatoes can be broiled, fried, baked, stuffed, stewed and made into sauces and soups. They add color and flavor to almost any savory dish.

BUYING AND STORING

Tomatoes are at their best in summer, when they have ripened naturally in the sun. Choose your tomatoes according to how you wish to prepare them. Salad tomatoes should be very firm and easy to slice. The best tomatoes for cooking are plum tomatoes, which hold their shape well and should have a fine flavor. Tomatoes will only ripen properly if left for long enough on the vine, so try to buy "vine-ripened" varieties. If you can find only unripe

tomatoes, you can ripen them by putting them in a brown paper bag with a ripe tomato or leaving them in a fruit bowl with a banana; the gases the ripe fruits give off will ripen the tomatoes but, alas, they cannot improve the flavor.

Try to buy tomatoes loose so that you can smell them. They should have a wonderful aroma. If the flavor is not all it should be, add a good pinch of sugar to enhance it. For cooked recipes, if you cannot find really flavorful tomatoes, use canned instead. The best are San Marzano plum tomatoes, which are grown near Salerno. In Italy, you will often find large knobby green tomatoes, which are sold as *pomodori da insalata.* Although you can let them ripen in the usual way, Italians prefer to slice these tomatoes thinly and eat them in their unripe state as a crunchy and refreshing salad.

Large tomatoes
Not always as smooth as these, locally grown Italian tomatoes bought at a market can be very ridged and almost pumpkin-shaped

PEELING TOMATOES

It is easy to remove the skin from tomatoes. Prick the tomatoes with the point of a sharp knife, plunge them into a bowl of boiling water for about 30 seconds, then refresh in cold water. Peel away the skins, cut the tomatoes into quarters or halves and remove the seeds using a teaspoon.

Vine-ripened tomatoes
Tomatoes sold on the vine are likely to have a far better flavor than those sold loose

Vegetables

Spinaci (spinach)

Spinach and its close relatives, *bietola* (Swiss chard) and *biete* (spinach beet), are dark green leafy vegetables, rich in minerals (especially iron) and vitamins. Unlike many other vegetables, they are often served in Italy as side dishes to a main course, although they appear in numerous composite dishes as well. All spinach, whether flat-leafed or curly-leafed, has a distinctive metallic flavor, which people either love or loathe. The latter should avoid dishes *alla fiorentina*, which use spinach in large quantities.

Curly-leaf spinach is a summer variety with very dark green leaves. Winter spinach has flat, smooth leaves, but tastes very similar. Usually, only the leaves are eaten and the stalks are discarded. Spinach has a delicate, melting quality and should be cooked only very briefly.

The coarser *bietola* contains less iron and has a less pronounced flavor than spinach. The leaves have broad, tender creamy or pale green midribs, and both the leaves and stalks are eaten, but are cooked in different ways. *Bietola* is available all year round, but is particularly popular in autumn and winter, when more delicate spinach is not available. No one is quite sure why it is called Swiss chard; the Swiss certainly eat it, but in much smaller quantities than the French or Italians.

Biete (spinach beet) has a much smaller stalk and more closely resembles spinach. The stalks are usually left attached to the leaves for cooking. The coarser texture of *biete* makes it more suitable than spinach for recipes that require more than the briefest cooking. Balls of ready-cooked *biete* are often sold in Italian delicatessens.

HISTORY

Spinach was originally cultivated in Persia in the sixth century and was brought to Europe by Arab traders some thousand years later. It had become very popular in France, Spain and England by the sixteenth century, when it was used for both sweet and savory dishes, but it did not reach Italy until the eighteenth century.

CULINARY USES

Tender young spinach leaves can be eaten raw in salads or cooked and served cold with a dressing of olive oil and lemon. Cooked spinach is used to make gnocchi and is often combined with ricotta to make fillings for pasta and *crespoline*

(pancakes). Florentine-style recipes usually contain spinach, and it is a classic partner for eggs, fish, poultry and white meats. Spinach, *biete* and *bietola* are all used in savory tarts, such as *torta alla pasqualina*, an Easter speciality. They make excellent soups and soufflés. *Bietola* stalks are delicious sautéed in butter and baked in a white sauce sprinkled with Parmesan.

Spinach
The tender young leaves can be eaten raw; larger leaves need to be cooked

Spinach beet
The coarse texture of biete *makes it more suitable than spinach for slower-cooked recipes*

BUYING AND STORING

All types of spinach should look very fresh and green, with no signs of wilting. The leaves should be unblemished and the stalks crisp. Spinach and spinach beets contain a very high proportion of water and wilt down to about half their weight during cooking, so always buy far more than you think you will need—at least 9 oz per serving. Loose spinach should be used as soon as possible after buying. Packed loosely into a plastic bag, it will keep in the refrigerator for a couple of days. Unopened bags of pre-packaged spinach will keep for up to a week.

Bietola (Swiss chard)

Pull off the green leaves from the stems. Snap the veins and leafstalks and remove the stringy parts (do not cut with a knife, or the strings will not come off). Wash as you would spinach and cut the stalks into 2½–3½ in lengths.

PREPARING AND COOKING SPINACH AND SWISS CHARD

Spinach and spinach beet: Carefully pick over the spinach, discarding any withered or damaged leaves and tough stalks. Wash thoroughly in several changes of water until no signs of earth or grit remain. Spinach should be cooked with only the water that clings to the leaves after washing. Sauté it in butter with a clove of chopped garlic for about 5 minutes; overcooked spinach will be unpleasantly watery. To stew spinach, put it in a large saucepan, cover and cook gently until wilted, turning it over halfway through cooking. Drain and gently squeeze out the excess moisture with your hands. Toss in butter or olive oil, season with freshly grated nutmeg or chop finely and use for gnocchi and pasta fillings.

Swiss chard leaves can be cooked exactly like spinach. The prepared stalks should be blanched until tender in salted water or vegetable stock, then baked in a sauce or tart, sautéed in butter or used as a stuffing. A popular bietola *dish is a* sformato, *a savory, molded, baked custard.*

Swiss chard
Available all year round, this vegetable is particularly popular in winter when the more tender spinach is not available

Vegetables

Zucca (squash) and zucchini

Squashes and zucchini are widely used in northern Italian cooking. Both have large, open, deep-yellow flowers, which are considered a great delicacy. Squashes come in a variety of shapes and sizes, from huge orange pumpkins to small, pale butternut squashes and green acorn squashes. They all have dense, sweet-tasting flesh. Zucchini are especially versatile, with shiny green skin and a sweet, delicate flavor. In Italy, tiny specimens are often sold with their flowers attached.

CULINARY USES

The pumpkin is the symbol of Mantua and recipes *alla mantovana* use the flesh a multitude of ways, from *tortelli alla zucca* (pumpkin-filled tortelli) to risotti, soups and sweet dessert tarts. Pumpkin flowers can be coated in batter and deep-fried, stuffed with a filling of ricotta, or chopped and added to risotti for extra color and flavor.

Zucchini combine well with other Mediterranean vegetables, like tomatoes and eggplants. They can be dipped in batter and deep-fried, made into fritters or served with a white sauce seasoned with Parmesan or nutmeg. Served cold with a mint-flavored vinaigrette (*zucchini a scapece*) or tomato sauce, they can be part of an *antipasto*. They can be halved and stuffed with a meat or vegetable filling. Young zucchini can also be thinly sliced or grated and eaten raw in a salad.

BUYING AND STORING

Zucchini are available almost all year round, but are at their best in spring and summer. The smaller and skinnier zucchini are, the better they taste. They should have very glossy green skins and feel very firm. Do not buy flabby zucchini or those with blemished skins. Larger specimens are useful for stuffing.

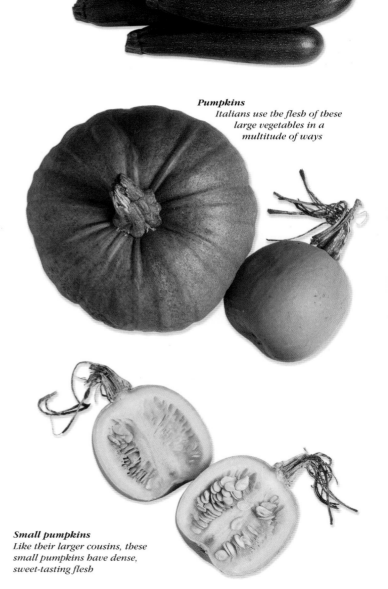

Zucchini
These familiar vegetables combine well with other Mediterranean vegetables

Pumpkins
Italians use the flesh of these large vegetables in a multitude of ways

Small pumpkins
Like their larger cousins, these small pumpkins have dense, sweet-tasting flesh

If you can find them in markets, buy tiny zucchini with their flowers attached. Allow 9 oz zucchini per serving. They will keep in the vegetable compartment of the refrigerator for up to a week.

Squashes should feel firm and heavy for their size. It is not worth buying enormous pumpkins (other than for decorative purposes), as their flesh tends to be stringy and flavorless. All whole squashes keep well, but once they are opened, they should be wrapped in plastic wrap and kept in the refrigerator for no more than three days.

If you are lucky enough to find squash or zucchini flowers (the best way is to grow your own), they must be cooked immediately, as they are extremely perishable.

PREPARING ZUCCHINI, SQUASHES AND PUMPKINS

Zucchini should be trimmed, then sliced, diced, cut into batons or grated as appropriate. They do not need peeling.

Flowers may contain small insects, so wash them quickly under cold running water and gently pat dry with paper towels. Cut off all but 1 in of the stems. Zucchini are best sautéed in butter or olive oil flavored with plenty of chopped garlic and parsley. Zucchini deep fried in a light batter are a

favorite appetizer or side dish in Italy. The flowers can be prepared in the same way. To make zucchini a scapece, slice 2¼ lb zucchini and brown in hot olive oil. Place in a dish and scatter on about 20 torn mint leaves and 1 finely chopped garlic clove. Season and dress with one part red wine vinegar and two parts olive oil. Mix well and let the flavors develop for 2 hours before serving.

Squashes and pumpkins should be peeled and the seeds and fibrous parts removed. Cut the flesh into chunks or slices. The skin of large pumpkins may be too hard to peel; if so, break open the pumpkin with a hammer or drop it on the floor, and scoop out the flesh, discarding the seeds.

Pumpkin and squash should be blanched in boiling salted water, then sweated in butter until soft and made into soup or stuffing, cooked au gratin or grated raw and added to a risotto. Pumpkin can also be sweetened and used as a pie filling.

Butternut squash
The brightly colored flesh of butternut squashes is widely used in northern Italian cooking

Acorn squash
Once halved, these small squashes need to be seeded and peeled before cooking

Salad Greens

Italians grow salad greens in profusion and gather them from the wild to create inventive and interesting combinations, such as *misticanza*, a potpourri of wild greens and cultivated leaves. In high season, you will find at least a dozen different salad greens at an Italian market, ranging from fresh green round garden lettuces to bitter dark green grass-like leaves and purplish-red radicchio. Such salads are served after the main course, simply dressed with olive oil and vinegar to cleanse the palate.

Cicoria di campo or dente di leone (dandelion)

Dandelion leaves are rich in iron and vitamins, and are also reputed to be a powerful diuretic. They have a pungent, peppery taste and long, fresh green indented leaves (hence the name "lion's tooth"). They can be picked in the wild before the plant has flowered, but only the young leaves should be eaten. Cultivated dandelion leaves are available. They are more tender than wild leaves, but have a less intense flavor.

CULINARY USES

Young dandelion leaves are usually served raw in salads together with other leaves; they are particularly good with crisply cooked bacon and hard-cooked eggs. They can also be cooked like spinach.

Radicchio

This variety of red-leafed chicory comes originally from Treviso. *Radicchio di Treviso* has elongated purplish-red leaves with pronounced cream-colored veins. The more familiar round variety is known as *radicchio di Verona*. Both types of red-leafed chicory have a bitter taste, and for salads are best used in small quantities together with other leaves. They look particularly attractive when combined with frilly-leafed curly endive, pale whitish-green chicory leaves, or the darker arugula.

Dandelion leaves
Pick these peppery-tasting leaves from the wild before the plant has flowered

Radicchio di Verona
The more familiar round red-leafed chicory

Radicchio di Treviso
This elongated variety is delicious grilled with olive oil

CULINARY USES

Radicchio can also be eaten as a hot vegetable, either quartered and grilled with olive oil, or stuffed with a mixture of bread crumbs, anchovies, capers and olives and baked—but it loses its beautiful color when cooked. A little radicchio added to a risotto made with red wine will add to the pretty pink color.

BUYING AND STORING

Radicchio leaves should be fresh-looking with no trace of brown at the edges. *Radicchio di Verona* should be firm with tightly packed leaves. Both types will keep in the refrigerator for up to a week.

Rucola *(arugula)*

Arugula has dark green elongated, indented leaves and a hot, pungent flavor and aroma. Like dandelions, it grows wild in the Italian countryside, but it is also cultivated commercially. Home-grown arugula has a much better flavor than the immature leaves usually found in supermarkets, but it bolts easily and should be picked as soon as the leaves are large enough.

CULINARY USES

Arugula adds zest to any green salad and can be eaten on its own with a dressing of olive oil and lemon juice or balsamic vinegar. Combined with radicchio, lamb's lettuce and fresh herbs, arugula makes a good substitute for *misticanza*. It can be added to pasta sauces and risotto, or cooked like spinach, but cooking does diminish the pungent flavor.

BUYING AND STORING

In Italy, arugula is always sold in small bunches. The leaves should look very fresh with no sign of wilting. Arugula does not keep well unless it has been pre-packaged. To keep it for a day or two, wrap it in damp newspaper or damp paper towels and store in the refrigerator.

Arugula
This hot, pungent salad leaf grows wild in the Italian countryside, but it is also cultivated commercially

Lamb's Lettuce
The delicate but distinctive flavor of this salad plant adds interest to winter salads

Valeriana *(lamb's lettuce)*

This delicate salad plant, called lamb's lettuce, has tender green rounded leaves bunched together in a rosette shape. It grows wild in fields in Italy, but is also cultivated and is an essential ingredient of *misticanza*. It has a delicate but distinctive flavor, which adds interest to winter salads.

CULINARY USES

Lamb's lettuce is usually served by itself or in a mixed green salad, but it can also be cooked like spinach. The tender leaves will blacken if damaged, so take care when tossing a salad not to bruise them.

BUYING AND STORING

Lamb's lettuce should look fresh and green, with no drooping leaves. The smaller and rounder the leaves, the better the flavor. It will keep in the salad compartment of the refrigerator for several days, but take care not to squash it.

PREPARING LAMB'S LETTUCE

Lamb's Lettuce is sold with the root attached, so it must be washed before use. Dunk it in several changes of cold water to remove all the grit, then dab the leaves dry with paper towels, handling them very gently.

Mushrooms

Italian country-dwellers have always been passionate collectors of edible wild mushrooms; in spring and autumn, the woods and fields are alive with furtive fungi hunters in search of these flavorful delicacies. Cultivated button mushrooms are rarely eaten in Italy, even when fresh wild varieties are out of season; Italians prefer to use dried or preserved wild fungi with their robust, earthy taste.

The most prized mushroom for use in Italian cooking is the *porcino* (cepe). Since these are extremely expensive, they are most often dried and used in small quantities to add flavor to field or other wild mushrooms. Drying actually intensifies the flavor of *porcini*, so they are not regarded as inferior to the fresh mushrooms—quite the reverse. Other popular wild fungi include *gallinacci* (chanterelles), *prataioli* (field mushroooms) and *ovoli* (Caesar's mushrooms).

HISTORY
From earliest times, man gathered and ate wild mushrooms. The Greeks and Romans enjoyed many fungi, including *amanita caesarea* (Caesar's mushroom), which was popular with the Emperor Claudius and ultimately his downfall; his wife Agrippina poisoned him by adding deadly *amanita phalloides* (the aptly named deathcap) to a dish of his favorite fungi. The Romans succeeded in cultivating several types of mushrooms, but cultivation on a large scale really began in the seventeenth century, when a French botanist discovered how to grow mushrooms in compost all year round.

STORING
Never store mushrooms in a plastic bag, as they will sweat and turn mushy. Put them into a paper bag and keep in the vegetable compartment of the refrigerator for no more than two days.

Chanterelles
These orangey-yellow mushrooms have a delicious, delicate flavor and a distinct apricot aroma

COOKING CHANTERELLES

Chanterelles have a delicious, delicate flavor and a slightly chewy texture; they should be cooked slowly or they may become hard. Fry them gently in butter with chopped garlic or shallots for about 10 minutes, adding some finely chopped parsley, marjoram or thyme toward the end of the cooking time. Serve them on hot buttered toast, or add to omelets or scrambled eggs. They are particularly good with poultry, rabbit or veal and can also be dressed with a herb-flavored vinaigrette and served warm in a salad.

CULINARY USES

Ovoli can be thinly sliced and eaten raw in a salad. They combine very well with hazelnuts.

Dried chanterelles
Dried chanterelles can be used to flavor soups, stew and pasta dishes

Ovoli (Caesar's mushrooms; Latin name amanita caesarea)

These large mushrooms with an orangey-yellow cap have an excellent flavor and were a favorite of the Roman emperors. They are still found in Italy, but are very rare elsewhere.

Mushroom powder

Well-flavored dried mushrooms can be crushed to a powder and used to flavor sauces, soups and stews. Some Italian delicatessens stock mushroom powder. If you make your own, store it in an airtight container.

RECONSTITUTING DRIED MUSHROOMS

Soak 1 oz dried mushrooms in 1 cup hot water for about 20 minutes until soft, then drain and use like fresh mushrooms. Keep the soaking water to use in sauces, stocks or soups; it will have an intense mushroom flavor.

DRYING CHANTERELLES

Leave the chanterelles whole, or halve them if they are large.

Lay them on a double thickness of newspaper and let sit in a very warm, airy place (above the heater is ideal), turning them over every few hours until they have become completely dry and brittle. Alternatively, string them like necklaces and hang them up to dry, or place in a very cool convection oven (maximum 250°F), leaving the door ajar. When the chanterelles are completely dry, store them in jars or paper bags. All mushrooms can be dried in this way; slice them thinly before drying. It is only worth drying perfect specimens.

Mushrooms

Porcini (cepes)

These are the king of mushrooms in Italian cooking. Their Italian name means "little piglets," which aptly describes their bulbous stalks and rounded brown caps. In autumn, they are found in woodlands, where they can grow to an enormous size, weighing more than 1¼ lb each (although mushroom-hunters rarely leave them for long enough to grow to these proportions). There are many different varities of *porcini*, all of which have a fine flavor and meaty texture.

CULINARY USES

All cepes can be cooked in the same way as other mushrooms. Young ones can be thinly sliced and eaten raw, dressed with extra virgin olive oil. Larger caps are delicious brushed with olive oil, grilled and served with a grinding of salt and pepper. Don't discard the stalks, which have an excellent flavor; chop them and cook with the caps, or use them for sauces, stocks and soups; just trim off the earthy bits from the base.

DRYING

Cepes can be thinly sliced and dried in the same way as *gallinacci*. Dried *porcini* are commercially available. They are very expensive, but a little goes a long way. Just 1 oz dried porcini, soaked and drained, will enhance the flavor of 1¼ lb cultivated mushrooms beyond recognition. Don't be tempted to buy cheap packages of dried *porcini*, which may contain a high proportion of inferior dried mushrooms and bits of twig from the forest floor.

STORING

Fresh *porcini* can be kept in the vegetable compartment of the refrigerator for up to two days. Dried mushrooms will keep in an airtight container for at least a year.

Porcini *(cepes)*
Italian cooks consider these to be the king of mushrooms

FREEZING

Small *porcini* in perfect condition can be frozen whole. Large or blemished specimens should be sliced and lightly sautéed in butter, then drained and frozen. Do not defrost before use, or they will become mushy. Simply cook the frozen mushrooms in hot olive oil or butter. Frozen mushrooms will only keep for about one month.

Dried porcini *(cepes)*
These dried porcini are expensive to buy, but since drying actually accentuates their flavor, a little goes a long way

---

PICKLING *PORCINI*

Unblemished fresh porcini *can be preserved by pickling. Choose unblemished fungi (if you don't have enough* porcini, *use a mixture of mushrooms), leaving small ones whole and slicing or quartering large ones.*

2¼ lb mushrooms
 generous 2 cups white wine
  vinegar
 generous 2 cups water
2 tsp salt
1 tsp peppercorns,
  lightly crushed
2 bay leaves
2 tsp coriander seeds
2 garlic cloves, peeled
  and halved
4 small dried red chilies
olive oil

1 Put the mushrooms in a saucepan with all the ingredients except the olive oil. Bring to a boil and simmer for 5–10 minutes, until the mushrooms are tender but still firm. Drain them, reserving the pickling aromatics, and let cool completely.

2 Spoon the mushrooms and aromatics into a sterilized preserving jar and fill up the jar with olive oil. Seal and let sit for at least a month. Pickled mushrooms will keep for at least six months.

Black truffles
No one has succeeded in cultivating truffles, so they remain rare and expensive—the black variety is more highly prized than the white

White truffles
Found in Piedmont, northern Italy, these delicately flavored truffles are usually served raw

Chiodini (honey fungus; Latin name armillaria mellea)

No gardener welcomes the sight of honey fungus (the Italian name means "little nails"), as it is a parasitic fungus that destroys the trees on whose roots it grows. However, the caps of these small golden mushrooms are good to eat (the fibrous stalks should be discarded). In their raw state they are mildly toxic, but once they have been blanched in very hot oil or boiling water, then stewed in butter with a little garlic, seasoning and parsley, they make good eating.

CULINARY USES

Honey fungus makes a good filling for a *frittata* (Italian omelet). Allow 5 oz *chiodini* caps and 4 large eggs for two people. Season the eggs and beat them lightly with 1 oz grated Parmesan. Heat 2 tbsp olive oil in a frying pan and sauté the blanched mushroom caps with 1 chopped garlic clove and 1 tbsp chopped parsley for about 3 minutes. Season with salt and pepper, pour in the eggs and stir well. Cook the *frittata* until set on the bottom, then sprinkle with a little more Parmesan and place under a hot grill until golden brown. Cut into wedges and serve hot or cold.

Tartufi (truffles)

Truffles grow 8 in underground, usually near oak trees. They are in season from October to late December. Their irregular, knobby, round shape conceals a pungent, earthy and delicious aroma and flavor. There are two main varieties, black and white. The more highly prized black truffles (*tuber melanosporum*) grow mostly in the Périgord region of France, but they are also found in northern Italy, in Tuscany and Piedmont. The more common Piedmont truffle is the white variety (*tuber magnatum*), which has a more delicate flavor.

No one has yet succeeded in cultivating truffles commercially, so they remain rare and expensive. They are sniffed out by trained pigs or dogs, who can detect their subterranean scent. In order to develop their full aroma and flavor, the truffles must be left to mature, so truffle-hunters often cover up those that the animals have unearthed (praying that nobody else will find their buried treasure) until they reach full maturity.

HISTORY

Truffles have been eaten since ancient times. They were a favorite dish of the ancient Egyptians. The Greeks and Romans believed them to have aphrodisiac properties, but in the Middle Ages they were thought to be manifestations of the devil. Louis XIV of France, however, subscribed to the earlier theory, and from his reign on truffles were enthusiastically consumed by all those rich enough to afford this luxury food.

CULINARY USES

Truffles can be eaten raw or cooked. White Piedmont truffles are usually served raw, shaved very thinly over fresh pasta, a *fonduta* or eggs. They can be heated briefly in butter and seasoned with salt, white pepper and nutmeg. Black or white truffles are delicious with all poultry and white meat. A few slivers of truffle will add a touch of luxury to almost any savory sauce. A classic rich Italian dish using truffles is *vincisgrassi*, sheets of fresh pasta layered with butter, cream, slivers of truffle, ham and chicken livers. It is a speciality of the Marches and the Abruzzi.

BUYING AND STORING

If you are lucky enough to find a fresh truffle, use it as soon as possible, as the flavor is volatile. Brush off the earth from the skin and peel the truffle (keep the peelings to use in a sauce). To give whole fresh eggs the most wonderful flavor, put them in a bowl with the truffle, cover and let sit overnight; they will absorb the superb musty aroma.

You are more likely to buy canned or bottled truffles than fresh. Whole ones are extremely expensive, but cheaper pieces and even peelings are available. The most economical way to enjoy the flavor of truffles is to buy Italian oil scented with white truffles. A drop or two of this added to a dish will transform it into something really special.

Truffle oil
The most economical way to enjoy the flavor of truffles— a drop or two of this scented oil will enhance sauces, pastas and salads

Fruits & Nuts

Italians prefer to buy only those fruits and nuts that are in season, and who can blame them? Italy produces an abundance of berries, pitted fruits and citrus fruits, all bursting with flavor and often available fresh from the tree. There are apples and pears from the orchards of the northern regions; nuts, peaches, plums and figs from the central plains; while the south and Sicily produce almost every kind of fruit—grapes, cherries, oranges and lemons—as well as pistachios and almonds. Many of these fruits are indigenous to Italy and have been grown there since time immemorial.

After a full meal of *antipasto*, pasta and a *secondo* (main course), it is hardly surprising that Italian desserts very often consist of nothing but a bowl of seasonal fresh fruit served on its own or made into a refreshing *macedonia* (fruit salad). Berries form the basis of ice creams, sorbets, *granite* and *frullati* (fresh fruit milkshakes), while nuts and winter fruits (often dried or candied) are baked into tarts and pastries.

Amarena *(Morello cherry)*

Although Italy does produce sweet dessert cherries, it is best known for the bitter Morello variety, which are preserved in syrup or brandy, or made into ice cream and Maraschino liqueur. These cherries are small, with dark red skins and firm flesh. They are in season from late June to early July, and can be eaten raw, although they have quite a sharp flavor.

CULINARY USES

Morello cherries can be poached in sugar syrup and served whole, or puréed and made into a rich, dark, cherry syrup. Pit the cherries and purée them. Strain the cherries through a fine sieve and let the juice sit at room temperature for about 24 hours. Strain through muslin and add 1 lb, 10 oz sugar per generous 2 cups cherry juice. Heat gently. When the sugar has dissolved, bring the cherry syrup to a boil, strain again and pour into airtight bottles or containers. These cherries also

make excellent jam. A popular Venetian dish is Morello cherries poached in a red wine syrup flavored with cinnamon. Bottled cherries in vinegar can be used in sauces for meat, duck and game.

BUYING AND STORING

Choose fresh cherries with unwrinkled and unblemished skins, which look shiny and feel firm. Stored in a plastic bag, they will keep in the refrigerator for up to a week.

Morello cherries
These dark red cherries are usually preserved in syrup and used for desserts. Those bottled in vinegar can be used for savory recipes

Arancia *(orange)*

Many varieties of oranges are grown in Sicily and southern Italy. The best-known Sicilian oranges are the small blood oranges with their bright ruby-red flesh. Other types of sweet oranges include seedless navels, which take their name from the umbilical-like end which contains an embryonic orange, and seeded late oranges, which have paler flesh and are available throughout the winter. Bitter oranges (*arance amare*) are also grown; these rough-skinned varieties are made into preserves (although rarely marmalade in Italy), candied peel and *liquore all'arancia* (orange liqueur).

HISTORY

Oranges originated in China, but bitter oranges may possibly have been known in Ancient Greece; the mythical "golden apples of the Hesperides" are said by some to have been Seville oranges, although this seems historically far-fetched. They were certainly brought to Italy by Arab traders during the Roman Empire and over the centuries became a symbol of wealth and opulence— so much so that the Medici family incorporated them into their coat of arms as five golden balls. Sweet oranges did not arrive in Italy until the seventeenth century.

Oranges
Sweet varieties are used for both sweet and savory recipes—they are a favorite addition to salads

Bitter oranges
This rough-skinned variety can be used to add zest to savory dishes—it combines well with white fish, liver, duck and game—and is used for preserves

CULINARY USES

A favorite Sicilian recipe is *insalata di arance alla siciliana*, a salad of thinly sliced oranges and red onion rings dressed with black olives and their oil. Oranges also combine well with raw fennel and chicory. They can be sliced and served *alla veneziana*, coated with caramel, or simply macerated in a little lemon juice with a sliver of lemon peel for a refreshing dessert. They can be squeezed for juice, or made into sorbet and *granita*. Bitter oranges combine well with white fish, calf's liver, duck or game, and add zest to a tomato sauce.

BUYING AND STORING

Oranges are available all year round, but are at their best in winter. They should have unblemished shiny skins and feel heavy for their size (this indicates that they contain plenty of juice and that the flesh is not dry). If you intend to candy the peel or incorporate it into a recipe, choose unwaxed oranges. Oranges will keep at room temperature for a week and for at least two weeks in the refrigerator. Bring them back to room temperature or warm them slightly before eating them.

Preparing Fresh Oranges

1 When peeling an orange it is important to remove all the bitter white pith and membrane. Hold the orange over a bowl to catch the juice and use a very sharp knife to cut off the peel, pith and the membrane enclosing the flesh.

2 To segment the orange, cut down between the membranes of the segments and ease out the flesh. Squeeze the membranes into the bowl to extract the juice.

3 To remove strips of orange rind, run a paring knife down the orange, or use a zester for finer shreds. If you cannot find unwaxed fruit, wash the oranges in warm water, rinse and dry well before removing strips of rind.

Fruit

Fico (fig)

Figs are grown all over Italy, but thanks to the hot climate Sicilian figs are perhaps the most luscious of all. During the summer months you will often find Italian farmers at the roadside selling containers of ripe figs from their own trees. There are two types of Italian figs, green and purple. Both have thin, tender skins and very sweet, succulent, red flesh, and are rich in Vitamins A, B and C. They are in season from July to October and are best eaten straight off the tree when they are perfectly ripe.

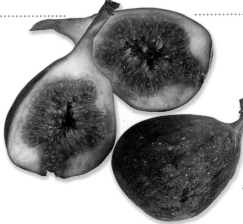

Purple figs
The sweet succulent flesh of this variety makes a perfect partner to nuts of all kinds

HISTORY

Figs were said to grow in the Garden of Eden, where Adam and Eve used the leaves to cover their nakedness. In fact they probably originated in Asia Minor, although the oldest fig tree in the world is reputed to be growing in a garden in Palermo in Sicily. The Greeks and Romans certainly enjoyed figs, which are still as highly prized today.

Green figs
Delicious served raw with prosciutto or salami as an antipasto

CULINARY USES

Fresh figs are delicious served on their own, but they have an affinity with nuts such as walnuts, pistachios and almonds. They can be served raw with prosciutto or salami as an *antipasto*, or stuffed with raspberry coulis or mascarpone as a dessert. Poached in a little water or wine flavored with cinnamon or nutmeg, they make an excellent accompaniment to duck, game or lamb.

BUYING AND STORING

Ripe figs are extremely delicate and do not travel well, so it is hard to find imported fruit at a perfect stage of maturity. In season in Italy, however, you can find local figs that are just ripe for eating; they should be soft and yielding, but not squashy. Sometimes the skin may have split, revealing the luscious red or pink flesh. As long as you are going to eat the fig immediately, this does not matter. Take great care not to squash the figs on your way home, or you will end up with a squishy, inedible mess.

Under-ripe figs can be kept at room temperature for a day or two until the skin softens, but they will never develop the fine flavor of tree-ripened figs. Ripe figs should be eaten on the day they are bought.

PREPARING AND COOKING FIGS

Wash the figs briefly and gently pat dry. Discard the stalk and peel the figs, if desired.

To serve as an antipasto *or dessert, cut them downward from the stalk end into quarters, leaving them attached at the base. Open them out like flowers.*

Perfectly ripe figs are best eaten raw, but less perfect specimens can be improved by cooking. They can be gently poached in syrup or red wine flavored with a cinnamon stick or vanilla pod, or rolled in sugar and baked in the oven until caramelized. Barely ripe figs also make excellent jam.

Limone (lemon)

Lemons are grown all over Italy, even in the northern regions. Lake Garda even boasts a town called Limone, named for its abundance of lemon trees. But the most famous Italian lemons come from the Amalfi coast, where they grow to an extraordinary size and have such a sweet flavor that they can almost be eaten as a dessert fruit. Their aromatic flavor enhances almost any dish, and they have the added advantage of being rich in Vitamin C.

HISTORY

Lemons originated in India or Malaysia and were brought by the Assyrians to Greece, which in turn took them to Italy. The Greeks and Romans greatly appreciated their culinary and medicinal qualities. Later seafarers ate them in large quantities to protect against scurvy, and society ladies used them as a beauty treatment to whiten their skin, bleach their hair and redden their lips.

CULINARY USES

Lemons are extraordinarily versatile. The juice can be squeezed to make a refreshing *spremuta di limone*, or it can be added to other cold drinks or tea. It is an antioxidant, which prevents discoloration when applied to other fruits and vegetables. The juice is used for dressings and for flavoring all sorts of drinks and sauces. A squeeze of lemon juice adds a different dimension to intrinsically bland foods, such as fish, poultry, veal or certain vegetables. Its acidity also helps to bring out the flavor of other fruits. The zest makes a wonderfully aromatic flavoring for cakes and pastries, and is an essential ingredient of *gremolata*, a topping of grated zest, garlic and parsley for *osso buco*. Quartered lemons are always served with *fritto misto di mare* (mixed fried fish) and other foods fried in batter.

PREPARING LEMONS

Before squeezing a lemon, warm it gently: Either put it in a bowl, pour boiling water over the top and let stand for about 5 minutes or, if you prefer, microwave the lemon on full power for about 30 seconds—this will significantly increase the quantity of juice you will obtain.

For sweet dishes, when you want to add the flavor of lemons, but not the grated rind, rub a sugar lump over the skin of the lemon to absorb the oil, then use the sugar as part of the recipe.

To prepare grated lemon rind, thoroughly wash and dry unwaxed lemons. Grate the rind or peel it off with a zester, taking care not to include any white pith.

BUYING AND STORING

Depending on the variety, lemons may have thick indented skin, or be perfectly smooth. Their appearance does not affect the flavor, but they should feel heavy for their size. If you intend to use the zest, buy unwaxed lemons. Lemons will keep in the refrigerator for up to two weeks.

Lemons
Lemons are grown all over Italy— their aromatic flavor enhances almost any dish

Fruits

Melone (melon)

Many different varieties of sweet, aromatic melons are grown in Italy, and each has its own regional name. *Napoletano* melons have a smooth pale green rind and delicately scented orange flesh. *Cantalupo* (cantaloupe) melons have a warty skin, which is conveniently marked into segments, and highly scented deep yellow flesh. A similar Tuscan melon with gray-green rind and orange flesh is called *popone*. These melons are all perfect for eating with Prosciutto or salami as an *antipasto*.

Watermelons (*anguria* or *cocomero*) are grown in Tuscany. These huge green melons with their refreshing bright pink or red flesh and edible brown seeds can be round or sausage-shaped. In Florence, the feast of San Lorenzo, the patron saint of cooks, is

celebrated with an orgy of watermelons on August 10th. During this season, roadside stalls groan under the weight of hundreds of these gigantic fruits.

CULINARY USES

Italians eat melon as an appetizer, usually accompanied by wafer-thin *prosciutto crudo* or cured meats. Melons and watermelons are occasionally served as a dessert fruit on their own, but more often appear in a *macedonia* (fruit salad).

BUYING AND STORING

The best way to tell whether a melon is ripe is to smell it; it should have a mild, sweet scent. If it smells highly perfumed and musky, it will be over-ripe. The fruit should feel heavy for its size and the

skin should not be bruised or damaged. Gently press the rind with your thumbs at the stalk end; it should give a little. Melons will ripen quickly at room temperature and should be eaten within two or three days. Wrap cut melon tightly in plastic wrap before storing in the refrigerator, or its scent may permeate other foods.

> #### PREPARING MELON
>
> *For serving as an* antipasto, *cut the melon into wedges, scoop out the seeds and run a flexible knife between the rind and flesh. Remove the rind before serving.*

Napoletano melon
The sweet scented flesh of this and the similar cantaloupe melon is perfect for eating with prosciutto as an antipasto

Pesche (peaches) and pesche noci (nectarines)

Peaches, with their velvety skin and sweet, juicy flesh, are a summer fruit grown in central and southern Italy. The most common variety is the *pesca gialla* (yellow peach), which has succulent, yellow flesh. More highly prized are the *pesche bianche* (white peaches), whose pink-tinted flesh is full of juice and flavor.

Nectarines have smooth plum-like skins and taste very similar to peaches. They also come in yellow and white varieties and, like peaches, the white nectarines have a finer flavor. Some people prefer nectarines as a dessert fruit because they do not require peeling. Peaches and nectarines are interchangeable in cooked dishes.

CULINARY USES

Peaches and nectarines are delicious served as a dessert fruit, but can also be macerated in fortified wine or spirits or poached in white wine and syrup. They have a particular affinity with almonds; a favorite Italian dessert is *pesche ripiene alla piemontese*, halved peaches stuffed with crumbled almond-flavored amaretti cookies and baked in white wine. They are also delicious served with raspberries, or made into fruit drinks (the famous Bellini cocktail is made with fresh peach juice) and ice creams and sorbets.

BUYING AND STORING

Peaches are in season from June to September. Make sure they are ripe, but not too soft, with unwrinkled and unblemished skins. They should have a sweet, intense scent. Peaches and nectarines bruise very easily, so try to buy those that have been kept in compartmented trays rather than piled into crates.

Do not keep peaches and nectarines for more than a day or two. If they are very ripe, store them in the refrigerator; underripe fruit will ripen in a couple of days if kept in a brown paper bag at room temperature.

PREPARING PEACHES

To peel peaches, place them in a heatproof bowl and pour boiling water over them. Let sit for 15–30 seconds (depending on how ripe they are), then refresh in very cold water; the skins will slip off easily.

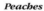

Peaches
This summer fruit is grown in central and southern Italy

Watermelon
Occasionally served on its own in wedges as a dessert, this vibrant red fruit is more usually chopped and added to a fruit salad

Nectarines
These smooth-skinned fruits are delicious served as a dessert fruit

Fruits

Uva (grapes)

Italy is the world's largest producer of grapes of all kinds. Almost every rural property boasts an expanse of vineyards, some producing wine-making grapes intended only for home consumption. Others (particularly in Chianti and the south) are destined for the enormous Italian wine-making industry. But Apulia, Abruzzo and Sicily produce sweet dessert grapes on a vast commercial scale, from large luscious Italia, with their fine muscat flavor, to Cardinal, named for its deep red color, purple Alphonse Lavallé, and various small seedless varieties.

Despite their high caloric value, grapes are extremely good for you, since they are rich in potassium, iron and vitamins.

HISTORY

Wild grapes grew in the Caucasus as early as the Stone Age, and early man soon discovered the secret of cultivating vineyards and making wine. The Greeks and Romans discovered that drying grapes transformed them into sweet raisins. The Gauls invented the wooden wine cask, and from that time on wine production became a major industry.

CULINARY USES

Dessert grapes are best eaten on their own or as an accompaniment to cheese, but they can be used in pastries or as a garnish for cooked quails, guinea fowl or other poultry. The seeds are pressed into grapeseed oil, which has a neutral taste and is high in polyunsaturated fatty acids.

BUYING AND STORING

Choosing white, black or red grapes is a matter of preference; beneath the skin, the flesh is always pale green and juicy. Buy bunches of grapes with fruit which is of equal size and not too densely packed on the stalk. Check that none is withered or rotten. The skin should have a delicate bloom and be firm to the touch. Try to eat one grape from a bunch to see how they taste. The flesh should be firm and very juicy and refreshing.

Grapes should be washed immediately after purchase, then placed in a bowl and kept in the refrigerator for up to three days. Keeping them in a plastic bag causes them to become overripe very quickly.

> #### PREPARING GRAPES
>
> *Grapes used for cooking should be peeled and deseeded. Put them in a bowl, pour in boiling water and let sit for 10–20 seconds, depending on the ripeness of the grapes. Peel off the skin. To remove the seeds, halve the grapes and scoop out the seeds with the tip of a pointed knife.*

Italia grapes
These luscious red and white grapes have a wonderful Muscat flavor

Nuts

Many different kinds of nuts are grown in Italy—chestnuts and hazelnuts in the north, pine nuts in the coastal regions, and almonds, pistachios and walnuts in the south. They are used in a wide variety of savory dishes, cakes and pastries, or served as a dessert with a glass of *vin santo* (sweet white wine).

Castagne (chestnuts)

These are a mainstay of Tuscan and Sardinian cooking, dating back to the days when the peasants could not afford wheat to make flour, so they ground up the chestnuts that grow in abundance throughout the region instead. Most varieties of sweet chestnut contain two or three

Chestnuts
A mainstay of Tuscan and Sardinian cooking

separate nuts inside the spiky green husk, but commercially grown varieties contain a single, large nut, which is easier to peel and better for serving whole.

Chestnuts have shiny, rich reddish-brown shells with a wrinkled, thin skin beneath, which can be very hard to remove. They cannot be eaten raw, but once cooked, the starchy nuts are highly nutritious and very sustaining.

Culinary Uses

Chestnuts roasted over an open fire conjure up the spirit of autumn. Peeled chestnuts can be boiled, poached in red wine or milk or fried in butter as a garnish. They make hearty soups, or can be puréed into sauces for game. In Piedmont, they are candied to make *marrons glacés*, and a favorite Italian dessert is *monte bianco*, a rich concoction of puréed chestnuts and cream.

Chestnut flour is still widely used in Tuscany and Liguria, where it is baked into cakes and pastries, such as *castagnaccio*, a confection with pine nuts and herbs.

Buying and Storing

The nicest chestnuts are those you gather yourself, but if you are buying them, look for large, shiny specimens, with no tiny holes in the shells. The chestnuts should feel heavy for their size and not rattle when you shake them. They will keep in a cool place for at least two weeks. If any holes appear in the shells, discard the nut immediately, or you will very soon have an infestation of maggots.

Mandorle (almonds)

Two varieties of almonds are grown in central and southern Italy. *Mandorle dolci* (sweet almonds) are eaten as a dessert or used in cooking and baking, while *mandorle amare* (bitter almonds) are used to flavor liqueurs such as amaretto or bittersweet confections such as amaretti cookies. These almonds are not edible in their raw state; in fact, they are poisonous if consumed in large quantities. Both types of almonds have a velvety pale green outer casing; the hard light brown shell within encloses one or two oval nuts.

Culinary Uses

Early in the season (late May), sweet almonds can be eaten raw as a dessert. They have a delicious fresh flavor and the brown skin is still soft enough to be palatable. Later, dried sweet almonds are blanched, slivered or ground to be used for cakes, pastries and all sorts of confectionery, including *marzapane* (marzipan) and *croccante* (almond brittle). They can be devilled or salted as an appetizing

Preparing Chestnuts

There are three possible ways to peel chestnuts.

Slit the domed side of the shells with a very sharp knife, then drop them into boiling water for 5 minutes, or put them in a roasting pan with a little hot water and cook in a very hot oven for about 10 minutes. Shell and skin the chestnuts as soon as they are cool enough to handle. Alternatively, shell the raw chestnuts and boil them in their skins for about 20 minutes, then peel off the skins.

snack with an *aperitivo*. Toasted almonds are the classic garnish for trout, and go well with chicken or rabbit. Dried bitter almonds are used in small quantities to add a more intense flavor to cookies and cakes.

Almonds
In Italy in late spring, fresh almonds are eaten raw as a dessert

Nuts

Buying and Storing
Fresh almonds in the shell are available from late May to late June. They are difficult to crack, so you may prefer to buy shelled nuts. They should look plump, and the skins should not feel too dry. Pre-blanched almonds can often be a disappointment; buy the nuts with their skins on and blanch them yourself. Store shelled almonds in an airtight container for no longer than a month.

Nocciole (hazelnuts)
Fresh hazelnuts are harvested in August and September and during these months are always sold in their frilled green husks. The small round nuts have a very sweet flavor and a milky texture when fresh. In Italy, they are generally dried and used in candy and cakes.

Culinary Uses
Hazelnuts are used in all sorts of confectionery, including *torrone* (a sort of nougat) and *gianduiotti*, a delicious fondant chocolate from Piedmont. The famous chocolate *baci* ("kisses") from Perugia contain a whole hazelnut in the center. Hazelnuts are finely ground to make cakes and cookies, and are excellent in stuffings for poultry and game.

Buying and Storing
If hazelnuts are sold in their fresh green husks, you can be sure they are fresh and juicy. Otherwise, look for shiny unblemished shells that are not too thick; cracked shells will cause the nut to shrivel and dry out. Shelled hazelnuts should be kept in an airtight container for no longer than one month.

Noci (walnuts)
Walnuts grow in abundance throughout central and southern Italy. The kernels, shaped like the two halves of a brain, grow inside a pale brown, heavily indented shell enclosed by a smooth green fleshy husk or "shuck." Fresh walnuts have a delicious milky sweetness and a soft texture, which hardens as the nuts mature. Walnuts do not need to be skinned before eating.

Shelled almonds
These dried almonds are used for cakes, pastries and candies

Walnuts
In Italy, fresh walnuts are very often eaten straight from the shell as a dessert

Shelled hazelnuts
These dried nuts are used for candies and cakes

Hazelnuts
When fresh, these small nuts have a very sweet flavor

Preparing Almonds

To blanch almonds, place them in a strainer and plunge into boiling water for a few seconds. As soon as the skin begins to loosen, transfer the almonds to a bowl of cold water and slip off the skins. Dry thoroughly before storing.

CULINARY USES

Fresh walnuts are usually eaten straight from the shell as a dessert. They can be ground or chopped and used in cakes and desserts, or halved and used for decoration. They are used to make savory sauces for pasta, such as *salsa di noci*, a rich combination of ground walnuts, butter and cream. Walnut oil has a distinctive flavor and, used sparingly, makes an excellent salad dressing. Unripe walnuts can be pickled, and they are used to make sweet, sticky liqueurs.

BUYING AND STORING

Fresh "wet" walnuts are available from late September to late October. They should be kept in a wicker basket and eaten within a week. Dried walnuts should not have cracked or broken shells. They will keep for at least two months. Never store walnuts in the refrigerator, as the oil they contain will harden and ruin the flavor. Dried walnut kernels will have the flavor and texture of fresh nuts if they are soaked in milk for at least 4 hours.

Pine nuts
The oily, slightly resinous flavor is accentuated by toasting

Pinoli (pine nuts)

Pine nuts (more accurately known as pine kernels) are actually the seeds from the stone pine trees that grow in profusion along the Adriatic and Mediterranean coasts of Italy. The small, oblong, cream-colored seeds grow inside a hard husk and are extracted from between the scales of the pine cones. The soft-textured kernels, which have an oily, slightly resinous flavor, are always sold de-husked. They can be eaten raw, but are usually toasted before use to bring out the flavor.

CULINARY USES

Pine nuts are used in many Italian dishes, both sweet and savory, but they are best known as an essential ingredient of pesto. They go well with meat and game, and make exceptionally delicious cookies and tarts.

Pistachio nuts
Grown in southern Italy, these sweet, delicately flavored nuts are used in mortadella

BUYING AND STORING

Pine nuts are always sold out of the husk. Because they are very oily, they go rancid quite quickly, so buy only as much as you need at any one time. Store them in an airtight container in the fridge for not more than a week.

Pistacchi (pistachios)

Pistachios are native to the Near East, but are grown in southern Italy, particularly Sicily. The small, bright green nut has a yellowish-red skin and is enclosed in a smooth, pale shell. Pistachios have a sweet, delicate flavor, which makes them ideal for desserts, but they are also used to stud mortadella and other pale cooked meat products.

CULINARY USES

Pistachios can be eaten raw or roasted and salted as a snack with an *aperitivo*. Their color enhances most white meats and poultry. They make deliciously rich ice cream and are used in *cassata gelata*, the famous Sicilian dessert.

BUYING AND STORING

If possible, buy pistachios still in their shells. These will be easier to open if they are already slightly ajar; once open, the nut is very easy to remove. Shelled, blanched pistachios are also available. They are useful for cooking, but lack the fine flavor of whole nuts. Store blanched pistachios in an airtight container for up to two weeks. Whole nuts will keep for well over a month.

Herbs & Seasonings

Herbs are vital to Italian cooking. Their aromatic flavor adds depth and interest to what is essentially plain cooking, based on fine, fresh ingredients. It is impossible to imagine roast chicken or veal without rosemary or sage, or tomatoes or pesto without basil. Many wild herbs grow in the Italian countryside, and these are often incorporated into Italian recipes. One of the most popular is mentuccia, *a wild mint with tiny leaves and the delicate favor of* marjoram. *If a recipe specifies* mentuccia *or its close relative* nepitella, *substitute a smaller quantity of mint.*

Always use fresh herbs whenever you can; the dried varieties have a stronger and often quite different taste, and lack the subtlety of fresh herbs. If you must use dried herbs, try to buy them freeze-dried; these taste much closer to the real thing. As a general rule, you will need only about one-third as much dried herb as fresh—in other words, allow about 1 tsp dried herbs for every 1 tbsp fresh.

Basilico (basil)

Basil, with its intense aroma and fresh, pungently sweet flavor, is associated with Italian cooking more than any other herb. It is an essential ingredient of pesto, but it also finds its way into soups, salads and almost all dishes based on tomatoes, with which it has an extraordinary affinity. There are over 50 varieties of this annual herb, but the one most commonly used in Italy is sweet basil, with its fresh broad green leaves and wonderfully spicy aroma.

CULINARY USES

Basil has a volatile flavor, so it is best added to dishes at the end of cooking. It can be used in any dish that contains tomatoes and is delicious sprinkled on a pizza. It adds a pungent, sweet note to almost all salads and is particularly good with white fish and seafood. It makes an excellent flavoring for omelets and is often added to

minestrone. The most famous of all basil dishes is pesto, the fragrant Genovese sauce made by pounding together fresh basil, garlic, Parmesan, pine nuts and olive oil.

BUYING AND STORING

In sunny climates, such as southern Italy, basil grows outdoors all through the summer. In other places it is available cut or growing in pots all year round, so there really is no reason to use dried basil. Look for sweet basil with bright green leaves—the larger the better. If you have grown your own and have a glut, you can freeze basil leaves to preserve the flavor, but they lose their fresh texture and darken in color. Alternatively, put a bunch of basil in a jar and fill up with olive oil for a fragrant flavored oil for dressings. To store fresh cut basil, wrap it in damp paper towels and keep in the vegetable compartment of the refrigerator for up to two days.

Basil
More than any other, this pungent, intensely flavored herb is associated with Italian cooking—it is an essential ingredient in many dishes, including pesto

---

PREPARING BASIL

Basil leaves are tender and bruise easily, so never chop them with a knife, but tear them lightly with your fingers immediately before using.

Pesto

To make enough pesto for 4–6 servings of pasta, put 2 cups basil leaves in a mortar with ½ cup pine nuts, 2 fat peeled garlic cloves and a large pinch of coarse salt, and crush to a paste with a pestle. Work in ½ cup freshly grated Parmesan. Gradually add about ½ cup extra virgin olive oil, working it in thoroughly with a wooden spoon to make a thick, creamy sauce. Put the pesto in a screwtop jar; it will keep for several weeks in the refrigerator.

Maggiorana (sweet marjoram) and origano (oregano)

These two highly aromatic herbs are closely related (oregano is the wild variety), but marjoram has a much milder flavor. Marjoram is more commonly used in northern Italy, while oregano is widely used in the south to flavor tomato dishes, vegetables and pizzas. Drying greatly intensifies the flavor of both herbs, so they should be used very sparingly.

CULINARY USES

In northern Italy, sweet marjoram is used to flavor meat, poultry, vegetables and soups; the flavor goes particularly well with carrots and cucumber. Despite its rather pungent aroma, marjoram has a delicate flavor, so it should be added to long-cooked foods toward the end of cooking.

Oregano is used exclusively in southern Italian cooking, especially in tomato-based dishes. It is a classic flavoring for pizza, but should always be used in moderation.

BUYING AND STORING

Marjoram and oregano are in season throughout the summer, but cut fresh herbs are available all year round at supermarkets. The leaves dry out quickly, so store them in plastic bags in the refrigerator; they will keep for up to a week. Dried oregano should be stored in small airtight jars away from the light. It loses its pungent flavor after a few months, so only buy a little at a time.

Oregano
Widely used in the south of Italy to flavor tomato dishes

Prezzemolo (parsley)

Italian parsley is the flat leaf variety, which has a more robust flavor than curly parsley. It has attractive dark green leaves, which resemble cilantro. It is used as a flavoring in innumerable cooked dishes, but rarely as a garnish. If flat leaf parsley is not available, curly parsley makes a perfectly adequate substitute. Parsley is an extremely nutritious herb, rich in iron and potassium and Vitamin C.

Marjoram
The aromatic flavor of this herb is very similar to that of oregano, but much milder

Parsley
Italian parsley is the flat leafed variety. It has a strong, robust flavor

Herbs & Seasonings

CULINARY USES

Parsley can be used to flavor innumerable savory dishes. It adds color and flavor to sauces, soups and risotto. The stalks can be used to flavor stocks and stews. Chopped parsley can be sprinkled over cooked savory dishes; whole leaves are rarely used as a garnish in Italy.

BUYING AND STORING

Parsley is available all year round, so it should never be necessary to use the dried variety. A large bunch of parsley will keep for up to a week in the fridge if washed and wrapped in damp paper towels. Chopped parsley freezes very well and can be added to cooked dishes straight from the freezer.

Rosmarino (rosemary)

Spiky evergreen rosemary bushes, with their attractive blue flowers, grow wild all over Italy. The herb has a delicious, highly aromatic flavor, which is intensifed when it is dried. The texture of rosemary leaves is quite hard and the flavor very pungent, so it is never used raw, but only in cooking. It can easily overpower a dish, so only a few leaves should be used in a dish.

CULINARY USES

Rosemary combines extremely well with roast or grilled lamb, veal and chicken. A few needles will enhance the flavor of baked fish or any tomato dish, and it adds a wonderful flavor to roast potatoes and onions. Some rosemary branches added to the charcoal on a barbecue impart a superb flavor to whatever is being cooked. Dried rosemary can always be substituted for fresh; it is extremely pungent, so should be used very sparingly.

Salvia (sage)

Wild sage grows in profusion in the Italian countryside. There are several varieties, including the common garden sage, with furry silvery-gray leaves and spiky purple flowers, and clary sage, with hairy curly leaves, which is used to make dry vermouth. All sages have a slightly bitter aromatic flavor, which contrasts well with fatty meats such as pork. In northern Italy, particularly Tuscany, it is used to flavor veal and chicken. It is an excellent medicinal herb (the Latin name means "good health"); an infusion of sage leaves makes a good gargle for a sore throat.

CULINARY USES

Used sparingly, sage combines well with almost all meat and vegetable dishes and is often used in minestrone. It has a particular affinity with veal (such as *osso buco*, *piccata* and, of course, calf's

Sage
Several varieties of this herb grow in profusion in the Italian countryside

liver) and is an essential ingredient of *saltimbocca alla romana*, veal scallops and *prosciutto crudo* topped with sage leaves and sautéed in butter and white wine. In Tuscany, white beans (*fagioli*) are often flavored with sage.

BUYING AND STORING

Fresh sage is very easy to grow on a sunny windowsill. It is available in both fresh and dried forms at supermarkets all year round. Dried sage is very strongly flavored, so should be used in tiny quantities. It starts to taste musty after a few weeks, so replace it fairly frequently. Fresh sage should be stored in a plastic bag in the refrigerator; it will keep for up to a week.

Rosemary
The highly aromatic flavor of this herb is intensified when it is dried

Aceto (vinegar)

Like all wine-making countries, Italy produces excellent red and white wine vinegar as a byproduct. The best vinegar is made from good wines, which are fermented in oak casks to give a depth of flavor. Good vinegar should be clean-tasting and aromatic, with no trace of bitterness, and it should be transparent, not cloudy. White wine vinegar is pale golden with a pinkish tinge; red wine vinegar ranges from deep pink to dark red.

Aceto balsamico (balsamic vinegar)

Balsamic vinegar is the king of vinegars. Its name means "balm-like," reflecting its digestive qualities. Indeed, the best has a flavor so mellow and sweet that it can be drunk on its own as a *digestivo*. Balsamic vinegar is made in the area around Modena; the boiled and concentrated juice of local *trebbiano* grapes is aged in a series of barrels of decreasing size and different woods over a long period— sometimes as long as 50 years —which gives it a slightly syrupy texture and a

rich, deep mahogany color. Like Parmigiano Reggiano and prosciutto, genuine balsamic vinegar (*aceto balsamico tradizionale di Modena*) is strictly controlled by law; it must have been aged in the wood for at least 12 years. Vinegar aged 20 years or more is called *stravecchio*.

CULINARY USES

Red and white wine vinegars are principally used to make salad dressings and marinades, or to preserve vegetables *sott'aceto* for *antipasti*. They also add the requisite sharpness to sauces such as *agrodolce* (sweet-and-sour). Good balsamic vinegar is also used as a dressing, sometimes on its own. It can be used to finish a delicate sauce for white fish, poultry or calf's liver. A few drops

sprinkled over ripe strawberries will enhance their flavor.

BUYING AND STORING

Price is usually an indication of quality where vinegar is concerned, so always buy the best you can afford. Genuine balsamic vinegar must be labeled *aceto balsamico tradizionale di Modena*; products that purport to be the real thing but are not labeled as such have either not been aged for long enough or, worse, are just red wine vinegar colored and flavored with caramel. Proper balsamic vinegar is expensive, but the flavor is so concentrated that a little goes a long way, and it is worth paying more for the genuine article. Vinegar will keep in a cool dark place for many months.

Balsamic vinegar
This is the king of vinegars and has a wonderfully sweet and mellow flavor

Red and white wine vinegars
These vinegars have a sharp flavor and are used primarily for salad dressings

Herbs & Seasonings

Aglio (garlic)

Garlic is not, as you might suppose, a type of onion, but is a member of the lily family. The bulb or "head" is a collection of cloves held together by a papery white or purplish skin. When crushed or chopped it releases a pungent, slightly acrid oil with a very distinctive flavor and smell. Freshly picked garlic is milder than older, dried garlic, and the large, mauve-tinged variety has a more delicate flavor than the smaller white variety.

Garlic finds its way into many Italian dishes, but it is generally used with discretion so as not to flavor the food too aggressively. It is indispensable to certain dishes such as *bagna cauda* (hot anchovy and garlic dip), *spaghetti all'aglio e olio* (garlic and olive oil) and pesto. In the south, garlic is used to flavor tomato sauces and fish soups.

CULINARY USES

Used in small quantities, garlic enlivens almost any sauce, soup or stew. It can be roasted with lamb and potatoes, or baked in its skin for a mellower flavor. Blanched, crushed garlic will aromatize olive oil to make an excellent dressing for salads or to use in cooking where only a hint of garlic flavor is required. Raw, skinned garlic cloves can be rubbed over toasted croutons to make flavorful *bruschetta* bases.

BUYING AND STORING

Garlic sold loose by the head is usually fresher and better than pre-packaged varieties. The heads should feel firm and the skin should not be too papery. Do not buy garlic that is sprouting green shoots; the cloves will be soft and of no culinary value.

Stored in a cool dry place, garlic will keep for many months. If possible, hang the heads in bunches to keep them aerated. Once garlic has become soft or withered, it is useless, so throw it away.

Garlic
Italian cooks prefer to use garlic with discretion, but it is indispensable to many dishes. The purple-skinned variety has a more delicate flavor than the white variety

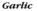

PREPARING AND COOKING GARLIC

To peel garlic, cut off the root end with a small sharp knife and peel the skin upward.

Alternatively, lay a garlic clove on the work surface, place the flat side of a heavy knife blade on top and bring the side of your fist sharply down on to the blade. This will flatten the garlic and split the skin.

To chop garlic, halve the clove and remove the bitter-tasting green shoot. Chop the garlic as finely as possible.

For very fine garlic, crush it in a garlic press.

Garlic should be softened gently in oil or butter; it will become very bitter if allowed to brown. For a subtle flavor, heat a whole clove of garlic in the oil, then remove it before adding the other ingredients. The flavor of garlic dissipates quite quickly during cooking, so for long-cooked dishes add it toward the end of the cooking time.

Olive (olives)

A wide variety of olives is cultivated all over Italy. Most are destined to be pressed into oil (nearly 20 percent of their weight is oil), but some are kept as table olives to be salted, pickled or marinated, and served as part of an *antipasto* or used in cooking. There are two main types of olive, green (immature) and black (mature); both are bitter and inedible in their natural state. All olives have a high caloric content and are rich in iron, potassium and vitamins.

Green olives are the unripe fruit, which are picked in October or November. They have a sharper flavor and crunchier texture than black olives, which continue to ripen on the tree and are not harvested until December. Among the best Italian table olives are the small, shiny black Gaeta olives from Liguria. Wrinkled black olives from Lazio have a strong, salty flavor, while Sardinian olives are semi-ripened and are brown or purplish in color. The largest olives come from Apulia and Sicily, where giant, green specimens are grown. These are sometimes pitted and stuffed with pimento, anchovy or almonds. Cured olives can be flavored with all sorts of aromatics, such as garlic, local herbs, orange or lemon zest and dried chilies.

HISTORY

Olive trees have been grown in the Mediterranean since Biblical times, when they were brought there from the East by the Romans. Ancient civilizations venerated the olive tree; the Egyptians believed that the goddess Isis discovered the secret of extracting oil from the fruit.

CULINARY USES

Olives can be served on their own or as a garnish or topping for pizza. They are used as an ingredient in many Italian recipes, such as *caponata*. Sicilian *caponata* is a dome-shaped salad of fried eggplants with celery, onions, tomatoes, capers and green olives, while the Ligurian dish of the same name consists of stale crackers or bread soaked in olive oil and topped with a mixture of chopped olives, garlic, anchovies and oregano. Olives combine well with Mediterranean ingredients such as tomatoes, eggplants, anchovies and capers and are used in sauces for rabbit, chicken and firm-fleshed fish. Made into a paste with red wine vinegar, garlic and olive oil, they make an excellent topping for *crostini*.

BUYING AND STORING

Cured olives vary enormously in flavor, so ask to taste one before making your selection. Loose olives can be kept in an airtight container in the refrigerator for up to a week.

Green olives
These unripe olives have a sharper flavor than black olives

Capperi (capers)

Capers are the immature flower buds of a wild Mediterranean shrub. They are pickled in white wine vinegar or preserved in brine, which gives them a piquant, peppery flavor. Sicilian capers are packed in whole salt, which should be rinsed off before using the capers. Bottled nasturtium flower buds are sometimes sold as a cheaper alternative to true capers. Caper berries look like large, fat capers on a long stalk, but they are actually the fruit of the caper shrub. They can be served as an hors d'oeuvre or in a salad.

Black olives
Olives are among the oldest fruits known to man. They are grown all over Italy

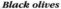

Caper berries
The pickled fruit of the caper shrub can be served as an hors d'oeuvre.

Herbs & Seasonings

CULINARY USES

Capers are mainly used as a
condiment or garnish, but they also
add zest to seafood and fish dishes,
salads, pizzas and pasta sauces such
as the famous Sicilian *pasta colle
sarde*, a mixture of sardines, parsley,
tomatoes, pine nuts and raisins.

BUYING AND STORING

Choosing pickled or brined capers is
a matter of taste, as is whether or not
you should rinse them before use.
Large capers are usually cheaper than
small ones; there is no difference in
flavor, but small capers make a more
attractive garnish. Salt-packed capers
are always sold loose by the *etto*
(3½ oz); they should be used as
soon as possible. Once opened, jars
of capers should be kept in the
refrigerator. Make sure any capers
left in the jar are covered with the
preserving liquid.

Pickled capers
*Rinsing these capers before use
softens their sharp, piquant flavor*

Olio di oliva *(olive oil)*

Unlike other oils, which are extracted
from the seeds or dried fruits of
plants, olive oil is pressed from the
pulp of ripe olives, which gives it an
inimitable richness and flavor.
Different regions of Italy produce
distinctively different olive oils;
Tuscan oil (considered the best) is
pungent and peppery, Ligurian oil is
lighter and sweeter, while the oils
from the south and Sicily are
powerful and nutty.

The best olive oil is *extra vergine*,
which is strictly controlled and
regulated like wine. This is made
simply by pressing the olives to
extract the oil, with no further
processing. Extra virgin olive oil must
have an acidity level of less than
1 percent. The distinctive fruity flavor
of this oil makes it ideal for dressings
and using raw. Virgin olive oil is
pressed in the same way, but has a
higher acidity level and a less refined
flavor. It, too, can be used
as a condiment, but is also suitable
for cooking. Unclassified olive oil
is refined, then blended with virgin
oil to add flavor. It has an
undistinguished taste, but is ideal
for cooking; it should not be used
as a condiment.

BUYING AND STORING

The best olive oil comes from Lucca
in Tuscany and is very expensive. It is
made with slightly under-ripe olives,
which give it a luminous green color.
If your budget does not stretch to
this, buy the best extra virgin oil you
can afford to use "neat" or in
dressings. Experiment with small
bottles of different extra virgin oils to
see which you prefer. For cooking,
pure olive oil is fine. Once opened,
olive oil should be kept in a cool
place away from the light. The best
oil will soon lose its savor, so use it
within six months.

Extra virgin olive oil
*The distinctive fruity flavor makes
this oil ideal for salad dressings*

COOKING WITH OLIVE OIL

*Olive oil can be heated to very
high temperatures without
burning or smoking, which
makes it ideal for frying, sauce-
making and other cooking.
Extra virgin olive oil should be
saved for dressing fish,
vegetables and salads.*

Peperoncini (dried red chilies)

Hot flakes of dried chilies are added to many southern Italian dishes, such as *arrabbiata* sauce and the famous *pasta all'aglio, olio e peperoncino* (dressed with garlic, oil and chilies). Chilies are unusual in that their "hotness" is usually in inverse proportion to their size, so larger dried varieties are generally milder than the smaller ones. In summer, bunches of tiny fresh red chilies can be bought in Italian markets. These can be used fresh, preserved in olive oil to make a spicy dressing or to drizzle over a pizza, or hung up to dry and crumbled to add "oomph" to a dish. Crushed chili flakes are available in jars.

CULINARY USES

A small pinch of dried chili flakes spices up stews and sauces, particularly those made with tomatoes. For a really hot pizza, crumble a few flakes over the top. Dried chilies are extremely fiery and should be used very sparingly.

BUYING AND STORING

Dried chilies will last for years, but they do lose their savor over a period of time, so buy only small quantities. Whole *peperoncini* should be hung up in bunches and crumbled directly into the dish you are cooking.

Dried chilies
These are often used in fiery southern Italian dishes, such as arrabbiata *sauce*

Dried red chili flakes
Just a small pinch of these fiery flakes spices up stews and sauces

Zafferano (saffron)

Saffron consists of the dried stigmas of the saffron crocus. It takes about 80,000 crocuses to produce about 1¼ lb of spice and these have to be hand-picked, so it is hardly surprising that saffron is the world's most expensive spice. Saffron stigmas or threads are a vivid orangey-red color with a pungent aroma. They are also sold ground into powder. Saffron has a highly aromatic flavor and will impart a wonderful, rich golden color to risotti and sauces.

Saffron threads
Used to flavor and color the classic risotto alla milanese

HISTORY

Saffron originated in Asia Minor, where it was used by ancient civilizations as a flavoring, as a dye, in perfumery and for medicinal purposes. Arab traders brought the spice to the Mediterranean in the tenth century; for centuries it was so highly prized that stealing or adulterating it was punishable by death. The best saffron is nowadays cultivated in Spain, but it is also grown in Italy.

CULINARY USES

In Italy, saffron is mainly used to flavor and color risotti, such as the classic *risotto alla milanese*. It is excellent in sauces for fish and poultry and can be used to flavor cookies and cakes.

BUYING AND STORING

Saffron threads are sold in small boxes or jars containing only a few strands. The wiry threads should be a deep orangey-red in color; paler yellowish-orange threads are probably the much cheaper and less desirable safflower, which will add color but not flavor to a dish. Powdered saffron is convenient to use, but less reliable, as it may have been adulterated with safflower. Stored in small, airtight containers, saffron will keep for months.

COOKING WITH SAFFRON

Do not add saffron directly to a dish. Infuse threads in a little hot water for at least 5 minutes before blending into a dish to bring out the flavor and ensure even coloring. Add the soaking water together with the threads. Never fry saffron in hot oil or butter; this will ruin the flavor.

Cakes, Cookies & Breads

In Italy it is perfectly normal and acceptable for a hostess to buy a dolce *(cake or dessert) to serve at the end of a meal, rather than make it herself. Pastry shops and bakeries sell a wide variety of traditional tarts, spiced yeast cakes and cookies to be enjoyed with coffee or a glass of vin santo, sweet dessert wine or a liqueur. Some of these, such as* panettone *and* colomba, *are reserved for special occasions like Christmas and Easter, and almost every town has its own specialty for its local saint's day.*

Amaretti *(macaroons)*

Amaretti cookies are made from ground almonds, egg whites and sugar. They have a distinctive flavor, which comes from the addition of bitter almonds. They originated in Venice during the Renaissance and their English name of macaroons comes from the Venetian *macerone*, meaning "fine paste." They come in dozens of different forms, from the famous crunchy sugar-encrusted cookies wrapped in pairs in twists of crisp white paper to soft-centered macaroons wrapped in brightly-colored foil. Amaretti are delicious dipped into hot coffee. They can also be crumbled to make a stuffing for baked peaches or apricots.

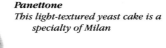

Panettone
This light-textured yeast cake is a specialty of Milan

Cantucci

These hard, high-baked lozenge-shaped cookies from Tuscany are designed to be dipped into *espresso* coffee or vin santo. When moistened, they become deliciously soft and crumbly. They are usually studded with almonds or other nuts and flavored with aniseed or vanilla.

Amaretti
These crunchy sugar-encrusted cookies are delicious dipped into hot coffee

Cantucci

Panettone

Literally meaning "big bread," *panettone* is a light-textured spiced yeast bread containing raisins and candied fruit. Originally a specialty of Milan, it is now sold all over Italy as a Christmas delicacy and is traditionally given as a gift. *Panettoni* can vary in size from small to enormous. They are sometimes sold in pastel-colored dome-shaped boxes, which are often hung from the ceiling of bakeries and delicatessens, and look very festive. At Easter, they are baked into the shape of a lamb (*agnello*) or a dove (*colomba*). *Panettone* is sliced into wedges and eaten like cake.

Crumiri

These sweet elbow-shaped cookies are a speciality of Piedmont. The rich golden brown dough is made with polenta and honey and piped through a fluted nozzle to give the cookies their characteristic ridged texture. Although the cookies seem hard on the outside, the polenta flour gives the *crumiri* a pleasantly crunchy texture. *Crumiri* are good snack cookies, but they are also excellent dipped in hot coffee.

Panforte

Somewhat resembling a Christmas pudding in flavor, but shaped like a flat disc, *panforte* is a rich, dark spiced cake crammed with dried fruit and toasted nuts. It is a speciality of Siena and is sold in a colorful glossy wrapping, often depicting Sienese scenes. It is extremely rich, so can only be eaten in small quantities, which is just as well, since it is also quite expensive.

Panettone
The characteristic box often hangs from the ceiling in Italian delicatessens

Panforte
This Italian spice cake is packed full of fruit and nuts

Savoiardi
These soft-textured, Italian sponge finger cookies are used as a base for tiramisù

Savoiardi (sponge cookies)

As their name suggests, *savoiardi* come from the Savoy region of Piedmont. They are plumper and wider than sponge fingers and have a softer texture. They are excellent dunked into tea or coffee, and are traditionally served with *zabaglione*; but they are best of all used as a base for tiramisù, the wickedly rich Italian coffee and mascarpone dessert.

Pane (Bread)

No Italian meal is ever served without bread to accompany the food. Indeed, it often constitutes one of the dishes in a meal in the form of *crostini* and *bruschetta* (toasted canapés), soups such as *pancotto*, *panzanella* (bread salad) or pizza. In Tuscany, bread plays a more important part in the food of the region than pasta. A favorite antipasto is *fettunta*, toasted or grilled bread rubbed with garlic, anointed with plenty of olive oil and sprinkled with coarse salt. When a topping is added, it becomes *bruschetta*.

Italians buy or make fresh bread every day, but stale or leftover loaves are never wasted. Instead they are made into bread crumbs and used for thickening sauces and stews, or for stuffings, salads or wonderfully sustaining soups.

There are hundreds of different types of Italian bread with many regional variations to suit the local food. Traditional Tuscan country bread is made without salt, since it is designed to be served with salty cured meats such as salami and *prosciutto crudo*. (If you prefer salted bread, ask for *pane salato*.) Southern Italian breads often contain olive oil, which goes well with tomatoes. *Pane integrale* (whole-wheat bread) is traditionally baked in a wood oven. The texture and flavor of the bread depends on the type of flour used and the amount of seasoning, but nearly all Italian breads are firm-textured with substantial crusts. You will never find flabby damp white sandwich loaves in an Italian bakery, although the inside of traditional white *panini* (bread rolls) can sometimes resemble cotton balls.

Ciabatta

These flattish, slipper-shaped loaves with squared or rounded ends are made with olive oil and are often flavored with fresh or dried herbs, olives or sun-dried tomatoes. They have an airy texture inside and a pale, crisp crust. *Ciabatta* is delicious served warm, and is excellent for sandwiches.

Ciabatta
These popular loaves are available plain or flavored with olives or sun-dried tomatoes

Whole-wheat bread
In Italy this bread is traditionally baked in a wooden oven

Focaccia

A dimpled flat bread similar to pizza dough, *focaccia* is traditionally oiled and baked in a wood oven. A whole *focaccia* from a bakery weighs several pounds and is sold by weight, cut into manageable pieces. A variety of ingredients can be worked into the dough or serve as a topping— onions, *pancetta*, rosemary or oregano, ham, cheese or olives. *Focaccine* are small versions, which are split and served with fillings like a sandwich. In Apulia, *focaccia del Venerdì Santo*, with its topping of fennel, chicory, anchovies, olives and capers, is traditionally served on Good Friday.

Focaccia
In Italy these large flat breads are sold by weight, cut into manageable pieces. It can be plain, as here, or flavored with herbs, sun-dried tomatoes or olives

White bread
Like nearly all Italian breads, this one is firm-textured, with a substantial crust

Grissini
The cover charge in every Italian restaurant invariably includes packages of bread sticks

Grissini

These crisp golden bread sticks originated in Turin, but are now found in almost every Italian restaurant, packaged in long envelopes. They range in size from matchstick-thin to hefty, knobby, homemade batons. Italian bakers often use up any leftover dough to make *grissini*, which are sold loose by weight. They can be rolled in sesame or poppy seeds for extra flavor.

Pantry

One of the great joys of Italian food is that you can create a delicious meal almost instantly using ingredients from your pantry. Rice and pasta can be combined with any number of jarred or canned vegetables, seafood or sauces to make a speedy and nutritious meal. Unopened jars and cans last for months, if not years, so it is worth keeping a selection in your pantry for an impromptu meal that you can create in moments.

Pesto

Although nothing is as good as homemade pesto, there are some excellent jarred varieties of this fragrant green basil sauce. Traditional pesto is made with basil, pine nuts, Parmesan or Pecorino cheese and olive oil, but you may also find a red version based on red bell peppers.

CULINARY USES

Pesto can be used as an instant dressing for any type of pasta or potato gnocchi. It gives a lift to risotti and tomato sauces, and is delicious stirred into minestrone or tomato-based soups. A spoonful of pesto will add a new dimension to bottled mayonnaise, creating a rich, pungent *maionese verde*. For a quick, attractive hors d'oeuvre, halve some cherry tomatoes, scoop out the seeds and fill the tomatoes with pesto.

Pomodori secchi (sun-dried tomatoes)

Sun-drying tomatoes intensifies their flavor to an astonishing sweetness and pungency and allows you to enjoy the full savor of tomatoes even in winter. If you are extremely lucky, you may still find in markets in southern Italy locally grown tomatoes that have been spread out to dry in the sun, but the commercially produced "sun-dried" tomatoes are actually air-dried by machine. Wrinkled red dried tomatoes are available dry in packages or preserved in olive oil. Dry tomatoes are brick-red in color and have a chewy texture. They can be eaten on their own as a snack, but for cooking they should be soaked in hot water until soft (the tomato-flavored soaking water can be used for a soup or sauce). Jarred sun-dried tomatoes are sold in chunky pieces or as a paste.

Sun-dried tomatoes
These strong-flavored tomatoes add extra piquancy to dishes

CULINARY USES

Sun-dried tomatoes add piquancy to vegetable dishes, soups or sauces. They can be chopped and added to a simple *sugo di pomodoro* or a meaty *ragù* for extra flavor. They make an excellent *antipasto* combined with sliced fresh tomatoes, mozzarella and basil or with other preserved or pickled vegetables. They go well with fresh Mediterranean vegetables like fennel, eggplants and zucchini, and add a special something to egg dishes, such as *frittata*. Use the oil in which the tomatoes are preserved for salad dressings or for sweating vegetables for a soup or sauce.

The paste can be used in small quantities for sauces and soups, or used on its own or with a little butter as a dressing for pasta.

Pesto
Both the traditional green version shown here and a red type based on red bell peppers are used to flavor sauces and pasta

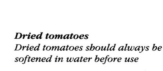

Dried tomatoes
Dried tomatoes should always be softened in water before use

Black olive paste

Passata
This rich tomato pureé varies in fineness from the ultra-smooth to the chunkier sugocasa

Green olive paste

Passata *(tomato pulp)*

Rich red passata is simply sieved ripe tomatoes, a wonderfully convenient shortcut whenever tomato pulp is required. Depending on the degree of sieving, it can be perfectly smooth or slightly chunky (*polpa di pomodoro* or *passata rustica*: "rustic passata"). The chunky variety is sold in tall jars, while the smoothest type is available in cartons or jars. More highly concentrated tomato paste (*concentrato di pomodoro*) is packed in small cans or tubes. This product is extremely strong and should only be used in small quantities.

CULINARY USES

Passata can be used as a basis for soups and sauces, and as a substitute for fresh tomatoes in all recipes where they require long cooking. For a very quick pasta sauce, sweat some finely chopped onion and garlic in olive oil, add a jar of passata and bubble the sauce while the pasta is cooking. Flavor with fresh basil, oregano, parsley or some chopped olives, capers and/or anchovies. For more body and depth and a richer color, stir in a spoonful or two of tomato concentrate.

Pasta di olive *(olive paste)*

Green or, more usually, black olives are pounded to a paste with salt and olive oil and packed in small jars. Olive paste tends to be very salty and rich, so a little goes a long way.

CULINARY USES

Olive paste can be spread very thinly over pizza bases, or scraped onto toasted croutons and topped with tomatoes or mushrooms to make *crostini*. Mixed with olive oil and a little lemon juice, it can be a dip for raw vegetables. For an interesting *antipasto*, mash a little olive paste into the yolks of halved hard-cooked eggs, spoon the mixture back into the cavity and top with a few capers.

A little olive paste adds a rich flavor to a tomato sauce, while a spoonful stirred into a vinaigrette makes a good dressing for a robust salad. If you are a real olive lover, stir a small amount into hot pasta for the simplest of dressings.

Legumi sott'olio *(vegetables preserved in oil)*

Italians produce a wide variety of vegetables preserved in olive or sunflower oil, or a mixture of both. The choicest are often cooked *alla brace* (grilled) before being packed in the best olive oil—tiny *carciofini* (artichokes), *funghi* and *porcini* (button and wild mushrooms), *peperoni* (red and yellow bell peppers) and *melanzane* (eggplants)—and look as beautiful as they taste. You will sometimes find large bulbous jars containing colorful layers of different vegetables in oil; these are packed by hand and are extremely expensive.

CULINARY USES

A mixture of oil-preserved vegetables combined with a selection of cured meats makes a wonderful *antipasto*. They can also be chopped or sliced and used to dress hot or cold pasta, or stirred into rice for a substantial cold salad. They make a delicious topping for *crostini* or pizza.

Artichoke hearts
These olive oil-packed vegetables are often combined with sliced cured meats to make an antipasto

Pantry

Giardiniera (pickled vegetables)

Mixed pickled vegetables are sold packed *in agrodolce* (vinegar and oil). Single varieties such as peeled or unpeeled eggplants and zucchini are available, but a mixture of these vegetables along with artichokes, baby onions, carrots, celery and peppers is more colorful. These vegetables are sometimes described as *alla contadina* (peasant-style).

CULINARY USES

Pickled vegetables can be served with salami and ham as an *antipasto*, or drained and mixed with raw vegetables and mayonnaise for a piquant version of *insalata russa* (Russian salad). Their vinegary taste makes an excellent counterpoint to plain cold roast meats or poultry.

Peppers
The vinegary flavor of these pickled vegetables goes well with cold roast meats

Filetti di acciughe (anchovy fillets)

Anchovy fillets are available preserved in salt or oil. The salted fillets have a superior flavor, but they are are only available in catering tins to be sold by the *etto* (3½ oz) at delicatessens. You can buy these and soak them for 30 minutes, then dry them thoroughly and pack them in olive oil, but it is more practical to buy canned or jarred anchovies.

CULINARY USES

Anchovies can be chopped and added to tomato sauces and salad dressings. They can be stirred into a fish risotto, or mixed with tomatoes and capers for a topping for pizzas or *crostini*. They are best of all made into *bagna cauda*, a delicious and quick hot dip for raw vegetables. For six people, heat ⅔ cup olive oil with 4 tbsp unsalted butter. As soon as it begins to foam, add 3 finely chopped garlic cloves and soften but do not brown. Drain and roughly chop a 2-oz can of anchovy fillets, add to the pan and stir over low heat until they have disintegrated to a paste. Keep the sauce hot and dip in the vegetables.

Anchovy fillets
Usually chopped and added to sauces or salads for extra flavor. These are available packed in oil or salt—the salted variety have a better flavor

Bottarga (salted roe)

The pressed, salted and dried roe of the gray mullet or tuna, also known as *buttariga, butarega* and *ovotarica*, is a speciality of Sardinia, Sicily and the Veneto, where it is regarded as a great delicacy. It is usually packed in a sausage shape inside a skin that should be removed before preparing. Wrapped in plastic wrap, it will keep for several months.

CULINARY USES

Bottarga can be served as an *antipasto* thinly sliced and dressed with a little extra virgin olive oil and lemon juice. In Sicily, it is served with *caponata*, a dome-shaped salad of fried eggplant and celery. It is delicious simply grated over hot pasta with a pat of unsalted butter and a little chopped fresh parsley or dried chili flakes.

Baccalà
(salted dried cod)

Air-drying is the oldest known method of preserving fish. Before the days of deep-freezing, dried fish was invaluable for people who wished to observe meatless days, but who lived far from the sea, because the salting and drying process ensures that it remains edible for many months. The most popular dried fish in Italy is salt cod, which is traditionally eaten on Good Friday. It is sometimes known confusingly as *stoccafisso* (although true stockfish is unsalted). It looks rather unappealing, like a flat, grayish board, but once it has been soaked and reconstituted it is absolutely delicious. Unlike other pantry ingredients, *baccalà* must be prepared a day in advance, but it is worth the effort.

Clams in brine

Salt cod
This is the favorite Italian dried fish—it looks unappealing, but once it is soaked and cooked, it is delicious

CULINARY USES

Before using *baccalà*, it must be soaked under cold running water for at least 8 hours to rehydrate it and remove the excess salt. Once this has been done, it can be creamed with olive oil, garlic, cream and parsley to make *baccalà mantecato*, a famous Venetian dish, which is served on fried polenta. In the Florentine version, the salt cod is cut into chunks, coated with flour and fried with tomatoes and onions. *Baccalà* combines well with all Mediterranean flavors and can be stewed or baked with red bell peppers, potatoes, fennel or celery, capers, olives and anchovies. Many recipes also include pine nuts and raisins. For a simple pasta sauce, mix some flaked salt cod with cream and chopped herbs and stir it into the hot pasta.

Vongole (clams)

Tiny clams are sold packed in brine in glass jars. These miniature golden nuggets need no further cooking and can be simply heated through and tossed into hot pasta or risotto, or combined with tomato sauce. If you have time, drain the clams and reduce the juice in which they are packed with finely chopped garlic and a few dried chili flakes to make a more intense sauce.

Mostarda di Cremona
(mustard fruit chutney)

This sweet crystallized fruit chutney with its piquant undertone of the mustard was first produced over a hundred years ago in Cremona and Venice. Its vibrant colors come from the assortment of candied fruits from which it is made—cherries, pears, melons, figs, apricots and clementines, infused in mustard seed oil. Also known as *mostarda di frutta*, the chutney is traditionally served with sausages such as zampone and cotechino, or roast and boiled beef, veal and pork. For an unusual and delicious dessert, serve the chutney as a topping for creamy mascarpone.

Mustard fruit chutney

Aperitifs & Liqueurs

Behind every bar in Italy is displayed row upon row of bottles containing dozens of different aperitivi *and* digestivi, *many of them never found outside Italy. They are consumed at any hour of the day; a favorite Italian morning drink is* caffè corretto, espresso *coffee laced with grappa or* Stock *(Italian brandy). Many of the vermouths and spirits are made from local ingredients, including herbs, nuts, lemons, artichokes or regional wines. The Italians have an unshakeable belief in the digestive properties of such drinks, many of which are so bitter that most non-Italians find them completely unpalatable. At the end of a restaurant meal, you will always find the men clustered around the bar aiding their digestion with a small glass of spirit or liqueur.*

Amaro

A very bitter *aperitivo* much beloved by the Italians, *amaro* is flavored with gentian, herbs and orange peel and contains quinine and iron. Marginally less bitter than straight *amaro* are the wine-based *amari* such as Campari, which is usually mixed with soda water and drunk before a meal to stimulate the appetite and cleanse the palate. Others, such as Fernet-Branca, are served as a pick-me-up and cure for stomach aches. *Amaro* is reputed to have excellent digestive and tonic properties, to cure hangovers and to have aphrodisiac qualities, which probably explains its popularity in Italy.

Campari

A bright crimson *aperitivo* from the *amaro* family, wine-based Campari has a bitter, astringent flavor. It was first produced in the nineteenth century by the Campari brothers from Milan, and has been produced by the same family ever since. Campari is sold in triangular single-portion bottles ready-mixed with soda (Campari soda). The neat bitters are an essential ingredient of cocktails such as *Negroni* and *Americano*.

Amaro

Fernet-Branca

Campari soda

Cynar

This dark brown, intensely bitter, aperitif with an alcoholic content of 17 percent is made from artichokes. Too bitter to swallow on its own, it is usually served as a long drink with ice and soda water.

Punt e Mes

The name of this intensely bitter red *aperitivo* means "point and a half." It is said to have been created by the Carpano distillery when customers ordered their drinks to be mixed according to their own specification. Punt e Mes is usually drunk on its own, but can be served with ice and soda.

Vermouth

All vermouths, both white and red, are made from white wine flavored with aromatic herbal extracts and spices. The first vermouth was made in Turin in the eighteenth century, and vermouth is still produced there. Red vermouths, such as Cinzano and sweet Martini, are sweetened with sugar and tinted with caramel to give them a deep red color. These sweet red varieties are generically called "Italian" vermouth—the "it" in gin and it. Dry vermouth is white and contains less sugar. It is known as "French," but is also produced in Italy by companies such as Martini and Rossi. Other well-known brands include Riccadonna and Gancia.

CULINARY USES

Although the Italians tend to use white wine rather than vermouth in their cooking, dry white vermouth can be substituted in sauces and veal, rabbit or poultry dishes. It adds a touch of dryness and intensity.

Cynar

Punt e Mes

Extra-dry white vermouth

Fortified Wines

Marsala

This rich brown fortified wine has a sweet, musky flavor and an alcoholic content of about 18 percent. It is made in the west of Sicily, near the town from which it takes its name. The best Marsala (*vergine*) has been matured for at least five years to give an intensity of flavor and color. Although sweet Marsala is better known, dry varieties (*ambra secco*) are also produced; their flavor is reminiscent of medium sherry. The sweetest version is *Marsala all'uovo*, an intensely rich and sticky dessert wine enriched with egg yolks, which can only be drunk in tiny quantities. Dry Marsala is generally served as an *aperitivo*, while the sweet version is served after a meal, usually with little cookies to dip into the wine. Unlike sherry, sweet Marsala does not deteriorate once the bottle is opened, so it makes a very useful standby in the kitchen.

Vin santo

This "holy wine" from Tuscany is made from semi-dried grapes with a long slow fermentation, followed by many years of aging to produce a syrupy golden wine. Although not a fortified wine, its intense flavor has some similarity to sherry and it is drunk in much the same way. Vin santo can be dry or sweet, but the sweet version is more common. It is generally served with a plate of *cantucci* or *biscotti di Prato*, hard slipper-shaped cookies studded with nuts. These are dunked into the wine to make a delicious dessert.

Culinary Uses

Sweet Marsala is probably best known as an essential ingredient of *zabaglione*, a light frothy dessert made from whisked egg yolks, sugar and Marsala. It is used in *zuppa inglese* (trifle) and many other desserts. Dry Marsala is widely used in Italian cooking, particularly in veal dishes such as *scaloppina* and *piccata al Marsala* and sautéed chicken livers. A few spoonfuls of Marsala added to the pan in which veal or poultry has been sautéed will mingle with the pan juices to make a delicious syrupy sauce. It adds extra flavor to wild mushrooms or a mushroom risotto.

Marsala
The sweet variety is used to flavor zabaglione

Marsala
Widely used by Italian cooks for flavoring veal and poultry dishes

Vin santo

Liqueurs & Digestivi

Amaretto

This sweet liqueur is made from apricot pits and flavored with almonds and aromatic extracts. There are several brands produced, but the best is Disaronno Amaretto, which comes in a distinctive squarish rippled glass bottle with a square cap.

CULINARY USES

The distinctive almond flavor of Amaretto enhances many desserts, such as *macedonia* (fruit salad), *zuppa inglese* (trifle) and *panna* (whipped cream).

Galliano

A bright yellow liqueur from Lombardy, Galliano is flavored with herbs and spices and tastes a little like a bittersweet Chartreuse. It is occasionally drunk on its own as a *digestivo*, but is best known as an ingredient for cocktails such as Harvey Wallbanger and Golden Cadillac.

Galliano

Amaretto

Liqueurs & Digestivi

Grappa

A pungent colorless brandy with an alcoholic content of about 40 percent, distilled from the pressed skins and seeds of the grapes left after wine-making. At its crudest, grappa tastes of raw spirit, but after maturing the taste becomes refined and the best grappa can be as good as a fine French *marc*. Grappa is made in many regions, usually from local grapes, which lend each variety its characteristic flavor. On the whole, you get what you pay for; cheap grappa is fiery and pungent, while expensive, well-matured varieties can be very smooth. The very best grappa often comes in exquisite hand-blown bottles. The spirit can be flavored with various aromatics, including rose petals and lemon peel.

CULINARY USES

Grappa is not used in Italian cooking, except in *capretto alla piemontese* (braised goat). It can be used for flambéeing and for preserving berries. The spirit takes on the flavor of the berries and can be drunk as a *digestivo* after the berries have been eaten.

Liquore al limone or Cedro

This sticky sweet liqueur is made from the peel of the lemons that grow in profusion around the Amalfi coast. Almost every delicatessen in the region sells a homemade version of this opaque yellow drink, whose sweetness is tempered by the tangy citrus fruit. It should be served ice-cold straight from the refrigerator or freezer and makes a refreshing *aperitivo* or *digestivo*.

Maraschino

This sweet, colorless cherry liqueur is made from fermented bitter Maraschino cherries. It can be drunk on its own as a *digestivo*, but is more commonly used for flavoring cocktails or sweet dishes.

Maraschino

Liquore al limone

Grappa

Nocino

This sticky, dark brown liqueur from Emilia-Romagna is made from unripe green walnuts steeped in spirit. It has an aromatic but bittersweet flavor.

Sambuca

The colorless liqueur has a strong taste of aniseed, although it is actually distilled from witch elder. Traditionally it is served in a schooner-shaped glass, flambéed and with a coffee bean floating on top. The coffee bean is crunched as the Sambuca is drunk, so that its bitterness counteracts the intense sweetness of the liqueur. This method of serving Sambuca is known as *colla mosca* ("with the fly"), the "fly" being the coffee bean.

Strega

A bright yellow liqueur made from herbs and flowers, strega (meaning "witch"), has a bittersweet flavor and is definitely an acquired taste.

Sambuca

Nocino

Strega

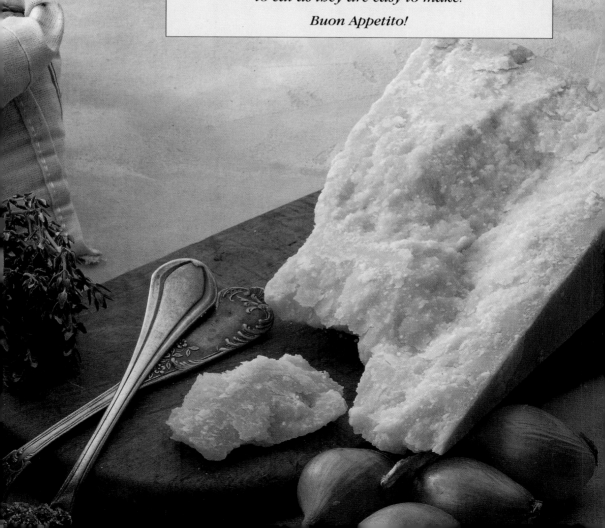

The Recipes

The recipes in this collection cover a range of styles, from regional specialities to popular modern classics. More unusual, innovative offerings are here too, destined to become future favorites. All of the recipes use ingredients that can be found easily outside Italy, and all are as delicious to eat as they are easy to make.

Buon Appetito!

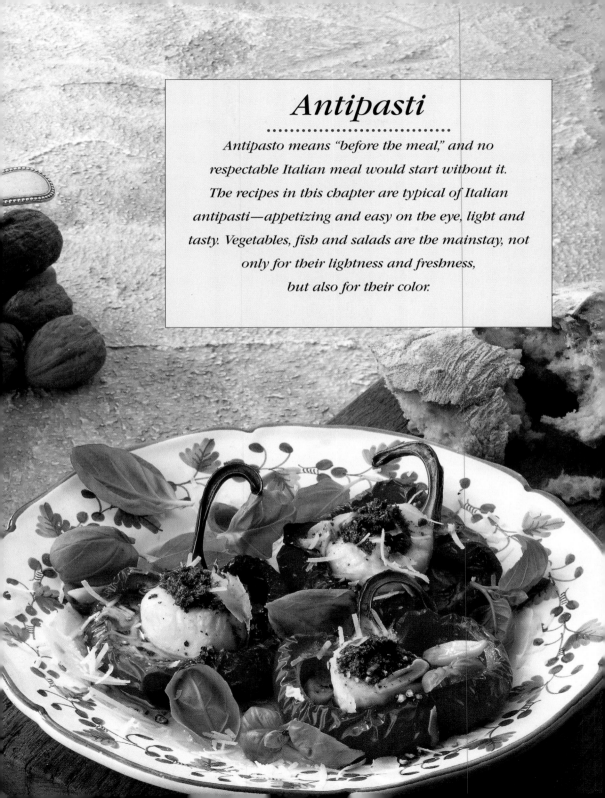

Antipasti

Antipasto means "before the meal," and no
respectable Italian meal would start without it.
The recipes in this chapter are typical of Italian
antipasti—appetizing and easy on the eye, light and
tasty. Vegetables, fish and salads are the mainstay, not
only for their lightness and freshness,
but also for their color.

Roasted Bell Pepper Salad

Insalata di peperoni arrostiti

Jars of Italian mixed peppers in olive oil are now a common sight in many supermarkets.

None, however, can compete with this colorful, freshly made version, perfect as an appetizer

on its own, or with thinly sliced Italian salami and cold meats.

Ingredients

3 red bell peppers
2 yellow or orange bell peppers
2 green peppers
½ cup sun-dried tomatoes in
    oil, drained
1 garlic clove
2 tbsp balsamic vinegar
5 tbsp olive oil
few drops of chili sauce
4 canned artichoke hearts, drained
    and sliced
salt and freshly ground black pepper
basil leaves, to garnish
serves 4

1 ▲ Preheat the oven to 400°F. Lightly oil a foil-lined baking sheet or baking tray and place the whole peppers on the foil. Bake for about 45 minutes until beginning to char. Cover with a dish towel and let cool for 5 minutes.

2 ▲ Cut the sun-dried tomatoes into thin strips and thinly slice the garlic. Set the tomatoes and garlic aside.

3 ▲ Beat together the vinegar, oil and chili sauce, then season with a little salt and pepper.

4 ▲ Peel, seed and slice the peppers. Mix with the artichokes, tomatoes and garlic. Pour the dressing over and scatter with the basil leaves.

Fontina Cheese Dip

Fonduta

Fontina is an Italian medium-fat cheese with a rich salty flavor, a little like Gruyère, which makes a good substitute. This delicious cheese dip needs only some warm ciabatta or focaccia, a salad and some robust red wine for a thoroughly enjoyable meal.

Ingredients
9 oz Fontina cheese, diced
8 fl oz/1 cup milk
1 tbsp butter
2 eggs, lightly beaten
freshly ground black pepper
bread, to serve
serves 4

Cook's Tip
This sauce needs to be cooked over a very gentle heat – don't overheat it, or the eggs might curdle. Cook slowly, stirring all the time.

1 ▲ Put the cheese in a bowl with the milk and allow to soak for 2–3 hours. Transfer to a double boiler or a heatproof bowl set over a pan of simmering water.

2 ▲ Add the butter and eggs and cook gently, stirring until the cheese has melted to a smooth sauce with the consistency of custard.

3 Remove from the heat and season with pepper. Transfer to a serving dish and serve immediately with chunks of bread.

Sautéed Mussels with Garlic

Cozze in padella all'aglio

These mussels are served without their shells in a delicious sauce flavored with garlic and paprika. Eat them with toothpicks or small forks.

Ingredients

2 lb fresh mussels
1 lemon slice
6 tbsp olive oil
2 shallots, finely chopped
1 garlic clove, finely chopped
1 tbsp chopped fresh parsley
½ tsp sweet paprika
¼ tsp dried red pepper flakes

serves 4

1 Scrub the mussels. Discard any that do not close when tapped sharply with the back of a knife.

2 ▲ Put the mussels in a large saucepan, with 1 cup water and the slice of lemon. Bring to a boil and cook for 3–4 minutes; remove the mussels as they open. Discard any that remain closed. Take the mussels out of the shells and drain them on paper towels.

3 ▲ Heat the oil in a sauté pan, add the mussels and cook, stirring, for a minute. Remove from the pan. Add the shallots and garlic and cook, covered, over low heat, for about 5 minutes, until soft. Remove from the heat and stir in the parsley, paprika and red pepper flakes. Return to the heat and stir in the mussels with any juice. Cook briefly to heat through, then serve at once.

Chicken Liver and Shrimp Toasts

Crostini

Crostini are Italian canapés, consisting of toasted slices of bread, spread with various

toppings. The following recipes are for a chicken liver pâté and a shrimp butter.

Ingredients

12 slices crusty Italian bread, cut
   ½ in thick
6 tbsp butter, melted
salt and freshly ground black pepper
sage leaves and flat leaf parsley,
   to garnish

For the chicken liver pâté

⅔ cup butter
1 small onion, finely chopped
1 garlic clove, crushed
8 oz chicken livers
4 sage leaves, chopped

For the shrimp butter

8 oz cooked, peeled shrimp
2 drained canned anchovies
¼ cup butter, softened
1 tbsp lemon juice
1 tbsp chopped fresh parsley
serves 6

1 ▲ To make the chicken liver pâté, melt half the butter in a frying pan, add the onion and garlic, and fry gently until soft. Add the chicken livers and chopped sage and sauté for about 8 minutes, until the livers are brown and firm. Cool slightly, then season with salt and pepper and process in a blender or food processor with the remaining butter.

2 ▲ To make the shrimp butter, chop the shrimp and anchovies finely. Put in a bowl with the butter and beat together until well blended. Add the lemon juice and parsley and season with salt and pepper. Preheat the oven to 400°F. Arrange the bread slices on baking sheets and brush with the melted butter.

3 Bake for 8–10 minutes, until pale golden. Spread half the hot crostini with the pâté and the rest with the shrimp butter, garnishing with sage and parsley, respectively. Serve the crostini immediately.

Cook's Tip
Both the chicken liver pâté and the shrimp butter can be made ahead, but should be used within two days. Cover both toppings tightly and store them in the fridge.

Crostini with Cheese

Crostini con formaggio

Crostini are small pieces of toasted bread. They can be made with various toppings, and are served hot or cold with drinks. This cheese-topped version is always popular.

Ingredients
4–6 slices day-old white or brown bread
³/₄ cup thinly sliced cheese (fontina,
    Cheddar or Gruyère)
anchovy fillets
strips of grilled red pepper
freshly ground black peppèr
serves 6

1 ▲ Cut the bread into small shapes (triangle, circle, oval etc.). Preheat the oven to 375°F.

2 ▲ Place a thin slice of cheese on each piece of bread, cutting it to fit.

~ VARIATION ~

For a colorful addition use strips of green or yellow pepper.

---

3 ▲ Cut the anchovy fillets and strips of pepper into small decorative shapes and place on top of the cheese. Grind a little pepper on each.

4 ▲ Butter a cookie sheet. Place the crostini on it, and bake for 10 minutes, or until the cheese has melted. Serve straight from the oven, or allow to cool before serving.

Crostini with Mussels or Clams

Crostini con cozze o vongole

Each of these seafood crostini is topped with a mussel or clam, and then baked. This recipe comes from Genoa. Use fresh seafood whenever possible.

Ingredients

16 large mussels or clams, in their shells
4 large slices bread, 1in thick
3 tbsp butter
2 tbsp chopped fresh parsley
1 shallot, very finely chopped
olive oil, for brushing
lemon sections, to serve
makes 16

3 ▲ Break the scooped-out bread into crumbs, and reserve. In a small frying pan, heat the butter. Cook the parsley with the shallot and the breadcrumbs until the shallot softens.

4 ▲ Brush each piece of bread with olive oil. Place one mussel or clam in each hollow. Spoon a small amount of the parsley and shallot mixture onto each mollusc. Place on an oiled cookie sheet. Bake for 10 minutes. Serve at once, while still hot, with the lemon sections.

1 ▲ Wash the mussels or clams well in several changes of water. Cut the "beards" off the mussels. Place the shellfish in a pan with a cupful of water, and heat until the shells open. (Discard any that do not open.) As soon as they open, lift the molluscs out of the pan. Spoon out of their shells, and set aside. Preheat the oven to 375°F.

2 ▲ Cut the crusts off the bread. Cut each slice into quarters. Scoop out a hollow from the top of each piece large enough to hold a mussel or clam. Do not cut through to the bottom.

Broiled Eggplant Packages

Pacchetti di melanzane alla griglia

These are delicious and flavorful bundles of plum tomatoes, mozzarella cheese and fresh basil, wrapped up smartly in thin slices of eggplant.

Ingredients

2 large, long eggplants
8 oz mozzarella cheese
2 plum tomatoes
16 large basil leaves
2 tbsp olive oil
salt and freshly ground black pepper
2 tbsp toasted pine nuts and torn basil
    leaves, to garnish

For the dressing

4 tbsp extra virgin olive oil
1 tsp balsamic vinegar
1 tbsp sun-dried tomato paste
1 tbsp lemon juice
serves 4

1 ▲ Remove the stalks from the eggplants and cut the eggplants lengthwise into thin slices – the aim is to get 16 slices in total, disregarding the first and last slices (each about ¼ in thick). (If you have a mandoline, it will cut perfect, even slices for you, otherwise, use a long-bladed, sharp knife.

2 Bring a large pan of salted water to the boil, add the eggplant slices and cook for about 2 minutes, until just softened. Drain the sliced eggplants, then dry them on paper towels.

3 Cut the mozzarella into eight slices. Cut each tomato into eight thin slices, not counting the first and last slices.

4 ▲ Take two eggplant slices and place on a flameproof tray or dish, in a cross. Place a slice of tomato in the center, season with salt and pepper, then add a basil leaf, followed by a slice of mozzarella, another basil leaf, a slice of tomato and a little more seasoning.

5 ▲ Fold the ends of the eggplant slices around the mozzarella and tomato filling to make a neat package. Repeat with the rest of the assembled ingredients to make eight packages. Chill the packages for at least 20 minutes.

6 To make the tomato dressing, whisk together the olive oil, vinegar, sun-dried tomato paste and lemon juice. Season to taste.

7 Preheat the broiler. Brush the packages with olive oil and cook them for about 5 minutes on each side, until golden. Serve hot, with the dressing, sprinkled with toasted pine nuts and torn basil leaves.

Cook's Tip

If the eggplants are very large they may have a slightly bitter flavor. To draw out the bitter juices, spread out the raw slices on a tray and sprinkle lightly with salt. Set aside for about 30 minutes, then rinse the eggplant slices thoroughly under cold running water before cooking.

Roasted Bell Peppers with Tomatoes *Insalata di peperoni arrostiti*

This is a Sicilian-style salad, using some typical ingredients from the Italian island. The flavor improves if the salad is made and dressed an hour or two before serving.

Ingredients

1 red bell pepper
1 yellow bell pepper
4 sun-dried tomatoes in oil, drained
4 ripe plum tomatoes, sliced
2 canned anchovies, drained
  and chopped
1 tbsp capers, drained
1 tbsp pine nuts
1 garlic clove, very thinly sliced

For the dressing

5 tbsp extra virgin olive oil
1 tbsp balsamic vinegar
1 tsp lemon juice
chopped fresh mixed herbs
salt and freshly ground black pepper

serves 4

1 ▲ Cut the peppers in half, and remove the seeds and stalks. Cut into quarters and cook, skin side up, under a hot broiler until the skin chars. Transfer to a bowl, and cover with a plate. Allow to cool. Peel the peppers and cut into strips.

2 ▲ Thinly slice the sun-dried tomatoes. Arrange the pepper strips and fresh tomatoes on a serving dish. Scatter the anchovies, sun-dried tomatoes, capers, pine nuts and garlic over the top.

3 To make the dressing, mix together the olive oil, vinegar, lemon juice, herbs and seasoning. Pour over the salad just before serving.

Sweet-and-sour Onion Salad

Insalata di cipolle in agrodolce

The best Italian onions are grown in Piedmont. Baby onions are traditionally cooked in this piquant sugar and vinegar sauce and served either warm or cold.

Ingredients

1 lb baby onions, peeled
¼ cup wine vinegar
3 tbsp olive oil
3 tbsp sugar
3 tbsp tomato paste
1 bay leaf
2 parsley sprigs
½ cup raisins
salt and freshly ground black pepper
serves 6

1 ▲ Put the onions in a pan with the wine vinegar, olive oil, sugar, tomato paste, herbs, raisins, salt and pepper and 1¼ cups water. Bring to a boil and simmer gently, uncovered, for 45 minutes, or until the onions are tender and most of the liquid has evaporated.

2 ▲ Remove the bay leaf and parsley, check the seasoning, and transfer to a serving dish. Serve at room temperature.

Frittata with Sun-dried Tomatoes   *Frittata con pomodori secchi*

Adding just a few sun-dried tomatoes gives this frittata a distinctly Mediterranean flavor.

Ingredients

6 sun-dried tomatoes, dry or in oil and
    drained
4 tbsp olive oil
1 small onion, finely chopped
pinch of fresh thyme leaves
salt and freshly ground black pepper
6 eggs
¹/₂ cup freshly grated Parmesan or
    Romano cheese
serves 3–4

3 ▲ Break the eggs into a bowl and beat lightly with a fork. Stir in 3–4 tbsp of the tomato soaking water and the grated Parmesan or Romano. Raise the heat under the pan. When the oil is sizzling pour in the eggs. Mix them quickly into the other ingredients, and stop stirring. Lower the heat to moderate, and cook for about 4–5 minutes, or until the frittata is puffed and golden brown underneath.

4 ▲ Take a large plate, place it upside down over the pan, and holding it firmly with oven mitts, turn the pan and the frittata over onto it. Slide the frittata back into the pan, and continue cooking until golden brown on the second side, 3–4 minutes more. Remove from the heat. The frittata can be served hot, at room temperature, or cold. Cut it into wedges to serve.

1 ▲ Place the tomatoes in a small bowl, and pour on enough hot water to just cover them. Soak for about 15 minutes. Lift the tomatoes out of the water, and slice them into thin strips. Reserve the soaking water.

2 ▲ Heat the oil in a large non-stick or heavy frying pan. Stir in the onion, and cook for 5–6 minutes or until soft and golden. Add the tomatoes and thyme, and stir over moderate heat for 2–3 minutes. Season with salt and pepper.

Tomato and Basil Tart

Torta di pomodoro e basilico

This tart is similar to a pizza, but uses shortcrust pastry instead of yeast dough for the base.

Ingredients

$1^{1}/_{2}$ cups white unbleached flour
$^{1}/_{2}$ tsp salt, plus more to sprinkle
$^{1}/_{2}$ cup butter or margarine, chilled
3–5 tbsp cold water
2 tbsp extra-virgin olive oil

For the filling

1 cup mozzarella cheese, sliced as
   thinly as possible
12 leaves fresh basil
4–5 medium tomatoes, cut into
   $^{1}/_{4}$in slices
salt and freshly ground black pepper
4 tbsp freshly grated Parmesan cheese
serves 6–8

4 ▲ Line the pastry with a sheet of parchment paper. Fill with dried beans. Place the pie pan on a cookie sheet and bake about 15 minutes. Remove from the oven.

5 Remove the beans and paper. Brush the pastry with oil. Line with the mozzarella. Tear half of the basil into pieces, and sprinkle on top.

6 ▲ Arrange the tomato slices over the cheese. Dot with the remaining whole basil leaves. Sprinkle with salt and pepper, Parmesan and oil. Bake for about 35 minutes. If the cheese exudes a lot of liquid during baking, tilt the pan and spoon it off to keep the pastry from becoming soggy. Serve hot or at room temperature.

1 ▲ Make the pastry by placing the flour and salt in a mixing bowl. Using a pastry blender, cut the butter or margarine into the dry ingredients until the mixture resembles coarse meal. Add 3 tbsp of water, and combine with a fork until the dough holds together. If it is too crumbly, mix in a little more water.

2 Gather the dough into a ball and flatten it into a disc. Wrap in waxed paper and refrigerate for at least 40 minutes. Preheat the oven to 375°F.

3 Roll the pastry out between two sheets of waxed paper to a thickness of $^{1}/_{4}$ inch. Line an 11 in tart or pie pan, trimming the edges evenly. Refrigerate for 20 minutes. Prick the bottom all over with a fork.

Potato Pizza

Pizza di patate

This "pizza", made of mashed potatoes with a filling of anchovies, capers and tomatoes, is a speciality of Puglia.

Ingredients
2lb potatoes, scrubbed
$1/2$ cup extra-virgin olive oil
salt and freshly ground black pepper
2 garlic cloves, finely chopped
12oz tomatoes, chopped
3 anchovy fillets, chopped
2 tbsp capers, rinsed
serves 4

2 Heat another 3 tbsp of the oil in a medium pan. Add the garlic and the chopped tomatoes, and cook over moderate heat until the tomatoes soften and begin to dry out, 12–15 minutes. Meanwhile, preheat the oven to 400°F.

3 ▲ Oil a shallow baking dish. Spread half the mashed potatoes into the dish in an even layer. Cover with the tomatoes, and dot with the chopped anchovies and the capers.

4 ▲ Spread the rest of the potatoes in a layer on top of the filling. Brush the top with the remaining oil. Bake in the preheated oven for 20–25 minutes, or until the top is golden brown. Serve hot, directly from the baking dish.

~ VARIATION ~

For a vegetarian version of this dish, omit the anchovies. A few pitted and chopped olives may be added to the filling instead.

1 ▲ Boil the potatoes in their skins until tender. Peel and mash or pass through a food mill. Beat in 3 tbsp of the oil, and season.

Bruschetta with Tomato

Bruschetta con pomodoro

Bruschetta is toasted or broiled bread, rubbed with garlic and sprinkled with olive oil or chopped fresh tomatoes. It is eaten as an appetizer or accompaniment.

Ingredients
3–4 medium tomatoes, chopped
salt and freshly ground black pepper
a few leaves fresh basil, torn
8 slices crusty white bread
2 or 3 garlic cloves, peeled and cut
     in half
6 tbsp extra-virgin olive oil
serves 4

1 Place the chopped tomatoes with their juice in a small bowl. Season with salt and pepper, and stir in the basil. Allow to stand for 10 minutes.

2 ▲ Toast or broil the bread until it is crisp on both sides. Rub one side of each piece of toast with the cut garlic.

3 ▲ Arrange on a platter. Sprinkle with the olive oil. Spoon on the chopped tomatoes, and serve at once.

Broiled Cheese Sandwiches

Panini alla griglia

Garlic, herbs and tomatoes make these open sandwiches very Mediterranean.

Ingredients
3 tbsp olive oil
4 or 5 canned plum tomatoes, finely chopped
a few leaves fresh basil, torn
salt and freshly ground black pepper
4–6 medium slices of Italian or crusty bread
1 garlic clove, peeled and cut in half
1/2 cup scamorza, mozzarella or Cheddar cheese, sliced
serves 4

1 Heat the oil in a small frying pan. Add the tomatoes and basil, and season with salt and pepper. Cook over low to moderate heat for about 8–10 minutes, or until the tomatoes start to dry out. Preheat the broiler.

2 ▲ Lightly toast the bread. When it has cooled slightly rub it on one side with the garlic.

3 ▲ Spread some of the tomatoes on each piece of bread, and top with the sliced cheese. Place under the hot broiler until the cheese melts and begins to bubble, 5–8 minutes. Serve hot.

Mozzarella, Tomato and Basil Salad

Insalata caprese

This very popular and easy salad is considered rather patriotic in Italy, as its three ingredients are the colors of the national flag.

Ingredients
4 large tomatoes
2 cups mozzarella cheese, from cow or buffalo milk
8–10 leaves fresh basil
4 tbsp extra-virgin olive oil
salt and freshly ground black pepper
serves 4

1 ▲ Slice the tomatoes and mozzarella into thick rounds.

2 ▲ Arrange the tomatoes and cheese in overlapping slices on a serving dish. Decorate with basil.

3 ▲ Sprinkle with olive oil and a little salt. Serve with the black pepper passed separately.

> ~ COOK'S TIP ~
>
> In Italy the most sought-after mozzarella is made from the milk of water buffalo. It is found mainly in the south and in Campania.

Fonduta with Steamed Vegetables

Fonduta con verdure

Fonduta is a creamy cheese sauce from the mountainous Val d'Aosta region. Traditionally it is garnished with slices of white truffles and eaten with toasted bread rounds.

Ingredients

assorted vegetables, such as fennel,
    broccoli, carrots, cauliflower
    and zucchini
$1/2$ cup butter
12–16 rounds of Italian or French
    baguette

For the fonduta

$1^2/_3$ cups fontina cheese
1 tbsp flour
milk, as required
$1/4$ cup butter
$1/2$ cup freshly grated Parmesan or
    Romano cheese
pinch of grated nutmeg
salt and freshly ground black pepper
2 egg yolks, at room temperature
a few slivers of white truffle (optional)
serves 4

1 ▲ About 6 hours before you want to serve the fonduta, cut the fontina into chunks and place in a bowl. Sprinkle with the flour. Pour in enough milk to barely cover the cheese, and set aside in a cool place. If you put the bowl in the refrigerator, take it out at least 1 hour before cooking the fonduta. It should be at room temperature before being cooked.

2 Just before preparing the fonduta, steam the vegetables until tender. Cut into pieces. Place on a serving platter, dot with butter, and keep warm.

3 Butter the bread rounds and toast lightly in the oven or under the broiler.

4 ▲ For the fonduta, melt the butter in a mixing bowl set over a pan of simmering water, or in the top of a double boiler. Strain the fontina and add it, with 3–4 tbsp of its soaking milk. Cook, stirring, until the cheese melts. When it is hot, and has formed a homogeneous mass, add the Parmesan or Romano and stir until melted. Season with nutmeg, salt and pepper.

5 ▲ Strain the egg yolks into a bowl. Remove the cheese mixture from the heat and immediately beat in the egg yolks. Spoon into warmed individual serving bowls, garnish with the white truffle if using, and serve with the vegetables and toasted bread.

Fried Mozzarella

Mozzarella fritta

These cheese slices make a good informal lunch. They originate from the Neapolitan area, where much mozzarella is produced. They must be made just before serving.

Ingredients

1³/₄ cups mozzarella cheese
oil, for deep-frying
2 eggs
flour seasoned with salt and freshly
　　ground black pepper, for coating
plain dry breadcrumbs, for coating
serves 2–3

1 ▲ Cut the mozzarella into slices about ¹/₂ inch thick. Gently pat off any excess moisture with a paper towel.

2 ▲ Heat the oil until a small piece of bread sizzles as soon as it is dropped in (about 360°F). While the oil is heating beat the eggs in a shallow bowl. Spread some flour on one plate, and some breadcrumbs on another.

3 ▲ Press the cheese slices into the flour, coating them evenly with a thin layer of flour. Shake off any excess. Dip them into the egg, then into the breadcrumbs. Dip them once more into the egg, and then again into the breadcrumbs.

4 ▲ Fry immediately in the hot oil until golden brown. (You may have to do this in two batches but do not let the breaded cheese wait for too long or the breadcrumb coating will separate from the cheese while it is being fried.) Drain quickly on paper towels, and serve hot.

Baked Eggs with Tomatoes

Uova al piatto con pomodori

These eggs simply baked over a fresh tomato sauce make an easy dish for a light supper.

Allow 1 or 2 eggs per person.

Ingredients
4 tbsp olive oil
1 small onion, finely chopped
1lb tomatoes, peeled, seeded and
    chopped
2 tbsp chopped fresh basil
6 eggs
salt and freshly ground black pepper
1 tbsp butter
chopped fresh parsley, to garnish
3 large or 6 small servings

1 ▲ Heat the oil in a shallow flame-proof dish, and add the onion.

2 ▲ Preheat the oven to 375°F. When the onion is soft and golden, add the tomatoes and cook for 5–10 minutes, or until the tomatoes are very soft. Remove from the heat and stir in the chopped basil.

~ VARIATION ~

Sprinkle 2–3 tbsp of freshly grated Parmesan cheese over the eggs before baking for a richer, tastier dish.

3 ▲ Break the eggs one at a time into a large spoon, and slip them into the dish in one layer on top of the tomatoes. Season with salt and pepper. Dot with butter. Cover the dish, and bake in the oven for 7–10 minutes, or until the egg whites have just set, but the yolks are still soft. Serve at once, garnished with chopped fresh parsley.

Baked Eggs with Cheese

Uova al piatto alla parmigiana

Grated Parmesan or Romano makes a tasty addition to this simple dish.

Ingredients
6 eggs
salt and freshly ground black pepper
3 tbsp baked or boiled ham, cut
    into thin matchsticks
6 tbsp freshly grated Parmesan or
    Romano cheese
2 tbsp butter
3–4 leaves fresh basil, to garnish
rounds of warm crusty bread, to serve
3 large or 6 small servings

1 Preheat the oven to 400°F. Butter a shallow ovenproof dish (or dishes, if you prefer to bake the eggs individually).

2 ▲ Break the eggs into the dish. Season with salt and pepper. Sprinkle the ham over the whites. Sprinkle the top with the Parmesan or Romano.

3 ▲ Dot with butter. Cover the dish, and bake for 7–10 minutes, or until the whites have set and the cheese has melted. Garnish with the basil. Serve hot with warmed bread.

Frittata with Spinach and Ham

Frittata con spinaci e prosciutto

In Italy, frittate are often used as fillings for sandwiches. This hearty version would make an excellent filling.

Ingredients

1 cup cooked leaf spinach, fresh or frozen
3 tbsp olive oil
4 scallions, finely sliced
1 garlic clove, finely chopped
$^1\!/_3$ cup ham or prosciutto, cut into
   small dice
salt and freshly ground black pepper
8 eggs
serves 6

1 ▲ Squeeze any excess moisture out of the spinach with your hands. Chop it roughly and set aside.

2 ▲ Heat the oil in a large non-stick or heavy frying pan. Stir in the scallions, and cook for 3–4 minutes. Add the garlic and ham, and stir over moderate heat until just golden. Stir in the spinach, and cook for 3–4 minutes, or until just heated through. Season with salt and pepper.

3 ▲ Break the eggs into a bowl and beat lightly with a fork. Raise the heat under the vegetables. After about 1 minute pour in the eggs. Mix them quickly into the other ingredients, and stop stirring. Cook over moderate heat for about 5–6 minutes, or until the frittata is puffed and golden brown underneath. If the frittata seems to be sticking to the pan, shake the pan backwards and forwards to release it.

4 ▲ Take a large plate, place it upside down over the pan and, holding it firmly with oven mitts, turn the pan and the frittata over onto it. Slide the frittata back into the pan, and continue cooking until golden brown on the second side, 3–4 minutes more. Remove from the heat. The frittata can be served hot, at room temperature, or cold. Cut it into wedges to serve.

Sliced Frittata Salad

Frittata fredda in insalata

This dish – cold frittata with a tomato sauce – is ideal for a light summer lunch.

Ingredients

6 eggs
2 tbsp mixed fresh herbs,such as
   basil, parsley, thyme or tarragon,
   very finely chopped
$1/4$ cup freshly grated Parmesan or
   Romano cheese
salt and freshly ground black pepper
3 tbsp olive oil
For the tomato sauce
2 tbsp olive oil
1 small onion, finely chopped
12oz fresh tomatoes, or 14oz can
   tomatoes, chopped
1 garlic clove, chopped
4 tbsp water
salt and freshly ground black pepper
serves 3–4

1 To make the frittata, break the eggs into a bowl, and beat them lightly with a fork. Beat in the herbs and cheese. Season with salt and pepper. Heat the oil in a large non-stick or heavy frying pan until hot but not smoking.

2 ▲ Pour in the egg mixture. Cook, without stirring, until the frittata is puffed and golden brown underneath.

3 Take a large plate, place it upside down over the pan, and holding it firmly with oven mitts, turn the pan and the frittata over onto it. Slide the frittata back into the pan, and continue cooking until golden brown on the second side, 3–4 minutes more. Remove from the heat and allow to cool completely.

4 ▲ To make the tomato sauce, heat the oil in a medium heavy pan. Add the onion, and cook slowly until it is soft. Add the tomatoes, garlic and water, and season with salt and pepper. Cover the pan and cook over moderate heat until the tomatoes are soft, about 15 minutes (or 5 minutes for canned tomatoes).

5 Remove from the heat, and cool slightly before passing the sauce through a food mill or strainer. Leave to cool completely.

6 ▲ To assemble the salad, cut the frittata into thin slices. Place them in a serving bowl and toss lightly with the sauce. Serve the salad at room temperature or chilled.

Frittata of Leftover Pasta

Frittata di pasta avanzata

This is a great way to use up cold leftover pasta, whatever the sauce.

Ingredients
5–6 eggs
1¹/₂–2 cups cold cooked pasta, with any
   sauce
¹/₂ cup freshly grated Parmesan cheese
salt and freshly ground black pepper
5 tbsp butter
serves 4

1 ▲ In a medium bowl beat the eggs lightly with a fork. Stir in the pasta and the Parmesan. Season to taste.

2 ▲ Heat half the butter in a large non-stick or heavy frying pan. As soon as the foam subsides pour in the pasta mixture. Cook over moderate heat, without stirring, for 4–5 minutes, or until the bottom is golden brown. Loosen the frittata by shaking the pan backwards and forwards.

3 ▲ Take a large plate, place it upside down over the pan and, holding it firmly with oven mitts, turn the pan and the frittata over onto it. Add the remaining butter to the pan. As soon as it stops foaming slide the frittata back into the pan, and continue cooking until golden brown on the second side, 3–4 minutes more. Remove from the heat. The frittata can be served hot, at room temperature, or cold. Cut it into wedges to serve.

Frittata with Onions

Frittata con cipolle

Gently cooked onions add a sweet flavor to the basic frittata mixture.

Ingredients
4 tbsp olive oil
2 medium onions, thinly sliced
salt and freshly ground black pepper
2 tbsp chopped fresh parsley or basil
6 eggs
serves 3–4

1 Heat the oil in a large non-stick or heavy frying pan. Stir in the onions, and cook over low heat until they are soft and golden. This may take 10–15 minutes. Season with salt and pepper. Stir in the herbs.

2 Break the eggs into a bowl, and beat them lightly with a fork. Raise the heat under the onions to moderate, and when they are sizzling pour in the eggs. Quickly stir them into the onions to distribute them. Stop stirring.

3 ▲ Cook for about 5 minutes, or until the frittata is puffed and golden brown underneath. If the frittata seems to be sticking to the pan, shake the pan back and forth to release it.

4 ▲ Take a large plate, place it upside down over the pan and, holding it firmly with oven mitts, turn the pan and the frittata over onto it. Slide the frittata back into the pan, and continue cooking until golden brown on the second side, 3–4 minutes more. Remove from the heat. Cut it into wedges to serve.

Roast Bell Pepper Terrine

Torta di peperoni al forno

This terrine is perfect for a dinner party because it tastes better if made ahead. Prepare the salsa on the day of serving. Serve with hot Italian bread.

Ingredients

8 bell peppers (red, yellow and orange)
3 cups mascarpone cheese
3 eggs, separated
2 tbsp each roughly chopped flat-leaf
    parsley and shredded basil
2 large garlic cloves, roughly chopped
2 red, yellow or orange bell peppers,
    seeded and roughly chopped
2 tbsp extra virgin olive oil
2 tsp balsamic vinegar
a few basil sprigs
pinch of sugar
salt and freshly ground black pepper
serves 8

1 Place the peppers under a hot broiler for 8–10 minutes, turning them frequently until the skins are charred and blistered on all sides. Put the hot peppers in ziplock bags, seal and set aside until cold.

2 ▲ Rub off the pepper skins under cold running water. Break open the flesh and rub out the cores and seeds. Drain the peppers, dry them on paper towels, then cut seven of them lengthwise into thin, even-size strips. Reserve the remaining pepper for the salsa.

Variation

For a low-fat version of this terrine, use ricotta cheese instead of the mascarpone.

3 Put the mascarpone cheese in a bowl with the egg yolks, herbs and half the garlic. Add salt and pepper to taste. Beat well. In a separate bowl, whisk the egg whites to a soft peak, then fold into the cheese mixture until evenly incorporated.

4 ▲ Preheat the oven to 350°F. Line the base of a lightly oiled 2-pound loaf pan. Put one-third of the cheese mixture in the pan and spread level. Arrange half the pepper strips on top in an even layer. Repeat until all the cheese and peppers are used.

5 Cover the pan with foil and place in a roasting pan. Pour in boiling water to come halfway up the sides of the pan. Bake for 1 hour. Let cool in the water bath, then lift out and chill overnight.

6 A few hours before serving, make the salsa. Place the remaining roast pepper and fresh peppers in a food processor. Add the remaining garlic, oil and vinegar. Set aside a few basil leaves for garnishing and add the rest to the processor. Process until finely chopped. Transfer the mixture to a bowl, add sugar and salt and pepper to taste and mix well. Cover and chill until ready to serve.

7 Turn out the terrine, peel off the paper and slice thickly. Garnish with the basil leaves and serve cold, with the sweet pepper salsa.

Pan-fried Chicken Liver Salad

Insalata di fegatini

This Florentine salad uses vin santo, a sweet dessert wine from Tuscany, but this is not essential—any dessert wine will do, or a sweet or cream sherry.

Ingredients

3 oz fresh baby spinach leaves
3 oz lollo rosso or red leaf lettuce
5 tbsp olive oil
1 tbsp butter
8 oz chicken livers, trimmed and thinly
    sliced
3 tbsp vin santo
2–3 oz fresh Parmesan cheese, shaved
    into curls
salt and freshly ground black pepper
serves 4

1 ▲ Wash and dry the spinach and lollo rosso. Tear the leaves into a large bowl, season with salt and pepper to taste and toss gently to mix.

2 ▲ Heat 2 tablespoons of the oil with the butter in a large heavy frying pan. When foaming, add the chicken livers and toss over medium to high heat for 5 minutes or until the livers are browned on the outside but still pink in the center. Remove from the heat.

3 ▲ Remove the livers from the pan with a slotted spoon, drain them on paper towels, then place on top of the spinach.

4 ▲ Return the pan to medium heat, add the remaining oil and the vin santo and stir until sizzling.

5 Pour the hot dressing over the spinach and livers and toss to coat. Put the salad in a serving bowl and sprinkle the Parmesan shavings on top. Serve immediately.

Salad Leaves with Gorgonzola
Insalata verde con gorgonzola

Crispy fried pancetta makes tasty croutons, which contrast well in texture and flavor with the softness of mixed salad greens and the sharp taste of Gorgonzola.

Ingredients
8 oz pancetta strips, any rinds removed,
    coarsely chopped
2 large garlic cloves, roughly chopped
3 oz arugula leaves
3 oz radicchio leaves
$1/2$ cup walnuts, roughly chopped
4 oz Gorgonzola cheese
4 tbsp olive oil
1 tbsp balsamic vinegar
salt and freshly ground black pepper
serves 4

Variation
Use walnut oil instead of olive oil, or
hazelnuts and hazelnut oil instead of
walnuts and olive oil.

1 ▲ Put the chopped pancetta
and garlic in a non-stick or heavy
frying pan and heat gently, stirring
constantly, until the pancetta fat
runs. Increase the heat and fry until
the pancetta and garlic are crisp.
Remove with a slotted spoon and
drain on paper towels. Leave the
pancetta fat in the pan, off the heat.

2 ▲ Tear the arugula and radicchio
leaves into a large salad bowl. Sprinkle
on the walnuts, pancetta and garlic.
Add salt and pepper to taste and
toss to mix. Crumble the Gorgonzola
over the top.

3 Return the frying pan to medium
heat and add the oil and balsamic
vinegar to the pancetta fat. Stir until
sizzling, then pour over the salad.
Serve immediately, toss at the table.

Tomato and Mozzarella Toasts
Bruschetta casalinga

These resemble mini pizzas and are good with drinks before a dinner party. Prepare them several hours in advance and pop them in the oven just as your guests arrive.

Ingredients
3 *sfilatini* (thin ciabatta)
about 1 cup sun-dried tomato paste
3 5-oz packages mozzarella cheese,
    drained
about 2 tsp dried oregano or
    mixed herbs
2–3 tbsp olive oil
freshly ground black pepper
serves 6–8

Variations
Use red or green pesto instead of
the sun-dried tomato paste—a
combination of colors is especially
effective if the toasts are served on a
large platter. Halved olives or criss-
crossed strips of anchovy can be
pressed into the cheese.

1 ▲ Cut each *sfilatino* on the
diagonal into 12–15 slices, discarding
the ends. Toast lightly on both sides.

2 Preheat the oven to 425°F. Spread
sun-dried tomato paste on one side
of each slice of toast. Cut the
mozzarella into small pieces and
arrange over the tomato paste.

3 ▲ Put the toasts on baking sheets,
sprinkle with herbs and pepper to
taste and drizzle with oil. Bake for
5 minutes or until the mozzarella
has melted and is bubbling. Let the
toasts settle for a few minutes
before serving.

Genoese Squid Salad

Calamari in insalata alla genovese

This is a good salad for summer, when green beans and new potatoes are at their best. Serve it for a first course or light lunch.

Ingredients

1 lb prepared squid, cut into rings
4 garlic cloves, roughly chopped
1¼ cups Italian red wine
1 lb waxy new potatoes,
  scrubbed clean
8 oz green beans, trimmed and cut into
  short lengths
2–3 drained sun-dried tomatoes in oil,
  thinly sliced lengthwise
4 tbsp extra virgin olive oil
1 tbsp red wine vinegar
salt and freshly ground black pepper
serves 4–6

Cook's Tip

The French potato called Charlotte is perfect for this type of salad because it retains its shape and does not break up when boiled. Prepared squid can be bought at supermarkets with fresh fish counters, and at fishmongers.

1 ▲ Preheat the oven to 350°F. Put the squid rings in an earthenware dish with half the garlic, the wine and pepper to taste. Cover and cook for 45 minutes or until the squid is tender.

2 Put the potatoes in a saucepan, cover with cold water and add a good pinch of salt. Bring to a boil, cover and simmer for 15–20 minutes or until tender. Using a slotted spoon, lift out the potatoes and set aside. Add the beans to the boiling water and cook for 3 minutes. Drain.

3 ▲ When the potatoes are cool enough to handle, slice them thickly on the diagonal and place them in a bowl with the warm beans and sun-dried tomatoes. Whisk the oil, wine vinegar and the remaining garlic in a pitcher and add salt and pepper to taste. Pour over the potato mixture.

4 Drain the squid and discard the wine and garlic. Add the squid to the potato mixture and fold very gently to mix. Arrange the salad on individual plates and grind pepper liberally all over. Serve warm.

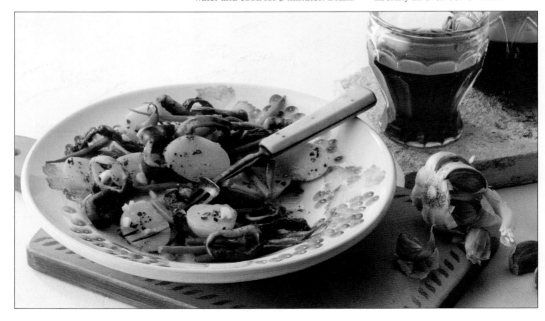

Tuna Carpaccio
Carpaccio di tonno

Fillet of beef is most often used for carpaccio, but meaty fish such as tuna—and swordfish—make an unusual change. The secret is to slice the fish wafer thin, made possible by freezing the fish first, a technique used by the Japanese for making sashimi.

Ingredients

2 fresh tuna steaks, about 1 pound total
    weight
4 tbsp extra virgin olive oil
1 tbsp balsamic vinegar
1 tsp superfine sugar
2 tbsp drained bottled green peppercorns
    or capers
salt and freshly ground black pepper
lemon wedges and green salad,
    to serve

serves 4

Cook's Tip

Raw fish is safe to eat as long as it is very fresh, so check with your fishmonger before purchase, and make and serve carpaccio on the same day. Do not buy fish that has been frozen and thawed.

1 ▲ Remove the skin from each tuna steak and place each steak between two sheets of plastic wrap or waxed paper. Pound with a rolling pin until flattened slightly.

2 Roll up the tuna as tightly as possible, then wrap tightly in plastic wrap and place in the freezer for 4 hours or until firm.

3 ▲ Unwrap the tuna and cut vertically into the thinnest possible slices. Arrange on individual plates.

4 Whisk together the remaining ingredients, season and pour over the tuna. Cover and let come to room temperature for 30 minutes before serving with lemon wedges and green salad.

Marinated Vegetable Antipasto
Verdura marinata per antipasto

Antipasto means "before the meal" and traditionally consists of a selection of marinated vegetable dishes served with good Italian salami and thin slices of prosciutto. Serve in attractive bowls, with plenty of fresh crusty bread.

Ingredients
For the peppers
3 red bell peppers
3 yellow bell peppers
4 garlic cloves, sliced
handful fresh basil, plus extra to garnish
extra virgin olive oil
salt and freshly ground black pepper

For the mushrooms
1 lb open cap mushrooms
4 tbsp extra virgin olive oil
1 large garlic clove, crushed
1 tbsp chopped fresh rosemary
1 cup dry white wine
fresh rosemary sprigs, to garnish

For the olives
1 dried red chili, crushed
grated rind of 1 lemon
1/2 cup extra virgin olive oil
1 1/3 cups Italian black olives
2 tbsp chopped fresh flat-leaf parsley
1 lemon wedge, to serve
serves 4

1 ▲ Place the peppers under a hot broiler. Turn occasionally until they are blackened and blistered all over. Remove from the heat and place in a large plastic bag. When cool, remove the skin, halve the peppers and remove the seeds. Cut the flesh into strips lengthwise and place them in a bowl with the sliced garlic and basil leaves. Add salt, to taste, cover with oil and marinate for 3–4 hours before serving, tossing occasionally. When serving, garnish with more basil leaves.

2 Thickly slice the mushrooms and place in a large bowl. Heat the oil in a small pan and add the garlic and rosemary. Pour in the wine. Bring the mixture to a boil, then lower the heat and simmer for 3 minutes. Add salt and pepper to taste.

3 ▲ Pour the mixture over the mushrooms. Mix well and let cool, stirring occasionally. Cover and marinate overnight. Serve at room temperature, garnished with rosemary sprigs.

4 ▲ Prepare the olives. Place the chili and lemon rind in a small pan with the oil. Heat gently for about 3 minutes. Add the olives and heat for 1 more minute. Pour into a bowl and let cool. Marinate overnight. Sprinkle on the parsley just before serving with the lemon wedge.

Cook's Tip
The pepper antipasto can be stored in the refrigerator for up to 2 weeks covered in olive oil in an airtight jar.

Stuffed Roast Peppers with Pesto

Peperoni arrostiti con pesto

Serve these scallop- and pesto-filled red bell peppers with Italian bread, such as ciabatta or focaccia, to mop up the garlicky juices.

Ingredients

4 squat red bell peppers
2 large garlic cloves, cut into thin slivers
4 tbsp olive oil
4 shelled scallops
3 tbsp pesto
salt and freshly ground black pepper
freshly grated Parmesan cheese,
    to serve
salad leaves and fresh basil sprigs,
    to garnish
serves 4

Cook's Tip

Scallops are available at most fishmongers and supermarkets with fresh fish counters. Never cook scallops for longer than the time stated in the recipe or they will be tough and rubbery.

1 Preheat the oven to 350°F. Cut the peppers in half lengthwise, through their stalks. Scrape out and discard the cores and seeds. Wash the pepper shells and pat dry.

2 ▲ Put the peppers, cut-side up, in an oiled roasting pan. Divide the slivers of garlic equally among them and sprinkle with salt and pepper to taste. Spoon the oil into the peppers, then roast for 40 minutes.

3 ▲ Cut each of the shelled scallops in half to make two flat discs. Remove the peppers from the oven and place a scallop half in each pepper half. Top with pesto.

4 Return the pan to the oven and roast for 10 more minutes. Transfer the peppers to individual serving plates, sprinkle with grated Parmesan and garnish each plate with a few salad leaves and fresh basil sprigs. Serve warm.

Mozzarella Skewers

Spiedini alla romana

Stacks of flavor—layers of oven-baked mozzarella, tomatoes, basil and bread.

Ingredients
12 slices white country bread, each about
  $1/2$ inch thick
3 tbsp olive oil
8 oz mozzarella cheese, cut into
  $1/4$-inch slices
3 plum tomatoes, cut into
  $1/4$-inch slices
$1/2$ cup fresh basil leaves, plus extra to
  garnish
salt and freshly ground black pepper
2 tbsp chopped fresh flat-
  leaf parsley, to garnish
serves 4

Cook's Tip
If you use wooden skewers, soak
them in water first, to prevent
scorching.

1 ▲ Preheat the oven to 425°F. Trim
the crusts from the bread and cut
each slice into four equal squares.
Arrange on a baking sheet and brush
on one side (or both sides) with half
the olive oil. Bake for 3–5 minutes,
until the squares are pale gold.

2 Remove from the oven and place
the bread squares on a board with
the other ingredients.

3 ▲ Make 16 stacks, each starting
with a square of bread, then a slice of
mozzarella topped with a slice of
tomato and a basil leaf. Sprinkle with
salt and pepper, then repeat, ending
with the bread. Push a skewer
through each stack and place on
the baking sheet. Drizzle with the
remaining oil and bake for
10–15 minutes, until the cheese
begins to melt. Garnish with fresh
basil leaves and serve scattered with
chopped fresh flat leaf parsley.

Eggplant Fritters

Frittelle di melanzane

These simply delicious fritters make a superb appetizer or vegetarian supper dish.

Ingredients
1 large eggplant, about $1^1/2$ lb, cut into
  $1/2$ inch thick slices
2 tbsp olive oil
1 egg, lightly beaten
2 garlic cloves, crushed
4 tbsp chopped fresh parsley
$2^1/4$ cups fresh white bread crumbs
generous 1 cup grated
  Parmesan cheese
generous 1 cup feta cheese, crumbled
3 tbsp flour
sunflower oil, for shallow frying
salt and freshly ground black pepper

To serve
plain yogurt, flavored with fried red
  chilies and cumin seeds
lime wedges
serves 4

1 ▲ Preheat the oven to 375°F.
Brush the eggplant slices with the
olive oil, then place them on a
baking sheet and bake for about
20 minutes until golden and tender.
Chop the slices finely and place them
in a bowl with the egg, garlic, parsley,
bread crumbs, Parmesan and feta.
Add salt and pepper to taste, and mix
well. Let the mixture rest for about
20 minutes. If the mixture looks very
sloppy, add more bread crumbs.

2 ▲ Divide the mixture into eight
balls and flatten them slightly. Place
the flour on a plate and season with
salt and pepper. Coat the fritters in
the flour, shaking off any excess.

3 Shallow fry the fritters in batches
for 1 minute on each side, until
golden brown. Drain on paper
towels and serve with the flavored
yogurt and lime wedges.

Raw Vegetables with Olive Oil Dip   *Pinzimonio*

Use a combination of any fresh seasonal vegetables for this colorful antipasto from Rome,

where the dip usually consists only of olive oil and salt. The vegetables should be raw or

lightly blanched, and the olive oil of the best quality available.

Ingredients
3 large carrots, peeled
2 fennel bulbs
6 tender stalks celery
1 pepper
12 radishes, trimmed of roots
2 large tomatoes, or 12 cherry tomatoes
8 scallions
12 small cauliflower florets
For the dip
1/2 cup extra-virgin olive oil
salt and freshly ground black pepper
3 tbsp fresh lemon juice (optional)
4 leaves fresh basil, torn into small
    pieces (optional)
serves 6–8

1 Prepare the vegetables by slicing
the carrots, fennel, celery and pepper
into small sticks.

2 ▲ Cut the large tomatoes into
sections if using. Trim the roots and
dark green leaves from the scallions.
Arrange the vegetables on a large
platter, leaving a space in the center
for the dip.

3 ▲ Make the dip by pouring the
olive oil into a small bowl. Add salt and
pepper. Stir in the lemon juice and
basil, if using. Place the bowl in the
center of the vegetable platter.

Celery Stuffed with Gorgonzola   *Sedano ripieno di Gorgonzola*

These celery stalks are very easy to make. Serve them with drinks, or take them to a picnic.

Ingredients
12 crisp stalks celery, leaves left on
1/2 cup Gorgonzola
1/2 cup cream cheese
fresh chives, to garnish
serves 4–6

1 ▲ Wash and dry the celery stalks,
and trim the root ends.

2 ▲ In a small bowl, mash the cheeses
together until smooth.

3 ▲ Fill the celery stalks with the
cheese mixture, using a spatula to
smooth the filling. Chill before serving.
Garnish with chopped chives.

Broiled Vegetable Terrine

Terrina di verdure alla griglia

A colorful, layered terrine, using the flavorful vegetables associated with the south of Italy:

red and yellow bell peppers, zucchini and eggplants.

Ingredients
2 large red bell peppers, quartered, cored
   and seeded
2 large yellow bell peppers, quartered,
   cored and seeded
1 large eggplant, sliced lengthwise
2 large zucchini, sliced lengthwise
6 tbsp olive oil
1 large red onion, thinly sliced
½ cup raisins
1 tbsp tomato paste
1 tbsp red wine vinegar
1⅔ cups tomato juice
2 tbsp gelatin
fresh basil leaves, to garnish

For the dressing
6 tbsp extra virgin olive oil
2 tbsp red wine vinegar
salt and freshly ground black pepper
serves 6

1 Place the prepared red and yellow
peppers skin side up under a hot
broiler and cook until the skins are
blackened. Transfer to a bowl and
cover with a plate. Allow to cool.

2 ▲ Preheat the broiler. Arrange the
eggplant and zucchini slices on
separate baking sheets. Brush them
with a little oil and broil, in batches if
necessary, turning occasionally, until
tender and golden.

3 When the peppers are cool, peel
off the skins and then rinse the
peppers under running water. Cut
into thick strips and set aside.

4 ▲ Heat the remaining olive oil in a
frying pan, and add the sliced onion,
raisins, tomato paste and red wine
vinegar. Cook gently until soft and
syrupy. Let the mixture cool in the
frying pan.

5 Line a 7½ cup terrine with plastic
wrap (it helps to lightly oil the
terrine first), leaving a little hanging
over the sides.

6 Pour half the tomato juice into a
small saucepan and sprinkle the
gelatin over the top. Dissolve gently
over a low heat, stirring occasionally.
Do not allow the gelatin mixture to
boil or it may not set properly.

7 ▲ Place a thin layer of red peppers
in the bottom of the terrine, and
pour in enough of the tomato juice
and gelatin mixture to cover.
Continue layering the eggplant,
zucchini, yellow peppers and onion
mixture, finishing with another layer
of red peppers. Pour a little of the
tomato juice and gelatin mixture
over each layer of vegetables.

8 ▲ Add the remaining tomato juice
to any left in the pan, and pour into
the terrine. Give the terrine a sharp
tap, to disperse the juice, then cover
and transfer to the fridge to set.

9 To make the dressing, whisk
together the oil and vinegar, and
season. Turn out the terrine and
remove the plastic wrap. Cut the
terrine into thick slices and serve,
drizzled with a little of the dressing.
Garnish with basil leaves.

Mixed Seafood Salad

Insalata di frutti di mare

All along Italy's coasts versions of this salad appear. Use fresh seafood that is in season, or use a combination of fresh and frozen.

Ingredients
12oz small squid
1 small onion, cut into quarters
1 bay leaf
7oz shrimp, in their shells
1¹/₂lb fresh mussels, in their
 shells
1lb fresh small clams
³/₄ cup white wine
1 fennel bulb
For the dressing
5 tbsp extra-virgin olive oil
3 tbsp fresh lemon juice
1 garlic clove, finely chopped
salt and freshly ground black pepper
serves 6–8

1 ▲ Working near the sink, clean the squid by first peeling off the thin skin from the body section. Rinse well. Pull the head and tentacles away from the sac section. Some of the intestines will come away with the head. Remove and discard the translucent quill and any remaining insides from the sac. Sever the tentacles from the head. Discard the head and intestines. Remove the small hard beak from the base of the tentacles. Rinse the sac and tentacles well under cold running water. Drain.

2 Bring a large pan of water to a boil. Add the onion and bay leaf. Drop in the squid and cook for about 10 minutes, or until tender. Remove with a slotted spoon, and allow to cool before slicing into rings ¹/₂in wide. Cut each tentacle section into 2 pieces. Set aside.

3 ▲ Drop the shrimp into the same boiling water, and cook until they turn pink, about 2 minutes. Remove with a slotted spoon. Peel and devein. (The cooking liquid may be strained and kept for soup.)

4 ▲ Cut off the "beards" from the mussels. Scrub and rinse the mussels and clams well in several changes of cold water. Place in a large pan with the wine. Cover, and steam until all the shells have opened. (Discard any that do not open.) Lift the clams and mussels out.

5 ▲ Remove all the clams from their shells with a small spoon. Place in a large serving bowl. Remove all but 8 of the mussels from their shells, and add them to the clams in the bowl. Leave the remaining mussels in their half shells, and set aside. Cut the green, ferny part of the fennel away from the bulb. Chop finely and set aside. Chop the bulb into bite-size pieces, and add it to the serving bowl with the squid and shrimp.

6 ▲ Make a dressing by combining the oil, lemon juice, garlic and chopped fennel green in a small bowl. Add salt and pepper to taste. Pour over the salad, and toss well. Decorate with the remaining mussels in the half shell. This salad may be served at room temperature or slightly chilled.

Prosciutto with Figs

Prosciutto crudo con fichi

The hams cured in the region of Parma are held to be the finest in Italy. Prosciutto makes an excellent appetizer sliced paper-thin and served with fresh figs or melon.

Ingredients
12 paper-thin slices prosciutto crudo
8 ripe green or black figs
crusty bread and unsalted butter,
   to serve
serves 4

1 ▲ Arrange the slices of prosciutto on a serving plate.

2 ▲ Wipe the figs with a damp cloth. Cut them almost into quarters but do not cut all the way through the base. If the skins are tender, they may be eaten along with the inner fruit. If you prefer, you may peel each quarter carefully by pulling the peel gently away from the pulp.

3 ▲ Arrange the figs on top of the prosciutto. Serve with bread and unsalted butter.

Cherry Tomatoes with Pesto

Pomodorini con pesto

These make a colorful and tasty appetizer to go with drinks, or as part of a buffet. Make the pesto when fresh basil is plentiful, and freeze it in batches.

Ingredients
1lb cherry tomatoes (about 36)
For the pesto
1 cup fresh basil
3–4 garlic cloves
4 tbsp pine nuts
1 tsp salt, plus extra to taste
7 tbsp olive oil
3 tbsp freshly grated Parmesan
   cheese
6 tbsp freshly grated Pecorino
   cheese
freshly ground black pepper
serves 8–10 as an appetizer

1 Wash the tomatoes. Slice off the top of each tomato, and carefully scoop out the seeds with a melon baller or small spoon.

2 ▲ Place the basil, garlic, pine nuts, salt and olive oil in a blender or food processor and process until smooth. Remove the contents to a bowl with a rubber spatula. If desired, the pesto may be frozen at this point, before the cheeses are added. To use when frozen, allow to thaw, then proceed to step 3.

3 Fold in the grated cheeses (use all Parmesan if Pecorino is not available). Season with pepper, and more salt if necessary.

4 ▲ Use a small spoon to fill each tomato with a little pesto. This dish is at its best if chilled for about an hour before serving.

Hard-boiled Eggs with Tuna Sauce

Uova sode tonnate

The combination of eggs with a tasty tuna mayonnaise makes a nourishing first course that is quick and easy to prepare.

Ingredients

6 extra large eggs
7oz can tuna in olive oil
3 anchovy fillets
1 tbsp capers, drained
2 tbsp fresh lemon juice
4 tbsp olive oil
salt and freshly ground black pepper

For the mayonnaise

1 egg yolk, at room temperature
1 tsp Dijon mustard
1 tsp white wine vinegar or fresh lemon
    juice
2/3 cup olive oil
capers and anchovy fillets, to garnish
    (optional)

serves 6

4 ▲ Fold the tuna sauce into the mayonnaise. Season with black pepper, and extra salt if necessary. Refrigerate for at least 1 hour.

5 ▲ To serve, cut the eggs in half lengthwise. Arrange on a serving platter. Spoon on the sauce, and garnish with capers and anchovy fillets, if desired. Serve chilled.

1 Boil the eggs for 12–14 minutes. Drain under cold water. Peel carefully and set aside.

2 ▲ Make the mayonnaise by whisking the egg yolk, mustard and vinegar or lemon juice together in a small bowl. Whisk in the oil a few drops at a time until 3 or 4 tablespoons of oil have been incorporated. Pour in the remaining oil in a slow stream, whisking constantly.

3 Place the tuna with its oil, the anchovies, capers, lemon juice and olive oil in the bowl of a blender or food processor. Process until smooth.

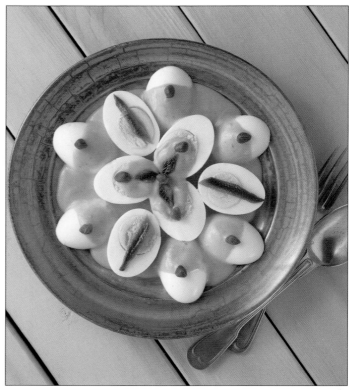

Tuna and Bean Salad

Tonno e fagioli

This substantial salad makes a good light meal, and can be very quickly assembled from canned ingredients.

Ingredients

2 × 14oz cans cannellini or borlotti
    beans
2 × 7oz cans tuna fish, drained
4 tbsp extra-virgin olive oil
2 tbsp fresh lemon juice
salt and freshly ground black pepper
1 tbsp chopped fresh parsley
3 scallions, thinly sliced
serves 4–6

1 ▲ Pour the beans into a large strainer and rinse under cold water. Drain
well. Place in a serving dish.

2 ▲ Break the tuna into fairly large
flakes and arrange over the beans.

3 ▲ In a small bowl make the dressing
by combining the oil with the lemon
juice. Season with salt and pepper, and
stir in the parsley. Mix well. Pour over
the beans and tuna.

4 ▲ Sprinkle with the scallions. Toss
well before serving.

Carpaccio with Arugula

Carpaccio con rucola

Carpaccio is a fine dish of raw beef in lemon juice and olive oil. It is traditionally served with flakes of fresh Parmesan cheese. Use very fresh meat of the best quality.

Ingredients
1 garlic clove, peeled and cut in half
1¹/₂ lemons
¹/₄ cup extra-virgin olive oil
salt and freshly ground black pepper
2 bunches arugula
4 very thin slices of beef top round
1 cup Parmesan cheese, thinly
    shaved
serves 4

1 Rub a small bowl all over with the cut side of the garlic. Squeeze the lemons into the bowl. Whisk in the olive oil. Season with salt and pepper. Allow the sauce to stand for at least 15 minutes before using.

2 ▲ Carefully wash the arugula and tear off any thick stalks. Spin or pat dry. Arrange the arugula around the edge of a serving platter, or divide on 4 individual plates.

3 ▲ Place the beef in the center of the platter, and pour on the sauce, spreading it evenly over the meat. Arrange the shaved Parmesan on top of the meat slices. Serve at once.

Tuna in Rolled Red Peppers

Peperoni rossi ripieni di tonno

This savory combination originated in southern Italy. Grilled peppers have a sweet, smoky taste that combines particularly well with fish.

Ingredients
3 large red peppers
7oz can tuna fish, drained
2 tbsp fresh lemon juice
3 tbsp olive oil
6 green or black olives, pitted and
    chopped
2 tbsp chopped fresh parsley
1 garlic clove, finely chopped
1 medium stalk celery, very finely
    chopped
salt and freshly ground black pepper
serves 4–6

1 Place the peppers under a hot broiler, and turn occasionally until they are black and blistered on all sides. Remove from the heat and place in a paper bag.

2 ▲ Leave for 5 minutes, and then peel. Cut the peppers into quarters, and remove the stems and seeds.

3 Meanwhile, flake the tuna and combine with the lemon juice and oil. Stir in the remaining ingredients. Season with salt and pepper.

4 ▲ Lay the pepper segments out flat, skin side down. Divide the tuna mixture equally between them. Spread it out, pressing it into an even layer. Roll the peppers up. Place the pepper rolls in the refrigerator for at least 1 hour. Just before serving, cut each roll in half with a sharp knife.

Stuffed Mussels

Cozze gratinate

This tasty appetizer is a speciality of southern Italy. It can be made equally well using large clams. Always use the freshest seafood available.

Ingredients

1¹/₂lb large fresh mussels in their
   shells
¹/₃ cup unsalted butter, at room
   temperature
¹/₄ cup dry breadcrumbs
2 garlic cloves, finely chopped
3 tbsp chopped fresh parsley
¹/₄ cup freshly grated Parmesan
   cheese
salt and freshly ground black pepper
serves 4

1 ▲ Scrub the mussels well under cold running water, cutting off the "beard" with a small knife. Preheat the oven to 450°F.

2 ▲ Place the mussels with a cupful of water in a large pan over moderate heat. As soon as they open, lift them out one by one. Remove and discard the empty half shells, leaving the meat in the other half. (Discard any mussels that do not open.)

3 ▲ Combine all the remaining ingredients in a small bowl. Blend well. Place in a small pan and heat gently until the stuffing mixture begins to soften.

4 ▲ Arrange the mussel halves on a flat cookie sheet. Spoon a small amount of the stuffing over each mussel. Bake for about 7 minutes, or until lightly browned. Serve hot or at room temperature.

Lemon and Herb Risotto Cake

Budino di riso al limone

This unusual dish can be served as a main course with salad, or as a satisfying side dish.

It is also good served cold, and packs well for picnics.

Ingredients

1 small leek, thinly sliced
2½ cups chicken stock
1 cup short-grain rice
finely grated rind of 1 lemon
2 tbsp chopped fresh chives
2 tbsp chopped fresh parsley
¾ cup grated mozzarella cheese
salt and freshly ground black pepper
parsley and lemon wedges,
    to garnish
serves 4

1 Preheat the oven to 400°F. Lightly oil an 8½ in round cake pan with a removable base.

2 ▲ Cook the leek in a large pan with 3 tbsp of the stock, stirring over moderate heat, to soften. Add the rice and the remaining stock.

3 ▲ Bring to a boil. Cover the pan and simmer gently, stirring occasionally for about 20 minutes, or until all the liquid is absorbed.

◀ 4 Stir in the lemon rind, herbs, cheese and seasoning. Spoon the mixture into the pan, cover with foil and bake for 30–35 minutes or until lightly browned. Turn out and serve in slices, garnished with parsley and lemon wedges.

Cook's Tip
The best type of rice to choose is one of the round grain risotto rices, such as Arborio.

Soups

· ·

The Italians are avid soup eaters, and some of the best soups in the world come from Italy. Clear broth, brodo, *and delicate puréed soups are served as a first course before a main meal. More substantial chunky soups,* minestre, *are often main meals in themselves, usually served in the evening if the main meal of the day has been at lunchtime.*

Wild Mushroom Soup

Zuppa di porcini

Wild mushrooms are expensive. Dried porcini have an intense flavor, so only a small quantity is needed. The beef stock may seem unusual in a vegetable soup, but it helps to strengthen the earthy flavor of the mushrooms.

Ingredients

2 cups dried porcini mushrooms
2 tbsp olive oil
1 tbsp butter
2 leeks, thinly sliced
2 shallots, roughly chopped
1 garlic clove, roughly chopped
3 cups fresh wild mushrooms
5 cups beef stock
$\frac{1}{2}$ tsp dried thyme
$\frac{2}{3}$ cup heavy cream
salt and freshly ground black pepper
fresh thyme sprigs, to garnish
serves 4

Cook's Tip

Porcini are cepes. Italian cooks would make this soup with a combination of fresh and dried cepes, but if fresh cepes are difficult to obtain, you can use other wild mushrooms, such as chanterelles.

1 ▲ Put the dried porcini in a bowl, add 1 cup warm water and let soak for 20–30 minutes. Lift them out of the liquid and squeeze over the bowl to remove as much of the soaking liquid as possible. Strain all the liquid and reserve to use later. Finely chop the porcini.

2 Heat the oil and butter in a large saucepan until foaming. Add the sliced leeks, chopped shallots and garlic and cook gently for about 5 minutes, stirring frequently, until softened but not colored.

3 ▲ Chop or slice the fresh mushrooms and add to the pan. Stir over medium heat for a few minutes until they begin to soften. Pour in the stock and bring to a boil. Add the porcini, soaking liquid, dried thyme and salt and pepper. Lower the heat, half cover the pan and simmer gently for 30 minutes, stirring occasionally.

4 ▲ Pour about three-quarters of the soup into a blender or food processor and process until smooth. Return to the soup remaining in the pan, stir in the cream and heat through. Check the consistency and add more stock if the soup is too thick. Taste for seasoning. Serve hot, garnished with thyme sprigs.

Cream of Zucchini Soup

Vellutata di zucchini

The beauty of this soup is its delicate color, rich and creamy texture and subtle taste. If you prefer a more pronounced cheese flavor, use Gorgonzola instead of Dolcelatte.

Ingredients

2 tbsp olive oil
1 tbsp butter
1 medium onion, roughly chopped
2 pounds zucchini, trimmed and sliced
1 tsp dried oregano
about 2¹/₂ cups vegetable or chicken
   stock
4 oz mild blue cheese (such as
   Dolcelatte), rind removed, diced
1¹/₄ cups light cream or half-and-half
salt and freshly ground black pepper
fresh oregano and extra cheese,
   to garnish

serves 4–6

1 ▲ Heat the oil and butter in a large saucepan until foaming. Add the onion and cook gently for about 5 minutes, stirring frequently, until softened but not brown.

2 ▲ Add the zucchini and oregano, with salt and pepper to taste. Cook over medium heat for 10 minutes, stirring frequently.

3 ▲ Pour in the stock and bring to a boil, stirring. Lower the heat, half cover the pan and simmer gently, stirring occasionally, for about 30 minutes. Stir in the diced Dolcelatte until melted.

Cook's Tip

To save time, trim off and discard the ends of the zucchini, cut them into thirds, then chop in a food processor fitted with the metal blade.

4 ▲ Process the soup in a blender or food processor until smooth, then press through a sieve into a clean pan.

5 Add two-thirds of the cream and stir over low heat until hot, but not boiling. Check the consistency and add more stock if the soup is too thick. Taste for seasoning, then pour into heated bowls. Swirl in the remaining cream. Garnish with oregano and extra cheese and serve.

Minestrone with Pasta and Beans

Minestrone alla milanese

This classic minestrone from Lombardy includes pancetta for a pleasant touch of saltiness.

Milanese cooks vary the recipe according to what is at hand, and you can do the same.

Ingredients

3 tbsp olive oil
4 oz pancetta, any rinds removed, roughly chopped
2–3 celery stalks, finely chopped
3 medium carrots, finely chopped
1 medium onion, finely chopped
1–2 garlic cloves, crushed
2 cans (14 oz each) chopped tomatoes
about 4 cups chicken stock
1 can (14 oz) cannellini beans, drained and rinsed
1/2 cup macaroni
2–4 tbsp chopped flat-leaf parsley, to taste
salt and freshly ground black pepper
shaved Parmesan cheese, to serve
serves 4

Variation

Use long-grain rice instead of the pasta, and borlotti beans instead of cannellini.

1 ▲ Heat the oil in a large saucepan. Add the pancetta, celery, carrots and onion and cook over low heat for 5 minutes, stirring constantly, until the vegetables are softened.

2 Add the garlic and tomatoes, breaking them up well with a wooden spoon. Pour in the stock. Add salt and pepper to taste and bring to a boil. Half cover the pan, lower the heat and simmer gently for about 20 minutes, until the vegetables are soft.

3 ▲ Drain the beans and add them to the pan with the macaroni. Bring to a boil again. Cover, lower the heat and continue to simmer for about 20 more minutes. Check the consistency and add more stock if necessary. Stir in the parsley and taste for seasoning.

4 Serve hot, sprinkled with plenty of Parmesan cheese. This makes a meal in itself if served with chunks of crusty Italian bread.

Summer Minestrone

Minestrone estivo

This brightly colored, fresh-tasting soup makes the most of summer vegetables.

Ingredients

3 tbsp olive oil
1 large onion, finely chopped
1 tbsp sun-dried tomato paste
1 lb ripe Italian plum tomatoes, peeled and finely chopped
8 oz green zucchini, trimmed and roughly chopped
8 oz yellow summer squash,trimmed and roughly chopped
3 waxy new potatoes, diced
2 garlic cloves, crushed
about 5 cups chicken stock or water
1/4 cup shredded fresh basil
2/3 cup grated Parmesan cheese
salt and freshly ground black pepper
serves 4

1 ▲ Heat the oil in a large saucepan, add the onion and cook gently for about 5 minutes, stirring constantly, until softened. Stir in the sun-dried tomato paste, chopped tomatoes, zucchini, squash, diced potatoes and garlic. Mix well and cook gently for 10 minutes, uncovered, shaking the pan frequently to prevent the vegetables from sticking to the base.

2 ▲ Pour in the stock. Bring to a boil, lower the heat, half cover the pan and simmer gently for 15 minutes or until the vegetables are just tender. Add more stock if necessary.

3 Remove the pan from the heat and stir in the basil and half the cheese. Taste for seasoning. Serve hot, sprinkled with the remaining cheese.

Clam and Pasta Soup

Zuppa alle vongole

This soup is a play on a popular pasta dish—spaghetti alle vongole—using pantry ingredients. Serve it with hot focaccia or ciabatta for an informal supper with friends.

Ingredients

2 tbsp olive oil
1 large onion, finely chopped
2 garlic cloves, crushed
1 can (14 oz) chopped tomatoes
1 tbsp sun-dried tomato paste
1 tsp sugar
1 tsp dried mixed herbs
about 3 cups fish or vegetable stock
²/₃ cup red wine
¹/₂ cup small pasta shapes
1 jar or can (5 oz) clams in
    natural juice
2 tbsp finely chopped flat-leaf parsley,
    plus a few whole leaves,
    to garnish
salt and freshly ground black pepper

serves 4

1 ▲ Heat the oil in a large saucepan. Cook the onion gently for 5 minutes, stirring frequently, until softened.

2 ▲ Add the garlic, tomatoes, tomato paste, sugar, herbs, stock and wine, with salt and pepper to taste. Bring to a boil. Lower the heat, half cover the pan and simmer for 10 minutes, stirring occasionally.

3 ▲ Add the pasta and continue simmering, uncovered, for about 10 minutes or until *al dente*. Stir occasionally, to prevent the pasta shapes from sticking together.

Cook's Tip

This soup has a fuller flavor if it is made the day before and reheated.

4 ▲ Add the clams and their juice to the soup and heat through for 3–4 minutes, adding more stock if required. Do not let it boil or the clams will be tough. Remove from the heat, stir in the parsley and taste the soup for seasoning. Serve hot, sprinkled with coarsely ground black pepper and parsley leaves.

Tuscan Bean Soup

Zuppa di fagioli alla toscana

There are lots of versions of this wonderful soup. This one uses cannellini beans, leeks,

cabbage and good olive oil—and tastes even better reheated.

Ingredients

3 tbsp extra virgin olive oil
1 onion, roughly chopped
2 leeks, roughly chopped
1 large potato, peeled and diced
2 garlic cloves, finely chopped
5 cups vegetable stock
1 can (14 oz) cannellini beans, drained,
    liquid reserved
1/2 (6 oz) Savoy cabbage, shredded
3 tbsp chopped fresh flat-
    leaf parsley
2 tbsp chopped fresh oregano
1 cup Parmesan cheese, shaved
salt and freshly ground black pepper

For the garlic toasts

2–3 tbsp extra virgin olive oil
6 thick slices country bread
1 garlic clove, peeled and bruised
serves 4

3 ▲ Stir in the cabbage and beans, with half the herbs, season and cook for 10 more minutes. Spoon about one-third of the soup into a food processor or blender and process until fairly smooth. Return to the soup in the pan, taste for seasoning and heat through for 5 minutes.

4 ▲ Meanwhile, make the garlic toasts. Drizzle a little oil over the slices of bread, then rub both sides of each slice with the garlic. Toast until browned on both sides. Ladle the soup into bowls. Sprinkle with the remaining herbs and the Parmesan shavings. Add a drizzle of olive oil and serve with the toasts.

1 ▲ Heat the oil in a large saucepan and gently cook the onion, leeks, potato and garlic for 4–5 minutes.

2 ▲ Pour in the stock and liquid from the beans. Cover and simmer for 15 minutes.

Lentil Soup with Tomatoes

Minestra di lenticchie

A classic rustic Italian soup flavored with rosemary, delicious served with garlic bread.

Ingredients
1 cup dried green or
    brown lentils
3 tbsp extra virgin olive oil
3 strips bacon, diced
1 onion, finely chopped
2 celery stalks, finely chopped
2 carrots, finely diced
2 rosemary sprigs, finely chopped
2 bay leaves
1 can (14 oz) chopped plum tomatoes
8 cups vegetable stock
salt and freshly ground black pepper
bay leaves and rosemary sprigs,
    to garnish
serves 4

Cook's Tip
Look for the small green lentils sold
at Italian groceries or delicatessens.

1 Place the lentils in a bowl and
cover with cold water. Let soak for
2 hours. Rinse and drain well.

2 ▲ Heat the oil in a large saucepan.
Add the bacon and cook for about
3 minutes, then stir in the onion and
cook for 5 minutes, until softened.
Stir in the celery, carrots, rosemary,
bay leaves and lentils. Toss over the
heat for 1 minute until thoroughly
coated in the oil.

3 ▲ Pour in the tomatoes and stock
and bring to a boil. Lower the heat,
half cover the pan, and simmer for
about 1 hour or until the lentils are
perfectly tender.

4 Remove the bay leaves, add salt
and pepper to taste and serve with a
garnish of fresh bay leaves and
rosemary sprigs.

Spinach and Rice Soup

Minestra di riso e spinaci

Use very fresh, young spinach leaves to prepare this light and fresh-tasting soup.

Ingredients
1¹/₂ lb fresh spinach, washed
3 tbsp extra virgin olive oil
1 small onion, finely chopped
2 garlic cloves, finely chopped
1 small fresh red chili, seeded and
    finely chopped
generous 1 cup risotto rice
5 cups vegetable stock
¹/₄ cup grated Pecorino cheese
salt and freshly ground black pepper
serves 4

1 Place the spinach in a large pan
with just the water that clings to its
leaves after washing. Add a large
pinch of salt. Heat gently until the
spinach has wilted, then remove
from the heat and drain, reserving
any liquid.

2 ▲ Either chop the spinach finely
using a large knife or place in a food
processor and process to a fairly
coarse purée.

3 ▲ Heat the oil in a large saucepan
and gently cook the onion, garlic and
chili for 4–5 minutes until softened.
Stir in the rice until well coated, then
pour in the stock and reserved
spinach liquid. Bring to a boil,
lower the heat and simmer for
10 minutes. Add the spinach, with
salt and pepper to taste. Cook for
5–7 more minutes, until the rice is
tender. Check the seasoning and
serve with the Pecorino cheese.

Onion Soup

La cipollata

This warming winter soup comes from Umbria, where it is sometimes thickened with beaten eggs and lots of grated Parmesan cheese. It is then served on top of hot toasted croutons— rather like savory scrambled eggs.

Ingredients

4 oz pancetta slices, any rinds removed,
   roughly chopped
2 tbsp olive oil
1 tbsp butter
1¹/₂ lb onions, thinly sliced
2 tsp sugar
about 5 cups chicken stock
12 oz ripe Italian plum tomatoes, peeled
   and roughly chopped
a few basil leaves, shredded
salt and freshly ground black pepper
freshly grated Parmesan cheese,
   to serve
serves 4

3 ▲ Add the stock, tomatoes and salt and pepper and bring to a boil, stirring. Lower the heat, half cover the pan and simmer, stirring occasionally, for about 30 minutes.

4 Check the consistency of the soup and add a little more stock or water if it is too thick.

5 Just before serving, stir in most of the basil and taste for seasoning. Serve hot, garnished with the remaining shredded basil. Serve the freshly grated Parmesan separately.

Cook's Tip

Look for Vidalia onions to make this soup. They are available at large supermarkets, and have a very sweet flavor and attractive yellowish flesh.

1 ▲ Put the chopped pancetta in a large saucepan and heat gently, stirring constantly, until the fat runs. Increase the heat to medium, add the oil, butter, onions and sugar and stir well to mix.

2 ▲ Half cover the pan and cook the onions gently for about 20 minutes, until golden. Stir frequently and lower the heat if necessary.

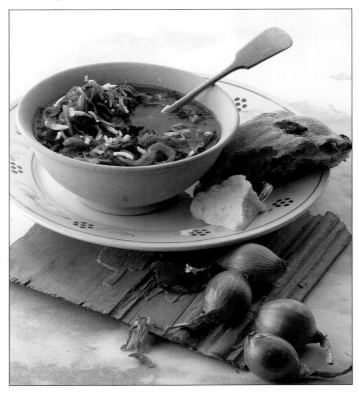

Tomato and Fresh Basil Soup

Crema di pomodori al basilico

A soup for late summer when fresh tomatoes are at their most flavorful.

Ingredients

1 tbsp olive oil
2 tbsp butter
1 medium onion, finely chopped
2 pounds ripe Italian plum tomatoes,
　　roughly chopped
1 garlic clove, roughly chopped
about 3 cups chicken or vegetable stock
$1/_2$ cup dry white wine
2 tbsp sun-dried tomato paste
2 tbsp shredded fresh basil, plus a few
　　whole leaves, to garnish
$2/_3$ cup heavy cream
salt and freshly ground black pepper
serves 4–6

1 ▲ Heat the oil and butter in a large saucepan until foaming. Add the onion and cook gently for about 5 minutes, stirring frequently, until softened but not brown.

2 ▲ Stir in the chopped tomatoes and garlic, then add the stock, white wine and sun-dried tomato paste, with salt and pepper to taste. Bring to a boil, then lower the heat, half cover the pan and simmer gently for 20 minutes, stirring occasionally to prevent the tomatoes from sticking to the base of the pan.

3 ▲ Process the soup with the shredded basil in a blender or food processor, then press through a sieve into a clean pan.

4 ▲ Add the heavy cream and heat through, stirring. Do not let the soup approach the boiling point. Check the consistency and add more stock if necessary and then taste for seasoning. Pour into heated bowls and garnish with basil. Serve immediately.

Variation
The soup can also be served chilled. Pour it into a container after straining and chill for at least 4 hours. Serve in chilled bowls.

Mediterranean Broth

Minestrone con prosciutto salato

This delicious main course soup is very similar to the warming, chunky meat and potato broths of cooler climates. For extra color, a few onion skins can be added when cooking the ham, but remember to remove them before serving.

Ingredients

1 lb ham, in one piece
2 bay leaves
2 onions, sliced
2 tsp paprika
1½ lb potatoes, cut into
    large chunks
8 oz collard greens
15 oz can haricot or cannellini
    beans, drained
salt and freshly ground black pepper
serves 4

1 Soak the ham overnight in cold water. Drain and put in a large saucepan with the bay leaves and onions. Pour on 6¼ cups cold water.

2 Bring to a boil, then reduce the heat and simmer very gently for about 1½ hours until the meat is tender. Keep an eye on the pan to make sure it doesn't boil over.

Cook's Tip

Bacon pieces can be used instead of the ham. The bones will give the juices a delicious flavor.

3 ▲ Drain the meat, reserving the cooking liquid and let cool slightly. Discard the skin and any excess fat from the meat and cut into small chunks. Return to the pan with the paprika and potatoes. Cover and simmer gently for 20 minutes.

4 ▲ Cut away the cores from the collard greens. Roll up the leaves and cut into thin shreds. Add to the pan with the beans and simmer for about 10 minutes. Season with salt and pepper to taste and serve hot.

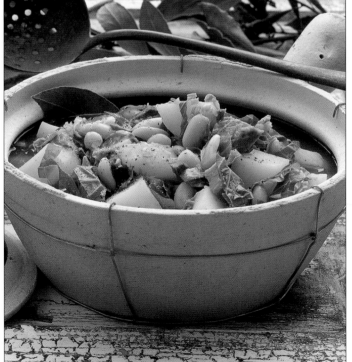

Egg and Cheese Soup

Stracciatella

*In this classic Roman soup, eggs and cheese are beaten into hot broth, producing a slightly
"stringy" texture characteristic of the dish.*

Ingredients

3 eggs
3 tbsp fine semolina
6 tbsp freshly grated Parmesan cheese
pinch of nutmeg
6¼ cups fresh or canned beef or
    chicken stock
salt and freshly ground black pepper
12 rounds of French bread, to serve
serves 6

3 ▲ When the stock is hot, and a few
minutes before you are ready to serve
the soup, whisk the egg mixture into
the broth. Raise the heat slightly, and
bring it barely to a boil. Season with
salt and pepper. Cook for 3–4
minutes. As the egg cooks, the soup
will not be completely smooth.

4 ▲ To serve, toast the rounds of
French bread and place 2 in the
bottom of each soup plate. Ladle on
the hot soup, and serve immediately.

1 ▲ Beat the eggs in a bowl with
the semolina and the cheese. Add
the nutmeg. Beat in 1 cupful of the
cool stock.

2 ▲ Meanwhile heat the remaining
stock to simmering point in a large pan.

Minestrone with Pesto

Minestrone con pesto

Minestrone is a thick mixed vegetable soup using almost any combination of seasonal vegetables. Short pasta or rice may also be added. This version includes pesto sauce.

Ingredients
$6^{1}/_{4}$ cups stock or water, or
  a combination
3 tbsp olive oil
1 large onion, finely chopped
1 leek, sliced
2 carrots, finely chopped
1 stalk celery, finely chopped
2 garlic cloves, finely chopped
2 potatoes, peeled and cut into small dice
1 bay leaf
1 sprig fresh thyme, or $^{1}/_{4}$ tsp dried
  thyme leaves
salt and freshly ground black pepper
$^{3}/_{4}$ cup peas, fresh or frozen
2-3 zucchini, finely chopped
3 medium tomatoes, peeled and
  finely chopped
2 cups cooked or canned beans
  such as cannellini
3 tbsp pesto sauce
freshly grated Parmesan cheese,
  to serve
serves 6

1 In a medium pan, heat the stock or water to simmering.

2 ▲ Heat the olive oil in a large pan. Stir in the onion and leek, and cook for 5-6 minutes, or until the onion softens. Add the carrots, celery and garlic, and cook over moderate heat, stirring often, for another 5 minutes. Add the potatoes and cook for 2-3 minutes more.

3 Pour in the hot stock or water, and stir well. Add the herbs and season with salt and pepper. Bring to a boil, reduce the heat slightly, and cook for 10-12 minutes.

4 Stir in the peas, if fresh, and the zucchini. Simmer for 5 minutes more. Add the frozen peas, if using, and the tomatoes. Cover the pan, and boil for 5-8 minutes.

5 ▲ About 10 minutes before serving the soup, uncover, and stir in the beans. Simmer for 10 minutes. Stir in the pesto sauce. Taste for seasoning. Simmer for another 5 minutes then remove from the heat. Allow the soup to stand for a few minutes, then serve with the grated Parmesan.

Pumpkin Soup

Minestrone di zucca

This beautifully colored soup would be perfect for an autumn dinner.

Ingredients
1lb piece of peeled pumpkin
$^{1}/_{4}$ cup butter
1 medium onion, finely chopped
$3^{1}/_{2}$ cups fresh or canned chicken stock
  or water
2 cups milk
pinch of grated nutmeg
salt and freshly ground black pepper
$1^{1}/_{2}$ oz spaghetti, broken into small pieces
6 tbsp freshly grated Parmesan cheese
serves 4

1 Chop the piece of pumpkin into 1in cubes.

2 ▲ Heat the butter in a large pan. Add the onion, and cook over moderate heat until it softens, about 6-8 minutes. Stir in the pumpkin, and cook for 2-3 minutes more.

3 Add the stock or water, and cook until the pumpkin is soft, for about 15 minutes. Remove from the heat.

4 Purée the soup in a blender or food processor. Return it to the pan. Stir in the milk and nutmeg. Season with salt and pepper. Bring the soup back to a boil.

5 Stir the broken spaghetti into the soup. Cook until the pasta is done. Stir in the Parmesan and serve at once.

Broccoli Soup

Zuppa di broccoletti

Around Rome broccoli grows abundantly and is served in this soup with garlic toasts.

Ingredients
1½lb broccoli spears
7½ cups fresh or canned chicken or
    vegetable stock
salt and freshly ground black pepper
1 tbsp fresh lemon juice
To serve
6 slices white bread
1 large garlic clove, cut in half
freshly grated Parmesan cheese
    (optional)
serves 6

1 Using a small sharp knife, peel the
broccoli stems, starting from the base
of the stalks and pulling gently up
towards the florets. (The peel comes
off very easily.) Chop the broccoli into
small chunks.

2 Bring the stock to a boil in a large
pan. Add the broccoli and simmer for
30 minutes, or until soft.

3 ▲ Purée about half of the soup and
mix into the rest of the soup. Season
with salt, pepper and lemon juice.

4 ▲ Just before serving, reheat the
soup to just below boiling point. Toast
the bread, rub with garlic and cut into
quarters. Place 3 or 4 pieces of toast in
the bottom of each soup plate. Ladle
on the soup. Serve at once, with
Parmesan if desired.

Tomato and Bread Soup

Pappa al pomodoro

This colorful Florentine recipe was created to use up stale bread. It can be made with very ripe

fresh or canned plum tomatoes.

Ingredients
6 tbsp olive oil
small piece of dried chili, crumbled
    (optional)
1½ cups stale coarse white bread,
    cut into 1 in cubes
1 medium onion, finely chopped
2 garlic cloves, finely chopped
1½ lb ripe tomatoes, peeled and
    chopped, or 2 × 14 oz cans peeled
    plum tomatoes, chopped
3 tbsp chopped fresh basil
6¼ cups fresh or canned stock or
    water, or a combination of both
salt and freshly ground black pepper
extra-virgin olive oil, to serve (optional)
serves 4

1 Heat 4 tbsp of the oil in a large
pan. Add the chili, if using, and stir for
1-2 minutes. Add the bread cubes and
cook until golden. Remove to a plate
and drain on paper towels.

2 ▲ Add the remaining oil, the onion
and garlic, and cook until the onion
softens. Stir in the tomatoes, bread
and basil. Season with salt. Cook over
moderate heat, stirring occasionally,
for about 15 minutes.

3 Meanwhile, heat the stock or water
to simmering. Add it to the pan with
the tomato mixture, and mix well.
Bring to a boil. Lower the heat slightly
and simmer for 20 minutes.

4 ▲ Remove the soup from the heat.
Use a fork to mash the tomatoes and
the bread together. Season with
pepper, and more salt if necessary.
Allow to stand for 10 minutes. Just
before serving swirl in a little extra-
virgin olive oil, if desired.

White Bean Soup

Minestrone di fagioli

A thick purée of cooked dried beans is at the heart of this substantial country soup from Tuscany. It makes a warming winter lunch or supper dish.

Ingredients
1½ cups dried cannellini or other
  white beans
1 bay leaf
5 tbsp olive oil
1 medium onion, finely chopped
1 carrot, finely chopped
1 stalk celery, finely chopped
3 medium tomatoes, peeled and
  finely chopped
2 garlic cloves, finely chopped
1 tsp fresh thyme leaves, or ½ tsp
  dried thyme
3½ cups boiling water
salt and freshly ground black pepper
extra-virgin olive oil, to serve
serves 6

1 ▲ Pick over the beans carefully, discarding any stones or other particles. Soak the beans in a large bowl of cold water overnight. Drain. Place the beans in a large pan of water, bring to a boil, and cook for 20 minutes. Drain. Return the beans to the pan, cover with cold water, and bring to a boil again. Add the bay leaf, and cook until the beans are tender, 1–2 hours. Drain again. Remove the bay leaf.

2 Purée about three-quarters of the beans in a food processor, or pass through a food mill, adding a little water if necessary.

3 Heat the oil in a large pan. Stir in the onion, and cook until it softens. Add the carrot and celery, and cook for 5 minutes more.

4 ▲ Stir in the tomatoes, garlic and thyme. Cook for 6–8 minutes more, stirring often.

5 ▲ Pour in the boiling water. Stir in the beans and the bean purée. Season with salt and pepper. Simmer for 10–15 minutes. Serve in individual soup bowls, sprinkled with a little extra-virgin olive oil.

Fish Soup

Ciuppin

Liguria is famous for its fish soups. In this one the fish are cooked in a broth with vegetables and then puréed. This soup can also be used to dress pasta.

Ingredients
2lb mixed fish or fish pieces (such
    as pollock, whiting, red mullet,
    red or white snapper, cod etc)
6 tbsp olive oil, plus extra to serve
1 medium onion, finely chopped
1 stalk celery, chopped
1 carrot, chopped
4 tbsp chopped fresh parsley
$^{3}/_{4}$ cup dry white wine
3 medium tomatoes, peeled and chopped
2 garlic cloves, finely chopped
$6^{1}/_{4}$ cups boiling water
salt and freshly ground black pepper
rounds of French bread, to serve
serves 6

3 ▲ Pour in the wine, raise the heat, and cook until it reduces by about half. Stir in the tomatoes and garlic. Cook for 3–4 minutes, stirring occasionally. Pour in the boiling water, and bring back to a boil. Cook over moderate heat for 15 minutes.

4 Stir in the fish, and simmer for 10–15 minutes, or until the fish are tender. Season with salt and pepper.

5 ▲ Remove the fish from the soup with a slotted spoon. Discard any bones. Purée in a food processor. Taste for seasoning. If the soup is too thick, add a little more water.

6 To serve, heat the soup to simmering. Toast the rounds of bread, and sprinkle with olive oil. Place 2 or 3 in each soup plate before pouring over the soup.

1 ▲ Scale and clean the fish, discarding all innards, but leaving the heads on. Cut into large pieces. Rinse well in cool water.

2 Heat the oil in a large pan and add the onion. Cook over low to moderate heat until it begins to soften. Stir in the celery and carrot, and cook for 5 minutes more. Add the parsley.

~ VARIATION ~

To use the soup as a pasta dressing, cook until it reduces to the consistency of a sauce.

Barley and Vegetable Soup

Minestrone d'orzo

This soup comes from the Alto Adige region, in Italy's mountainous north. It is a thick, nourishing and warming winter soup. Serve with crusty bread.

Ingredients
1 cup pearl barley, preferably organic
9 cups fresh or canned beef stock or
    water, or a combination
3 tbsp olive oil
2 carrots, finely chopped
1 large onion, finely chopped
2 stalks celery, finely chopped
1 leek, thinly sliced
1 large potato, finely chopped
$1/2$ cup diced ham
1 bay leaf
3 tbsp chopped fresh parsley
1 small sprig fresh rosemary
salt and freshly ground black pepper
freshly grated Parmesan cheese,
    to serve (optional)
serves 6–8

1 Pick over the barley, and discard any stones or other particles. Wash it in cold water. Put the barley to soak in cold water for at least 3 hours.

2 Drain the barley and place in a large pan with the stock or water. Bring to a boil, lower the heat and simmer for 1 hour. Skim off any scum.

3 ▲ Stir in the oil, all the vegetables and the ham. Add the herbs. If necessary add more water. The ingredients should be covered by at least 1 in. Simmer for 1–1$1/2$ hours, or until the vegetables and barley are very tender.

4 ▲ Taste for seasoning, adding salt and pepper as necessary. Serve hot with grated Parmesan, if desired.

> ~ VARIATION ~
>
> An excellent vegetarian version of this soup can be made by using vegetable stock instead of beef stock, and omitting the ham.

Rice and Fava Bean Soup

Minestra di riso e fave

This thick soup makes the most of fresh fava beans while they are in season. It works well with frozen beans for the rest of the year.

Ingredients
2lb fava beans in their pods, or 14oz
    shelled frozen fava beans, thawed
6 tbsp olive oil
1 medium onion, finely chopped
salt and freshly ground black pepper
2 medium tomatoes, peeled and
    finely chopped
1 cup risotto or other non-parboiled
    rice
2 tbsp butter
4 cups boiling water
freshly grated Parmesan cheese, to
    serve (optional)
serves 4

1 ▲ Shell the beans if they are fresh. Bring a large pan of water to a boil, and blanch the beans, fresh or frozen, for 3–4 minutes. Rinse under cold water, and peel off the skins.

2 Heat the oil in a large pan. Add the chopped onion, and cook over low to moderate heat until it softens. Stir in the fava beans, and cook for about 5 minutes, stirring often to coat them with the oil. Season with salt and pepper. Add the tomatoes, and cook for 5 minutes more, stirring often.

3 Stir in the rice. After 1–2 minutes add the butter, and stir until it melts. Pour in the water, a little at a time, until the whole amount has been added. Taste for seasoning. Continue cooking the soup until the rice is tender. Serve hot, with grated Parmesan if desired.

Pasta and Dried Bean Soup

Pasta e fagioli

This peasant soup is very thick. In Italy it is made with dried or fresh beans, never canned, and served hot or at room temperature.

Ingredients

1$\frac{1}{2}$ cups dried borlotti or cannellini beans
14oz can plum tomatoes, chopped, with their juice
3 garlic cloves, crushed
2 bay leaves
pinch coarsely ground black pepper
6 tbsp olive oil, plus extra to serve (optional)
3$\frac{1}{2}$ cups water
2 tsp salt
2$\frac{1}{4}$ cups ditalini, pastina, or other small pasta
3 tbsp chopped fresh parsley
freshly grated Parmesan cheese, to serve
serves 4–6

1 Soak the beans in water overnight. Rinse and drain well.

2 Place the beans in a large saucepan and cover with water. Bring to a boil and cook for 10 minutes. Rinse and drain again.

3 ▲ Return the beans to the pan. Add enough water to cover them by 1 in. Stir in the coarsely chopped tomatoes with their juice, the garlic, bay leaves, black pepper and the oil. Simmer for 1$\frac{1}{2}$-2 hours, or until the beans are tender. If necessary, add more water.

4 ▲ Remove the bay leaves. Pass about half of the bean mixture through a food mill, or purée in a food processor. Stir into the pan with the remaining bean mixture. Add the water, and bring the soup to a boil.

5 Add the salt and the pasta. Stir well, and cook until the pasta is just done. Stir in the parsley. Allow to stand for at least 10 minutes before serving. Serve with grated Parmesan passed separately. In Italy a little olive oil is poured into each serving.

Pasta and Lentil Soup

Pasta e lenticchie

The small brown lentils which are grown in central Italy are usually used in this wholesome soup, but green lentils may be substituted if preferred.

Ingredients

1 cup dried green or brown lentils
6 tbsp olive oil
$\frac{1}{4}$ cup ham or salt pork, cut into
    small dice
1 medium onion, finely chopped
1 stalk celery, finely chopped
1 carrot, finely chopped
9 cups chicken stock or water, or a
    combination of both
1 leaf fresh sage or $\frac{1}{8}$ tsp dried
1 sprig fresh thyme or $\frac{1}{4}$ tsp dried
salt and freshly ground black pepper
$2\frac{1}{2}$ cups ditalini, pastina, or other
    small pasta

serves 4–6

1 ▲ Carefully check the lentils for small stones. Place them in a bowl, covered with cold water, and soak for 2–3 hours. Rinse and drain well.

2 ▲ In a large pan, heat the oil and sauté the ham or salt pork for 2–3 minutes. Add the onion, and cook gently until it softens.

3 ▲ Stir in the celery and carrot, and cook for 5 minutes more, stirring frequently. Add the lentils, and stir to coat them in the fats.

4 ▲ Pour in the stock or water and the herbs, and bring the soup to a boil. Cook over moderate heat for about 1 hour or until the lentils are tender. Add salt and pepper to taste.

5 Stir in the pasta, and cook it until it is just done. Allow the soup to stand for a few minutes before serving.

Pasta and Chickpea Soup

Pasta e ceci

Another thick soup from central Italy. The addition of a sprig of fresh rosemary provides a typically Mediterranean flavor.

Ingredients
1 cup dried chickpeas
3 garlic cloves, peeled
1 bay leaf
6 tbsp olive oil
pinch of freshly ground black pepper
$1/4$ cup salt pork, pancetta or bacon, diced
1 sprig fresh rosemary
$2^1/_2$ cups water
2 cups ditalini, tubetti, or other short
    hollow pasta
salt, to taste
freshly grated Parmesan cheese,
    to serve (optional)
serves 4–6

2 ▲ Return the chickpeas to the pan. Add water to cover, 1 clove of garlic, the bay leaf, 3 tbsp of the oil and the ground pepper.

4 ▲ Sauté the diced pork gently in the remaining oil with the rosemary and 2 cloves of garlic until just golden. Discard the rosemary and garlic.

1 ▲ Soak the chickpeas in water overnight. Rinse well and drain. Place the chickpeas in a large pan with water to cover. Boil for 15 minutes. Rinse and drain.

3 ▲ Simmer until tender, about 2 hours, adding more water as necessary. Remove the bay leaf. Pass about half the chickpeas through a food mill or purée in a food processor with a few tablespoons of the cooking liquid. Return the purée to the pan with the rest of the peas and the remaining cooking water.

5 ▲ Stir the pork with its oils into the chickpea mixture.

~ COOK'S TIP ~

Allow the soup to stand for about 10 minutes before serving. This will allow the flavor and texture to develop.

6 ▲ Add $2^1/_2$ cups of water to the chickpeas, and bring to a boil. Correct the seasoning if necessary. Stir in the pasta, and cook until just *al dente*. Pass the Parmesan separately, if desired.

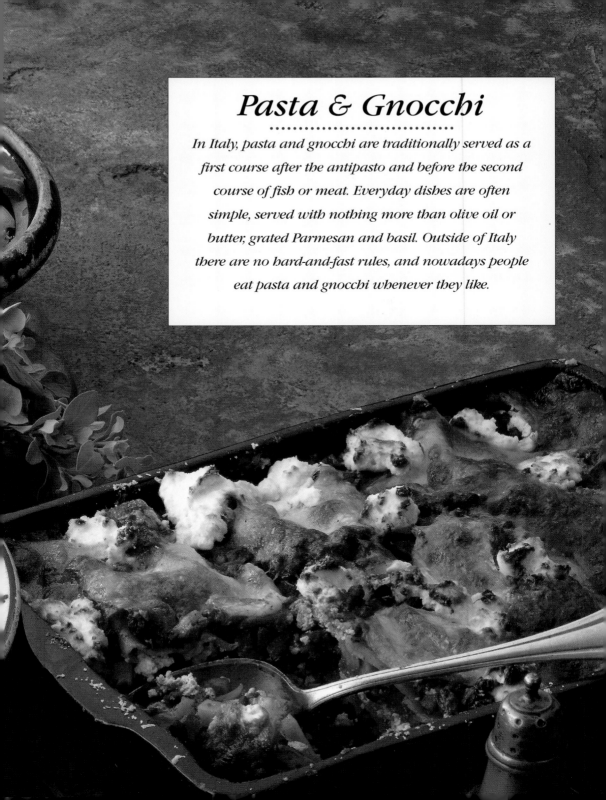

Pasta & Gnocchi

In Italy, pasta and gnocchi are traditionally served as a
first course after the antipasto and before the second
course of fish or meat. Everyday dishes are often
simple, served with nothing more than olive oil or
butter, grated Parmesan and basil. Outside of Italy
there are no hard-and-fast rules, and nowadays people
eat pasta and gnocchi whenever they like.

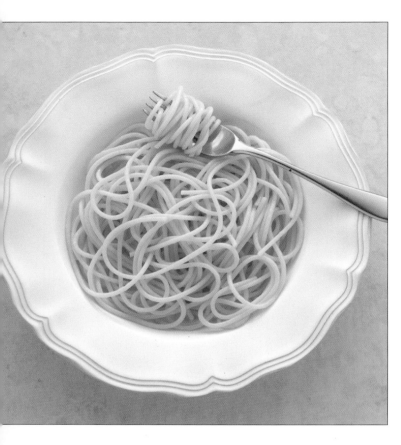

How to Make Egg Pasta by Hand

This classic recipe for egg noodles from Emilia-Romagna calls for just three ingredients: flour and eggs, with a little salt. In other regions of Italy water, milk or oil are sometimes added. Use plain unbleached white flour, and large eggs. As a general guide, use $1/2$ cup of flour to each egg. Quantities will vary with the size of the eggs.

To serve 3–4
2 eggs, salt
1 cup flour

To serve 4–6
3 eggs, salt
$1 1/2$ cups flour

To serve 6–8
4 eggs, salt
2 cups flour

1 Place the flour in the center of a clean smooth work surface. Make a well in the middle. Break the eggs into the well. Add a pinch of salt.

2 ▲ Start beating the eggs with a fork, gradually drawing the flour from the inside walls of the well. As the paste thickens, continue the mixing with your hands. Incorporate as much flour as possible until the mixture forms a mass. It will still be lumpy. If it still sticks to your hands, add a little more flour. Set the dough aside. Scrape off all traces of the dough from the work surface until it is perfectly smooth. Wash and dry your hands.

About Pasta

Most pasta is made from durum wheat flour and water – durum is a special kind of wheat with a very high protein content. Egg pasta, *pasta all'uova*, contains flour and eggs, and is used for flat noodles such as tagliatelle, or for lasagne. Very little whole wheat pasta is eaten in Italy, but it is quite popular in other countries.

All these types of pasta are available dried in packets, and will keep almost indefinitely. Fresh pasta is now more widely available and can be bought in most supermarkets. It can be very good, but can never compare to home-made egg pasta.

Pasta comes in countless shapes and sizes. It is very difficult to give a definite list, as the names for the shapes vary from country to country. In some cases, just within Italy, the same shape can appear with several different names, depending upon which region it is in. The pasta shapes called for in this book, as well as many others, are illustrated in the introduction. The most common names have been listed.

Most of the recipes in this book specify the pasta shape most appropriate for a particular sauce. They can, of course, be replaced with another kind. A general rule is that long pasta goes better with tomato or thinner sauces, while short pasta is best for chunkier, meatier sauces. But this rule should not be followed too rigidly. Part of the fun of cooking and eating pasta is in the endless combinations of sauce and pasta shapes.

3 ▲ Lightly flour the work surface. Knead the dough by pressing it away from you with the heel of your hands, and then folding it over towards you. Repeat this action over and over, turning the dough as you knead. Work for about 10 minutes, or until the dough is smooth and elastic.

4 ▲ If you are using more than 2 eggs, divide the dough in half. Flour the rolling pin and the work surface. Pat the dough into a disc and begin rolling it out into a flat circle, rotating it one quarter turn after each roll to keep its shape round. Roll until the disc is about 1/8 in thick.

5 ▲ Roll out the dough until it is paper-thin by rolling up onto the

rolling pin and simultaneously giving a sideways stretching with the hands. Wrap the near edge of the dough around the center of the rolling pin, and begin rolling the dough up away from you. As you roll back and forth, slide your hands from the center towards the outer edges of the pin, stretching and thinning out the pasta.

6 ▲ Quickly repeat these movements until about two-thirds of the sheet of pasta is wrapped around the pin. Lift and turn the wrapped pasta sheet about 45° before unrolling it. Repeat the rolling and stretching process, starting from a new point of the sheet each time to keep it evenly thin. By the end (this process should not last more than 8 to 10 minutes or the dough will lose its elasticity) the whole sheet should be smooth and almost transparent. If the dough is still sticky, lightly flour your hands as you continue rolling and stretching.

7 ▲ If you are making noodles (tagliatelle, fettuccine etc.) lay a clean dish towel on a table or other flat surface, and unroll the pasta sheet on it, letting about a third of the sheet hang over the edge of the table. Rotate

the dough every 10 minutes. Roll out the second sheet of dough if you are using more than 2 eggs. After 25–30 minutes the pasta will have dried enough to cut. Do not overdry or the pasta will crack as it is cut.

8 ▲ To cut tagliatelle, fettuccine or tagliolini, fold the sheet of pasta into a flat roll about 4 in wide. Cut across the roll to form noodles of the desired width. Tagliolini is 1/8 in; Fettuccine is 1/6 in; Tagliatelle is 1/4 in. After cutting, open out the noodles, and let them dry for about 5 minutes before cooking. These noodles may be stored for some weeks without refrigeration. Allow them to dry completely before storing them, uncovered, in a dry cupboard.

9 ▲ To cut the pasta for lasagne or pappardelle, do not fold or dry the rolled out dough. Lasagne is made by cutting rectangles approximately 5 in by 3 1/2 in. Pappardelle are large noodles cut with a fluted pastry wheel. They are about 3/4 in wide.

Egg Pasta Made by Machine

Making pasta with a machine is quick and easy. The results are perhaps not quite as fine as with handmade pasta, but they are certainly better than store-bought pastas.

You will need a pasta-making machine, either hand-cranked or electric. Use the same proportions of eggs, flours and salt as for Handmade Egg Pasta.

1 ▲ Place the flour in the center of a clean smooth work surface. Make a well in the middle. Break the eggs into the well. Add a pinch of salt. Start beating the eggs with a fork, gradually drawing the flour from the inside walls of the well. As the paste thickens, continue mixing with your hands. Incorporate as much flour as possible until the mixture forms a mass. It will still be lumpy. If it sticks to your hands, add a little more flour. Set the dough aside and scrape the work surface clean.

2 ▲ Set the machine rollers at their widest (kneading) setting. Pull off a piece of dough the size of a small

orange. Place the remaining dough between two soup plates. Feed the dough through the rollers. Fold it in half, end to end, and feed it through again 7 or 8 times, turning it and folding it over after each kneading. The dough should be smooth and fairly evenly rectangular. If it sticks to the machine, brush with flour. Lay it out on a lightly floured work surface or on a clean dish towel, and repeat with the remaining dough, broken into pieces the same size.

3 ▲ Adjust the machine to the next line setting. Feed each strip through once only, and replace on the drying surface. Keep them in the order in which they were first kneaded.

4 ▲ Reset the machine to the next setting. Repeat, passing each strip through once. Repeat for each remaining roller setting until the pasta is the right thickness – for most purposes this is given by the next to last setting, except for very delicate strips such as tagliolini, or for ravioli. If the pasta strips get too long, cut them in half to facilitate handling.

5 ▲ When all the strips are the desired thickness they may be machine-cut into noodles, or hand-cut for lasagne or pappardelle, as described for handmade pasta earlier. When making noodles, be sure the pasta is fairly dry, but not brittle, or the noodles may stick togther when cut. Select the desired width of cutter, and feed the strips through.

6 Separate the noodles, and leave to dry for at least 15 minutes before using. They may be stored for some weeks without refrigeration. Allow them to dry completely before storing them, uncovered, in a dry cupboard. They may also be frozen, first loose on trays and then packed together.

7 If you are making stuffed pasta (ravioli, cannelloni etc.) do not let the pasta strips dry out before filling them, but proceed immediately with the individual recipes.

~ PASTA VERDE ~

Follow the same recipe, adding $1/_4$ cup cooked, very finely chopped spinach (after having been squeezed very dry) to the eggs and flour. You may have to add a little more flour to absorb the moisture from the spinach. This pasta is very suitable for stuffed recipes, as it seals better than plain egg pasta.

How to Cook Dried Pasta

Store-bought and home-made pasta are cooked in the same way, though the timings vary greatly. Home-made pasta cooks virtually in the time it takes for the water to return to a boil after it is put in.

1 Always cook pasta in a large pot with a generous amount of rapidly boiling water. Use at least 5 cups of water to each $^1/_2$ cup pasta.

2 ▲ The water should be salted at least 2 minutes before the pasta is added, to give the salt time to dissolve. Add about $1^1/_2$ tbsp salt per 2 cups of pasta. You may want to vary the saltiness of the cooking water.

3 ▲ Drop the pasta into the boiling water all at once. Use a wooden spoon to help ease long pasta in as it softens, to prevent it from breaking. Stir frequently to prevent the pasta sticking to itself or to the pan. Cook the pasta at a fast boil, but be prepared to lower the heat if it boils over.

4 Timing is critical in pasta cooking. Follow package indications for store-bought pasta, but it is best in all cases to test for doneness by tasting, several times if necessary. In Italy pasta is always eaten *al dente*, which means firm to the bite. Cooked this way it is just tender, but its "soul" (the innermost part) is still firm.

5 ▲ Place a colander in the sink before the pasta has finished cooking. As soon as the pasta tastes done, tip it all into the colander (you may first want to reserve a cupful of the hot cooking water to add to the sauce if it needs thinning). Shake the colander lightly to remove most but not all of the cooking water. Pasta should never be over-drained.

6 ▲ Quickly turn the pasta into a warmed serving dish, and immediately toss it with a little butter or oil, or the prepared sauce. Alternatively, turn it into the cooking pan with the sauce, where it will be cooked for 1–2 minutes more as it is mixed into the sauce. Never allow pasta to sit undressed, as it will stick together and become unpalatable.

How to Cook Egg Pasta

Fresh egg pasta, especially home-made, cooks very much faster than dried pasta. Make sure everything is ready (the sauce, serving dishes etc) before you start boiling egg pasta, as there will not be time once the cooking starts, and egg pasta becomes soft and mushy very quickly.

1 Always cook pasta in a large pot with a generous amount of rapidly boiling water. Use at least 5 cups of water to a quantity of pasta made with 1 cup of flour. Salt the water as for dried pasta.

2 ▲ Drop the pasta into the boiling water all at once. Stir gently to prevent the pasta sticking to itself or to the pan. Cook the pasta at a fast boil.

3 ▲ Freshly made pasta can be done as little as 15 seconds after the cooking water comes back to a boil. Stuffed pasta takes a few minutes longer. When done, turn the pasta into the colander and proceed as for dried pasta.

Basic Tomato Sauce

Sugo di pomodoro alla napoletana

Tomato sauce is without a doubt the most popular dressing for pasta in Italy. This sauce is best made with fresh tomatoes, but works well with canned plum tomatoes.

Ingredients
4 tbsp olive oil
1 medium onion, very finely
  chopped
1 garlic clove, finely chopped
1lb tomatoes, fresh or canned,
  chopped, with their juice
salt and freshly ground black pepper
a few leaves fresh basil or sprigs
  parsley
for 4 servings of pasta

1 Heat the oil in a medium pan. Add the chopped onion, and cook over moderate heat until it is translucent, 5–8 minutes.

2 ▲ Stir in the garlic and the tomatoes with their juice (add 3 tbsp of water if you are using fresh tomatoes). Season with salt and pepper. Add the herbs. Cook for 20–30 minutes.

3 ▲ Pass the sauce through a food mill or purée in a food processor. To serve, reheat gently, correct the seasoning and pour over the drained pasta.

Special Tomato Sauce

Sugo di pomodoro

The tomatoes in this sauce are enhanced by the addition of extra vegetables. It is good served with all types of pasta or could be served as an accompaniment to stuffed vegetables.

Ingredients
1¼lb tomatoes, fresh or canned,
  chopped
1 carrot, chopped
1 stalk celery, chopped
1 medium onion, chopped
1 garlic clove, crushed
5 tbsp olive oil
salt and freshly ground black pepper
a few leaves fresh basil or a small
  pinch dried oregano
for 6 servings of pasta

1 Place all the ingredients in a medium heavy pan, and simmer together for 30 minutes.

2 ▲ Purée the sauce in a food processor, or press through a sieve.

3 ▲ Return the sauce to the pan, correct the seasoning, and simmer again for about 15 minutes.

~ COOK'S TIP ~

This sauce may be spooned into freezer bags and frozen until required. Allow to thaw to room temperature before re-heating.

Linguine with Pesto Sauce

Linguine con pesto

Pesto originates in Liguria, where the sea breezes are said to give the local basil a particularly fine flavor. It is traditionally made with a mortar and pestle, but it is easier to make in a food processor or blender. Freeze any spare pesto in an ice cube tray.

Ingredients

$3/4$ cup fresh basil leaves
3–4 garlic cloves, peeled
3 tbsp pine nuts
$1/2$ tsp salt
5 tbsp olive oil
$1/2$ cup freshly grated Parmesan cheese
4 tbsp freshly grated Pecorino cheese
freshly ground black pepper
$1 1/4$ lb linguine
serves 5–6

1 ▲ Place the basil, garlic, pine nuts, salt and olive oil in a blender or food processor and process until smooth. Remove to a bowl. (If desired, the sauce may be frozen at this point, before the cheeses are added.)

2 ▲ Stir in the cheeses (use all Parmesan if Pecorino is not available). Taste for seasoning.

3 ▲ Cook the pasta in a large pan of rapidly boiling salted water until it is *al dente*. Just before draining it, take about 4 tbsp of the cooking water and stir it into the sauce.

4 ▲ Drain the pasta and toss with the sauce. Serve immediately.

Bolognese Meat Sauce

Ragù alla bolognese

This great meat sauce is a speciality of Bologna. It is delicious with tagliatelle or short pastas

such as penne or conchiglie as well as spaghetti, and is indispensable in baked lasagne. It

keeps well in the refrigerator for several days and can also be frozen.

Ingredients

2 tbsp butter
4 tbsp olive oil
1 medium onion, finely chopped
2 tbsp pancetta or unsmoked bacon,
  finely chopped
1 carrot, finely sliced
1 stalk celery, finely sliced
1 garlic clove, finely chopped
12oz lean ground beef
salt and freshly ground black pepper
$2/_3$ cup red wine
$1/_2$ cup milk
14oz can plum tomatoes, chopped,
  with their juice
1 bay leaf
$1/_4$ tsp fresh thyme leaves
for 6 servings of pasta

3 ▲ Pour in the wine, raise the heat slightly, and cook until the liquid evaporates, 3–4 minutes. Add the milk, and cook until it evaporates.

4 ▲ Stir in the tomatoes with their juice, and the herbs. Bring the sauce to a boil. Reduce the heat to low, and simmer, uncovered for $1^1/_2$–2 hours, stirring occasionally. Correct the seasoning before serving.

1 ▲ Heat the butter and oil in a heavy pan or earthenware pot. Add the onion, and cook over moderate heat for 3–4 minutes. Add the pancetta, and cook until the onion is translucent. Stir in the carrot, celery and garlic. Cook for 3–4 minutes more.

2 Add the beef, and crumble it into the vegetables with a fork. Stir until the meat loses its red color. Season with salt and pepper.

Spaghetti with Garlic and Oil

Spaghetti con aglio e olio

This is one of the simplest and most satisfying pasta dishes of all. It is very popular throughout Italy. Use the best quality oil available for this dish.

Ingredients
1lb spaghetti
6 tbsp extra-virgin olive oil
3 garlic cloves, chopped
4 tbsp chopped fresh parsley
salt and freshly ground black pepper
freshly grated Parmesan cheese, to
    serve (optional)
serves 4

1 Drop the spaghetti into a large pan of rapidly boiling salted water.

2 ▲ In a large frying pan heat the oil and gently sauté the garlic until it is barely golden. Do not let it brown or it will taste bitter. Stir in the parsley. Season with salt and pepper. Remove from the heat until the pasta is ready.

3 ▲ Drain the pasta when it is barely *al dente*. Add it to the pan with the oil and garlic, and cook together for 2–3 minutes, stirring well to coat the spaghetti with the sauce. Serve immediately in a warmed serving bowl, with Parmesan, if you like.

Spaghetti with Walnut Sauce

Spaghetti con salsa di noci

Like pesto, this sauce is traditionally ground in a mortar and pestle, but works just as well made in a food processor. It is also very good on tagliatelle and other noodles.

Ingredients
1 cup walnut pieces or halves
3 tbsp plain breadcrumbs
3 tbsp olive or walnut oil
3 tbsp chopped fresh parsley
1–2 garlic cloves (optional)
$1/4$ cup butter, at room temperature
2 tbsp cream
salt and freshly ground black pepper
14oz whole wheat spaghetti
freshly grated Parmesan cheese,
    to serve
serves 4

1 Drop the nuts into a small pan of boiling water, and cook for 1–2 minutes. Drain. Slip off the skins. Dry on paper towels. Coarsely chop and set aside about a quarter of the nuts.

2 ▲ Place the remaining nuts, the breadcrumbs, oil, parsley and garlic, if using, in a food processor or blender. Process to a paste. Remove to a bowl, and stir in the softened butter and the cream. Season with salt and pepper.

3 ▲ Cook the pasta in a large pan of rapidly boiling salted water until *al dente*. Drain, and toss with the sauce. Sprinkle with the reserved chopped nuts, and pass the Parmesan separately.

Fusilli with Peppers and Onions

Fusilli con peperoni

Peppers are characteristic of southern Italy. When broiled and peeled they have a delicious smoky flavor, and are easier to digest.

Ingredients

1lb red and yellow peppers
6 tbsp olive oil
1 large red onion, thinly sliced
2 garlic cloves, minced
1lb fusilli or other short pasta
salt and freshly ground black pepper
3 tbsp finely chopped fresh parsley
freshly grated Parmesan cheese,
   to serve

serves 4

3 ▲ Heat the oil in a large frying pan. Add the onion, and cook over moderate heat until it is translucent, 5–8 minutes. Stir in the garlic, and cook for 2 minutes more.

5 ▲ Meanwhile, add the peppers to the onions, and mix together gently. Stir in about 3 tbsp of the pasta cooking water. Season with salt and pepper. Stir in the parsley.

1 ▲ Place the peppers under a hot broiler and turn occasionally until they are black and blistered on all sides. Remove from the heat, place in a paper bag and leave for 5 minutes.

4 ▲ Add salt and the pasta to the boiling water, and cook until the pasta is just *al dente*.

6 ▲ Drain the pasta. Add it to the frying pan with the vegetables, and cook over moderate heat for 1–2 minutes, stirring constantly to mix the pasta into the sauce. Serve with the Parmesan passed separately.

2 ▲ Peel the peppers. Cut them into quarters, remove the stems and seeds, and slice into thin strips. Bring a large pan of water to a boil.

~ COOK'S TIP ~

Peppers belong to the *Capsicum annuum* species. They were brought to Europe by Columbus who discovered them in Haiti. The large red, yellow and orange peppers are usually sweeter than the green varieties, and have a fuller flavor.

Orecchiette with Broccoli

Pasta e broccoli

Puglia, in southern Italy, specializes in imaginative pasta and vegetable combinations. Using the broccoli cooking water for boiling the pasta gives it more of the vegetable's flavor.

Ingredients

1³/₄lb broccoli
1lb orecchiette or penne
6 tbsp olive oil
3 garlic cloves, finely chopped
6 anchovy fillets in oil
salt and freshly ground black pepper
serves 6

1 Peel the stems of the broccoli, starting from the base and pulling up towards the florets with a knife. Discard the woody parts of the stem. Cut florets and stems into 2 in pieces.

2 ▲ Bring a large pan of water to a boil. Drop in the broccoli, and boil until barely tender, about 5–8 minutes. Remove the broccoli pieces from the pan to a serving bowl. Do not discard the cooking water.

3 ▲ Add salt to the broccoli cooking water. Bring it back to a boil. Drop in the pasta, stir well, and cook until it is *al dente*.

4 ▲ While the pasta is boiling, heat the oil in a small pan. Add the garlic and, after 2–3 minutes, the anchovy fillets. Using a fork, mash the anchovies and garlic to a paste. Cook for 3–4 minutes more.

5 ▲ Before draining the pasta, ladle 1–2 cupfuls of the cooking water over the broccoli. Add the drained pasta and the hot anchovy and oil mixture. Mix well, and season with salt and pepper if necessary. Serve at once.

Spaghetti with Eggs and Bacon

Spaghetti alla carbonara

One of the classic pasta sauces, about which a debate remains: whether or not it should contain cream. Purists believe that it should not.

Ingredients

2 tbsp olive oil
generous $1/2$ cup bacon, cut into
　　matchsticks
1 garlic clove, crushed
1lb spaghetti
3 eggs, at room temperature
$3/4$ cup freshly grated Parmesan cheese
salt and freshly ground black pepper
serves 4

3 ▲ While the pasta is cooking, warm a large serving bowl and break the eggs into it. Beat in the Parmesan cheese with a fork, and season with salt and pepper.

4 ▲ As soon as the pasta is done, drain it quickly, and mix it into the egg mixture. Pour on the hot bacon and its fat. Stir well. The heat from the pasta and bacon fat will cook the eggs. Serve immediately.

1 ▲ Bring a large pan of water to a boil. In a medium frying pan, heat the oil and sauté the bacon and the garlic until the bacon renders its fat and starts to brown. Remove and discard the garlic. Keep the bacon and its fat hot until needed.

2 ▲ Add salt and the spaghetti to the boiling water, and cook until it is *al dente*.

Short Pasta with Cauliflower   *Pennoni rigati con cavolfiore*

This is a pasta version of cauliflower cheese. The cauliflower water is used to boil the pasta.

Ingredients
1 medium cauliflower
2 cups milk
1 bay leaf
$1/4$ cup butter
$1/2$ cup flour
salt and freshly ground black pepper
$3/4$ cup freshly grated Parmesan or
   Romano cheese
$1^1/4$lb pennoni rigati, tortiglioni, or
   other short pasta
serves 6

1 Bring a large pan of water to a boil.
Wash the cauliflower well, and
separate it into florets. Boil the florets
until they are just tender, about 8–10
minutes. Remove them from the pan
with a strainer or slotted spoon. Chop
the cauliflower into bite-size pieces
and set aside. Do not discard the
cooking water.

2 ▲ Make a béchamel sauce by gently
heating the milk with the bay leaf in a
small saucepan. Do not let it boil. Melt
the butter in a medium heavy
saucepan. Add the flour, and mix it in
well with a wire whisk ensuring there
are no lumps. Cook for 2–3 minutes,
but do not let the butter burn.

3 Strain the hot milk into the flour
and butter mixture all at once, and
mix smoothly with the whisk.

4 Bring the sauce to a boil, stirring
constantly, and cook for 4–5 minutes
more. Season with salt and pepper.
Add the cheese, and stir over low heat
until it melts. Stir in the cauliflower.

5 ▲ Bring the cooking water back
to a boil. Add salt, and stir in the pasta.
Cook until it is *al dente*. Drain, and
place the pasta in a warm serving bowl.
Pour over the sauce. Mix well, and
serve at once.

Spaghetti with Bacon and Onion   *Spaghetti all'amatriciana*

This easy sauce is quickly made from ingredients that are almost always at hand.

Ingredients
2 tbsp olive oil
$1/2$ cup unsmoked lean bacon, cut
   into matchsticks
1 small onion, finely chopped
$1/2$ cup dry white wine
1lb fresh or canned tomatoes,
   chopped
$1/4$ tsp thyme leaves
salt and freshly ground black pepper
$1^1/4$lb spaghetti
freshly grated Parmesan, to serve
serves 6

1 In a medium frying pan, heat the oil.
Add the bacon and onion, and cook
over low to moderate heat until the
onion is golden and the bacon has
rendered its fat and is beginning to
brown, about 8–10 minutes. Bring a
large pan of water to a boil.

2 ▲ Add the wine to the bacon and
onion, raise the heat, and cook rapidly
until the liquid boils off. Add the
tomatoes, thyme, salt and pepper.
Cover, and cook over moderate heat
for 10–15 minutes.

3 ▲ Meanwhile, add salt to the boiling
water, and cook the pasta until it is
al dente. Drain, toss with the sauce, and
serve with the grated Parmesan.

Spaghetti with Olives and Capers

Spaghetti alla puttanesca

This spicy sauce originated in the Naples area, where it was named for the local women of easy virtue. It can be quickly assembled using a few kitchen cupboard staples.

Ingredients

4 tbsp olive oil
2 garlic cloves, finely chopped
small piece of dried chili, crumbled
2oz can of anchovy fillets, chopped
12oz tomatoes, fresh or canned,
    chopped
²/₃ cup pitted black olives
2 tbsp capers, rinsed
1 tbsp tomato paste
1lb spaghetti
2 tbsp chopped fresh parsley, to serve
serves 4

3 ▲ Add the tomatoes, olives, capers and tomato paste. Stir well and cook over moderate heat.

4 Add salt to the boiling water, and put in the spaghetti. Stir, and cook until the pasta is just *al dente*. Drain.

5 ▲ Turn the spaghetti into the sauce. Raise the heat, and cook for 1–2 minutes, turning the pasta constantly. Sprinkle with parsley if desired and serve. Traditionally, no cheese is served with this sauce.

1 ▲ Bring a large pan of water to a boil. Heat the oil in a large frying pan. Add the garlic and the dried chili, and cook for 2–3 minutes until the garlic is just golden.

2 ▲ Add the anchovies, and mash them into the garlic with a fork.

Linguine with Clam and Tomato Sauce
Linguine con vongole

There are two types of traditional Italian clam sauce for pasta: one with and one without

tomatoes. This tomato version can be made with canned clams if fresh are not available.

Ingredients
2lb fresh clams in their shells, or 12oz
   canned clams, with their liquid
6 tbsp olive oil
1 garlic clove, crushed
14oz tomatoes, fresh or canned, very
   finely chopped
1lb linguine
4 tbsp chopped fresh parsley
salt and freshly ground black pepper
serves 4

1 ▲ Scrub and rinse the clams well under cold running water. Place them in a large pan with a cupful of water, and heat until the clams begin to open. Lift each clam out as soon as it opens, and scoop it out of its shell using a small spoon. Place in a bowl.

2 If the clams are large, chop them into 2 or 3 pieces. Reserve any liquids from the shells in a separate bowl. When all the clams have opened (discard any that do not open) pour the cooking liquids into the juices from the clams, and strain them through a piece of paper towel to remove any sand. If using canned clams, use the liquid from the can.

3 Bring a large pot of water to a boil for the pasta. Place the olive oil in a medium pan with the crushed garlic. Cook over a moderate heat until the garlic is just golden.

4 ▲ Remove the garlic and discard. Add the chopped tomatoes to the oil, and pour in the clam liquid. Mix well and cook over low to moderate heat until the sauce begins to dry out and thicken slightly. Add salt and the pasta to the boiling water.

5 ▲ A minute or two before the pasta is ready to be drained, stir the parsley and the clams into the tomato sauce, and raise the heat. Add some freshly ground black pepper, and taste for seasoning. Drain the pasta, and turn it into a serving bowl. Pour on the hot sauce, and mix well before serving.

Spaghetti with Mussels

Spaghetti con cozze

Mussels are popular in all the coastal regions of Italy, and are delicious with pasta. This simple dish is greatly improved by using the freshest mussels available.

Ingredients
2lb fresh mussels, in their shells
5 tbsp olive oil
3 garlic cloves, finely chopped
4 tbsp finely chopped fresh parsley
4 tbsp white wine
1lb spaghetti
salt and freshly ground black pepper
serves 4

1 ▲ Scrub the mussels well under cold running water, cutting off the "beard" with a small sharp knife.

2 ▲ Bring a large pan of water to a boil for the pasta. Place the mussels with a cupful of water in another large pan over moderate heat. As soon as they open, lift them out one by one.

3 ▲ When all the mussels have opened (discard any that do not), strain the liquid in the pan through a layer of paper towels and reserve until needed.

4 ▲ Heat the oil in a large frying pan. Add the garlic and parsley, and cook for 2–3 minutes. Add the mussels, their strained juices and the wine. Cook over moderate heat. Meanwhile add salt to the boiling water, and drop in the pasta.

5 ▲ Add a generous amount of freshly ground black pepper to the sauce. Taste for seasoning, adding salt as necessary.

6 ▲ Drain the pasta when it is *al dente*. Add it to the frying pan with the sauce, and stir well over moderate heat for 1–2 minutes more. Serve at once, without cheese.

> ### ~ COOK'S TIP ~
> Mussels should be firmly closed when fresh. If a mussel is slightly open, pinch it closed. If it remains closed on its own, it is alive. If it remains open, discard it. Fresh mussels should be consumed as soon as possible after being purchased. They may be kept in a bowl of cold water in the refrigerator.

Pasta with Fresh Sardine Sauce

Pasta con sarde

In this classic Sicilian dish, fresh sardines are combined with golden raisins and pine nuts.

Ingredients

3 tbsp golden raisins
1lb fresh sardines
6 tbsp breadcrumbs
1 small fennel bulb
6 tbsp olive oil
1 medium onion, very thinly sliced
3 tbsp pine nuts
$1/2$ tsp fennel seeds
salt and freshly ground black pepper
1lb long hollow pasta such as percatelli,
   ziti, or bucatini

serves 4

1 Soak the golden raisins in warm
water for 15 minutes. Drain and pat dry.

2 ▲ Clean the sardines. Open each
one out flat and remove the back bone
and head. Wash well and shake dry.
Sprinkle with breadcrumbs.

3 ▲ Coarsely chop the top fronds of
fennel and reserve. Pull off a few outer
leaves and wash. Fill a large pan with
enough water to cook the pasta. Add
the fennel leaves and bring to a boil.

4 ▲ Heat the oil in a large frying
pan and sauté the onion lightly until
soft. Remove to a side dish. Add the
sardines, a few at a time, and cook over
moderate heat until golden on both
sides, turning them once carefully.
When all the sardines have been
cooked, gently return them to the pan.
Add the onion, and the golden raisins,
pine nuts and fennel seeds. Season with
salt and pepper.

5 ▲ Take about 4 tbsp of the boiling
water for the pasta, and add it to the
sauce. Add salt to the boiling water,
and drop in the pasta. Cook until it is
al dente. Drain, and remove the fennel
leaves. Dress the pasta with the sauce.
Divide between individual serving
plates, arranging several sardines
on each. Sprinkle with the reserved
chopped fennel tops before serving.

Baked Macaroni with Cheese

Maccheroni gratinati al forno

This delicious dish is perhaps less common in Italy than other pasta dishes, but has become a family favorite around the world.

Ingredients

2 cups milk
1 bay leaf
3 blades mace, or pinch of grated nutmeg
4 tbsp butter
$1/3$ cup flour
salt and freshly ground black pepper
$1^1/2$ cups grated Parmesan or Cheddar cheese, or a combination of both
$1/3$ cup breadcrumbs
1 lb macaroni or other short hollow pasta
serves 6

1 Make a béchamel sauce by gently heating the milk with the bay leaf and mace in a small saucepan. Do not let it boil. Melt the butter in a medium heavy saucepan. Add the flour, and mix it in well with a wire whisk. Cook for 2–3 minutes, but do not let the butter burn. Strain the hot milk into the flour and butter mixture all at once, and mix smoothly with the whisk. Bring the sauce to a boil, stirring constantly, and cook for 4–5 minutes more.

3 ▲ Bring a large pan of water to a boil. Preheat the oven to 400°F. Grease an ovenproof dish, and sprinkle with some breadcrumbs. Add salt and the pasta to the boiling water, and cook until it is barely *al dente*. Do not overcook, as the pasta will get a second cooking in the oven.

4 ▲ Drain the pasta, and combine it with the sauce. Pour it into the prepared ovenproof dish. Sprinkle the top with the remaining breadcrumbs and grated cheese, and place in the center of the preheated oven. Bake for 20 minutes.

2 ▲ Season with salt and pepper, and the nutmeg if no mace has been used. Add all but 2 tbsp of the cheese, and stir over low heat until it melts. Place a layer of plastic wrap right on the surface of the sauce to stop a skin from forming, and set aside.

Penne with Tuna and Mozzarella   *Penne con tonno e mozzarella*

This tasty sauce is quickly made from kitchen cupboard staples, with the addition of fresh mozzarella. If possible, use tuna canned in olive oil.

Ingredients
1lb penne, or other short pasta
1 tbsp capers, in brine or salt
2 garlic cloves
3 tbsp chopped fresh parsley
7oz can of tuna, drained
5 tbsp olive oil
salt and freshly ground black pepper
$2/3$ cup mozzarella cheese, cut into
    small dice
serves 4

1 Bring a large pan of salted water to a boil and drop in the pasta.

2 ▲ Rinse the capers well in water. Chop them finely with the garlic. Combine with the parsley and the tuna. Stir in the oil, and season with salt and pepper, if necessary.

3 ▲ Drain the pasta when it is just *al dente*. Turn it into a large frying pan. Add the tuna sauce and the diced mozzarella, and cook over moderate heat, stirring constantly, until the cheese just begins to melt. Serve at once.

Spaghettini with Vodka and Caviar   *Spaghettini con vodka e caviale*

This is an elegant yet easy way to serve spaghettini. In Rome it is an after-theater favorite.

Ingredients
4 tbsp olive oil
3 scallions, thinly sliced
1 garlic clove, finely chopped
$1/2$ cup vodka
$2/3$ cup heavy cream
$1/2$ cup black or red caviar
salt and freshly ground black pepper
1lb spaghettini
serves 4

1 ▲ Heat the oil in a small pan. Add the scallions and garlic, and cook gently for 4–5 minutes.

2 ▲ Add the vodka and cream, and cook over low heat for about 5–8 minutes more.

~ COOK'S TIP ~

The finest caviar is salted sturgeon roe. Red "caviar" is salmon roe, cheaper and often saltier than sturgeon roe, as is the black-dyed lump fish roe.

3 ▲ Remove from the heat and stir in half the caviar. Season with salt and pepper as necessary.

4 Meanwhile, cook the spaghettini in a large pan of rapidly boiling salted water until *al dente*. Drain the pasta, and toss with the sauce. Spoon the remaining caviar on top and serve immediately.

Pasta Bows with Shrimp and Peas   *Farfalle con gamberetti e piselli*

A small amount of saffron in the sauce gives this dish a lovely golden color.

Ingredients
3 tbsp olive oil
2 tbsp butter
2 scallions, chopped
1¼ cups frozen petits pois or peas,
    thawed
1lb farfalle
12oz fresh or frozen peeled shrimp
1 cup dry white wine
a few whole strands saffron or
    ⅛ tsp powdered saffron
salt and freshly ground black pepper
2 tbsp chopped fresh fennel or dill,
    to serve
serves 4

1 Bring a large pan of water to a
boil. Heat the oil and butter in a large
frying pan and sauté the scallions
lightly. Add the peas, and cook for
2–3 minutes.

2 ▲ Add salt and the pasta to the
boiling water. Add the shrimp, wine and
saffron to the peas. Raise the heat and
cook until the wine is reduced by about
half. Add salt and pepper to taste. Cover
the pan and reduce the heat to low.

3 ▲ Drain the pasta when it is *al
dente*. Add it to the pan with the sauce.
Stir over high heat for 1–2 minutes,
coating the pasta with the sauce.
Sprinkle with the fresh herbs, and
serve at once.

Short Pasta with Spring Vegetables   *Pasta primavera*

This colorful sauce makes the most of new crops of fresh tender spring vegetables.

Ingredients
1 or 2 small young carrots
2 scallions
1 cup zucchini
2 tomatoes
½ cup shelled peas, fresh or frozen
½ cup green beans
1 yellow pepper
4 tbsp olive oil
2 tbsp butter
1 garlic clove, finely chopped
5–6 leaves fresh basil, torn into pieces
salt and freshly ground black pepper
1¼lb short colored or plain pasta
    such as fusilli, penne or farfalle
freshly grated Parmesan, to serve
serves 6

1 Cut all the vegetables into small,
bite-size pieces.

2 ▲ Heat the oil and butter in a large
frying pan. Add the chopped
vegetables, and cook over moderate
heat for 5–6 minutes, stirring
occasionally. Add the garlic and the
basil, and season with salt and pepper.
Cover the pan, and cook for 5–8
minutes more, or until the vegetables
are just tender.

3 ▲ Meanwhile, cook the pasta in a
large pan of rapidly boiling salted
water until *al dente*. Before draining it,
reserve a cupful of the pasta water.

4 Turn the pasta into the pan with the
sauce, and mix well to distribute the
vegetables. If the sauce seems too dry,
add a few tablespoons of the reserved
pasta water. Serve with the Parmesan
passed separately.

Baked Seafood Spaghetti

Spaghetti cartoccio

In this dish, each portion is baked and served in an individual packet which is then opened at the table. Use parchment paper or aluminum foil to make the packets.

Ingredients

1lb fresh mussels
1/2 cup dry white wine
4 tbsp olive oil
2 garlic cloves, finely chopped
1lb tomatoes, fresh or canned,
    peeled and finely chopped
1lb spaghetti or other long pasta
2 tbsp chopped fresh parsley
8oz peeled and deveined shrimp,
    fresh or frozen
salt and freshly ground black pepper
serves 4

1 ▲ Scrub the mussels well under cold running water, cutting off the "beard" with a small sharp knife. Place the mussels and the wine in a large pan and heat until they open.

2 ▲ Lift out the mussels and remove to a side dish. (Discard any that do not open.) Strain the cooking liquid through paper towels, and reserve until needed. Preheat the oven to 300°F.

3 ▲ Bring a large pan of water to a boil. In a medium pan, heat the olive oil and garlic together for 1–2 minutes. Add the tomatoes, and cook over moderate to high heat until they soften. Stir in 3/4 cup of the cooking liquid from the mussels. Add salt and the pasta to the boiling water, and cook until it is just *al dente*.

4 ▲ Just before draining the pasta, add the parsley and shrimp, if uncooked, to the tomato sauce. Cook for 2 minutes. Taste for seasoning, adding salt and black pepper as desired. Remove from the heat.

~ VARIATION ~

Canned mussels or clams may be substituted for fresh shellfish in this recipe. Add them to the tomato sauce with the shrimp.

5 ▲ Prepare 4 pieces of parchment paper or foil approximately 12 in × 18 in. Place each sheet in the center of a shallow bowl. Turn the drained pasta into a mixing bowl. Add the tomato sauce and mix well. Stir in the mussels and shrimp, if pre-cooked.

6 ▲ Divide the pasta and seafood between the four pieces of paper, placing a mound in the center of each, and twisting the paper ends together to make a closed packet. (The bowl under the paper will stop the sauce from spilling while the paper parcels are being closed.) Arrange on a large cookie sheet, and place in the center of the preheated oven. Bake for 10 minutes. Place one unopened packet on each individual serving plate.

Tuna Pasta Salad

Insalata di pasta con tonno

This easy pasta salad uses canned beans and tuna for a quick main dish.

Ingredients
1lb short pasta, such as ruote,
   macaroni or farfalle
4 tbsp olive oil
2 × 7oz cans tuna, drained and flaked
2 × 14oz cans cannellini or borlotti
   beans, rinsed and drained
1 small red onion
2 stalks celery
juice of 1 lemon
2 tbsp chopped fresh parsley
salt and freshly ground black pepper
serves 6–8

1 Cook the pasta in a large pan of
rapidly boiling salted water until it is
al dente. Drain, and rinse under cold
water to stop cooking. Drain well and
turn into a large bowl. Toss with the
olive oil, and set aside. Allow to cool
completely before mixing with the
other ingredients.

2 ▲ Mix the flaked tuna and the beans
into the cooked pasta. Slice the onion
and celery very thinly and add them to
the pasta.

3 ▲ Combine the lemon juice with
the parsley. Mix into the other
ingredients. Season with salt and
pepper. Allow the salad to stand for
at least 1 hour before serving.

Chicken Pasta Salad

Insalata di pasta con pollo

This salad uses leftover chicken from a roast, or a cold poached chicken breast.

Ingredients
12oz short pasta, such as mezze
   rigatoni, fusilli or penne
3 tbsp olive oil
1$\frac{1}{2}$ cups cold cooked chicken
2 small red and yellow peppers
   (about 7oz)
$\frac{1}{3}$ cup pitted green olives
4 scallions, chopped
3 tbsp mayonnaise
1 tsp Worcestershire sauce
1 tbsp wine vinegar
salt and freshly ground black pepper
a few leaves fresh basil, to garnish
serves 4

1 Cook the pasta in a large pan of
rapidly boiling salted water until it is
al dente. Drain, and rinse under cold
water to stop the cooking. Drain well
and turn into a large bowl. Toss with
the olive oil, and set aside. Allow to
cool completely.

2 ▲ Cut the chicken into bite-size
pieces, removing any bones. Cut the
peppers into small pieces, removing
the seeds and stems.

3 ▲ Combine all the ingredients
except the pasta in a medium bowl.
Taste for seasoning, then mix into the
pasta. Garnish with the basil, and
serve chilled.

Whole Wheat Pasta Salad

Insalata di pasta integrale

This substantial vegetarian salad is easily assembled from any combination of seasonal vegetables. Use raw or lightly blanched vegetables, or a mixture of both.

Ingredients

1lb short whole wheat pasta, such
   as fusilli or penne
3 tbsp olive oil
2 medium carrots
1 small head broccoli, halved
1 cup shelled peas, fresh or frozen
1 red or yellow pepper
2 stalks celery
4 scallions
1 large tomato
$^1/_2$ cup pitted olives, halved

For the dressing

3 tbsp balsamic or wine vinegar
4 tbsp olive oil
1 tbsp Dijon style mustard
1 tbsp sesame seeds
2 tsp finely chopped mixed fresh herbs,
   such as parsley, thyme and basil
salt and freshly ground black pepper
$^2/_3$ cup diced Cheddar or mozzarella,
   or a combination

serves 8

1 Cook the pasta in a large pan of rapidly boiling salted water until it is *al dente*. Drain, and rinse under cold water to stop the cooking. Drain well and turn into a large bowl. Toss with 3 tbsp of the olive oil, and set aside. Allow to cool completely before mixing with the other ingredients.

2 ▲ Lightly blanch the carrots, broccoli and peas in a large pan of boiling water. Refresh under cold water. Drain well.

3 ▲ Chop the carrots and broccoli into bite-size pieces and add to the pasta with the peas. Slice the pepper, celery, scallions and tomato into small pieces. Add them to the salad with the olives.

4 ▲ Make the dressing in a small bowl by combining the vinegar with the oil and mustard. Stir in the sesame seeds and herbs. Mix the dressing into the salad. Taste for seasoning, adding salt, pepper or more oil and vinegar as necessary. Stir in the cheese. Allow the salad to stand for 15 minutes before serving.

Pasta Salad with Olives

Insalata di pasta con olive

This delicious salad combines all the flavors of the Mediterranean. It is an excellent way of serving pasta and is particularly nice on hot summer days.

Ingredients

1lb short pasta, such as medium
    shells, farfalle or penne
4 tbsp extra-virgin olive oil
10 sun-dried tomatoes, thinly sliced
2 tbsp capers, in brine or salted
$^2/_3$ cup black olives, pitted
2 garlic cloves, finely chopped
3 tbsp balsamic vinegar
salt and freshly ground black pepper
3 tbsp chopped fresh parsley
serves 6

3 ▲ Combine the olives, tomatoes, capers, garlic and vinegar in a small bowl. Season with salt and pepper.

4 ▲ Stir this mixture into the pasta, and toss well. Add 2 or 3 spoons of the tomato soaking water if the salad seems too dry. Toss with the parsley, and allow to stand for 15 minutes before serving.

1 ▲ Cook the pasta in a large pan of rapidly boiling salted water until it is *al dente*. Drain, and rinse under cold water to stop the cooking. Drain well and turn into a large bowl. Toss with the olive oil, and set aside.

2 ▲ Soak the tomatoes in a bowl of hot water for 10 minutes. Do not discard the water. Rinse the capers well. If they have been preserved in salt, soak them in a little hot water for 10 minutes. Rinse again.

Cannelloni with Tuna

Cannelloni sorpresa

Children love this pasta dish. Fontina cheese has a sweet, nutty flavor and melts perfectly.

Look for it at large supermarkets and Italian delicatessens.

Ingredients

¼ cup butter
½ cup flour
about 3 ¾ cups hot milk
2 cans (7 oz each) tuna, drained
1 cup Fontina cheese, grated
¼ tsp grated nutmeg
12 cannelloni tubes
⅔ cup grated Parmesan cheese
salt and freshly ground black pepper
fresh herbs, to garnish

serves 4–6

1 ▲ Melt the butter in a heavy saucepan, add the flour and stir over low heat for 1–2 minutes. Remove the pan from the heat and gradually add 1½ cups of the milk, beating vigorously after each addition. Return the pan to the heat and whisk for 1–2 minutes, until the sauce is very thick and smooth. Remove from the heat.

2 ▲ Mix the drained tuna with about ½ cup of the warm white sauce in a bowl. Add salt and black pepper to taste. Preheat the oven to 350°F.

3 ▲ Gradually whisk the remaining milk into the rest of the sauce, then return to the heat and simmer, whisking constantly, until thickened. Add the grated Fontina and nutmeg, with salt and pepper to taste. Simmer for a few more minutes, stirring frequently. Pour about one-third of the sauce into a baking dish and spread to the corners.

4 ▲ Fill the cannelloni tubes with the tuna mixture, pushing it in with the handle of a teaspoon. Place the cannelloni in a single layer in the dish. Thin the remaining sauce with a little more milk if necessary, then pour it over the cannelloni. Sprinkle with Parmesan cheese and bake for 30 minutes or until golden. Serve hot, garnished with herbs.

Seafood Lasagne

Lasagne alla marinara

Rich and creamy, this flavorful lasagne makes a good dinner party dish.

Ingredients

5 tbsp butter
1 lb monkfish fillets, skinned and diced small
8 oz large shrimp, shelled, deveined and roughly chopped
3 cups button mushrooms, chopped
3 tbsp flour
2 ¹/₂ cups hot milk
1 ¹/₄ cups heavy cream
1 can (14 oz) chopped tomatoes
2 tbsp shredded fresh basil
8 sheets no-cook lasagne
1 cup grated Parmesan cheese
salt and freshly ground black pepper
fresh herbs, to garnish

serves 6

1 ▲ Melt 1 tbsp of the butter in a large, deep sauté pan, add the monkfish and shrimp and sauté over medium to high heat for 2–3 minutes. As soon as the shrimp turn pink, remove them with a slotted spoon and place in a bowl.

2 Add the mushrooms to the pan and sauté for about 5 minutes, until the juices run and the mushrooms are soft. Remove with a slotted spoon and add to the fish in the bowl.

3 Melt the remaining butter in a saucepan, add the flour and stir over low heat for 1–2 minutes. Remove the pan from the heat and gradually whisk in the milk. Return to the heat and bring to a boil, whisking. Lower the heat and simmer for 2–3 minutes, whisking occasionally, until thick. Whisk in the cream and cook over low heat for 2 more minutes.

4 ▲ Remove the sauce from the heat and stir in the fish and mushroom mixture with all the juices that have collected in the bowl. Add salt to taste, and plenty of pepper. Preheat the oven to 375°F.

5 Spread half the chopped tomatoes over the bottom of a baking dish. Sprinkle with half the basil and add salt and pepper to taste. Ladle one-third of the sauce over the tomatoes.

6 ▲ Cover the sauce with four lasagne sheets. Spread the remaining tomatoes over the lasagne and sprinkle with the basil and salt and pepper to taste. Ladle half the sauce over. Arrange the remaining lasagne sheets on top, top with the remaining sauce and cover with the cheese. Bake for 30–40 minutes until golden and bubbling. Serve hot, garnished with fresh herbs.

Fettuccine with Ham and Cream

Fettuccine con prosciutto

Prosciutto is perfect for this rich and delicious dish, which makes an elegant first course.

Ingredients
4oz slice prosciutto crudo or other
   unsmoked ham
$1/4$ cup butter
2 shallots, very finely chopped
salt and freshly ground black pepper
$3/4$ cup heavy cream
12oz fettuccine
$1/2$ cup grated Parmesan cheese
sprig fresh parsley, to garnish
serves 4

1 ▲ Cut the fat from the ham, and chop both lean and fat parts separately into small squares.

2 ▲ Melt the butter in a medium frying pan, and add the shallots and the squares of ham fat. Cook until golden. Add the lean ham, and cook for 2 minutes more. Season with black pepper. Stir in the cream, and keep warm over low heat while the pasta is cooking.

3 ▲ Boil the pasta in a large pan of rapidly boiling salted water. Drain when *al dente*. Turn into a warmed serving bowl, and toss with the sauce. Stir in the cheese and serve at once, garnished with a sprig of parsley.

~ VARIATION ~

Substitute 6 oz fresh or frozen peas for the ham. Add to the pan with the shallots.

Tagliatelle with Smoked Salmon

Tagliatelle con salmone affumicato

In Italy smoked salmon is imported, and quite expensive. This elegant creamy sauce makes a little go a long way.

Ingredients
$3/4$ cup smoked salmon slices or ends,
   fresh or frozen
$1 1/4$ cups light cream
pinch of ground mace or nutmeg
12oz green and white tagliatelle
salt and freshly ground black pepper
3 tbsp chopped fresh chives, to garnish
serves 4–5

1 Cut the salmon into thin strips about 2 in long. Place in a bowl with the cream and the mace or nutmeg. Stir, cover, and allow to stand for at least 2 hours in a cool place.

2 ▲ Bring a large pan of water to a boil for the pasta. While the water is heating, gently warm the cream and salmon mixture in a small saucepan without boiling it.

3 ▲ Add salt to the boiling water. Drop in the pasta all at once. Drain when it is just *al dente*. Pour the sauce over the pasta and mix well. Season and garnish with the chives.

Spaghetti with Clams and White Wine *Spaghetti alle vongole*

Raid the pantry to make this quick and easy pasta dish with an intense flavor.

Ingredients

2 tbsp olive oil
1 onion, very finely chopped
2 garlic cloves, crushed
1 can (14 oz) chopped tomatoes
²/₃ cup dry white wine
1 jar or can (5 oz) clams in natural juice,
    drained with juice reserved
12 oz dried spaghetti
2 tbsp finely chopped fresh flat-leaf
    parsley, plus extra
    to garnish
salt and freshly ground black pepper
serves 4

Cook's Tip

The tomato sauce can be made several days ahead of time and kept in the refrigerator. Add the clams and heat them through at the last minute—but don't let the sauce boil or they will toughen.

1 Heat the oil in a saucepan, add the onion and cook gently, stirring frequently for about 5 minutes, until softened, but not brown.

2 ▲ Stir in the garlic, tomatoes, wine and reserved clam juice, with salt to taste. Add a generous grinding of black pepper. Bring to a boil, stirring, then lower the heat. Cover the pan and simmer the sauce gently for about 20 minutes, stirring occasionally.

3 ▲ Meanwhile, coil the spaghetti into a large saucepan of rapidly boiling salted water and cook for 12 minutes or until it is *al dente*.

4 Drain the spaghetti. Add the clams and finely chopped parsley to the tomato sauce and heat through, then taste for seasoning. Pour the drained spaghetti into a warmed serving bowl, pour on the tomato sauce and toss to mix. Serve immediately, sprinkled with more parsley.

Pasta with Cream and Parmesan *Pasta Alfredo*

This popular classic originated in Rome. It is incredibly quick and simple, perfect for a

midweek supper.

Ingredients

12 oz dried fettuccine
2 tbsp butter
1¹/₄ cups heavy cream
²/₃ cup grated Parmesan cheese, plus
    extra to serve
2 tbsp finely chopped fresh flat-leaf
    parsley, plus extra
    to garnish
salt and freshly ground black pepper
serves 3–4

Variation

In Rome, fettuccine would traditionally be served with this sauce, but tagliatelle can be used if you prefer. Pasta shapes, such as penne, rigatoni or farfalle, are also suitable.

1 Cook the fettuccine in a large pan of rapidly boiling salted water for 8–10 minutes or until *al dente*.

2 ▲ Meanwhile, melt the butter in a large flameproof casserole and add the cream and Parmesan, with salt and pepper to taste. Stir over medium heat until the cheese has melted and the sauce has thickened.

3 ▲ Drain the fettuccine and add it to the sauce with the chopped parsley. Fold the pasta and sauce together over medium heat until the strands of pasta are generously coated. Grind more black pepper over the pasta and garnish with the extra chopped parsley. Serve immediately, with a bowl of grated Parmesan served separately.

Tagliatelle with Bolognese Sauce

Tagliatelle alla bolognese

Most people think of bolognese sauce, the famous ragù from Bologna, as being served with spaghetti. Traditionally, it is served with tagliatelle.

Ingredients

2 tbsp olive oil
1 onion, finely chopped
1 carrot, finely chopped
1 celery stick, finely chopped
1 garlic clove, crushed
12 oz ground beef
²/₃ cup red wine
1 cup milk
1 can (14 oz) chopped tomatoes
1 tbsp sun-dried tomato paste
12 oz dried tagliatelle
salt and freshly ground black pepper
shredded fresh basil, to garnish
grated Parmesan cheese, to serve
serves 4

1 ▲ Heat the oil in a large saucepan. Add the onion, carrot, celery and garlic and cook gently, stirring frequently, for about 10 minutes, until softened. Do not let the vegetables color.

2 ▲ Add the ground beef to the pan with the vegetables and cook over medium heat until the meat changes color, stirring constantly and breaking up any lumps with a wooden spoon.

3 ▲ Pour in the wine. Stir frequently until it has evaporated, then add the milk and continue cooking and stirring until this has evaporated, too.

Cook's Tip

Don't skimp on the cooking time—it is essential for a full-flavored bolognese sauce. Some Italian cooks insist on cooking it for 3–4 hours, so the longer the better.

4 ▲ Stir in the tomatoes and tomato paste, with salt and pepper to taste. Simmer the sauce uncovered, over the lowest possible heat for at least 45 minutes.

5 Cook the tagliatelle in a large pan of rapidly boiling salted water for 8–10 minutes or until *al dente*. Drain thoroughly and pour into a warmed large bowl. Pour on the sauce and toss to combine. Garnish with basil and serve immediately, with Parmesan cheese served separately.

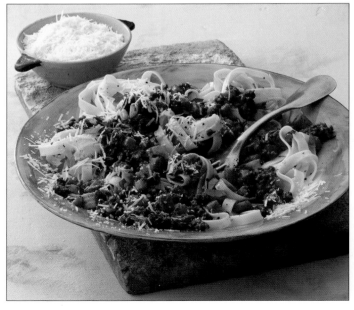

Penne with Pancetta and Cream

Penne alla carbonara

This makes a gloriously rich supper dish. Follow it with a simple salad.

Ingredients

12 oz dried penne
2 tbsp olive oil
1 small onion, finely chopped
6 oz pancetta slices, any rinds removed,
    cut into bite-size strips
1–2 garlic cloves, crushed
5 egg yolks
³/₄ cup heavy cream
1¹/₃ cups grated Parmesan cheese, plus
    extra to serve
salt and freshly ground black pepper

serves 3–4

1 ▲ Cook the penne in a large pan of rapidly boiling salted water for about 10 minutes or until *al dente*.

2 Meanwhile, heat the oil in a large flameproof casserole. Add the onion and cook gently for about 5 minutes, stirring frequently, until softened. Add the pancetta and garlic. Cook over medium heat until the pancetta is cooked but not crisp. Remove the pan from the heat and set aside.

3 ▲ Put the egg yolks in a bowl and add the cream and Parmesan cheese. Grind in plenty of black pepper. Beat well to mix.

4 ▲ Drain the penne thoroughly, pour into the casserole and toss over medium to high heat until the pancetta mixture is evenly mixed with the pasta.

5 Remove from the heat, pour in the egg yolk mixture and toss well to combine. Spoon into a large shallow serving dish, grind a little black pepper on top and sprinkle with some of the extra Parmesan. Serve the rest of the Parmesan separately.

Cook's Tip
Serve this dish the moment it is ready or it will not be hot enough. Having added the egg yolks, don't return the pan to the heat or attempt to reheat the pasta and sauce together or the egg yolks will scramble and give the pasta a curdled appearance.

Baked Lasagne with Meat Sauce

Lasagne al forno

This lasagne made from egg pasta with home-made meat and béchamel sauces is exquisite.

Ingredients
1 recipe Bolognese Meat Sauce
egg pasta sheets made with 3 eggs,
    or 1lb dried lasagne
1 cup grated Parmesan
3 tbsp butter
For the béchamel sauce
3 cups milk
1 bay leaf
3 blades mace
$1/2$ cup butter
$3/4$ cup flour
salt and freshly ground black pepper
serves 8–10

1 Prepare the meat sauce and set aside. Butter a large shallow baking dish, preferably rectangular or square.

2 Make the béchamel sauce by gently heating the milk with the bay leaf and mace in a small pan. Melt the butter in a medium heavy pan. Add the flour, and mix it in well with a wire whisk. Cook for 2–3 minutes. Strain the hot milk into the flour and butter mixture, and combine smoothly with the whisk. Bring the sauce to a boil, stirring constantly, and cook for 4–5 minutes more. Season with salt and pepper, and set aside.

3 ▲ Make the pasta. Do not let it dry out before cutting it into rectangles approximately $4^{1}/_{2}$ in wide and the same length as the baking dish (this will make it easier to assemble). Preheat the oven to 400°F.

4 ▲ Bring a very large pan of water to a boil. Place a large bowl of cold water near the stove. Cover a large work surface with a tablecloth. Add salt to the rapidly boiling water. Drop in 3 or 4 of the egg pasta rectangles. Cook very briefly, about 30 seconds. Remove them from the pan using a slotted spoon, and drop them into the bowl of cold water for about 30 seconds. Pull them out of the water, shaking off the excess water. Lay them out flat without overlapping on the tablecloth. Continue with all the remaining pasta and trimmings.

5 ▲ To assemble the lasagne, have all the elements at hand: the baking dish, béchamel and meat sauces, pasta strips, grated Parmesan and butter. Spread one large spoonful of the meat sauce over the bottom of the dish. Arrange a layer of pasta in the dish, cutting it with a sharp knife so that it fits well inside the dish.

6 ▲ Cover with a thin layer of meat sauce, then one of béchamel. Sprinkle with a little cheese. Repeat the layers in the same order, ending with a layer of pasta coated with béchamel. Do not make more than about 6 layers of pasta. (If you have a lot left over, make another small lasagne in a little ovenproof dish.) Use the pasta trimmings to patch any gaps in the pasta. Sprinkle the top with Parmesan, and dot with butter.

7 Bake in the preheated oven for 20 minutes or until brown on top. Remove from the oven and allow to stand for 5 minutes before serving. Serve directly from the baking dish, cutting out rectangular or square sections for each helping.

~ VARIATION ~

If you are using dried or bought pasta, follow step 4, but boil the lasagne in just two batches, and stop the cooking about 4 minutes before the recommended cooking time on the package has elapsed. Rinse in cold water and lay the pasta out the same way as for the egg pasta.

Tagliolini with Asparagus

Tagliolini con asparagi

Tagliolini are very thin home-made egg noodles, more delicate in texture than spaghetti. They go well with this subtle cream sauce flavored with asparagus.

Ingredients

1lb fresh asparagus
egg pasta sheets made with 2 eggs,
    or 12oz fresh tagliolini or other
    egg noodles
1/4 cup butter
3 scallions, finely chopped
3–4 leaves fresh mint or basil, finely
    chopped
2/3 cup heavy cream
salt and freshly ground black pepper
1/2 cup freshly grated Parmesan or
    Romano cheese
serves 4

3 Make the egg pasta sheets, and fold and cut into thin noodles, or feed them through the narrowest cutters of a machine. Open the noodles out, and let them dry for at least 5–10 minutes.

5 Bring the asparagus cooking water back to the boil. Add salt. Drop the noodles in all at once. Cook until just tender (freshly made noodles will cook in a few seconds). Drain.

1 ▲ Peel the asparagus by inserting a small sharp knife at the base of the stalks and pulling upwards towards the tips. Drop them into a large pan of rapidly boiling water, and boil until just tender, 4–6 minutes.

4 ▲ Melt the butter in a large frying pan. Add the scallions and herbs, and cook for 3–4 minutes. Stir in the cream and asparagus, and heat gently, but do not boil. Season to taste.

6 ▲ Turn the pasta into the pan with the sauce, raise the heat slightly, and mix well. Stir in the Parmesan or Romano. Mix well and serve at once.

2 ▲ Remove from the water, reserving the cooking water. Cut the tips off, and then cut the stalks into 1 1/2 in pieces. Set aside.

Ravioli with Ricotta and Spinach

Ravioli ripieni di magro

Home-made ravioli are fun to make, and can be stuffed with different meat, cheese or vegetable fillings. This filling is easy to make, and lighter than the normal meat variety.

Ingredients
14oz fresh spinach or 6oz frozen spinach
$3/4$ cup ricotta cheese
1 egg
$1/2$ cup grated Parmesan cheese
pinch of grated nutmeg
salt and freshly ground black pepper
egg pasta sheets made with 3 eggs
For the sauce
$1/3$ cup butter
5–6 sprigs fresh sage
serves 4

1 Wash fresh spinach well in several changes of water. Place in a saucepan with only the water that is clinging to the leaves. Cover, and cook until tender, about 5 minutes. Drain. Cook frozen spinach according to the instructions on the package. When the spinach is cool, squeeze out as much moisture as possible. Chop finely.

2 Combine the chopped spinach with the ricotta, egg, Parmesan and nutmeg. Mix well. Season with salt and pepper. Cover the bowl and set aside.

3 Prepare the sheets of egg pasta. Roll out very thinly by hand or machine. Do not let the pasta dry out.

4 ▲ Place small teaspoons of filling along the pasta in rows 2 in apart. Cover with another sheet of pasta, pressing down gently to avoid forming air pockets.

5 ▲ Use a fluted pastry wheel to cut between the rows to form small squares with filling in the center of each. If the edges do not stick well, moisten with milk or water, and press together with a fork. Place the ravioli on a lightly floured surface, and allow to dry for at least 30 minutes. Turn occasionally so they dry on both sides. Bring a large pan of salted water to a boil.

6 Heat the butter and sage together over very low heat, taking care that the butter melts but does not darken.

7 ▲ Drop the ravioli into the boiling water. Stir gently to prevent them from sticking. They will be cooked in very little time, about 4–5 minutes. Drain carefully and arrange in individual serving dishes. Spoon on the sauce, and serve at once.

Tagliatelle with Hazelnut Pesto

Tagliatelle al pesto di nocciale

Hazelnuts make an interesting addition to this variation on the classic pesto.

Ingredients
2 garlic cloves, crushed
1 cup fresh basil leaves
¼ cup shelled hazelnuts
scant 1 cup low-fat soft cheese
8 oz dried tagliatelle
salt and freshly ground black pepper
serves 4

Cook's Tip
If you buy fresh tagliatelle instead of dried, cook in boiling salted water for only 2–3 minutes until *al dente*.

1 Place the crushed garlic, basil leaves, hazelnuts and cheese in a blender or food processor and process to a thick paste.

2 ▲ Meanwhile, cook the tagliatelle in lightly salted boiling water for about 10 minutes until *al dente*, then drain well.

3 ▲ Spoon the pesto into the hot pasta and toss lightly until melted. Grind on plenty of black pepper and serve hot.

Spaghetti with Tuna Sauce

Spaghetti al sugo di tonno

This delicious pasta dish combines some of the simplest, but most delicious Italian ingredients, along with a little extra zing from the chili sauce.

Ingredients
8 oz dried spaghetti
1 garlic clove, crushed
14 oz can chopped tomatoes
15 oz can tuna fish in
  brine, drained
½ tsp chili sauce
4 black olives, pitted and chopped
salt and freshly ground black pepper
serves 4

Cook's Tip
If fresh tuna steaks are available, use 1 lb. Cut the steaks into small chunks and add to the sauce after step 2. Simmer for 6–8 minutes, then add the chili, olives and pasta.

1 ▲ Cook the spaghetti in lightly salted boiling water for about 10 minutes or until *al dente*. Drain well and keep hot.

2 ▲ Add the garlic and tomatoes to the pan and bring to a boil. Simmer uncovered for 2–3 minutes.

3 Add the tuna, chili sauce, olives and spaghetti to the pan. Heat well, season to taste with salt and plenty of black pepper and serve hot.

Farfalle with Mushrooms and Cheese   *Farfalle boscaiole*

Fresh wild mushrooms are very good in this sauce, but they are expensive. To cut the cost,

use half wild and half cultivated, or as many wild as you can afford—even a small handful

will intensify the mushroom flavor.

Ingredients

1 cup dried porcini mushrooms
2 tbsp butter
1 small onion, finely chopped
1 garlic clove, crushed
3 cups fresh mushrooms, thinly sliced
a few fresh sage leaves, very
    finely chopped, plus a few whole
    leaves, to garnish
²/₃ cup dry white wine
2 cups dried farfalle
¹/₂ cup mascarpone cheese
1 cup Gorgonzola or torta di Gorgonzola
    cheese, crumbled
salt and freshly ground black pepper
serves 4

3 ▲ Cook the farfalle in a large saucepan of rapidly boiling salted water, for about 10 minutes or until *al dente*.

Variation

For a lighter sauce, use crème fraîche instead of mascarpone.

4 ▲ Meanwhile, stir the mascarpone and Gorgonzola into the mushroom sauce. Heat through, stirring, until melted. Taste for seasoning. Drain the pasta thoroughly, add to the sauce and toss to mix. Serve immediately, with black pepper ground liberally on top. Garnish with sage leaves.

1 ▲ Put the dried porcini in a small bowl with 1 cup warm water and let soak for 20–30 minutes. Remove from the liquid and squeeze the porcini over the bowl to extract as much liquid as possible. Strain the liquid and set it aside. Finely chop the porcini.

2 Melt the butter in a large saucepan, add the onion and chopped porcini and cook gently, stirring for about 3 minutes, until the onion is soft. Add the garlic and fresh mushrooms, chopped sage, salt and plenty of black pepper. Cook over medium heat, stirring frequently, for about 5 minutes or until the mushrooms are soft and juicy. Stir in the soaking liquid and the wine and simmer.

Pasta with Tomato and Chili Sauce

Pasta all'arrabbiata

This is a speciality of Lazio—the word arrabbiata means rabid or angry, and describes the heat that comes from the chili. This quick version is made with jarred sugocasa.

Ingredients
1 lb sugocasa (see Cook's Tip)
2 garlic cloves, crushed
²/₃ cup dry white wine
1 tbsp sun-dried tomato purée
1 fresh red chili
12 oz penne or tortiglioni
¹/₄ cup finely chopped fresh flat-leaf
     parsley
salt and freshly ground black pepper
freshly grated Pecorino cheese, to serve
serves 4

1 ▲ Put the sugocasa, garlic, wine, tomato paste and whole chili in a saucepan and bring to a boil. Cover and simmer gently.

2 ▲ Drop the pasta into a large saucepan of rapidly boiling salted water and simmer for 10–12 minutes or until *al dente*.

Cook's Tip
Sugocasa is sold in jars sometimes labeled "crushed Italian tomatoes." It is finer than canned chopped tomatoes and coarser than passata, and so is ideal for pasta sauces, soups and stews.

3 ▲ Remove the chili from the sauce and add half the parsley. Taste for seasoning. If you prefer a hotter taste, chop some or all of the chili and return it to the sauce.

4 ▲ Drain the pasta and pour into a warmed large bowl. Pour the sauce over the pasta and toss to mix. Serve immediately, sprinkled with grated Pecorino and the remaining parsley.

Baked Vegetable Lasagne

Lasagne al forno con funghi e pomodori

Following the principles of the classic meat sauce lasagne, other combinations of ingredients can be used most effectively. This vegetarian lasagne uses fresh vegetables and herbs.

Ingredients

egg pasta sheets made with 3 eggs
2 tbsp olive oil
1 medium onion, very finely chopped
1¹⁄₄lb tomatoes, fresh or canned, chopped
salt and freshly ground black pepper
1¹⁄₂lb cultivated or wild mushrooms, or a combination of both
¹⁄₃ cup butter
2 garlic cloves, finely chopped
juice of ¹⁄₂ lemon
4¹⁄₂ cups béchamel sauce
1¹⁄₂ cups freshly grated Parmesan or Romano cheese, or a combination
serves 8

1 Butter a large shallow baking dish, preferably rectangular or square.

2 ▲ Make the egg pasta. Do not let it dry out before cutting it into rectangles approximately 4¹⁄₂in wide and the same length as the baking dish (this will make it easier to assemble).

3 In a small frying pan heat the oil and sauté the onion until translucent. Add the chopped tomatoes, and cook for 6–8 minutes, stirring often. Season with salt and pepper, and set aside.

4 ▲ Wipe the mushrooms carefully with a damp cloth. Slice finely. Heat 2 tbsp of the butter in a frying pan, and when it is bubbling, add the mushrooms. Cook until the mushrooms start to exude their juices. Add the garlic and lemon juice, and season with salt and pepper. Cook until the liquids have almost all evaporated and the mushrooms are starting to brown. Set aside.

5 ▲ Preheat the oven to 400°F. Bring a very large pan of water to a boil. Place a large bowl of cold water near the stove. Cover a large work surface with a tablecloth. Add salt to the rapidly boiling water. Drop in 3 or 4 of the egg pasta rectangles. Cook very briefly, about 30 seconds. Remove them from the pan using a slotted spoon, and drop them into the bowl of cold water for about 30 seconds. Remove and lay out to dry. Continue with the remaining pasta.

6 ▲ To assemble the lasagne have all the elements at hand: the baking dish, fillings, pasta, cheeses and butter. Spread one large spoonful of the béchamel sauce over the bottom of the dish. Arrange a layer of pasta in the dish, cutting it with a sharp knife so that it fits well. Cover the pasta with a thin layer of mushrooms, then one of béchamel sauce. Sprinkle with a little Parmesan or Romano cheese.

7 ▲ Make another layer of pasta, spread with a thin layer of tomatoes, and then one of béchamel. Sprinkle with cheese. Repeat the layers in the same order, ending with a layer of pasta coated with béchamel. Do not make more than about 6 layers of pasta. Use the pasta trimmings to patch any gaps in the pasta. Sprinkle with cheese, and dot with butter.

8 Bake for 20 minutes. Remove from the oven and allow to stand for 5 minutes before serving.

Tortelli with Pumpkin Stuffing

Tortelli di zucca

During autumn and winter the northern Italian markets are full of bright orange pumpkins, which are used to make soups and pasta dishes. This dish is a speciality of Mantua.

Ingredients
2lb pumpkin (weight with shell)
$1\frac{1}{2}$ cups amaretti, finely crushed
2 eggs
$\frac{3}{4}$ cup freshly grated Parmesan or
   Romano cheese
pinch of grated nutmeg
salt and freshly ground black pepper
plain breadcrumbs, as required
egg pasta sheets made with 3 eggs
To serve
$\frac{1}{2}$ cup butter
$\frac{3}{4}$ cup freshly grated Parmesan or
   Romano cheese
serves 6–8

1 Preheat the oven to 375°F. Cut the pumpkin into 4 in pieces. Leave the skin on. Place the pumpkin pieces in a covered casserole, and bake for 45–50 minutes. When cool, cut off the skins. Purée the flesh in a food mill or food processor or press through a sieve.

2 ▲ Combine the pumpkin purée with the cookie crumbs, eggs, cheese and nutmeg. Season with salt and pepper. If the mixture is too wet, add 1–2 tbsp of breadcrumbs. Set aside.

3 Prepare the sheets of egg pasta. Roll out very thinly by hand or machine. Do not let the pasta dry out before filling it.

4 ▲ Place tablespoons of filling every $2\frac{1}{2}$ in along the pasta in rows 2 in apart. Cover with another sheet of pasta, and press down gently. Use a fluted pastry wheel to cut between the rows to form rectangles with filling in the center of each. Place the tortelli on a lightly floured surface, and allow to dry for at least 30 minutes. Turn them occasionally so they dry on both sides.

5 Bring a large pan of salted water to a boil. Gently heat the butter over very low heat, taking care that it does not darken.

6 ▲ Drop the tortelli into the boiling water. Stir to prevent from sticking. They will be cooked in 4–5 minutes. Drain and arrange in individual dishes. Spoon on the melted butter, sprinkle with Parmesan or Romano, and serve.

Stuffed Pasta Half-moons

Mezzelune ripiene di formaggi

These stuffed egg pasta half-moons are filled with a delicate mixture of cheeses. They make an elegant first course.

Ingredients

1¼ cups fresh ricotta or cottage cheese
1¼ cups mozzarella cheese
1 cup freshly grated Parmesan or
   Romano cheese
2 eggs
3 tbsp finely chopped fresh basil
salt and freshly ground black pepper
egg pasta sheets made with 3 eggs

For the sauce

1lb fresh tomatoes
2 tbsp olive oil
1 small onion, very finely chopped
6 tbsp cream

serves 6–8

1 ▲ Press the ricotta or cottage cheese through a sieve or strainer. Chop the mozzarella into very small cubes. Combine all three cheeses in a bowl. Beat in the eggs and basil, season and set aside.

2 Make the sauce by dropping the tomatoes into a small pan of boiling water for 1 minute. Remove, and peel using a small sharp knife to pull the skins off. Chop the tomatoes finely. Heat the oil in a medium pan. Add the onion and cook over moderate heat until soft and translucent. Add the tomatoes and cook until soft, about 15 minutes. Season with salt and pepper. (The sauce may be pressed through a sieve to make it smooth.) Set aside.

3 Prepare the sheets of egg pasta. Roll out very thinly by hand or machine. Do not let the pasta dry out.

4 ▲ Using a water glass or pastry cutter, cut out rounds approximately 4in in diameter. Spoon one large tablespoon of the filling onto one half of each pasta round and fold over.

5 Press the edges closed with a fork. Re-roll any trimmings and use to make more rounds. Allow the half-moons to dry for at least 10–15 minutes. Turn them over so they dry evenly.

6 Bring a large pan of salted water to a boil. Place the tomato sauce in a small saucepan and heat gently while the pasta is cooking. Stir in the cream. Do not boil.

7 Gently drop the stuffed pasta into the boiling water, and stir carefully to prevent them from sticking. Cook for 5–7 minutes. Scoop them out of the water, drain carefully, and arrange in individual dishes. Spoon on some of the sauce, and serve at once.

Cannelloni Stuffed with Meat
Cannelloni ripieni di carne

Cannelloni are rectangles of egg pasta which are spread with a filling, rolled up and baked in a sauce. In this recipe, they are baked in a béchamel sauce.

Ingredients

2 tbsp olive oil
1 medium onion, very finely chopped
1¹⁄₂ cups very lean ground beef (preferably 80% lean)
¹⁄₂ cup cooked ham (either boiled or baked), finely chopped
1 tbsp chopped fresh parsley
2 tbsp tomato paste, softened in 1 tbsp warm water
1 egg
salt and freshly ground black pepper
egg pasta sheets made with 2 eggs
3¹⁄₂ cups béchamel sauce
¹⁄₂ cup freshly grated Parmesan or Romano cheese
3 tbsp butter
serves 6–8

2 ▲ Remove from the heat, and turn the beef mixture into a bowl with the ham and parsley. Add the tomato paste and the egg, and mix well. Season with salt and pepper. Set aside.

1 ▲ Prepare the meat filling by heating the oil in a medium pan. Add the onion, and sauté gently until translucent. Stir in the beef, crumbling it with a fork, and stirring constantly until it has lost its raw red color. Cook for 3–4 minutes.

3 ▲ Make the egg pasta sheets with a machine or by hand. Do not let the pasta dry before cutting it into rectangles 5–6 in long and as wide as they come from the machine (3 in if you are not using a machine).

4 Bring a very large pan of water to a boil. Place a large bowl of cold water near the stove. Cover a large work surface with a tablecloth. Add salt to the rapidly boiling water. Drop in 3 or 4 of the egg pasta rectangles. Cook very briefly, about 30 seconds. Remove and drop them into the bowl of cold water for about 30 seconds more. Pull them out of the water, shaking off the excess water. Lay them out flat on the tablecloth. Continue with the remaining pasta.

5 Preheat the oven to 425°F. Select a shallow baking dish large enough to accommodate all the cannelloni in one layer. Butter the dish, and smear 2–3 tbsp of béchamel sauce over the bottom.

6 ▲ Stir about one-third of the béchamel into the meat filling. Spread a thin layer of filling on each pasta rectangle. Roll the rectangles up loosely starting from the long side, jelly-roll style. Place the cannelloni into the baking dish with their open edges down.

7 ▲ Spoon the rest of the béchamel over the cannelloni, pushing a little down between each pasta roll. Sprinkle the top with the grated Parmesan or Romano, and dot with butter. Bake for about 20 minutes. Allow to rest for 5–8 minutes before serving.

Three-cheese Lasagne

Lasagne ai tre formaggi

The cheese makes this lasagne quite expensive, so reserve it for a special occasion.

Ingredients
2 tbsp olive oil
1 onion, finely chopped
1 carrot, finely chopped
1 celery stalk, finely chopped
1 garlic clove, crushed
1 1/2 lb ground beef
1 can (14 oz) chopped tomatoes
1 1/4 cups beef stock
1 1/4 cups red wine
2 tbsp sun-dried tomato paste
2 tsp dried oregano
9 sheets no-cook lasagne
3 5-oz packages mozzarella cheese, thinly sliced
2 cups ricotta cheese
4 ounces Parmesan cheese, grated
salt and freshly ground black pepper
serves 6–8

1 Heat the oil and gently cook the onion, carrot, celery and garlic, stirring for 10 minutes until softened.

2 Add the beef and cook until it changes color, stirring constantly and breaking up the meat.

3 ▲ Add the tomatoes, stock, wine, tomato paste, oregano and salt and pepper and bring to a boil, stirring. Cover, lower the heat and simmer gently for 1 hour, stirring occasionally.

4 ▲ Preheat the oven to 375°F. Check for seasoning, then ladle one-third of the meat sauce into a 9 x 13 in baking dish and cover with 3 sheets of lasagne. Arrange one-third of the mozzarella slices over the top, dot with one-third of the ricotta, then sprinkle with one-third of the Parmesan.

5 Repeat these layers twice, then bake for 40 minutes. Let cool for 10 minutes before serving.

Tortiglioni with Spicy Sausage Sauce

Tortiglioni alla siciliana

This heady pasta dish is not for the faint-hearted. Serve it with a robust Sicilian red wine.

Ingredients
2 tbsp olive oil
1 onion, finely chopped
1 celery stalk, finely chopped
2 large garlic cloves, crushed
1 fresh red chili, seeded and chopped
1 lb ripe Italian plum tomatoes, peeled and finely chopped
2 tbsp tomato paste
2/3 cup red wine
1 tsp sugar
12 oz dried tortiglioni
6 oz spicy salami, rind removed
salt and freshly ground black pepper
2 tbsp chopped fresh parsley, to garnish
grated Parmesan cheese, to serve
serves 4

Cook's Tip
Buy the salami for this dish in one piece so that you can chop it into large chunks.

1 ▲ Heat the oil, then add the onion, celery, garlic and chili and cook gently, stirring frequently, for about 10 minutes, until softened.

2 Add the tomatoes, tomato paste, wine, sugar and salt and pepper to taste and bring to a boil, stirring. Lower the heat, cover and simmer gently, stirring occasionally, for about 20 minutes. Add a few spoonfuls of water occasionally if the sauce becomes too thick.

3 ▲ Meanwhile, drop the pasta into a large saucepan of rapidly boiling salted water and simmer, uncovered, for 10–12 minutes.

4 Chop the salami into bite-size chunks and add to the sauce. Heat through, then taste for seasoning.

5 Drain the pasta, tip it into a large bowl, then pour on the sauce and toss to mix. Scatter over the parsley and serve with grated Parmesan.

Pasta and Bolognese Casserole

Pasticcio

Pasticcio is Italian for pie, and in some regions this is made with a pastry topping. This simple version makes a great family supper because it's such a favorite with children.

Ingredients
8 oz dried conchiglie
1 quantity hot Bolognese Sauce (see
    Tagliatelle with Bolognese Sauce,
    page 244)
salt and freshly ground black pepper

For the white sauce
4 tbsp butter
¹/₂ cup flour
3 cups milk
1 cup grated Parmesan cheese
1 egg, beaten
good pinch of grated nutmeg
mixed salad leaves, to serve
serves 4

1 Cook the conchiglie in a large pan of rapidly boiling salted water for 10–12 minutes or until *al dente*.

2 Meanwhile, make the white sauce. Melt the butter in a saucepan until foaming, add the flour and stir over low heat for 1–2 minutes. Remove the pan from the heat and gradually whisk in the milk. Return the pan to the heat and bring to a boil, whisking constantly. Lower the heat and simmer for 2–3 minutes, whisking occasionally, until the sauce thickens. Remove the pan from the heat.

3 ▲ Preheat the oven to 375°F. Drain the pasta thoroughly, pour it into a 8 x 12-in baking dish and mix in the hot bolognese sauce. Level the surface.

4 ▲ Stir about two-thirds of the Parmesan into the white sauce, then stir in the beaten egg and nutmeg, with salt and pepper to taste. Pour on top of the pasta and sauce and sprinkle with the remaining Parmesan. Bake for 20 minutes or until golden and bubbling. Serve hot, straight from the dish. Add a salad garnish to each plate.

Cook's Tip
This is a good way of using up leftover bolognese sauce and cooked pasta—the quantities do not need to be exact.

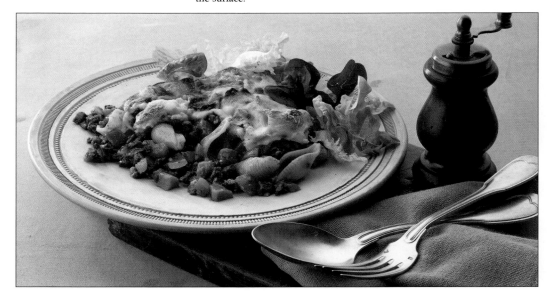

Pasta with Eggplants

Pasta alla Norma

This Sicilian recipe is traditionally made from fried eggplants. This version is lighter.

Ingredients

2 medium eggplants, about 8 ounces
    each, diced small
3 tbsp olive oil
10 oz dried macaroni or fusilli
²/₃ cup grated Pecorino cheese
salt and freshly ground black pepper
shredded fresh basil leaves, to garnish
crusty bread, to serve

For the tomato sauce

2 tbsp olive oil
1 onion, finely chopped
1 can (14 oz) chopped tomatoes or
    1 jar (14 oz) passata

serves 4

Cook's Tip

In Sicily, a cheese called ricotta salata
is used for this recipe. This is a
matured salted ricotta that is grated
like Pecorino and Parmesan. It is
unlikely that you will find ricotta
salata outside Sicily; Pecorino is the
best substitute because it tastes
slightly saltier than Parmesan.

1 Soak the diced eggplant in a bowl
of cold salted water for 30 minutes.

2 Meanwhile, preheat the oven to
425°F. Make the sauce. Heat the oil
in a large saucepan, add the onion
and cook gently for about 3 minutes,
until softened. Add the tomatoes,
with salt and pepper to taste. Bring
to a boil, lower the heat, cover and
simmer for 20 minutes. Stir the sauce
and add a few spoonfuls of water
occasionally, to prevent it from
becoming too thick. Remove from
the heat.

3 ▲ Drain the eggplants and pat dry.
Spread the pieces out in a roasting
pan, add the oil and toss to coat.
Bake for 20–25 minutes, turning the
eggplants every 4–5 minutes with a
spatula so that they brown evenly.

4 Cook the pasta in a large pan of
rapidly boiling salted water for
10–12 minutes or until *al dente*.
Reheat the tomato sauce.

5 ▲ Drain the pasta thoroughly and
add it to the tomato sauce, with half
the roasted eggplant and half the
Pecorino. Toss to mix, then taste for
seasoning.

6 Spoon the pasta and sauce
mixture into a warmed large serving
dish and top with the remaining
roasted eggplant. Scatter the
shredded fresh basil leaves on
top, followed by the remaining
Pecorino. Serve immediately, with
generous chunks of crusty bread.

Semolina Gnocchi

Gnocchi di semola

This famous Roman dish is made with coarsely ground semolina, which is cooked in a
similar way to polenta. The rich paste is cut into flat discs, and baked with butter and cheese.

Ingredients

4$\frac{1}{2}$ cups milk
pinch of salt
3 tbsp butter
generous 2 cups coarsely ground
    semolina
3 egg yolks
3 tbsp freshly grated Parmesan
    or Romano cheese

For baking

5 tbsp butter, melted
$\frac{1}{2}$ cup freshly grated Parmesan
    or Romano cheese
pinch of grated nutmeg

serves 4

1 ▲ Heat the milk with the salt and
a third of the butter in a heavy pan.
When it boils sprinkle in the semolina,
stirring with a wire whisk to prevent
lumps from forming. Bring the mixture
to a boil. Lower the heat and simmer
for 15–20 minutes, stirring occasionally.
The mixture should be very thick.

2 ▲ Remove from the heat and beat in
the remaining butter, and then the egg
yolks one at a time. Stir in the grated
Parmesan or Romano. Season with salt.
Sprinkle a little cold water onto a work
surface. Spread the hot semolina
mixture out onto it in an even layer
about $\frac{1}{2}$ inch thick. Allow to cool for
at least 2 hours.

3 ▲ Preheat the oven to 425°F, and
butter a shallow baking dish. Use a
cookie cutter to cut the semolina into
2$\frac{1}{2}$in rounds.

4 ▲ Place the trimmings in an even
layer in the bottom of the dish. Pour
over a little melted butter, and
sprinkle with cheese. Cover with a
layer of the cut-out circles,
overlapping them slightly. Sprinkle
with nutmeg, cheese and butter.
Continue the layering until all the
ingredients have been used up.

5 Bake for about 20 minutes, or until
the top is browned. Remove from the
oven and allow to stand for 5 minutes
before serving.

~ COOK'S TIP ~

Semolina is ground durum wheat,
which is the kind used to make
dried pasta. Buy semolina in small
batches and store in an air-tight
container as it goes stale when
kept for too long.

Potato Gnocchi

Gnocchi di patate

Gnocchi are little dumplings made either with mashed potato and flour, as here, or with semolina. They should be light in texture, and must not be overworked while being made.

Ingredients

2lb waxy potatoes, scrubbed
1 tbsp salt
2–2$^1/_2$ cups flour
1 egg
pinch of grated nutmeg
2 tbsp butter
freshly grated Parmesan, to serve
serves 4–6

1 Place the unpeeled potatoes in a large pot of water, with the salt. Bring to a boil, and cook until the potatoes are tender but not falling apart. Drain. Peel as soon as possible, while the potatoes are still hot.

2 On a work surface spread out 1$^1/_4$ cups of the flour. Mash the hot potatoes with a food mill, dropping them directly onto the flour. Sprinkle with $^3/_4$ cup flour and mix very lightly into the potatoes. Break the egg into the mixture, add the nutmeg, and knead lightly, drawing in more flour as necessary. When the dough is light to the touch and no longer moist or sticky it is ready to be rolled. Do not overwork or the gnocchi will be heavy.

3 ▲ Divide the dough into 4 parts. On a lightly floured board form each into a roll about $^3/_4$ inch in diameter. Cut the rolls crosswise into pieces about $^3/_4$ inch long.

4 ▲ Hold an ordinary table fork with long tines sideways, leaning on the board. One by one press and roll the gnocchi lightly along the tines of the fork towards the points, making ridges on one side, and a depression from your thumb on the other.

5 Bring a large pan of water to a fast boil. Add salt, and drop in about half the gnocchi.

6 ▲ When the gnocchi rise to the surface, after 3–4 minutes, they are cooked. Scoop them out of the water, allow to drain, and place in a warmed serving bowl. Dot with butter. Keep warm while the remaining gnocchi are boiling. As soon as they are cooked, toss the gnocchi with the butter or a heated sauce, sprinkle with grated Parmesan, and serve.

Potato and Spinach Gnocchi

Gnocchi di patate e spinaci

These green gnocchi are made in the same way as potato gnocchi, with the addition of fresh or frozen spinach. Serve tossed with butter or with a tomato sauce.

Ingredients

1½lb fresh spinach, or 14oz frozen leaf
   spinach
2lb waxy potatoes, scrubbed
salt, to taste
2–2½ cups flour
1 egg
pinch of grated nutmeg
¼ cup butter
freshly grated Parmesan cheese, to serve
serves 6

1 If using fresh spinach, wash it in several changes of cold water. Pull off any tough stalks. Place in a large pan with only the water that is clinging to the leaves. Cover the pan, and cook over moderate heat, stirring occasionally, until the spinach is tender, about 5–8 minutes. Cook uncovered for the last 2–3 minutes to boil off some of the water. Remove from the heat. Drain.

4 ▲ On a work surface spread out 1¼ cups of the flour. Mash the hot potatoes with a food mill, dropping them directly onto the flour. Add the spinach, and mix lightly into the potatoes. Sprinkle with ¾ cup flour and mix in lightly.

7 ▲ Hold an ordinary table fork with long tines sideways, leaning on the board. One by one press and roll the gnocchi lightly along the tines of the fork towards the points, making ridges on one side, and a depression from your thumb on the other.

5 Break the egg into the mixture, add the nutmeg, and knead lightly, drawing in more flour as necessary. When the dough is light to the touch and no longer moist or sticky it is ready to be rolled. Do not overwork or the gnocchi will be heavy.

2 ▲ Cook frozen spinach according to the instructions on the package. Spread the spinach over a clean dish towel, roll it up and wring out all excess moisture. Chop the spinach finely with a sharp knife.

8 ▲ Bring a large pan of water to a fast boil. Add salt and drop about half the gnocchi in. They will sink to the bottom of the pan. When they rise to the surface, after 3–4 minutes, the gnocchi are done. Scoop them out with a large slotted spoon, and place in a warmed serving bowl. Keep warm while the remaining gnocchi are boiling. As soon as they are cooked, toss the gnocchi with the butter or a heated sauce, sprinkle with grated Parmesan, and serve.

3 Place the unpeeled potatoes in a large pan of salted water. Bring to a boil, and cook until the potatoes are tender but not falling apart. Drain. Peel as soon as possible, while the potatoes are still hot.

6 ▲ Divide the dough into 4 parts. On a lightly floured board form each into a roll about ¾ inch in diameter. Cut the rolls crosswise into pieces about ¾ inch long.

Spinach and Ricotta Gnocchi *Gnocchi di spinaci e ricotta*

The mixture for these tasty little herb dumplings needs to be handled very carefully to

achieve light and fluffy results. Serve with sage butter and grated Parmesan.

Ingredients

6 garlic cloves, unpeeled
1 oz mixed fresh herbs, such as parsley,
    basil, thyme, coriander and chives,
    finely chopped
8 oz fresh spinach leaves
generous 1 cup ricotta cheese
1 egg yolk
$^2/_3$ cup grated Parmesan cheese
$^2/_3$ cup flour
$^1/_4$ cup butter
2 tbsp fresh sage, chopped
salt and freshly ground black pepper
serves 4

1 Cook the garlic cloves in boiling
water for 4 minutes. Drain and pop
out of the skins. Place in a food
processor with the herbs and blend
to a purée or mash the garlic with a
fork and add the herbs to mix well.

2 ▲ Place the spinach in a large pan
with just the water that clings to the
leaves and cook gently until wilted.
Let cool, then squeeze out as much
liquid as possible. Chop finely.

3 Place the ricotta in a bowl and beat
in the egg yolk, spinach, herbs and
garlic. Stir in half the Parmesan, sift
in the flour and mix well.

Cook's Tip
Squeeze the spinach dry to ensure
the gnocchi are not wet and to give a
lighter result. The mixture should be
fairly soft and will be easier to handle
if chilled for an hour before
preparing the dumplings.

4 ▲ Using floured hands, break off
pieces of the mixture slightly smaller
than a walnut and roll into small
dumplings.

5 Bring a large pan of salted water
to a boil and carefully add the
gnocchi. When they rise to the top of
the pan they are cooked, this should
take about 3 minutes.

6 ▲ The gnocchi should be light and
fluffy all the way through. If not,
simmer for another minute. Drain
well. Meanwhile, melt the butter in a
frying pan and add the sage. Simmer
gently for 1 minute. Add the gnocchi
to the frying pan and toss in the
butter over gentle heat for 1 minute,
then serve sprinkled with the
remaining Parmesan.

Gnocchi with Gorgonzola Sauce

Gnocchi al gorgonzola

Gnocchi are prepared all over Italy with different ingredients used in different regions. These are gnocchi di patate, *potato dumplings.*

Ingredients
1 lb potatoes, unpeeled
1 large egg
1 cup flour
salt and freshly ground black pepper
fresh thyme sprigs, to garnish

For the sauce
4 oz Gorgonzola cheese
¼ cup heavy cream
1 tbsp fresh thyme, chopped
¼ cup freshly grated
  Parmesan cheese, to serve
serves 4

1 Cook the potatoes in boiling salted water for about 20 minutes until they are tender. Drain and, when cool enough to handle, remove the skins.

2 ▲ Force the potatoes through a sieve, pressing through using the back of a spoon, into a mixing bowl. Add plenty of seasoning and then beat in the egg until completely incorporated. Add the flour a little at a time, stirring well with a wooden spoon after each addition until you have a smooth dough. (You may not need all the flour.)

3 Turn the dough out onto a floured surface and knead for about 3 minutes, adding more flour if necessary, until it is smooth and soft and not sticky to the touch.

Cook's Tips
Choose dry, floury potatoes. Avoid new or red-skinned potatoes, which do not have the right dry texture.

4 ▲ Divide the dough into 6 equal pieces. Flour your hands and gently roll each piece between your hands into a log shape measuring 6–8 in long and 1 in around. Cut each log into 6–8 pieces, about 1 in long, then gently roll each piece in the flour. Form into gnocchi by gently pressing each piece on to the floured surface with the tines of a fork to leave ridges in the dough.

5 ▲ To cook, drop the gnocchi into a pan of boiling water about 12 at a time. Once they rise to the surface, after about 2 minutes, cook for 4–5 more minutes. Remove and drain.

6 Place the Gorgonzola, cream and thyme in a large frying pan and heat gently until the cheese melts to form a thick, creamy consistency. Add the drained gnocchi and toss well to combine. Serve with Parmesan and garnish with thyme.

Rice, Polenta & Pizzas

· ·

*In the north of Italy, rice is served as a first course, as
a creamy risotto, but you can serve it as a main dish,
with a salad and Italian bread. Polenta, also from the
north of Italy, is most often served with the main
course, especially with meaty casseroles. Pizzas hail
from the south, where they are eaten at any time of
day, the ultimate convenience food.*

Risotto with Cheese

Risotto alla parmigiana

Risotto is distinguished from other rice dishes by its unique cooking method.

Ingredients
5$\frac{1}{2}$ cups beef, chicken or vegetable
  stock, preferably home-made
5 tbsp butter
1 small onion, finely chopped
1$\frac{1}{2}$ cups medium-grain risotto rice,
  such as Arborio
$\frac{1}{2}$ cup dry white wine
salt and freshly ground black pepper
$\frac{3}{4}$ cup freshly grated Parmesan or
  Romano cheese
serves 3–4

1 Heat the stock in a medium pan, and
keep it simmering until it is needed.

2 In a large heavy pan, melt two-thirds
of the butter. Stir in the onion, and
cook gently until it is soft and golden.
Add the rice, mixing it well to coat it
with butter. After 1–2 minutes pour in
the wine.

3 ▲ Raise the heat slightly, and cook
until the wine evaporates. Add one
small ladleful of the hot stock. Over
moderate heat cook until the stock is
absorbed or evaporates, stirring the
rice with a wooden spoon to prevent
it from sticking to the pan. Add a little
more stock, and stir until the rice dries
out again. Continue stirring and
adding the liquid a little at a time. After
about 20 minutes of cooking time,
taste the rice. Add salt and pepper.

4 Continue cooking, stirring and
adding the liquid until the rice is *al
dente*, or tender but still firm to the
bite. The total cooking time of the
risotto may be from 20–35 minutes.
If you run out of stock, use hot water,
but do not worry if the rice is done
before you have used up all the stock.

5 ▲ Remove the risotto pan from the
heat. Stir in the remaining butter and
the cheese. Taste again for seasoning.
Allow the risotto to rest for 3–4
minutes before serving.

Risotto with Shrimp

Risotto con gamberi

This shrimp risotto is given a soft pink color by the addition of a little tomato paste.

Ingredients
12oz fresh shrimp in their shells
5 cups water
1 bay leaf
1–2 sprigs of parsley
1 tsp whole peppercorns
2 garlic cloves, peeled
5 tbsp butter
2 shallots, finely chopped
1$\frac{1}{2}$ cups medium-grain risotto rice,
  such as Arborio
1 tbsp tomato paste softened in
  $\frac{1}{2}$ cup dry white wine
salt and freshly ground black pepper
serves 4

1 Place the shrimp in a large pan
with the water, bay leaf, parsley,
peppercorns and garlic cloves. Bring to
a boil and cook for about 1 minute.
Remove the shrimp, peel, and return
the shells to the pan. Boil the shells for
another 10 minutes. Strain. Return the
broth to a pan, and simmer until needed.

2 Slice the shrimp in half lengthwise,
removing the dark intestinal vein along
the back. Set 4 halves to one side for
garnishing the risotto, and roughly
chop the rest.

3 Heat two-thirds of the butter in a
large heavy pan. Add the shallots and
cook until golden. Stir in the shrimp.
Cook for 1–2 minutes.

4 ▲ Add the rice, mixing well to coat
it with butter. After 1–2 minutes pour
in the tomato paste and wine. Follow
steps 3–5 for Risotto with Cheese,
omitting the cheese and garnishing
with the reserved shrimp halves.

Risotto with Mushrooms

Risotto con funghi

The addition of wild mushrooms gives this risotto a wonderful woodsy flavor.

Ingredients

1/3 cup dried wild mushrooms,
   preferably porcini
1 1/2 cups fresh cultivated mushrooms
juice of 1/2 lemon
1/3 cup butter
2 tbsp finely chopped parsley
4 cups beef or chicken stock,
   preferably home-made
2 tbsp olive oil
1 small onion, finely chopped
1 1/2 cups medium-grain risotto rice,
   such as Arborio
1/2 cup dry white wine
salt and freshly ground black pepper
3 tbsp freshly grated Parmesan or
   Romano cheese
serves 3–4

1 Place the dried mushrooms in a small bowl with about 1 1/2 cups warm water. Soak for at least 40 minutes. Rinse the mushrooms thoroughly. Filter the soaking water through a strainer lined with paper towels, and reserve.

2 ▲ Wipe the fresh mushrooms with a damp cloth, and slice finely. Place in a bowl and toss with the lemon juice. In a large heavy pan melt one-third of the butter. Stir in the fresh sliced mushrooms and cook over moderate heat until they give up their juices, and begin to brown. Stir in the parsley, cook for 30 seconds more, and remove to a side dish.

3 Place the stock in a pan. Add the soaking water from the mushrooms, and simmer until needed.

4 ▲ Heat another third of the butter with the olive oil in the same pan the mushrooms were cooked in. Stir in the onion, and cook until it is soft and golden. Add the rice, stirring for 1–2 minutes to coat it with the oils. Add the soaked and sautéed mushrooms, and mix well.

5 ▲ Pour in the wine, and cook over moderate heat until it evaporates. Follow steps 3–4 for Risotto with Cheese.

6 Remove the risotto pan from the heat. Stir in the remaining butter and the Parmesan or Romano. Grind in a little black pepper, and taste again for salt. Allow the risotto to rest for 3–4 minutes before serving.

Risotto with Asparagus

Risotto con asparagi

This is an elegant risotto to make when asparagus is in season.

Ingredients

8oz fresh asparagus, peeled
3 cups vegetable or beef stock,
    preferably home-made
5 tbsp butter
1 small onion, finely chopped
2 cups medium-grain risotto rice,
    such as Arborio
salt and freshly ground black pepper
$3/4$ cup freshly grated Parmesan or
    Romano cheese
serves 4–5

1 Bring a large pan of water to a boil. Add the asparagus. Bring the water back to a boil, and blanch for 5 minutes. Lift the asparagus out, reserving the cooking water. Rinse the asparagus under cold water. Drain. Cut the asparagus diagonally into $1^1/_2$ in pieces. Keep the tip and next-highest sections separate from the stalk sections.

2 Place the vegetable or beef stock in a pan. Measure out $3^3/_4$ cups of the asparagus cooking water, and add it to the stock. Heat the liquid to simmering, and keep it hot until it is needed.

4 ▲ Stir in half a ladleful of the hot liquid. Using a wooden spoon, stir constantly until the liquid has been absorbed or evaporated. Add another half ladleful of the liquid, and stir until it has been absorbed. Continue stirring and adding the liquid, a little at a time, for about 10 minutes.

5 ▲ Add the remaining asparagus sections, and proceed as for step 4 of Risotto with Cheese.

6 Remove the risotto pan from the heat. Stir in the remaining butter and the Parmesan or Romano. Grind in a little black pepper, and taste again for salt. Serve at once.

3 ▲ Heat two-thirds of the butter in a large heavy pan. Add the chopped onion and cook until it is soft and golden. Stir in all the asparagus except the top two sections. Cook for 2–3 minutes. Add the Arborio rice, mixing well for 1–2 minutes to coat it thoroughly with butter.

Timballo of Rice with Peas

Timballo di riso con piselli

*The timballo is named because it looks like an inverted kettledrum (*timballo *or* timpano*).*

It is made like a risotto, but is given a final baking in the oven, and then unmolded.

Ingredients
1/3 cup butter
2 tbsp olive oil
1 small onion, finely chopped
1/3 cup ham, cut into small dice
3 tbsp finely chopped fresh parsley,
    plus a few sprigs to garnish
2 garlic cloves, very finely chopped
1 cup shelled peas, fresh or frozen
    and thawed
salt and freshly ground black pepper
4 tbsp water
5 1/2 cups fresh or canned low-salt
    beef or vegetable stock, preferably
    home-made
1 1/2 cups medium-grain risotto rice,
    such as Arborio
3/4 cup freshly grated Parmesan or
    Romano cheese
3/4 cup fontina cheese, very thinly sliced
a few sprigs parsley, to garnish
serves 4

1 ▲ Heat half the butter and all the oil in a large heavy pan. Add the chopped onion, and cook for a few minutes until it softens. Add the diced ham, and stir over moderate heat for 3–4 minutes. Stir in the parsley and garlic. Cook for 1 or 2 minutes. Add the peas, mix well, season with salt and pepper and add the water. Cover the pan, and cook for about 8 minutes for fresh peas, 4 minutes for frozen peas. Remove the cover, and cook until all the liquid has evaporated. Remove half the pea mixture to a dish.

2 Heat the stock, and keep it simmering until needed. Butter a round, flat-bottomed ovenproof dish and line the bottom with buttered waxed paper.

3 ▲ Stir the rice into the pea mixture remaining in the pan. After 1–2 minutes, add a small ladleful of the hot broth. Cook over moderate heat until the broth is absorbed, stirring the rice with a wooden spoon to prevent it from sticking. Add a little more stock, and stir until the rice dries out again. Continue stirring and adding the liquid.

4 ▲ Preheat the oven to 350°F. After about 20 minutes of cooking time, taste the rice. As soon as the rice is just *al dente*, or tender but still firm to the bite, remove the pan from the heat. Correct the seasoning. Mix most of the remaining butter and half the grated Parmesan or Romano into the rice.

5 Assemble by sprinkling a little grated cheese into the bottom of the dish. Spoon about half the rice into the dish. Follow with a thin layer of the fontina and a layer of reserved cooked peas and ham. Sprinkle with grated cheese.

6 ▲ Cover with the remaining fontina slices and end with the rice. Sprinkle with cheese, and dot with butter. Bake in the preheated oven for 10–15 minutes. Remove from the oven, and allow to stand for 10 minutes.

7 ▲ To unmold, slip a knife around between the rice and the dish. Place a serving plate upside down on top of the dish. Wearing oven mitts, pick up the dish and turn it over while still holding the plate. If the rice does not drop down, give it a sharp knock with your gloved hand. Peel off the waxed paper. Garnish with parsley. Serve by cutting the timballo into wedges.

Risotto with Spring Vegetables

Risotto primavera

This is one of the prettiest risottos, especially when made with yellow summer squash.

Ingredients

1 cup shelled fresh peas
1 cup green beans, cut into short lengths
2 tbsps olive oil
6 tbsp butter
2 small yellow summer squash, cut
    into matchsticks
1 onion, finely chopped
1¹/₂ cups risotto rice
¹/₂ cup Italian dry
    white vermouth
about 4 cups boiling chicken stock
1 cup grated Parmesan cheese
a small handful of fresh basil leaves,
    finely shredded, plus a few whole
    leaves, to garnish
salt and freshly ground black pepper
serves 4

1 Blanch the peas and beans in a large saucepan of lightly salted boiling water for 2–3 minutes, until just tender. Drain, refresh under cold running water, drain again and set aside for later.

2 ▲ Heat the oil and 2 tbsp of the butter in a medium saucepan until foaming. Add the squash and cook gently for 2–3 minutes or until just softened. Remove with a slotted spoon and set aside. Add the onion to the pan and cook gently for about 3 minutes, stirring frequently, until softened.

3 ▲ Stir in the rice until the grains start to swell and burst, then add the vermouth. Stir until the vermouth stops sizzling and most of it has been absorbed by the rice, then add a few ladlefuls of the stock, with salt and pepper to taste. Stir over low heat until the stock has been absorbed.

4 Continue cooking and stirring for 20–25 minutes, adding the remaining stock a few ladlefuls at a time. The rice should be *al dente* and the risotto should have a moist and creamy appearance.

5 ▲ Gently stir in the vegetables, the remaining butter and about half the grated Parmesan. Heat through, then stir in the shredded basil and taste for seasoning. Garnish with a few whole basil leaves and serve hot, with the remaining grated Parmesan served separately.

Variations

Shelled fava beans can be used instead of the peas, and asparagus tips instead of the green beans. Use green zucchini if yellow summer squash are unavailable.

Rice with Peas, Ham and Cheese
Risi e bisi

A classic risotto from the Veneto. Although it is traditionally served as an appetizer in Italy,

risi e bisi makes an excellent supper dish with hot crusty bread.

Ingredients

6 tbsp butter
1 small onion, finely chopped
about 4 cups boiling
    chicken stock
1¹/₂ cups risotto rice
²/₃ cup dry white wine
2 cups frozen peas, thawed
4 oz cooked ham, diced
salt and freshly ground black pepper
²/₃ cup Parmesan cheese,
    to serve

serves 4

1 ▲ Melt 4 tbsp of the butter in a saucepan until foaming. Add the onion and cook gently for about 3 minutes, stirring frequently, until softened. Have the hot stock ready in an adjacent pan.

2 ▲ Add the rice to the onion mixture. Stir until the grains start to burst, then pour in the wine. Stir until it stops sizzling and most of it has been absorbed, then pour in a little hot stock, with salt and pepper to taste. Stir over low heat until the stock has been absorbed.

3 ▲ Add the remaining stock, a little at a time, allowing the rice to absorb all the liquid before adding more, and stirring constantly. Add the peas toward the end. After 20–25 minutes, the rice should be *al dente* and the risotto moist and creamy.

4 ▲ Gently stir in the diced cooked ham and the remaining butter. Heat through until the butter has melted, then taste for seasoning. Transfer to a warmed serving bowl. Grate or shave a little Parmesan over the top and serve the rest separately.

Risotto with Four Cheeses

Risotto ai quattro formaggi

This is a very rich dish. Serve it for a dinner-party first course, with sparkling white wine.

Ingredients

3 tbsp butter
1 small onion, finely chopped
4 cups boiling chicken stock
1¾ cups risotto rice
scant 1 cup sparkling dry white wine
½ cup grated Gruyère cheese
½ cup Fontina cheese, diced small
½ cup Gorgonzola cheese, crumbled
⅔ cup grated Parmesan cheese
salt and freshly ground black pepper
fresh flat-leaf parsley, to garnish

serves 6

Cook's Tip

If you're feeling extravagant you can use Champagne for this risotto, although Asti spumante works quite well.

1 Melt the butter in a saucepan until foaming. Add the onion and cook gently, stirring frequently for about 3 minutes, until softened. Have the hot stock ready in an adjacent pan.

2 ▲ Add the rice and stir until the grains start to swell and burst, then add the sparkling wine. Stir until it stops sizzling and most of it has been absorbed by the rice, then pour in a little of the hot stock. Add salt and pepper to taste. Stir over low heat until the stock has been absorbed.

3 Add more stock, a little at a time, allowing the rice to absorb it before adding more, and stirring constantly. After 20–25 minutes the rice will be *al dente* and the risotto creamy.

4 ▲ Turn off the heat under the pan, then add the Gruyère, Fontina, Gorgonzola and 2 tbsp of the Parmesan. Stir gently until the cheeses have melted, then taste for seasoning. Pour into a serving bowl and garnish with parsley. Serve the remaining Parmesan separately.

Fried Rice Balls Stuffed with Cheese

Supplì

These deep-fried balls of risotto are stuffed with an inner filling of mozzarella cheese. They are very popular snacks in Rome and central Italy.

Ingredients
1 recipe Risotto with Cheese or
   Risotto with Mushrooms
3 eggs
plain breadcrumbs, as required
²/₃ cup mozzarella cheese, cut into
   small dice
oil, for deep-frying
flour, to coat
serves 4

3 Heat the oil until a small piece of bread sizzles as soon as it is dropped in (about 360°F).

5 ▲ Fry them a few at a time in the hot oil until golden and crisp. Drain on paper towels while the remaining balls are frying. Serve hot.

4 ▲ Spread some flour on a plate. Beat the remaining egg in a shallow bowl. Sprinkle another plate with breadcrumbs. Roll the balls in the flour, then in the egg, and finally in the breadcrumbs.

1 ▲ Allow the risotto to cool completely. (These are even better when formed from risotto made the day before.) Beat 2 of the eggs, and mix them well into the cold risotto.

2 ▲ Use your hands to form the rice mixture into balls the size of a large egg. If the mixture is too moist to hold its shape well, stir in a few tablespoons of breadcrumbs as necessary. Poke a hole into the center of each ball, fill it with a few small cubes of mozzarella, and close the hole over again with the rice mixture.

Saffron Risotto

Risotto alla milanese

This classic risotto is always served with osso buco, but makes a delicious first course or light supper dish in its own right.

Ingredients
about 5 cups beef or chicken stock
good pinch of saffron threads or
    1 envelope of saffron powder
6 tbsp butter
1 onion, finely chopped
1¹/₂ cups risotto rice
1 cup grated Parmesan cheese
salt and freshly ground black pepper
serves 4

1 Bring the stock to a boil, then reduce to a low simmer. Ladle a little stock into a small bowl. Add the saffron threads or powder and set aside to infuse.

2 Melt 4 tbsp of the butter in a large saucepan until foaming. Add the onion and cook gently for about 3 minutes, stirring frequently, until softened.

3 Add the rice. Stir until the grains start to swell and burst, then add a few ladlefuls of the stock, with the saffron liquid and salt and pepper to taste. Stir over low heat until the stock is absorbed. Add the remaining stock, a few ladlefuls at a time, allowing the rice to absorb all the liquid before adding more, and stirring constantly. After 20–25 minutes, the rice should be *al dente* and the risotto golden yellow, moist and creamy.

4 ▲ Gently stir in about two-thirds of the grated Parmesan and the remaining butter. Heat through until the butter has melted, then taste for seasoning. Transfer the risotto to a warmed serving bowl or platter and serve hot, with the remaining grated Parmesan sprinkled on top.

Polenta Elisa

Polenta Elisa

This dish comes from the valley around Lake Como. Serve it solo as an appetizer, or with a mixed salad and some sliced salami or prosciutto for a midweek supper.

Ingredients
1 cup milk
2 cups pre-cooked polenta
1 cup grated Gruyère cheese
1 cup torta di Dolcelatte cheese,
    crumbled
4 tbsp butter
2 garlic cloves, roughly chopped
a few fresh sage leaves, chopped
salt and freshly ground black pepper
prosciutto, to serve
serves 4

1 Preheat the oven to 400°F. Lightly butter an 8–10-in glass baking dish.

Cook's Tip
Pour the polenta into the boiling liquid in a continuous stream, stirring constantly with a wooden spoon or balloon whisk. If using a whisk, change to a wooden spoon once the polenta thickens.

2 ▲ Bring the milk and 3 cups water to a boil in a large saucepan, add 1 tsp salt, then pour in the polenta. Cook for about 8 minutes or according to the instructions on the package.

3 Spoon half the polenta into the baking dish and level. Cover with half the grated Gruyère and crumbled Dolcelatte. Spoon the remaining polenta evenly over the top and sprinkle with the remaining cheeses.

4 Melt the butter in a small saucepan until foaming, add the garlic and sage and fry, stirring, until the butter turns golden brown.

5 ▲ Drizzle the butter mixture over the polenta and cheese and grind black pepper liberally over the top. Bake for 5 minutes. Serve hot, with slices of prosciutto.

Polenta

Polenta

Polenta is a form of cornmeal. It is eaten in northern Italy in place of rice or pasta.

Ingredients
6$\frac{1}{4}$ cups water
1 tbsp salt
2$\frac{1}{2}$ cups polenta
serves 4–6

1 ▲ Bring the water to a boil in a large heavy pan. Add the salt. Reduce the heat to a simmer, and begin to add the polenta in a fine rain. Stir constantly with a whisk until the polenta has all been incorporated.

2 ▲ Switch to a long-handled wooden spoon, and continue to stir the polenta over low to moderate heat until it is a thick mass, and pulls away from the sides of the pan. This may take from 25–50 minutes, depending on the type of polenta used. For best results, never stop stirring the polenta until you remove it from the heat.

3 ▲ When the polenta is cooked, spoon it into a large slightly wet bowl, wait 5 minutes, and turn it out onto a serving platter. Serve it with a meat or tomato sauce, or follow the instructions given in the recipes on the following pages.

Fried Polenta

Polenta fritta

Leftover polenta can be fried, making a crispy appetizer to serve with drinks or antipasti.

Ingredients
cold leftover polenta
oil, for deep-frying
flour, for dredging
salt and freshly ground black pepper
serves 6–8 as an appetizer

2 Heat the oil until a small piece of bread sizzles as soon as it is dropped in (about 360°F).

1 ▲ Cut the polenta into slices about $\frac{1}{2}$ inch thick. Cut the slices into triangles or rounds.

3 ▲ Season the flour with salt and pepper. Dredge the polenta lightly in the flour, shaking off any excess.

4 ▲ Fry the polenta, a few pieces at a time, until golden and crisp. Drain on paper towels while the remaining pieces are frying. Serve at once.

Baked Polenta with Tomato Sauce

Polenta al forno

Polenta, or cornmeal, is a staple food in Italy. It is cooked like a sort of porridge, and eaten soft, or set, cut into shapes, then baked or broiled.

Ingredients

1 tsp salt
2¼ cups instant polenta
1 tsp paprika
½ tsp ground nutmeg
2 tbsp olive oil
1 large onion, finely chopped
2 garlic cloves, crushed
2 x 14 oz cans chopped tomatoes
1 tbsp tomato paste
1 tsp sugar
3 oz Gruyère cheese, grated
salt and freshly ground black pepper
serves 4

1 Preheat the oven to 400°F. Line a baking pan (11 x 7 in) with clear film. Bring 4 cups water to a boil with the salt.

2 ▲ Pour in the polenta in a steady stream and cook, stirring constantly, for 5 minutes. Beat in the paprika and nutmeg, then pour into the prepared pan and smooth the surface. Let cool.

3 Heat the oil in a pan and cook the onion and garlic until soft. Add the tomatoes, tomato paste and sugar. Season. Simmer for 20 minutes.

4 ▲ Turn out the polenta on to a chopping board, and cut into about 12 squares. Place half the squares in a greased ovenproof dish. Spoon on half the tomato sauce, and sprinkle with half the cheese. Repeat the layers. Bake in the oven for about 25 minutes, until golden.

Polenta with Mushroom Sauce

Polenta con salsa di funghi

Polenta, made from maize flour, fulfills the same function as rice, bread or potatoes in forming the starchy base for a meal. Here, it is cooked until it forms a soft dough, then flavored with Parmesan. Its subtle taste works well with the rich mushroom sauce.

Ingredients

5 cups vegetable stock
3 cups polenta
²/₃ cup grated Parmesan cheese
salt and freshly ground black pepper

For the sauce

1 cup dried porcini mushrooms
1 tbsp olive oil
4 tbsp butter
1 onion, finely chopped
1 carrot, finely chopped
1 celery stalk, finely chopped
2 garlic cloves, crushed
6 cups mixed chestnut and large flat
   mushrooms, roughly chopped
¹/₂ cup red wine
1 can (14 oz) chopped tomatoes
1 tsp tomato paste
1 tbsp chopped fresh thyme leaves
serves 4

1 ▲ Make the sauce. Put the dried mushrooms in a bowl, add ²/₃ cup of hot water and soak for 20 minutes. Drain the mushrooms, reserving the liquid, and chop them roughly.

2 Heat the oil and butter in a saucepan and add the onion, carrot, celery and garlic. Cook over low heat for about 5 minutes, until the vegetables are beginning to soften, then raise the heat and add the fresh and soaked dried mushrooms to the pan of vegetables. Cook for 8–10 minutes, until the mushrooms are softened and golden.

3 ▲ Pour in the wine and cook rapidly for 2–3 minutes, until reduced, then pour in the tomatoes and reserved mushroom liquid. Stir in the tomato paste with the thyme and plenty of salt and pepper. Lower the heat and simmer for 20 minutes, until the sauce is rich and thick.

Cook's Tip
The polenta will spit during cooking, so use a long-handled spoon and wrap a towel around your hand to protect it while stirring.

4 ▲ Meanwhile, heat the stock in a large heavy saucepan. Add a generous pinch of salt. As soon as it simmers, pour in the polenta in a fine stream, whisking until the mixture is smooth. Cook for 30 minutes, stirring constantly, until the polenta comes away from the pan. Remove from the heat and stir in half the Parmesan and some black pepper.

5 Divide among four heated bowls and top each with sauce. Sprinkle with the remaining Parmesan.

Polenta with Mushrooms

Polenta con funghi

This dish is delicious made with a mixture of wild and cultivated mushrooms. Just a few dried porcini mushrooms will help to give cultivated mushrooms a more interesting flavor.

Ingredients

2 tbsp dried porcini mushrooms
  (omit if using wild mushrooms)
4 tbsp olive oil
1 small onion, finely chopped
1½lb mushrooms, wild or
  cultivated, or a combination
2 garlic cloves, finely chopped
3 tbsp chopped fresh parsley
3 medium tomatoes, peeled and diced
1 tbsp tomato paste
¾ cup warm water
¼ tsp fresh thyme leaves, or ⅛ tsp
  dried thyme
1 bay leaf
salt and freshly ground black pepper
a few sprigs fresh parsley, to garnish

For the polenta

6¼ cups water
1 tbsp salt
2½ cups polenta

serves 6

3 ▲ Clean the fresh mushrooms by wiping them with a damp cloth. Cut into slices. When the onion is soft add the mushrooms to the pan. Stir over moderate to high heat until they give up their liquid. Add the garlic, parsley and diced tomatoes. Cook for 4–5 minutes more.

5 ▲ Bring the water to a boil in a large heavy pan. Add the salt. Reduce the heat to a simmer, and begin to add the polenta in a fine rain. Stir constantly with a whisk until the polenta has all been incorporated.

6 Switch to a long-handled wooden spoon, and continue to stir the polenta over low to moderate heat until it is a thick mass, and pulls away from the sides of the pan. This may take from 25–50 minutes, depending on the type of polenta used. For best results, never stop stirring the polenta until you remove it from the heat.

1 ▲ Soak the dried mushrooms, if using, in a small cup of warm water for 20 minutes. Remove the mushrooms with a slotted spoon, and rinse them well in several changes of cool water. Filter the soaking water through a layer of paper towels placed in a sieve, and reserve.

2 In a large frying pan heat the oil, and sauté the onion over low heat until soft and golden.

4 ▲ Soften the tomato paste in the warm water (use only ½ cup water if you are using dried mushrooms). Add it to the pan with the herbs. Add the dried mushrooms and soaking liquid, if using them. Mix well and season with salt and pepper. Lower the heat to low to moderate and cook for 15–20 minutes. Set aside while you make the polenta.

7 ▲ When the polenta has almost finished cooking, gently reheat the mushroom sauce. To serve, spoon the polenta onto a warmed serving platter. Make a well in the center. Spoon some of the mushroom sauce into the well, and garnish with parsley. Serve at once, passing the remaining sauce in a separate bowl.

Broiled Polenta with Gorgonzola

Polenta alla griglia

Broiled polenta is delicious, and is a good way of using up cold polenta. Try it with any soft flavorful cheese. Plain broiled polenta is a good accompaniment to stews and soups.

Ingredients

6¼ cups water
1 tbsp salt
2½ cups polenta
1¼ cups Gorgonzola or other cheese,
    at room temperature
serves 6–8 as a snack or
appetizer

1 ▲ Bring the water to a boil in a large heavy pan. Add the salt. Reduce the heat to a simmer, and begin to add the polenta in a fine rain. Stir constantly with a whisk until the polenta has all been incorporated.

2 ▲ Switch to a long-handled wooden spoon, and continue to stir the polenta over low to moderate heat until it is a thick mass, and pulls away from the sides of the pan. This may take from 25–50 minutes, depending on the type of polenta used. For best results, never stop stirring the polenta until you remove it from the heat.

3 ▲ When the polenta is cooked, sprinkle a work surface or large board with a little water. Spread the polenta out onto the surface in a layer ³/₄in thick. Allow to cool completely. Preheat the broiler.

4 ▲ Cut the polenta into triangles. Broil until hot and speckled with brown on both sides. Spread with the Gorgonzola or other cheese. Serve immediately.

Polenta Baked with Cheese

Polenta pasticciata

Cold polenta can be cut into slices and baked in layers with cheese and other ingredients. The traditional way of cutting it is with a wooden knife or a piece of thick thread.

Ingredients

generous $1/3$ cup butter
cooked polenta, made with 2 cups
    cornmeal
3 tbsp olive oil
2 medium onions, thinly sliced
pinch of grated nutmeg
salt and freshly ground black pepper
$3/4$ cup mozzarella or sharp Cheddar
    cheese, cut into thin slices
3 tbsp finely chopped fresh parsley
$1/3$ cup freshly grated Parmesan or
    Romano cheese
serves 4–6

1 ▲ Stir a third of the butter into the cooked polenta. Sprinkle a work surface with a little water. Spread the polenta out in a layer $1/2$in thick. Allow to cool. Cut into $2^1/2$in rounds.

2 ▲ Heat the oil in a medium pan with 1 tbsp of the remaining butter. Add the onions, and stir over low heat until soft. Season the onions with nutmeg, salt and pepper.

3 ▲ Preheat the oven to 375°F. Butter an ovenproof dish. Spread a few of the onion slices in the bottom of the dish. Cover with a layer of polenta rounds. Dot with butter. Add a layer of mozzarella or Cheddar, and a sprinkling of parsley and Parmesan or Romano. Season with salt and pepper, and continue the layers in order.

4 ▲ Finish the layering with the cheese. Dot the top with butter and bake for 20–25 minutes, or until the cheese has melted. Serve from the baking dish.

Basic Pizza Dough

Pizza dough is leavened with yeast. It usually rises once before being rolled out and filled. The dough can be baked in pizza pans or on a flat cookie sheet.

Ingredients

2$\frac{1}{2}$ tbsp fresh bread yeast or 1$\frac{1}{2}$ tbsp
   active dried yeast
1 cup lukewarm water
pinch of sugar
1 tsp salt
3–3$\frac{1}{2}$ cups unbleached white
   bread flour

**serves 4 as a main course or 8
as an appetizer**

1 ▲ Warm a medium mixing bowl by swirling some hot water in it. Drain. Place the yeast in the bowl, and pour on the warm water. Stir in the sugar, mix with a fork, and allow to stand until the yeast has dispersed and starts to foam, 5–10 minutes.

2 ▲ Use a wooden spoon to mix in the salt and about one-third of the flour. Mix in another third of the flour, stirring with the spoon until the dough forms a mass and begins to pull away from the sides of the bowl.

3 ▲ Sprinkle some of the remaining flour onto a smooth work surface. Remove the dough from the bowl and begin to knead it, working in the remaining flour a little at a time. Knead for 8–10 minutes. By the end the dough should be elastic and smooth. Form it into a ball.

4 Lightly oil a mixing bowl. Place the dough in the bowl. Stretch a moistened and wrung-out dish towel across the top of the bowl, and leave it to stand in a warm place until the dough has doubled in volume, about 40–50 minutes or more, depending on the type of yeast used. (If you do not have a warm enough place, turn the oven on to medium heat for 10 minutes before you knead the dough. Turn it off. Place the bowl with the dough in it in the turned-off oven with the door closed and let it rise there.) To test whether the dough has risen enough, poke two fingers into the dough. If the indentations remain, the dough is ready.

5 ▲ Punch the dough down with your fist to release the air. Knead for 1–2 minutes.

6 Divide the dough, if you wish: for 2 medium pizzas, divide into 2 balls, and for 4 individual pizzas, divide into 4 balls. Pat the ball of dough out into a flat circle on a lightly floured surface. With a rolling pin, roll it out to a thickness of about $\frac{3}{8}$–$\frac{1}{4}$in. If you are using a pizza pan, roll the dough out about $\frac{1}{4}$in larger than the size of the pan to allow for the rim of the crust.

7 ▲ Place in the lightly oiled pan, folding the extra dough under to make a thicker rim around the edge. If you are baking the pizza without a round pan, press some of the dough from the center of the circle towards the edge, to make a thicker rim. Place it on a lightly oiled flat cookie sheet. The dough is now ready for filling.

~ COOK'S TIP ~

This basic dough can be used for other recipes in this book, such as Focaccia, Breadsticks, Calzone and Sicilian Closed Pizza. The dough may be frozen at the end of step 7, and thawed before filling.

Wholewheat Pizza Dough

Pizza dough can also be made with wholewheat flour, although it is easier to handle and more elastic if a proportion of white flour is used. This dough can be used in any recipe calling for Basic Pizza Dough.

Ingredients

2¹/₂ tbsp fresh bread yeast or
   1¹/₂ tbsp active dried yeast
1 cup lukewarm water
pinch of sugar
2 tbsp olive oil
1 tsp salt
1¹/₄ cups plain white bread flour
2 cups stoneground whole wheat
   bread flour
**serves 4 as a main course or 8
as an appetizer**

1 Warm a medium mixing bowl by swirling some hot water in it. Drain. Place the yeast in the bowl, and pour on the warm water. Stir in the sugar, mix with a fork, and allow to stand until the yeast has dispersed and starts to foam, 5–10 minutes.

2 ▲ Use a wooden spoon to mix in the olive oil and the salt, and the white flour. Mix in about half of the wholewheat flour, stirring with the spoon until the dough forms a mass and begins to pull away from the sides of the bowl.

3 ▲ Proceed with steps 3–7 as for Basic Pizza Dough, punching down the risen dough, and kneading until ready to roll out and place in a pan.

To Make the Dough in a Food Processor

1 ▲ Have all the ingredients ready and measured out. In a small pitcher or bowl add the yeast to the warm water. Stir in the sugar, and allow to stand until the yeast has dissolved, 5–10 minutes.

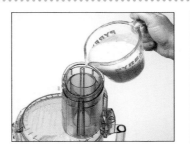

2 ▲ Fit the food processor with the metal blades. Place the salt and three-quarters of the flour in the bowl of the food processor. Turn it on, and pour in the yeast mixture and olive oil through the opening at the top. Continue processing until the dough forms one or two balls. Turn the machine off, open it, and touch the dough. If it still feels sticky, add a little more flour, and process again until it is incorporated.

3 ▲ Remove the dough from the processor. Knead it for about 2–3 minutes on a surface dusted with the remaining flour. Form the dough into a ball, and proceed with Step 4 of Basic Pizza Dough.

Cheese and Tomato Pizza

Pizza alla Margherita

The Margherita is named after the nineteenth-century Queen of Italy, and is one of the most popular of all pizzas.

Ingredients

1lb peeled plum tomatoes, fresh or canned, weighed whole, without extra juice
1 recipe Basic Pizza Dough, rolled out
1³/₄ cups mozzarella cheese, cut into small dice
10–12 leaves fresh basil, torn
4 tbsp freshly grated Parmesan cheese (optional)
salt and freshly ground black pepper
3 tbsp olive oil
serves 4

1 Preheat the oven to 475°F. Strain the tomatoes through the medium holes of a food mill placed over a bowl, scraping in all the pulp.

2 ▲ Spread the puréed tomatoes onto the prepared pizza dough, leaving the rim uncovered.

3 ▲ Sprinkle evenly with the mozzarella. Dot with basil. Sprinkle with Parmesan if using, salt and pepper and olive oil. Immediately place the pizzas in the oven. Bake for about 15–20 minutes, or until the crust is golden brown and the cheeses have melted and are bubbling.

Pizza with Mozzarella and Anchovies

Pizza alla napoletana

If you ask for a pizza in the Neapolitan manner anywhere in Italy other than in Naples, you will be given this pizza with anchovies.

Ingredients

1lb peeled plum tomatoes, fresh or canned, weighed whole, without extra juice
1 recipe Basic Pizza Dough, rolled out
3 tbsp anchovy fillets in oil, drained and cut into pieces
1³/₄ cups mozzarella cheese, cut into small dice
1 tsp fresh or dried oregano leaves
salt and freshly ground black pepper
3 tbsp olive oil
serves 4

1 Preheat the oven to 475°F. Strain the tomatoes through the medium holes of a food mill placed over a bowl, scraping in all the pulp.

2 ▲ Spread the puréed tomatoes on the pizza dough, leaving the rim uncovered. Dot with the anchovy pieces and the mozzarella.

3 ▲ Sprinkle with oregano, salt and pepper, and olive oil. Immediately place the pizza in the oven. Bake for about 15–20 minutes, or until the crust is golden brown and the cheese is bubbling.

Four Seasons Pizza

Pizza quattro stagioni

The topping on this pizza is divided into four quarters, one for each "season". You may replace the suggested ingredients with any other seasonal flavors.

Ingredients
1lb peeled plum tomatoes, fresh or canned, weighed whole, without extra juice
5 tbsp olive oil
1 cup mushrooms, thinly sliced
1 garlic clove, finely chopped
1 recipe Basic Pizza Dough, rolled out
1³/₄ cups mozzarella cheese, cut into small dice
4 thin slices of ham, cut into 2in squares
32 black olives, pitted and halved
8 artichoke hearts marinated in oil, drained and cut in half
1 tsp fresh or dried oregano leaves
salt and freshly ground black pepper
serves 4

1 ▲ Preheat the oven to 475°F. Strain the tomatoes through the medium holes of a food mill placed over a bowl, scraping in all the pulp.

2 Heat 2 tbsp of the oil in a frying pan and lightly sauté the mushrooms. Stir in the garlic, remove from the heat and set aside.

3 ▲ Spread the puréed tomato on the prepared pizza dough, leaving the rim uncovered. Sprinkle evenly with the mozzarella. Spread mushrooms over one-quarter of each pizza.

4 ▲ Arrange the ham on another quarter, and the olives and artichoke hearts on the two remaining quarters. Sprinkle with oregano, salt and pepper, and the remaining olive oil. Immediately place the pizza in the oven. Bake for about 15–20 minutes, or until the crust is golden brown and the topping is bubbling.

Pizza with Fresh Vegetables

Pizza all'ortolana

This pizza can be made with any combination of fresh vegetables. Most will benefit from being blanched or sautéed before being baked on the pizza.

Ingredients

14oz peeled plum tomatoes, fresh or canned, weighed whole, without extra juice
2 medium broccoli heads
8oz fresh asparagus
3 small zucchini
5 tbsp olive oil
$1/3$ cup shelled peas, fresh or frozen
4 scallions, sliced
1 recipe Basic Pizza Dough, rolled out
$1/2$ cup mozzarella cheese, cut into small dice
10 leaves fresh basil, torn
2 garlic cloves, finely chopped
salt and freshly ground black pepper
serves 4

4 ▲ Spread the puréed tomatoes onto the pizza dough, leaving the rim uncovered. Add the other vegetables, spreading them evenly over the tomatoes.

5 ▲ Sprinkle with the mozzarella, basil, garlic, salt and pepper, and remaining olive oil. Immediately place the pizza in the oven. Bake for about 20 minutes, or until the crust is golden brown and the cheese has melted.

1 Preheat the oven to 475°F. Strain the tomatoes through the medium holes of a food mill placed over a bowl, scraping in all the pulp.

2 ▲ Peel the broccoli stems and the lower parts of the asparagus, and blanch with the zucchini in a large pan of boiling water for 4–5 minutes. Drain. Cut into bite-size pieces.

3 Heat 2 tbsp of the olive oil in a small pan. Stir in the peas and scallions, and cook for 5–6 minutes, stirring often. Remove from the heat.

Pizza with Sausage

Pizza con salsicce

Use sausages with a high meat content for this topping.

Ingredients
1lb peeled plum tomatoes, fresh or
   canned, weighed whole, without
   extra juice
1 recipe Basic Pizza Dough, rolled out
$1^3/_4$ cups mozzarella cheese, cut into
   small dice
$1^1/_2$ cups sausage meat, removed
   from the casings and crumbled
1 tsp oregano leaves, fresh or dried
salt and freshly ground black pepper
3 tbsp olive oil
serves 4

1 Preheat the oven to 475°F. Strain the
tomatoes through the medium holes of
a food mill placed over a bowl, scraping
in all the pulp.

2 ▲ Spread some of the puréed
tomatoes on the prepared pizza
dough, leaving the rim uncovered.
Sprinkle evenly with the mozzarella.
Add the sausage meat in small lumps.

3 ▲ Sprinkle with oregano, salt and
pepper, and olive oil. Immediately
place the pizza in the preheated oven.
Bake for about 15–20 minutes, or until
the crust is golden brown and the
cheese is bubbling.

Pizza with Four Cheeses

Pizza con quattro formaggi

Any combination of cheeses can be used, but choose cheeses which are different in character.

Ingredients
1 recipe Basic Pizza Dough,
   rolled out
$1/_2$ cup Gorgonzola or other blue
   cheese, thinly sliced
$1/_2$ cup mozzarella cheese, finely
   diced
$1/_2$ cup goat's cheese, thinly sliced
$1/_2$ cup sharp Cheddar cheese,
   coarsely grated
1 tbsp fresh oregano leaves, or
   3 tbsp chopped fresh parsley
salt and freshly ground black pepper
3 tbsp olive oil
serves 4

1 Preheat the oven to 475°F. Arrange
the Gorgonzola on one quarter of the
pizza and the mozzarella on another,
leaving the edge free.

2 ▲ Arrange the goat's and Cheddar
cheeses on the remaining two
quarters.

~ VARIATION ~

For an unusual taste, substitute
3oz sliced smoked cheese for one
of the cheeses.

3 ▲ Sprinkle with the herbs, salt and
pepper, and olive oil. Immediately
place the pizza in the oven. Bake for
about 15–20 minutes, or until the
crust is golden brown and the cheeses
are bubbling.

Mediterranean Pizza

Pizza mediterranea

The combination of favorite Mediterranean ingredients makes a delicious modern pizza topping.

Ingredients
12 sun-dried tomatoes, dry or in oil, drained
1³/₄ cups goat's cheese, sliced as thinly as possible
1 recipe Basic Pizza Dough, rolled out
2 tbsp capers in brine or salt, rinsed
10 leaves fresh basil
salt and freshly ground black pepper
3 tbsp olive oil
serves 4

1 Preheat the oven to 475°F for at least 20 minutes before baking the pizza. Place the tomatoes in a small bowl, cover with hot water, and leave to soak for 15 minutes. Drain and cut into thin slices. (The soaking water may be saved to add to a pasta sauce or soup.)

2 ▲ Arrange the cheese on the prepared pizza dough, leaving the rim uncovered. Dot the pizza with the tomato slices.

3 ▲ Sprinkle with the capers and basil leaves. Allow to rise for 10 minutes before baking.

4 Sprinkle with salt, pepper and olive oil. Place the pizza in the oven. Bake for about 15–20 minutes, or until the crust is golden brown.

Pizza with Onions and Olives

Pizza con cipolle e olive

Onions cooked slowly to release their sweetness contrast with the salty bitterness of the olives.

Ingredients
6 tbsp olive oil
4 medium onions, finely sliced
salt and freshly ground black pepper
1 recipe Basic Pizza Dough, rolled out
1³/₄ cups mozzarella cheese, cut into small dice
32 black olives, pitted and halved
3 tbsp chopped fresh parsley
serves 4

1 Preheat the oven to 475°F. Heat half the olive oil in a large frying pan. Add the sliced onions, and cook over low heat until soft, translucent, and just beginning to turn brown, 12–15 minutes. Season with salt and pepper, and remove from the heat.

2 ▲ Spread the onions over the prepared pizza dough in an even layer, leaving the rim uncovered. Sprinkle with the mozzarella.

3 ▲ Dot with the olives. Sprinkle with parsley and the remaining olive oil. Immediately place the pizza in the oven. Bake for about 15–20 minutes, or until the crust is golden brown and the cheese is bubbling.

Pizza with Seafood

Pizza con frutti di mare

Any combination of shellfish or other seafood can be used as a pizza topping.

Ingredients

1lb peeled plum tomatoes, fresh or
　canned, weighed whole, without
　extra juice
6oz small squid
8oz fresh mussels
1 recipe Basic Pizza Dough, rolled out
6oz shrimp, raw or cooked, peeled
　and deveined
2 garlic cloves, finely chopped
3 tbsp chopped fresh parsley
salt and freshly ground black pepper
3 tbsp olive oil
serves 4

1 ▲ Preheat the oven to 475°F. Strain the tomatoes through the medium holes of a food mill placed over a bowl, scraping in all the pulp.

2 ▲ Working near the sink, clean the squid by first peeling off the thin skin from the body section. Rinse well. Pull the head and tentacles away from the sac section. Some of the intestines will come away with the head.

3 ▲ Remove and discard the translucent quill and any remaining insides from the sac. Sever the tentacles from the head, and discard the head and intestines. Remove the small hard beak from the base of the tentacles. Rinse the sac and tentacles under running water. Drain. Slice the sacs into rings ¹/₄ in thick.

4 ▲ Scrape any barnacles off the mussels, and scrub well with a stiff brush. Rinse in several changes of cold water. Place the mussels in a pan with 1 cup water and heat, covered, until they open. Lift them out with a slotted spoon, and remove to a side dish. (Discard any that do not open.) Break off the empty half shells, and discard.

5 ▲ Spread the puréed tomatoes on the prepared pizza dough, leaving the rim uncovered. Dot evenly with the shrimp and squid rings and tentacles. Sprinkle with the garlic, parsley, salt and pepper, and olive oil. Immediately place the pizza in the oven. Bake for about 8 minutes.

6 ▲ Remove from the oven, and add the mussels in the half shells. Return to the oven and bake for 7–10 minutes more, or until the crust is golden.

~ VARIATION ~

Fresh clams may be added: scrub them well under cold running water. Cook them in the same way as the mussels. Discard any that do not open. Break off the empty half shells, and discard. Add to the pizza after 8 minutes of baking.

Pizza with Herbs

Pizza in bianco con erbe aromatiche

This simple topping of mixed fresh herbs, olive oil and salt makes a delicious hot pizza which can also be eaten as a bread. In Italy it is often served in pizzerias as an appetizer.

Ingredients
1 recipe Basic Pizza Dough, rolled out
4 tbsp chopped mixed fresh herbs,
    such as thyme, rosemary, basil,
    parsley or sage
salt, to taste
6 tbsp extra-virgin olive oil
serves 4

1 ▲ Preheat the oven to 475°F. Sprinkle the prepared dough with the herbs, and salt.

2 ▲ Sprinkle with olive oil. Immediately place the pizza in the oven. Bake for about 20 minutes, or until the crust is golden brown.

Sicilian Closed Pizza

Sfinciuni

These can be stuffed with any pizza topping.

Ingredients
1 recipe Basic Pizza Dough, risen once
2 tbsp coarse cornmeal
3 hard-boiled eggs, peeled and sliced
$^1/_4$ cup anchovy fillets, drained
    and chopped
12 olives, pitted and halved
8 leaves fresh basil, torn into pieces
6 medium tomatoes, peeled, seeded
    and diced
2 garlic cloves, finely chopped
freshly ground black pepper
$1^1/_2$ cups grated caciocavallo or
    Pecorino cheese
olive oil, for brushing
serves 4–6

1 Preheat the oven to 450°F. Punch the dough and knead lightly for 3–4 minutes. Divide the dough into two pieces, one slightly larger than the other. Lightly oil a round pizza pan 15 inches in diameter. Sprinkle with the cornmeal. Roll or press the larger piece of dough into a round slightly bigger than the pan.

2 ▲ Transfer to the pan, bringing the dough up the sides of the pan to the rim. Fill the pie by placing the sliced eggs in the bottom in a layer, leaving the edges of the dough uncovered. Dot with the anchovies, olives and basil.

3 Spread the diced tomatoes over the other ingredients. Sprinkle with garlic and pepper. Top with the grated cheese.

4 ▲ Roll or press the other piece of dough into a circle the same size as the pan. Place it over the filling. Roll the edge of the bottom dough over it, and crimp together to make a border.

5 Brush the top and edges of the pie with olive oil. Bake for 30–40 minutes, or until the top is golden brown. Allow to stand for 5–8 minutes before slicing into wedges.

Calzones

Calzone

A calzone is a pizza folded over to enclose its filling. It can be made large or small, and stuffed with any of the flat pizza fillings. Calzones can be eaten hot or cold.

Ingredients

1 recipe Basic Pizza Dough, risen once
1¹⁄₂ cups ricotta cheese
³⁄₄ cup ham, cut into small dice
6 medium tomatoes, peeled, seeded and diced
8 leaves fresh basil, torn into pieces
1 cup mozzarella cheese, cut into small dice
4 tbsp freshly grated Parmesan or Romano cheese
salt and freshly ground black pepper
olive oil, for brushing
serves 4

3 ▲ Combine all the filling ingredients in a bowl, and mix well. Season with salt and pepper.

5 ▲ Fold the other half of the circle over. Crimp the edges of the dough together with your fingers to seal.

1 ▲ Preheat the oven to 475°F. Punch the dough down and knead it lightly on a floured surface. Divide the dough into 4 balls.

4 ▲ Divide the filling between the 4 circles of dough, placing it on half of each circle and allowing a border of 1 in all around.

6 ▲ Place the calzones on lightly oiled cookie sheets. Brush the tops lightly with olive oil. Bake in the preheated oven for about 15–20 minutes, or until the tops are golden brown and the dough is puffed.

2 ▲ Roll each ball out into a flat circle about ¹⁄₄ inch thick.

> ~ COOK'S TIP ~
>
> The calzone is a speciality of Naples. Calzone means "trouser leg" in Italian. This pizza was so named because it resembled a leg of the baggy trousers worn by Neapolitan men in the 18th and 19th centuries. Calzones are now usually round but were traditionally made from rectangular pieces of dough folded over a long central filling.

Butternut Squash and Sage Pizza   *Pizza con zucca e salvia*

The combination of the sweet butternut squash, sage and sharp goat cheese works

wonderfully on this pizza. Pumpkin and winter squashes are popular in northern Italy.

Ingredients

1 tbsp butter
2 tbsp olive oil
2 shallots, finely chopped
1 butternut squash, peeled, seeded and
    cubed, about 1 pound
    prepared weight
16 sage leaves
1 recipe risen Pizza Dough
1 recipe Tomato Sauce
1 cup mozzarella cheese, sliced
½ cup firm goat cheese
salt and freshly ground black pepper

serves 4

3 ▲ Transfer each round to a baking sheet and spread with the tomato sauce, leaving a ½-in border all around. Spoon the squash and shallot mixture over the crust.

4 ▲ Arrange the slices of mozzarella over the squash mixture and crumble the goat cheese on top. Scatter the remaining sage leaves on top and season with plenty of salt and pepper. Bake for 15–20 minutes, until the cheese has melted and the crust on each pizza is golden.

1 ▲ Preheat the oven to 400°F. Oil four baking sheets. Put the butter and oil in a roasting pan and heat in the oven for a few minutes. Add the shallots, squash and half the sage leaves. Toss to coat. Roast for 15–20 minutes, until tender.

2 ▲ Raise the oven temperature to 425°F. Divide the pizza dough into four equal pieces and roll out each piece on a lightly floured surface to a 10-in round.

Ricotta and Fontina Pizza

Pizza con ricotta e fontina

The flavor of the earthy mixed mushrooms is delicious with the creamy cheeses.

Ingredients

For the pizza dough

¹/₂ tsp active dried yeast
pinch of sugar
4 cups flour
1 tsp salt
2 tbsp olive oil

For the tomato sauce

1 can (14 oz) chopped tomatoes
²/₃ cup passata
1 large garlic clove, finely chopped
1 tsp dried oregano
1 bay leaf
2 tsp malt vinegar
salt and freshly ground black pepper

For the topping

2 tbsp olive oil
1 garlic clove, finely chopped
4 cups mixed mushrooms (chestnut, flat
    or button), sliced
2 tbsp chopped fresh oregano, plus
    whole leaves, to garnish
generous 1 cup ricotta cheese
8 oz Fontina cheese, sliced

**makes 4 10-in thin
    crust pizzas**

1 ▲ Make the dough. Put 1¹/₄ cups warm water in a measuring cup. Add the yeast and sugar and set aside for 5–10 minutes until frothy. Sift the flour and salt into a large bowl and make a well in the center. Gradually pour in the yeast mixture and the olive oil. Mix to make a smooth dough. Knead on a lightly floured surface for about 10 minutes until smooth, springy and elastic. Place the dough in a floured bowl, cover and let rise in a warm place for 1¹/₂ hours.

2 Meanwhile, make the tomato sauce. Place all the ingredients in a saucepan, cover and bring to a boil. Lower the heat, remove the lid and simmer for 20 minutes, stirring occasionally, until reduced.

3 ▲ Make the topping. Heat the oil in a frying pan. Add the garlic and mushrooms, with salt and pepper to taste. Cook, stirring, for about 5 minutes or until the mushrooms are tender and golden. Set aside.

4 ▲ Preheat the oven to 425°F. Brush four baking sheets with oil. Knead the dough for 2 minutes, then divide into four equal pieces. Roll out each piece to a 10-in round and place on a baking sheet.

5 Spoon the tomato sauce over each dough round. Brush the edge with a little olive oil. Add the mushrooms, oregano and cheese. Bake for about 15 minutes until golden brown. Scatter the oregano leaves on top.

Fried Pizza Pasties
Panzerotti

These tasty little morsels are served all over central and southern Italy as a snack food or as part of a hot antipasto. Although similar to calzone, they are fried instead of baked.

Ingredients
½ recipe Pizza Dough
½ recipe Tomato Sauce
8 oz mozzarella cheese, chopped
4 oz Italian salami, thinly sliced
handful of fresh basil leaves, roughly torn
sunflower oil, for deep frying
salt and freshly ground black pepper
serves 4

Cook's Tip
To test that the oil is ready, carefully drop a piece of bread into the oil. If it sizzles instantly, the oil is ready.

1 Preheat the oven to 400°F. Brush two baking sheets with oil. Divide the dough into 12 pieces and roll out each piece on a lightly floured surface to a 4-in round.

2 ▲ Spread the center of each round with a little of the tomato sauce, leaving a sufficient border all around for sealing the pasty, then top with a few pieces of mozzarella and salami slices. Sprinkle with salt and freshly ground black pepper and add a few fresh basil leaves to each round.

3 ▲ Brush the edges of the dough rounds with a little water, then fold over and press together to seal.

4 Heat oil to a depth of about 4 in in a heavy pan. When hot, deep-fry the pasties, a few at a time, for 8–10 minutes until golden. Drain on paper towels and serve hot.

Sicilian Pizza
Pizza alla siciliana

This robust-flavored pizza is topped with mozzarella and Pecorino cheeses.

Ingredients
1 small eggplant, cut into thin rounds
2 tbsp olive oil
½ recipe risen Pizza Dough
½ recipe Tomato Sauce
6 oz mozzarella cheese, sliced
½ cup pitted black olives
1 tbsp drained capers
¼ cup grated Pecorino cheese
salt and freshly ground black pepper
serves 2

Cook's Tip
For best results choose olives that have been marinated in extra virgin olive oil and flavored with herbs and garlic.

1 ▲ Preheat the oven to 400°F. Brush one or two baking sheets with oil. Brush the eggplant rounds with olive oil and arrange them on the baking sheet(s). Bake for 10–15 minutes, turning once, until browned and tender. Remove the eggplant slices from the baking sheet(s) and drain on paper towels.

2 Raise the oven temperature to 425°F. Roll out the pizza dough into two 10-in rounds. Transfer to baking sheets and spread with the tomato sauce.

3 ▲ Pile the eggplant slices on top of the tomato sauce and cover with the mozzarella. Dot with the black olives and capers. Sprinkle the Pecorino cheese liberally over the top, and season with plenty of salt and pepper. Bake for 15–20 minutes, until the crust on each pizza is golden.

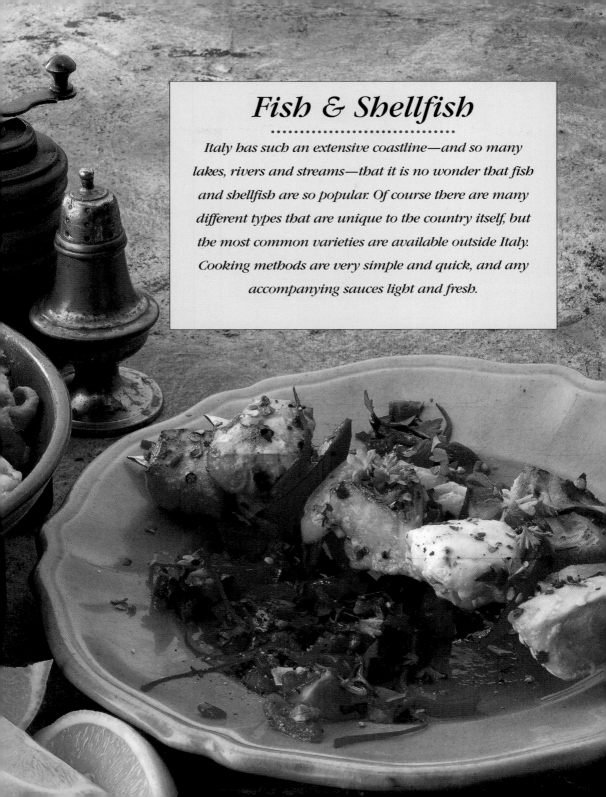

Fish & Shellfish

Italy has such an extensive coastline—and so many lakes, rivers and streams—that it is no wonder that fish and shellfish are so popular. Of course there are many different types that are unique to the country itself, but the most common varieties are available outside Italy. Cooking methods are very simple and quick, and any accompanying sauces light and fresh.

Sole with Sweet and Sour Sauce

Sfogi in saor

This Venetian dish should be prepared 1–2 days before it is to be eaten.

Ingredients
3–4 fillets of sole, about 1¼lb total,
    divided in half
4 tbsp flour
salt and freshly ground black pepper
pinch of ground cloves
6–8 tbsp olive oil
generous ¼ cup pine nuts
3 bay leaves
pinch of ground cinnamon
pinch of grated nutmeg
4 cloves
1 small onion, very finely sliced
¼ cup dry white wine
¼ cup white wine vinegar
⅓ cup golden raisins
serves 4

1 Dredge the sole fillets in the flour seasoned with salt and pepper and the ground cloves.

2 Heat 3 tbsp of the oil in a heavy frying pan or skillet. Cook the sole fillets a few at a time until golden, about 3 minutes on each side. Add more oil as necessary.

3 ▲ Remove with a slotted spatula to a large shallow serving dish. Sprinkle with the pine nuts, bay leaves, cinnamon, nutmeg and whole cloves.

4 ▲ Heat the remaining oil in a pan. Add the onion, and cook over low heat until golden. Add the wine, vinegar and golden raisins, and boil for 4–5 minutes. Pour over the fish. Cover the dish with foil, and leave in a cool place for 24–48 hours. Remove 2 hours before serving. This dish is traditionally eaten at room temperature.

Salt Cod with Parsley and Garlic

Baccalà alla bolognese

Salt cod is very popular all over Italy. For centuries it has been imported from Scandinavia.

The very salty fish must be soaked for 24 hours in water to reduce its salt content.

Ingredients
1½lb boneless and skinless salt
    cod, preferably in one piece
flour seasoned with freshly ground
    black pepper, for dredging
2 tbsp extra-virgin olive oil
3 tbsp finely chopped fresh parsley
2 garlic cloves, finely chopped
2 tbsp butter, cut into small pieces
serves 4–5

1 Cut the salt cod into 2in squares. Place them in a large bowl and cover with cold water. Allow to stand for at least 24 hours, changing the water several times.

2 ▲ Preheat the oven to 375°F. Drain the fish, shaking out the excess moisture. Remove any remaining bones or skin. Dredge lightly in the seasoned flour.

3 Spread 1 tbsp of the oil over the bottom of a baking dish large enough to hold the fish in one layer.

4 ▲ Place the fish in the dish. Combine the chopped parsley and garlic, and sprinkle evenly over the fish. Sprinkle with the remaining oil, and dot with butter. Bake for 15 minutes. Turn the fish, and bake for 15–20 minutes more, or until tender. Serve immediately, straight from the dish.

Fresh Tuna and Tomato Stew

Tonno e pomodori in umido

A deliciously simple dish that relies on good basic ingredients. For real Italian flavor serve with polenta or pasta.

Ingredients
12 baby onions, peeled
2 lb ripe tomatoes
1½ lb fresh tuna
3 tbsp olive oil
2 garlic cloves, crushed
3 tbsp chopped fresh herbs
2 bay leaves
½ tsp sugar
2 tbsp sun-dried tomato paste
⅔ cup dry white wine
salt and freshly ground black pepper
baby zucchini and fresh herbs,
    to garnish

serves 4

1 Leave the onions whole and cook in a pan of salted boiling water for 4–5 minutes until softened. Drain.

2 Plunge the tomatoes into boiling water for 30 seconds, then refresh in cold water. Peel off the skins and chop coarsely.

3 ▲ Cut the tuna into 1 in chunks. Heat the oil in a large frying or sauté pan and quickly fry the tuna until browned. Drain.

4 ▲ Add the onions, garlic, tomatoes, chopped herbs, bay leaves, sugar, tomato paste and wine and bring to a boil, breaking up the tomatoes with a wooden spoon.

5 Reduce the heat and simmer gently for 5 minutes. Return the fish to the pan and cook for another 5 minutes. Season, and serve hot, garnished with baby zucchini and fresh herbs.

Variation
Two large mackerel make a more readily available alternative to the tuna. Fillet them and cut into chunks or simply lay the whole fish on the sauce and cook, covered with a lid, until the mackerel is cooked through. Fresh sage, rosemary or oregano all go extremely well with this dish. Choose whichever you prefer, or use a mixture of two.

Red Mullet with Tomatoes

Triglie con pomodoro

Red mullet is a popular fish in Italy, and this recipe accentuates both its flavor and color.

Ingredients

4 red mullet or red snapper, about
    6–7oz each
1 lb tomatoes, peeled, or 14oz can
    plum tomatoes
4 tbsp olive oil
4 tbsp finely chopped fresh parsley
2 garlic cloves, finely chopped
salt and freshly ground black pepper
$^1/_2$ cup white wine
4 thin lemon slices, cut in half
serves 4

1 ▲ Scale and clean the fish without removing the liver. Wash and pat dry with paper towels.

2 ▲ Chop the tomatoes into small pieces. Heat the oil in a pan large enough to hold the fish in one layer. Add the parsley and garlic, and sauté for 1 minute. Stir in the tomatoes and cook over moderate heat for 15–20 minutes. Season with salt and pepper.

3 ▲ Add the fish to the tomato sauce and cook over moderate to high heat for 5 minutes. Add the wine and the lemon slices. Bring the sauce back to a boil, and cook for about 5 minutes more. Turn the fish over, and cook for 4–5 minutes more, until tender. Remove the fish to a warmed serving platter and keep warm until needed.

4 ▲ Boil the sauce for 3–4 minutes to reduce it slightly. Spoon it over the fish, and serve.

~ VARIATION ~

Small sea bass may be substituted.

Baked Cod with Garlic Mayonnaise

Merluzzo al forno

Although cod is not native to the Mediterranean, a similar species is used for this dish.

Ingredients
4 anchovy fillets
3 tbsp finely chopped fresh parsley
coarsely ground black pepper
6 tbsp olive oil
4 cod fillets, about 1$\frac{1}{2}$lb total, skinned
$\frac{1}{3}$ cup plain breadcrumbs
For the mayonnaise
2 garlic cloves, finely chopped
1 egg yolk
1 tsp Dijon mustard
$\frac{3}{4}$ cup vegetable oil
salt and freshly ground black pepper
serves 4

1 Make the mayonnaise. Mash the garlic to a paste using a pestle and mortar, then beat it with the egg yolk and mustard in a medium bowl. Add the oil, little by little, while whisking vigorously. When the mixture is thick and smooth, season with salt and pepper. Cover the bowl and keep cool.

2 ▲ Preheat the oven to 400°F. Chop the anchovy fillets very finely. Place in a small bowl with the parsley, and add pepper and 3 tbsp of the oil. Stir to a paste.

3 ▲ Place the cod fillets in one layer in an oiled baking dish. Spread the anchovy paste on the top of the cod fillets. Sprinkle with the breadcrumbs and the remaining oil. Bake for 20–25 minutes, or until the breadcrumbs are golden. Serve hot with the garlic mayonnaise.

Monkfish Medallions with Thyme

Pescatrice con timo

Monkfish has a sweet flesh that combines well with Mediterranean flavors.

Ingredients
1$\frac{1}{4}$lb monkfish fillet, preferably in one piece
3 tbsp extra-virgin olive oil
$\frac{1}{2}$ cup small black olives, pitted
1 large or 2 small tomatoes, seeded and diced
1 sprig fresh thyme, or 1 tsp dried thyme leaves
salt and freshly ground black pepper
1 tbsp very finely chopped fresh parsley, to serve
serves 4

1 Preheat the oven to 400°F. Remove the grey membrane from the monkfish, if necessary. Cut the fish into slices $\frac{1}{2}$ in thick.

2 Heat a non-stick frying pan quite hot, without oil. Sear the fish quickly on both sides. Remove to a side dish.

3 ▲ Spread 1 tbsp of the olive oil in the bottom of a shallow baking dish. Arrange the fish in one layer. Distribute the olives and diced tomato on top of the fish.

4 Sprinkle with thyme, salt and pepper, and the remaining oil. Bake for 10–12 minutes, until the fish is tender.

5 ▲ To serve, divide the medallions between 4 warmed plates. Spoon on the vegetables and any cooking juices. Sprinkle with the chopped parsley.

Broiled Salmon Steaks with Fennel

Salmone alla griglia

Fennel grows wild all over the south of Italy. Its mild aniseed flavor goes well with fish.

Ingredients
juice of 1 lemon
3 tbsp chopped fresh fennel herb, or the
    green fronds from the top of a
    fennel bulb
1 tsp fennel seeds
3 tbsp olive oil
4 salmon steaks of the same thickness,
    about 1½lb total
salt and freshly ground black pepper
lemon slices, to garnish
serves 4

1 Combine the lemon juice, chopped fennel and fennel seeds with the olive oil in a bowl. Add the salmon steaks, turning them to coat them with the marinade. Sprinkle with salt and pepper. Cover and place in the refrigerator. Allow to stand for 2 hours.

2 ▲ Preheat the broiler. Arrange the fish in one layer on a broiling pan or cookie sheet. Broil about 4 in from the heat source for 3–4 minutes.

3 ▲ Turn. Spoon on the remaining marinade and broil for 3–4 minutes on the other side, or until the edges begin to brown. Serve hot, garnished with lemon slices.

Octopus with Lemon and Garlic

Polpo con limone e aglio

Octopus is widely appreciated in Italy. Dressed with oil and lemon it is delicious.

Ingredients
2lb octopus (young and small
    if possible)
2 tbsp chopped fresh parsley
2 garlic cloves, very finely chopped
4 tbsp extra-virgin olive oil
3 tbsp fresh lemon juice
freshly ground black pepper
serves 3–4

1 Beat the octopus repeatedly against a strong table or marble surface. Clean, removing the eyes, beak and sacs. (Or ask your fishmonger to do this.) Wash carefully under cold running water.

2 Place the octopus in a large pan with cold water to cover. Bring to a boil, cover the pan tightly, and simmer gently until tender, 45 minutes for small octopus and up to 2 hours for larger ones. Skim off any scum which rises to the surface.

3 ▲ Remove from the pan, and allow to cool slightly. Rub the octopus lightly with a clean cloth to remove any loose dark skin. Slice the warm octopus into rounds ¾ inch wide.

4 ▲ Place the octopus pieces in a serving bowl. Toss with the parsley, garlic, olive oil and lemon juice. Sprinkle with pepper. Mix well. Allow to stand for at least 20 minutes before serving at room temperature.

~ COOK'S TIP ~

In Italy, a wine cork is placed in the pan with the octopus to reduce the scum.

Roast Sea Bass

Branzino al forno

Sea bass has meaty flesh. It is an expensive fish, best cooked as simply as possible. Avoid elaborate sauces, which would mask its delicate flavor.

Ingredients

1 fennel bulb with fronds, about 10 oz
2 lemons
$^1\!/_2$ cup olive oil
1 small red onion, diced
2 sea bass, about 1$^1\!/_4$ lb each, cleaned
  with heads left on
$^1\!/_2$ cup dry white wine
salt and freshly ground black pepper
lemon slices, to garnish

serves 4

1 ▲ Preheat the oven to 375°F. Cut the fronds off the top of the fennel and reserve for the garnish. Cut the fennel bulb lengthwise into thin wedges, then into dice. Cut one half lemon into four slices. Squeeze the juice from the remaining lemon half and the other lemon.

2 ▲ Heat 2 tbsp of the oil in a frying pan, add the diced fennel and onion and cook gently, stirring frequently, for about 5 minutes, until softened. Remove from the heat.

3 ▲ Make three diagonal slashes on both sides of each sea bass with a sharp knife. Brush a roasting pan generously with oil, add the fish and tuck two lemon slices in each cavity. Scatter the softened fennel and onion over the fish.

Cook's Tip

Farmed or wild sea bass are available year round from the fishmonger. They are expensive, but well worth buying for a special main course. Sizes vary from the ones used here, which are a very good size for two servings, to 3–4$^1\!/_2$ lb, which take up to 50 minutes to cook.

4 ▲ Whisk the remaining oil, the lemon juice and salt and pepper to taste and pour over the fish. Cover with foil and roast for 30 minutes or until the flesh flakes, removing the foil for the last 10 minutes. Discard the lemon slices, transfer the fish to a heated serving platter and keep hot.

5 Put the roasting pan on top of the stove. Add the wine and stir over medium heat to incorporate all the pan juices. Bring to a boil, then spoon the juices over the fish. Garnish with the reserved fennel fronds and lemon slices and serve immediately.

Stuffed Swordfish Rolls

Involtini di pesce spada

This is a very tasty dish, with strong flavors from the tomato, olive and caper sauce—and

from the salty Pecorino cheese. If desired, substitute Parmesan cheese, which is milder.

Ingredients

2 tbsp olive oil
1 small onion, finely chopped
1 celery stalk, finely chopped
1 lb ripe Italian plum
   tomatoes, chopped
4 oz pitted green olives, half roughly
   chopped, half left whole
3 tbsp drained bottled capers
4 large swordfish steaks, each about
   ¹/₂ inch thick and 4 ounces in weight
1 egg
²/₃ cup grated Pecorino cheese
¹/₂ cup fresh white bread crumbs
salt and freshly ground black pepper
sprigs of fresh parsley, to garnish
serves 4

Cook's Tip

This dish is not for the inexperienced
cook because the pounding, stuffing
and rolling of the fish is quite tricky.
If you prefer, you can omit the
stuffing and simply cook the
swordfish steaks in the sauce.

1 ▲ Heat the oil in a large heavy
frying pan. Add the onion and celery
and cook gently for about 3 minutes,
stirring frequently. Stir in the
tomatoes, olives and capers, with salt
and pepper to taste. Bring to a boil,
then lower the heat, cover and
simmer for about 15 minutes. Stir
occasionally and add a little water if
the sauce becomes too thick.

2 Remove the fish skin and place
each steak between two sheets of
plastic wrap. Pound lightly with a
rolling pin until each steak is
reduced to about ¹/₄ in thick.

3 ▲ Beat the egg in a bowl and add
the cheese, bread crumbs and a few
spoonfuls of the sauce. Stir well to
mix to a moist stuffing. Spread one-
quarter of the stuffing over each
swordfish steak, then roll up into a
sausage shape. Secure with wooden
toothpicks.

4 ▲ Add the rolls to the sauce in the
pan and bring to a boil. Lower the
heat, cover and simmer for about
30 minutes, turning once. Add a little
water as the sauce reduces.

5 Remove the rolls from the sauce
and discard the toothpicks. Place on
warmed dinner plates and spoon the
sauce over and around. Garnish with
the parsley and serve hot.

Pan-fried Sole with Lemon

Sogliole al limone

The delicate flavor and texture of sole is brought out in this simple, classic recipe. Lemon sole

is used here because it is easier to obtain—and less expensive—than Dover sole.

Ingredients

2–3 tbsp flour
4 lemon sole fillets
3 tbsp olive oil
4 tbsp butter
¼ cup lemon juice
2 tbsp rinsed bottled capers
salt and freshly ground black pepper
fresh flat-leaf parsley and lemon wedges,
    to garnish
serves 2

Cook's Tip

It is important to cook the pan juices
to the right color after removing the
fish. Too pale, and they will taste
insipid, too dark, and they may taste
bitter. Take great care not to be
distracted at this point so that you
can watch the color of the juices
change to a golden brown.

1 ▲ Season the flour with salt and
black pepper. Coat the sole fillets
evenly on both sides. Heat the oil
with half the butter in a large shallow
pan until foaming. Add two sole
fillets and fry over medium heat for
2–3 minutes on each side.

2 Lift out the sole fillets with a
spatula and place on a warmed
serving platter. Keep hot. Fry the
remaining sole fillets.

3 ▲ Remove the pan from the heat
and add the lemon juice and
remaining butter. Return the pan to
high heat and stir vigorously until the
pan juices are sizzling and beginning
to turn golden brown. Remove from
the heat and stir in the capers.

4 Pour the pan juices over the sole,
sprinkle with salt and pepper to taste
and garnish with the parsley. Add the
lemon wedges and serve immediately.

Three-color Fish Kebabs
Spiedini tricolori

Don't let the fish marinate for more than an hour. The lemon juice will start to break down the fibers of the fish after this time and it will be difficult not to overcook it.

Ingredients
$^1/_2$ cup olive oil
finely grated rind and juice of
    1 large lemon
1 tsp crushed chili flakes
12 oz monkfish fillet, cubed
12 oz swordfish fillet, cubed
12 oz thick salmon fillet or
    steak, cubed
2 red, yellow or orange bell peppers,
    cored, seeded and cut into squares
2 tbsp finely chopped fresh
    flat-leaf parsley
salt and freshly ground black pepper

For the sweet tomato and chili salsa
8 oz ripe tomatoes, finely chopped
1 garlic clove, crushed
1 fresh red chili, seeded and chopped
3 tbsp extra virgin olive oil
1 tbsp lemon juice
1 tbsp finely chopped fresh
    flat-leaf parsley
pinch of sugar
serves 4

1 ▲ Put the oil in a shallow glass or china bowl and add the lemon rind and juice, the chili flakes and pepper to taste. Whisk to combine, then add the fish chunks. Turn to coat evenly.

2 Add the pepper squares, stir, then cover and marinate in a cool place for 1 hour, turning occasionally.

Variation
Use tuna instead of swordfish. It has a similar meaty texture.

3 ▲ Thread the fish and peppers onto eight oiled metal skewers, reserving the marinade. Barbecue or grill the skewered fish for 5–8 minutes, turning once.

4 Meanwhile, make the salsa by mixing all the ingredients in a bowl, and seasoning to taste with salt and pepper. Heat the reserved marinade in a small pan, remove from the heat and stir in the parsley, with salt and pepper to taste. Serve the kebabs hot, with the marinade spooned over, accompanied by the salsa.

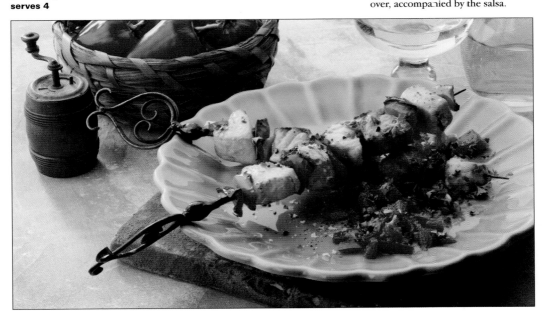

Seafood Stew

Zuppa di pesce

"Soups" – really stews – of mixed fish and shellfish are specialities of the Mediterranean.

Ingredients

3 tbsp olive oil
1 medium onion, sliced
1 carrot, sliced
$\frac{1}{2}$ stalk celery, sliced
2 garlic cloves, chopped
14oz can plum tomatoes, chopped,
  with their juice
8oz fresh shrimp, peeled and deveined
  (reserve the shells)
1lb white fish bones and heads,
  gills removed
1 bay leaf
1 sprig fresh thyme, or $\frac{1}{4}$ tsp dried
  thyme leaves
a few peppercorns
salt and freshly ground black pepper
$1\frac{1}{2}$lb fresh mussels, in their shells,
  scrubbed and rinsed
1 lb fresh small clams, in their shells,
  scrubbed and rinsed
1 cup white wine
2 lb mixed fish fillets, such as cod, monkfish, red snapper or hake, bones
  removed and cut into chunks
3 tbsp finely chopped fresh parsley
rounds of French bread, toasted, to serve
serves 6–8

2 ▲ Place the shrimp shells in a large pan with the fish bones and heads. Add the herbs and peppercorns, and pour in 3 cups of water. Bring to a boil, reduce the heat, and simmer for 25 minutes, skimming off any scum that rises to the surface. Strain and pour into a pan with the tomato sauce. Season to taste.

3 Place the mussels and clams in a pan with the wine. Cover, and steam until all the shells have opened. (Discard any that do not open.)

4 Lift the clams and mussels out and set aside. Filter the cooking liquid through a layer of paper towel and add it to the stock and tomato sauce. Check the seasoning.

5 ▲ Bring the sauce to a boil. Add the fish, and boil for 5 minutes. Add the shrimp and boil for 3–4 minutes. Stir in the mussels and clams and cook for 2–3 minutes more. Transfer the stew to a warmed casserole. Sprinkle with parsley, and serve with the toasted rounds of French bread.

1 ▲ Heat the olive oil in a medium pan. Add the sliced onion, and cook slowly until soft. Stir in the carrot and celery, and cook gently for 5 minutes more. Add the chopped garlic, the tomatoes and their juice, and 1 cup of water. Cook over moderate heat until the vegetables are soft, about 15 minutes. Purée in a food processor or pass through a food mill, and set aside.

Trout Baked in Paper with Olives

Trota in cartoccio con olive

Baking fish in paper packets keeps in all the flavor and moisture.

Ingredients

4 medium trout, about 10 oz each, gutted
5 tbsp olive oil
4 bay leaves
salt and freshly ground black pepper
4 slices pancetta or bacon
4 tbsp chopped shallots
4 tbsp chopped fresh parsley
$1/2$ cup dry white wine
24 green olives, pitted
serves 4

1 ▲ Preheat the oven to 400°F. Wash the trout well in cold running water. Drain. Pat dry with paper towels.

2 ▲ Lightly brush oil onto 4 pieces of parchment paper each large enough to enclose one fish. Lay one fish on each piece of oiled paper. Place a bay leaf in each cavity, and sprinkle with salt and pepper.

3 ▲ Wrap a slice of pancetta or bacon around each fish. Sprinkle with 1 tbsp each of chopped shallots and parsley. Drizzle each fish with 1 tbsp of oil and 2 tbsp of white wine. Add 6 olives to each packet.

4 ▲ Close the paper loosely around the fish, rolling the edges together to seal them completely. Bake for 25 minutes. Place each packet on an individual plate and open at the table.

Stuffed Squid

Calamari ripieni

Squid are popular in all the coastal regions of Italy. They are very tender and easy to cook.

Ingredients
2lb fresh squid (about 16 medium)
juice of $\frac{1}{2}$ lemon
2 anchovy fillets, chopped
2 garlic cloves, finely chopped
3 medium tomatoes, peeled, seeded
 and finely chopped
2 tbsp chopped fresh parsley
$\frac{1}{2}$ cup plain breadcrumbs
1 egg
salt and freshly ground black pepper
2 tbsp olive oil
$\frac{1}{2}$ cup dry white wine
few sprigs fresh parsley, to garnish
serves 4

1 Working near the sink, clean the
squid by first peeling off the thin skin
from the body section. Rinse well. Pull
the head and tentacles away from the
body sac. Some of the intestines will
come away with the head. Remove
and discard the translucent quill and
any remaining insides from the sac.
Sever the tentacles from the head.
Discard the head and intestines.

2 Remove and discard the small hard
beak from the base of the tentacles.
Place the tentacles in a bowl of water
with the lemon juice. Rinse the sacs
well under cold running water. Pat the
insides dry with paper towels.

3 ▲ Preheat the oven to 350°F. Drain
the tentacles. Chop them coarsely and
place in a mixing bowl. Stir in the next
6 ingredients and season. Use this
mixture to loosely stuff the squid sacs.
Close the opening to the sacs with
wooden toothpicks.

4 ▲ Oil a shallow baking dish large
enough to accommodate the squid in
one layer. Arrange the squid sacs in
the dish. Pour over the oil and wine.
Bake uncovered for 35–45 minutes, or
until tender. Remove the toothpicks
and serve garnished with parsley.

~ COOK'S TIP ~

Do not overstuff the squid sacs
or they may burst during cooking.

Deep-fried Shrimp and Squid

Fritto misto

The Italian name of this recipe means "mixed fry". Any mixture of seafood can be used.

Ingredients
vegetable oil, for deep-frying
$1\frac{1}{4}$lb medium-sized fresh shrimp,
 shelled and deveined
$1\frac{1}{4}$lb squid (about 12 medium),
 cleaned, cut into bite-size pieces
1 cup flour
lemon wedges, to serve
For the batter
2 egg whites
2 tbsp olive oil
1 tbsp white wine vinegar
scant 1 cup flour
2 tsp baking soda
$\frac{1}{3}$ cup cornstarch
salt and freshly ground black pepper
1 cup water
serves 6

1 Make the batter in a large bowl by
beating the egg whites, olive oil and
vinegar together lightly with a wire
whisk. Beat in the dry ingredients, and
whisk until well blended. Beat in the
water, a little at a time. Cover the
bowl, and allow to stand 15 minutes.

2 Heat the oil for deep-frying until a
small piece of bread sizzles as soon as
it is dropped in (about 360°F).

3 Dredge the shrimp and squid pieces
in the flour, shaking off any excess.
Dip them quickly into the batter. Fry
in small batches for about 1 minute,
stirring with a slotted spoon to keep
them from sticking to each other.

4 ▲ Remove and drain on paper
towels. Allow the oil to come back up
to the correct temperature between
batches. Sprinkle lightly with salt, and
serve hot with lemon wedges.

Pan-fried Red Mullet with Citrus

Triglie agli agrumi

Red mullet is extremely popular all over the Mediterranean. This recipe combines it with oranges and lemons, which grow in abundance in Italy.

Ingredients

4 red mullet, about 8 oz each, filleted
6 tbsp extra virgin olive oil
10 black peppercorns, crushed
2 medium oranges, one peeled and
    sliced and one squeezed
1 lemon
2 tbsp flour
1 tbsp butter
2 drained canned anchovies,
    chopped
4 tbsp shredded fresh basil or chopped
    fresh parsley
salt and freshly ground black pepper
serves 4

2 ▲ Cut the lemon in half. Remove the skin and pith from one half using a small sharp knife. Discard the pith and peel, then slice the lemon thinly. Squeeze the juice from the other lemon half.

1 ▲ Place the fish fillets in a shallow dish in a single layer. Pour over the olive oil and sprinkle with the crushed peppercorns. Lay the orange slices on top of the fish. Cover the dish, and allow to marinate in the fridge for at least 4 hours, or overnight, if you prefer.

3 ▲ Lift the fish out of the marinade, and pat dry on paper towels. Reserve the marinade and orange slices. Season the fish with salt and pepper and dust lightly with flour.

Cook's Tip

Ask to have the red mullet filleted for you. If red mullet is not available, use other small fish fillets for this dish, such as lemon sole, red bream, trout, haddock or hake.

4 Heat about 3 tbsp of the marinade in a large frying pan. Add the fish and fry for 2 minutes on each side until the fish is just cooked through. Carefully remove the fish fillets from the pan and keep them warm. Discard the marinade that is left in the pan.

5 Melt the butter in the frying pan with any of the remaining original marinade. Add the chopped anchovies to the pan and cook until they are completely softened.

6 Stir in the orange and lemon juice, then season to taste with salt and pepper. Reduce the heat and simmer until the cooking juices are slightly reduced. Stir in the shredded basil or chopped parsley.

7 To serve, pour the sauce over the fish, garnish with the reserved orange slices and lemon slices and serve immediately.

Black Pasta with Squid Sauce

Pasta nera con calamari

Tagliatelle flavored with squid ink looks amazing and tastes deliciously of the sea. You'll find it in good Italian delicatessens.

Ingredients

7 tbsp olive oil
2 shallots, chopped
3 garlic cloves, crushed
3 tbsp chopped fresh parsley
1½ lb cleaned squid, cut into rings
    and rinsed
⅔ cup dry white wine
14 oz can chopped tomatoes
½ tsp dried red pepper flakes or
    chili powder
1 lb dried squid ink tagliatelle
salt and freshly ground black pepper

serves 4

1 ▲ Heat the oil in a pan and add the shallots. Cook until pale golden, then add the garlic. When the garlic colors a little, add 2 tbsp of the parsley, stir, then add the squid and stir again. Cook for 3–4 minutes, then add the wine. Simmer for a few seconds, then add the tomatoes.

2 ▲ Add the red pepper flakes or chili powder and seasoning. Cover and simmer for 1 hour, or until the squid is tender. Add more water if necessary. Cook the tagliatelle in boiling, salted water, for 10 minutes or until *al dente*. Drain and return the tagliatelle to the pan. Add the squid sauce and mix well. Sprinkle each serving with the remaining parsley and serve immediately.

Sicilian Spaghetti with Sardines

Spaghetti alle sarde

A traditional dish from Sicily, made with the freshest ingredients and flavorings that are common to many parts of the Mediterranean.

Ingredients

12 fresh sardines, cleaned and boned
1 cup extra virgin olive oil
1 onion, chopped
¼ cup dill sprigs
½ cup pine nuts
2 tbsp raisins, soaked in water
½ cup fresh bread crumbs
1 lb dried spaghetti
flour, for dusting
salt
serves 4

1 ▲ Wash the sardines and pat dry on paper towels. Open them out flat, then cut in half lengthwise.

2 Heat 2 tbsp of the oil in a pan, add the onion and fry until golden. Add the dill and cook gently for a minute or two. Add the pine nuts and raisins and season with salt. Dry-fry the bread crumbs in a frying pan until golden. Set aside.

3 ▲ Cook the spaghetti in boiling salted water according to the instructions on the package, until *al dente*. Heat the remaining oil in a pan. Dust the sardines with flour and fry in the hot oil for 2–3 minutes. Drain on paper towels.

4 Drain the spaghetti and return to the pan. Add the onion mixture and toss well. Transfer the spaghetti mixture to a serving platter and arrange the fried sardines on top. Sprinkle with the toasted bread crumbs and serve immediately.

Broiled Fresh Sardines

Sarde alla griglia

Fresh sardines are flavorful and firm-fleshed, and quite different in taste and consistency from those canned in oil. They are excellent simply broiled and served with lemon.

Ingredients
2 lb very fresh sardines, gutted and with
  heads removed
olive oil, for brushing
salt and freshly ground black pepper
3 tbsp chopped fresh parsley, to serve
lemon wedges, to garnish
serves 4–6

1 Preheat the broiler. Rinse the sardines in water. Pat dry with paper towels.

2 ▲ Brush the sardines lightly with olive oil and sprinkle generously with salt and pepper. Place the sardines in one layer on the broiling pan. Broil for about 3–4 minutes.

3 ▲ Turn, and cook for 3–4 minutes more, or until the skin begins to brown. Serve immediately, sprinkled with parsley and garnished with lemon wedges.

Baked Aromatic Sea Bass

Branzino aromatizzato al forno

Sea bass is a firm white-fleshed fish which benefits from simple cooking. Use fresh herbs for this recipe, if possible.

Ingredients
1 large sea bass, about 3lb
4 bay leaves
few sprigs fresh thyme
8–10 sprigs fresh parsley
a few fresh fennel, tarragon
  or basil leaves
1 tbsp peppercorns
9 tbsp extra-virgin olive oil
salt and freshly ground black pepper
flour, for coating
herb sprigs or lemon wedges, to
  garnish
serves 5–6

1 Gut the fish, leaving the head on. Wash carefully in cold water. Pat dry with paper towels. Place half the herbs and peppercorns in the bottom of a shallow platter, and lay the fish on top. Arrange the remaining herbs on top of the fish and in its cavity. Sprinkle with 3 tbsp of the oil. Cover lightly with foil, and refrigerate for 2 hours.

2 ▲ Preheat the oven to 400°F. Remove and discard all the herbs from around the fish, and pat it dry with paper towels. Spread a little flour in a platter and season it with salt and pepper. Roll the fish in the flour, then shake off the excess.

3 ▲ Heat the remaining olive oil in a flameproof dish just large enough to hold the fish comfortably. When the oil is hot, add the fish, and brown it quickly on both sides. Transfer the dish to the oven, and bake for 25–40 minutes, depending on the size of the fish. The fish is cooked when the dorsal fin (in the middle of the backbone) comes out easily when pulled. Serve garnished with sprigs of herbs or lemon wedges.

Monkfish with Tomato and Olive Sauce   *Pesce alla calabrese*

This dish comes from the coast of Calabria in southern Italy. Garlic-flavored mashed potatoes

are delicious with its robust sauce.

Ingredients

1 lb fresh mussels, scrubbed
a few fresh basil sprigs
2 garlic cloves, roughly chopped
1¼ cups dry white wine
2 tbsp olive oil
1 tbsp butter
2 lb monkfish fillets, skinned and cut into
   large chunks
1 onion, finely chopped
1¼ lb jar sugocasa or passata
1 tbsp sun-dried tomato paste
1 cup pitted black olives
salt and freshly ground black pepper
extra fresh basil leaves, to garnish

serves 4

1 ▲ Put the mussels in a flameproof casserole with some basil leaves, the garlic and the wine. Cover and bring to a boil. Lower the heat and simmer for 5 minutes, shaking the pan frequently. Remove the mussels, discarding any that fail to open. Strain the cooking liquid and reserve.

2 ▲ Heat the oil and butter until foaming, add the monkfish pieces and sauté over a medium heat until they just change color. Remove.

3 ▲ Add the onion to the juices in the casserole and cook gently for about 5 minutes, stirring frequently, until softened. Add the sugocasa or passata, the reserved cooking liquid from the mussels and the tomato paste. Season with salt and pepper to taste. Bring to a boil, stirring, then lower the heat, cover and simmer for 20 minutes, stirring occasionally.

4 ▲ Pull off and discard the top shells from the mussels. Add the monkfish pieces to the tomato sauce and cook gently for 5 minutes. Gently stir in the olives and remaining basil, then taste for seasoning. Place the mussels in their half shells on top of the sauce, cover the pan and heat the mussels through for 1–2 minutes. Serve immediately, garnished with basil.

Char-grilled Squid

Grigliata di calamari

If you like your food hot, chop some—or all—of the chili seeds with the flesh. If not, cut the chilies in half lengthwise, scrape out the seeds and discard them before chopping the flesh.

Ingredients

2 whole prepared squid, with tentacles
5 tbsp olive oil
2 tbsp balsamic vinegar
2 fresh red chilies, finely chopped
1/4 cup dry white wine
salt and freshly ground black pepper
hot cooked risotto rice, to serve
sprigs of fresh parsley, to garnish
serves 2

3 ▲ Cut the squid bodies into diagonal strips. Pile the hot risotto rice in the center of heated soup plates and top with the strips of squid, arranging them in criss-cross fashion. Keep hot.

4 ▲ Add the chopped tentacles and chilies to the pan and toss over medium heat for 2 minutes. Stir in the wine, then drizzle over the squid and rice. Garnish with the parsley and serve immediately.

1 ▲ Make a lengthwise cut down the body of each squid, then open out the body flat. Score the flesh on both sides of the bodies in a criss-cross pattern with the tip of a sharp knife. Chop the tentacles. Place all the squid in a china or glass dish. Whisk the oil and vinegar in a small bowl. Add salt and pepper to taste and pour over the squid. Cover and let marinate for about 1 hour.

2 ▲ Heat a ridged cast-iron pan until hot. Add the body of one of the squid. Cook over medium heat for 2–3 minutes, pressing the squid with a spatula to keep it flat. Repeat on the other side. Cook the other squid body in the same way.

Pan-fried Shrimp in their Shells

Gamberi fritti in padella

Although expensive, this is a very quick and simple dish, ideal for an impromptu supper with friends. Serve with hot crusty Italian bread to scoop up the juices.

Ingredients
¹/₄ cup extra virgin olive oil
32 large fresh shrimp, in their shells
4 garlic cloves, finely chopped
¹/₂ cup Italian dry white vermouth
3 tbsp passata
salt and freshly ground black pepper
chopped fresh flat-leaf parsley, to garnish
crusty bread, to serve
serves 4

Cook's Tip
Shrimp in their shells are sweet and juicy, and fun to eat with your fingers. They can be quite messy though, so provide guests with finger bowls and napkins.

1 ▲ Heat the olive oil in a large heavy frying pan until just sizzling. Add the shrimp and toss over medium to high heat until their shells just begin to turn pink. Sprinkle the garlic over the shrimp in the pan and toss again, then add the vermouth and let it bubble, tossing the shrimp constantly so that they cook evenly and absorb the flavors of the garlic and vermouth.

2 ▲ Keeping the pan on the heat, add the passata, with salt and pepper to taste. Stir until the shrimp are thoroughly coated in the sauce. Serve immediately, sprinkled with the parsley and plenty of crusty bread.

Broiled Red Mullet with Rosemary

Triglie al rosmarino

This recipe is very simple—the taste of broiled red mullet is so good in itself that it needs very little to bring out the flavor.

Ingredients
4 red mullet, cleaned, about
     10 ounces each
4 garlic cloves, cut lengthwise into
     thin slivers
5 tbsp olive oil
2 tbsp balsamic vinegar
2 tsp very finely chopped fresh rosemary
     or 1 tsp dried rosemary
freshly ground black pepper
coarse sea salt, to serve
fresh rosemary sprigs and lemon
     wedges, to garnish
serves 4

Variation
Red mullet are extra delicious cooked on the barbecue. If possible, enclose them in a basket grill so that they are easy to turn over.

1 ▲ Cut three diagonal slits in both sides of each fish. Push the garlic slivers into the slits. Place the fish in a single layer in a shallow dish. Whisk the oil, vinegar and rosemary, with ground black pepper to taste.

2 ▲ Pour the marinade over the fish, cover with plastic wrap and let marinate in a cool place for 1 hour. Put the fish on the rack of a broiler pan and broil for 5–6 minutes on each side, turning once and brushing with the marinade. Serve hot, sprinkled with coarse sea salt and garnished with fresh rosemary sprigs and lemon wedges.

Baked Mussels and Potatoes

Cozze in tortiera con patate

This dish originates from Puglia, noted for its imaginative baked casseroles.

Ingredients
1¹/₂lb large mussels, in their shells
8oz potatoes, unpeeled
5 tbsp olive oil
2 garlic cloves, finely chopped
8 leaves fresh basil, torn
8oz tomatoes, peeled and thinly sliced
3 tbsp plain breadcrumbs
freshly ground black pepper
serves 2–3

1 Cut off the "beards" from the mussels. Scrub and soak in several changes of cold water. Discard any with broken shells. Place the mussels with a cupful of water in a large pan over moderate heat. As soon as they open, lift them out. Remove and discard the empty half shells, leaving the mussels in the other half. (Discard any mussels that do not open.) Strain any liquid in the pan through a layer of paper towels, and reserve.

2 ▲ Boil the potatoes. Remove them from the water when they are still quite firm and peel and slice them.

3 ▲ Preheat the oven to 350°F. Spread 2 tbsp of the olive oil in the bottom of a shallow ovenproof dish. Cover with the potato slices in one layer. Add the mussels in their half shells in one layer. Sprinkle with garlic and pieces of basil.

4 ▲ Cover with a layer of the tomato slices. Sprinkle with breadcrumbs and black pepper, the filtered mussel liquid and the remaining olive oil. Bake for about 20 minutes, or until the tomatoes are soft and the breadcrumbs golden. Serve directly from the baking dish.

Shrimp in Spicy Tomato Sauce

Gamberi alla marinara

The tomato sauce base can be sharpened up by adding hot chilies.

Ingredients

6 tbsp olive oil
1 medium onion, finely chopped
1 stalk celery, finely chopped
1 small red pepper, seeded and chopped
$^{1}/_{2}$ cup red wine
1 tbsp wine vinegar
14oz can plum tomatoes, chopped,
    with their juice
salt and freshly ground black pepper
2lb fresh shrimp, in their shells
2–3 garlic cloves, finely chopped
3 tbsp finely chopped fresh parsley
1 piece dried chili, crumbled or chopped
    (optional)
serves 6

1 In a heavy pan, heat half the olive oil. Add the chopped onion, and cook over low heat until soft. Stir in the chopped celery and pepper, and cook gently for 5 minutes more. Raise the heat to medium high, and add the wine, vinegar and tomatoes. Season with salt and pepper. Bring to a boil and cook for about 5 minutes.

2 ▲ Lower the heat, cover the pan, and simmer until the vegetables are soft, about 30 minutes. Purée the sauce through a food mill.

3 Shell the shrimp and devein them, either by using a deveiner or by making a shallow incision with a small sharp knife down the center of the back to disclose the long black vein. Remove and discard.

4 ▲ Heat the remaining oil in a clean heavy pan. Stir in the garlic, parsley and chili, if using. Cook over moderate heat, stirring constantly, until the garlic is golden. Do not let it brown. Add the tomato sauce and bring to a boil. Taste to check the seasoning.

5 ▲ Stir in the shrimp. Bring the sauce back to a boil. Reduce the heat slightly and simmer until the shrimp are pink and firm, 4–6 minutes, depending on their size. Remove from the heat and serve.

Stewed Mussels and Clams

Zuppa di cozze e vongole

Casseroles of mixed shellfish are very popular on the Ligurian coast.

Ingredients
1¹/₂lb fresh mussels, in their shells
1¹/₂lb fresh clams, in their shells
5 tbsp olive oil
3 garlic cloves, peeled and crushed
1¹/₄ cups dry white wine
5 tbsp chopped fresh parsley
freshly ground black pepper
rounds of crusty bread, toasted, to serve
serves 4

1 Cut off the "beards" from the mussels. Scrub and rinse the mussels and clams in cold water. Discard any with broken shells.

2 Heat the oil in a large pan with the garlic. As soon as this is golden, add the mussels, clams and the wine. Cover, and steam until all the shells have opened, about 5–8 minutes. (Discard any that do not open.)

3 Lift the clams and mussels out, pouring any liquid in the shells back into the pan. Place in a warmed serving bowl. Discard the garlic.

4 ▲ Strain the liquid in the pan through a layer of paper towels held in a sieve, pouring it over the clams and mussels in the bowl. Sprinkle with parsley and black pepper.

5 ▲ To serve, place rounds of toasted bread in the bottom of individual soup bowls, and ladle in the mussels and clams with some of the hot liquid.

Broiled Shrimp with Herbs

Gamberi con erbe aromatiche

Large shrimp are delicious marinated with fresh herbs, lemon and garlic. They can be broiled or grilled on a barbecue.

Ingredients
24 large raw shrimp, in their shells
3 garlic cloves, finely chopped
3 tbsp finely chopped fresh basil
1 tbsp fresh thyme leaves
2 tbsp finely chopped fresh parsley
1 tbsp coarsely crushed black pepper
juice of 1 lemon
4 tbsp olive oil
8 bay leaves
¹/₄ cup salt pork or pancetta, cut into 8
    small squares
serves 4

1 Shell the shrimp and devein them either by using a deveiner, or by making a shallow incision with a small sharp knife down the center of the back to disclose the long black vein. Remove and discard this.

2 ▲ Place the shrimp in a bowl with the garlic, chopped herbs, pepper, lemon juice and olive oil. Mix well, cover, and leave to marinate in the refrigerator for at least 6 hours, or preferably overnight.

3 ▲ Preheat the broiler. Arrange 6 shrimp on each of 4 skewers so that they lie flat, threading a bay leaf and a square of salt pork between every 2 shrimp. Brush with the remaining marinade. Place in one layer under the broiler or on a barbecue. Cook for about 3 minutes. Turn, and cook for 3 minutes more.

Poultry & Meat

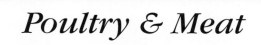

The Italians eat a wide variety of different meats, and tastes vary according to region. Veal, pork and poultry are popular all over the country, while beef is farmed and eaten more in the north, and lamb is a great Roman speciality. All meats are eaten as a second course—secondo piatto—usually simple and served solo, with vegetables to follow.

Pizzaiola Steak

Bistecchine alla pizzaiola

This dish comes from Naples, where tomato sauces are used in all kinds of dishes.

Ingredients

1lb beef steaks, preferably rump or
chuck, thinly sliced
3 tbsp flour, for dredging
3 tbsp olive oil
3 garlic cloves, peeled and crushed
14oz can plum tomatoes, with their
juice, passed through a food mill
2 tbsp chopped fresh basil or
parsley
salt and freshly ground black pepper
serves 4

1 Trim any excess fat from the steaks,
and notch the edges slightly with a
sharp knife to prevent them from
curling during cooking. Pat the steaks
dry with paper towels, and dredge
lightly in the flour.

2 ▲ In a large heavy frying pan or
skillet, heat 2 tbsp of the oil with the
garlic cloves. As soon as they are
golden, raise the heat, push them to
the side of the pan, and add the steaks.
Brown quickly on both sides. Remove
the meat to a dish.

3 ▲ Add the tomatoes, the remaining
oil, and the herbs to the pan. Season
with salt and pepper. Cook over
moderate heat for about 15 minutes.
Discard the garlic cloves. Return the
steaks to the pan, stir to cover them
with the sauce, and cook for 4–5
minutes more. Serve.

Herbed Burgers

Polpette

Dress up ground beef with fresh herbs and a tasty tomato sauce.

Ingredients

1½lb lean ground beef
1 garlic clove, finely chopped
1 scallion, very finely chopped
3 tbsp chopped fresh basil
2 tbsp chopped fresh parsley
salt and freshly ground black pepper
3 tbsp butter
For the tomato sauce
3 tbsp olive oil
1 medium onion, finely chopped
11oz tomatoes, chopped
a few leaves fresh basil
3–4 tbsp water
1 tsp sugar
1 tbsp white wine vinegar
salt and freshly ground black pepper
serves 4

1 To make the tomato sauce, heat
the oil in a large pan and sauté the
onion gently until translucent. Add the
tomatoes and cook for 2–3 minutes.
Add the basil, cover the pan, and cook
for 7–8 minutes over moderate heat.

2 Add the water, sugar and vinegar,
and cook for 2–3 minutes more.
Season with salt and pepper. Remove
from the heat, allow to cool slightly,
and pass the sauce through a food mill
or strainer. Check the seasoning.

3 ▲ Combine the meat with the
garlic, scallion and herbs in a mixing
bowl. Season with salt and pepper.
Form into 4 burgers, patting the meat
as lightly as possible.

4 ▲ Heat the butter in a frying pan.
When the foam subsides add the
burgers, and cook over moderate heat
until brown on the underside. Turn
the burgers over, and continue
cooking until done. Remove to a
warmed plate.

5 Tilt the frying pan, and spoon off
any surface fat. Pour in the sauce, raise
the heat and bring to a boil, scraping
up the meat residue from the bottom
of the pan. Serve with the burgers.

Meatballs

Polpettine

These meatballs are delicious served hot with pasta or rice. They are also good cold.

Ingredients

2 tbsp dried porcini mushrooms
²/₃ cup warm water
1lb lean ground beef
2 garlic cloves, finely chopped
4 tbsp chopped fresh parsley
3 tbsp chopped fresh basil
1 egg
6 tbsp plain breadcrumbs
2 tbsp freshly grated Parmesan cheese
salt and freshly ground black pepper
4 tbsp olive oil
1 medium onion, very finely chopped
¹/₄ cup dry white wine
chopped fresh parsley, to garnish
serves 3–4

1 Soak the dried mushrooms in the warm water for 15 minutes. Lift them out of the water and chop finely. Filter the soaking water through paper towels and reserve.

2 ▲ In a mixing bowl, combine the meat with the chopped mushrooms, garlic and herbs. Stir in the egg. Add the breadcrumbs and Parmesan, and season with salt and pepper. Form the mixture into small balls 1¹/₂ inches in diameter.

3 ▲ In a large heavy frying pan or skillet, heat the oil. Add the onion and cook over low heat until soft. Raise the heat and add the meatballs, rolling them often to brown them evenly on all sides. After about 5 minutes add the filtered mushroom soaking water. Cook for 5–8 minutes more, or until the meatballs are cooked through.

4 ▲ Remove the meatballs to a heated serving plate with a slotted spoon or spatula. Add the wine to the pan, and cook for 1–2 minutes, stirring to scrape up any residues on the bottom of the pan. Pour the sauce over the meatballs. Sprinkle with parsley, and serve at once.

Meatballs with Peperonata

Polpette di manzo

These taste very good with creamed potatoes. Use a potato ricer to get them really smooth.

Ingredients
14 oz ground beef
2 cups fresh white bread crumbs
²/₃ cup grated Parmesan cheese
2 eggs, beaten
pinch of paprika
pinch of grated nutmeg
1 tsp dried mixed herbs
2 thin slices of mortadella or prosciutto
(total weight about 2 ounces), chopped
vegetable oil, for shallow frying
salt and freshly ground black pepper
snipped fresh basil leaves, to garnish

For the peperonata
2 tbsp olive oil
1 small onion, thinly sliced
2 yellow bell peppers, cored, seeded and
cut lengthwise into thin strips
2 red bell peppers, cored, seeded and
cut lengthwise into thin strips
1¼ cups finely chopped tomatoes or
passata
1 tablespoon chopped fresh parsley
serves 4

1 ▲ Put the ground beef in a bowl. Add half the bread crumbs and all the remaining ingredients, including salt and ground black pepper to taste. Mix well with clean wet hands. Divide the mixture into 12 equal portions and roll each into a ball. Flatten the meat balls slightly so they are about ½ in thick.

2 Put the remaining bread crumbs on a plate and roll the meatballs in them, a few at a time, until they are evenly coated. Place on a plate, cover with plastic wrap and chill for about 30 minutes to firm up.

3 ▲ Meanwhile, make the peperonata. Heat the oil in a medium saucepan, add the onion and cook gently for about 3 minutes, stirring frequently, until softened. Add the pepper strips and cook for 3 minutes, stirring constantly. Stir in the tomatoes and parsley, with salt and pepper to taste. Bring to a boil, stirring. Cover and cook for 15 minutes, then remove the lid and continue to cook, stirring frequently, for 10 more minutes, or until reduced and thick. Taste for seasoning. Keep hot.

4 ▲ Pour oil into a frying pan to a depth of about 1 in. When hot but not smoking, shallow fry the meatballs for 10–12 minutes, turning them 3–4 times and pressing them flat with a spatula. Remove and drain on paper towels. Serve hot, with the peperonata alongside. Garnish with the basil.

Variation
Instead of ground beef, used half ground pork and half ground veal.

Beef Stew with Tomatoes, Wine and Peas   *Spezzatino*

It seems there are as many spezzatino recipes as there are Italian cooks. This one is very traditional, perfect for a winter lunch or dinner. Serve it with boiled or mashed potatoes to soak up the deliciously rich sauce.

Ingredients

2 tbsp flour
2 tsp chopped fresh thyme or
   1 tsp dried thyme
2¼ lb braising or stewing steak, cut into
   large cubes
3 tbsp olive oil
1 medium onion, roughly chopped
1 jar (1 lb) sugocasa or passata
1 cup beef stock
1 cup red wine
2 garlic cloves, crushed
2 tbsp tomato paste
2 cups shelled fresh peas
1 tsp sugar
salt and freshly ground black pepper
fresh thyme, to garnish

serves 4

1 ▲ Preheat the oven to 325°F. Put the flour in a shallow dish and season with the thyme and salt and pepper. Add the beef cubes and coat evenly.

2 ▲ Heat the oil in a large flameproof casserole, add the beef and brown on all sides over medium to high heat. Remove with a slotted spoon and drain on paper towels.

3 ▲ Add the onion to the pan, scraping the base of the pan to mix in any sediment. Cook gently for about 3 minutes, stirring frequently, until softened, then stir in the sugocasa, stock, wine, garlic and tomato paste. Bring to a boil, stirring. Return the beef to the pan and stir well to coat with the sauce. Cover and cook in the oven for 1½ hours.

4 ▲ Stir in the peas and sugar. Return the casserole to the oven and cook for 30 more minutes, or until the beef is tender. Taste for seasoning. Garnish with fresh thyme before serving.

Variation
Use thawed frozen peas instead of fresh. Add them 10 minutes before the end of cooking.

Beef Stew with Red Wine   *Spezzatino di manzo con vino rosso*

This rich, hearty dish should be served with mashed potatoes or polenta.

Ingredients
5 tbsp olive oil
2¹/₂lb boneless beef chuck, cut into
    1¹/₂in cubes
1 medium onion, very finely sliced
2 carrots, chopped
3 tbsp finely chopped fresh parsley
1 garlic clove, chopped
1 bay leaf
a few sprigs fresh thyme, or pinch
    of dried thyme leaves
pinch of grated nutmeg
1 cup red wine
14oz can plum tomatoes, chopped,
    with their juice
¹/₂ cup fresh or canned beef or
    chicken stock
about 15 black olives, pitted and halved
salt and freshly ground black pepper
1 large red sweet pepper, cut into strips
serves 6

1 ▲ Preheat the oven to 350°F. Heat 3 tbsp of the oil in a large, heavy casserole. Brown the meat in batches, turning it to color on all sides. Remove to a side plate while the remaining meat is being browned.

2 When all the meat has been browned and removed, add the remaining oil, the onion and carrots. Cook over low heat until the onion softens. Add the parsley and garlic, and cook for 3–4 minutes more.

3 ▲ Return the meat to the pan, raise the heat, and stir well to mix the vegetables with the meat. Stir in the bay leaf, thyme and nutmeg. Add the wine, bring to a boil and cook, stirring, for 4–5 minutes. Stir in the tomatoes, stock and olives, and mix well. Season with salt and pepper, and return to a boil. Cover the casserole, and bake in the oven for 1¹/₂ hours.

4 ▲ Remove the casserole from the oven. Stir in the strips of pepper. Return the casserole to the oven and cook, uncovered, for 30 minutes more, or until the beef is tender.

Corsican Beef Stew with Macaroni
Stufato di manzo alla corsa

Pasta is eaten in many parts of Italy. In Corsica, it is often served with gravy as a sauce and, in this case, a rich beef stew.

Ingredients

1 oz dried porcini mushrooms
6 garlic cloves
2 lb beef for stew, cut into
   2 in cubes
4 oz lardons, or thick bacon strips
3 tbsp olive oil
2 onions, sliced
1¼ cups dry white wine
30 ml/2 tbsp passata
pinch of ground cinnamon
sprig of rosemary
1 bay leaf
2 cups large macaroni
⅔ cup freshly grated
   Parmesan cheese
salt and freshly ground black pepper
serves 4

2 ▲ Heat the oil in a heavy-based pan, add half the beef and brown well on all sides. Repeat with the remaining beef. Transfer to a plate. Add the sliced onions to the pan and cook until lightly browned. Crush the remaining garlic and add to the onions with the meat.

4 ▲ Cook the macaroni in a large pan of boiling, salted water for 10 minutes, or until *al dente*. Lift the pieces of meat out of the gravy and transfer to a warmed serving platter. Drain the pasta and layer in a serving bowl with the gravy and cheese. Serve with the meat.

Cook's Tip

This recipe calls for 2 tbsp passata, thick puréed tomatoes. If you haven't a jar already open, substitute regular tomato paste or a tablespoon or two of sun-dried tomato paste.

1 ▲ Soak the dried mushrooms in warm water for 30 minutes. Drain, set the mushrooms aside and reserve the liquid. Cut three of the garlic cloves into thin strips and insert into the pieces of the beef by making little slits with a sharp knife. Push the lardons or pieces of bacon into the beef with the garlic. Season the meat with salt and pepper.

3 ▲ Stir in the white wine, passata, mushrooms, cinnamon, rosemary and bay leaf and season with salt and pepper. Cook gently for 30 minutes, stirring often. Strain the mushroom liquid and add to the stew with enough water to cover. Bring to a boil, cover and simmer the stew very gently for about 3 hours, or until the meat is very tender.

Roast Lamb with Herbs

Arrosto d'agnello con erbe e aglio

This dish, from southern Italy, is simple but full of flavor.

Ingredients
3lb leg of lamb
3–4 tbsp olive oil
4 garlic cloves, peeled and halved
2 sprigs fresh sage, or pinch of
　dried sage leaves
2 sprigs fresh rosemary, or
　1 tsp dried
2 bay leaves
2 sprigs fresh thyme, or $^1/_2$ tsp dried
salt and freshly ground black pepper
$^3/_4$ cup dry white wine
serves 4–6

1　Cut any excess fat from the lamb. Rub with olive oil. Using a sharp knife, make small cuts just under the skin all around the meat. Insert the garlic pieces in some of the cuts, and a few of the fresh herbs in the others. (If using dried herbs, sprinkle them over the surface of the meat.)

2　Rub the remaining fresh herbs all over the lamb, and allow it to stand in a cool place for at least 2 hours before cooking. Preheat the oven to 375°F.

3　▲ Place the lamb in a baking pan, surrounded by the herbs. Pour on 2 tbsp of the oil. Season. Place in the oven and roast for 35 minutes, basting occasionally.

4　▲ Pour the wine over the lamb. Roast for 15 minutes more, or until the meat is cooked. Remove the lamb to a heated serving dish. Tilt the pan, spooning off any fat on the surface. Strain the pan juices into a gravy boat. Slice the meat, and serve with the sauce handed separately.

Lamb Stewed with Tomatoes and Garlic

Spezzatino d'agnello

This rustic stew comes from the plateau of Puglia, where sheep graze alongside vineyards.

Ingredients
2 large garlic cloves
1 sprig fresh rosemary (or 3 tbsp
　chopped fresh parsley if fresh
　rosemary is not available)
6 tbsp olive oil
$2^1/_2$lb stewing lamb, trimmed of fat
　and gristle and cut into chunks
flour seasoned with freshly ground
　black pepper, for dredging
$^3/_4$ cup dry white wine
2 tsp salt
1lb fresh tomatoes, chopped, or
　14oz can tomatoes, chopped
$^1/_2$ cup beef stock, heated
serves 5–6

1　Preheat the oven to 350°F. Chop the garlic with the parsley, if using. Heat 4 tbsp of the oil in a wide flameproof casserole.

2　Add the garlic and rosemary or arsley and cook over moderate heat, until the garlic is golden.

3　▲ Dredge the lamb in the flour. Add a batch of lamb chunks to the pan in one layer, turning to brown them evenly. When brown, remove them to a side plate. Add a little more oil, and brown the remaining lamb.

4　▲ When all the lamb has been browned, return it to the casserole with the wine. Raise the heat and bring to a boil, scraping up any residues from the bottom. Sprinkle with the salt. Stir in the tomatoes and the stock. Stir well. Cover the casserole, and place in the center of the oven. Bake for $1^3/_4$–2 hours, or until the meat is tender.

Roast Lamb with Rosemary

Agnello al rosmarino

In Italy, lamb is traditionally served at Easter. This simple roast with potatoes owes its wonderful flavor to the fresh rosemary and garlic. It makes the perfect Sunday lunch at any time of year, served with one or two lightly cooked fresh vegetables, such as broccoli, spinach or baby carrots.

Ingredients

$1/2$ leg of lamb, about 3 lb
2 garlic cloves, cut lengthwise into
    thin slivers
7 tbsp olive oil
leaves from 4 sprigs of fresh rosemary,
    finely chopped
about 1 cup lamb or vegetable stock
$1^1/2$ pounds potatoes, cut into
    1-in cubes
a few fresh sage leaves, chopped
salt and freshly ground black pepper
lightly cooked baby carrots, to serve
serves 4

2 ▲ Put the lamb in a roasting pan and rub it all over with 3 tbsp of the oil. Sprinkle on about half of the chopped rosemary, patting it on firmly, and season with plenty of salt and pepper. Roast for 30 minutes, turning once.

5 ▲ Meanwhile, put the potatoes in a separate roasting pan and toss with the remaining oil and rosemary and the sage. Roast, on the same shelf as the lamb if possible, for 45 minutes, turning the potatoes several times until they are golden and tender.

1 ▲ Preheat the oven to 450°F. Using the point of a sharp knife, make deep incisions in the lamb, especially near the bone, and insert the slivers of garlic.

3 ▲ Lower the oven temperature to 375°F. Turn the lamb over again and add $1/2$ cup of the stock.

4 Roast for $1^1/4$ –$1^1/2$ hours longer until the lamb is tender, turning the joint two or three times more and adding the rest of the stock in two or three batches. Baste the lamb each time it is turned.

6 ▲ Transfer the lamb to a carving board, tent with foil and set aside in a warm place for 10 minutes so that the flesh firms for easier carving. Serve whole or carved into thin slices, surrounded by the potatoes and accompanied by baby carrots.

Cook's Tip
If desired, the cooking juices can be strained and used to make a thin gravy with stock and red wine.

Pork in Sweet-and-Sour Sauce   *Scaloppine di maiale in agrodolce*

The combination of sweet and sour flavors is popular in Venetian cooking, especially with

meat and liver. This recipe is given extra bite with the addition of crushed mixed

peppercorns. Served with shelled fava beans tossed with grilled bacon—it is delectable.

Ingredients
1 whole pork fillet, about 12 oz
1½ tbsp flour
2–3 tbsp olive oil
1 cup dry white wine
2 tbsp white wine vinegar
2 tsp sugar
1 tbsp mixed peppercorns, coarsely
    ground
salt and freshly ground black pepper
fava beans tossed with grilled bacon,
    to serve

serves 2

3 ▲ Heat 1 tbsp of the oil in a wide heavy saucepan or frying pan and add as many slices of pork as the pan will hold. Fry over medium to high heat for 2–3 minutes on each side, until crispy and tender. Remove with a spatula and set aside. Repeat with the remaining pork, adding more oil as necessary.

4 ▲ Mix the wine, wine vinegar and sugar in a bowl. Pour into the pan and stir vigorously over high heat until reduced, scraping the pan to incorporate the sediment. Stir in the peppercorns and return the pork to the pan. Spoon the sauce over the pork until it is evenly coated and heated through.

1 ▲ Cut the pork diagonally into thin slices. Place between two sheets of plastic wrap and pound lightly with a rolling pin to flatten them evenly.

2 ▲ Spread out the flour in a shallow bowl. Season well and coat the meat.

Cook's Tip
Grind the peppercorns in a pepper grinder, or crush them with a mortar and pestle.

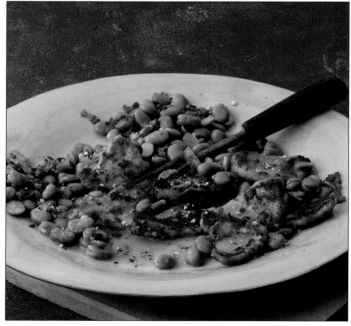

Pork with Marsala and Juniper

Marsale al marsala

Although most frequently used in desserts, Sicilian marsala gives savory dishes a rich, fruity and alcoholic tang. Use good quality pork from the butcher's that won't be overwhelmed by the richly aromatic flavor of the sauce.

Ingredients

1 oz dried porcini mushrooms
4 pork escalopes
2 tsp balsamic vinegar
8 garlic cloves
1 tbsp butter
3 tbsp marsala
several sprigs of rosemary
10 juniper berries, crushed
salt and freshly ground black pepper
noodles and green vegetables, to serve
serves 4

1 Put the dried mushrooms in a bowl and just cover with hot water. Let stand.

2 ▲ Brush the pork with 1 tsp of the vinegar and season with salt and pepper. Put the garlic cloves in a small pan of boiling water and cook for 10 minutes until soft. Drain and set aside.

3 ▲ Melt the butter in a large frying pan. Add the pork and fry quickly until browned on the bottom. Turn the meat over and cook for another minute.

4 Add the marsala, rosemary, mushrooms, 4 tbsp of the mushroom juices, the garlic cloves, juniper and remaining vinegar.

5 Simmer gently for about 3 minutes until the pork is cooked through. Season lightly and serve hot with noodles and green vegetables.

Pork Braised in Milk with Carrots

Lonza al latte con carote

This method of slowly cooking a joint of pork produces a deliciously creamy gravy. It is a speciality of the Veneto region.

Ingredients

1¹/₂lb lean loin of pork
3 tbsp olive oil
2 tbsp butter
1 small onion, finely chopped
1 stalk celery, finely chopped
8 carrots, cut into 2in strips
2 bay leaves
1 tbsp peppercorns
salt, to taste
2 cups milk, scalded
serves 4–5

3 ▲ Pour in the hot milk. Cover the casserole and place it in the center of the oven. Bake for about 90 minutes, turning and basting the pork with the sauce about once every 20 minutes. Remove the cover for the last 20 minutes of baking.

5 ▲ Discard the bay leaves. Press about one-third of the carrots and all the liquids in the pan through a strainer. Arrange the remaining carrots around the meat.

1 ▲ Trim any excess fat from the pork, and tie it into a roll with string.

6 ▲ Place the sauce in a small saucepan, taste for seasoning, and bring to a boil. If it seems too thin, boil it for a few minutes to reduce it slightly. Serve the sliced meat with the carrots, and hand the hot sauce separately.

4 ▲ Remove the meat from the casserole, and cut off the string. Place the meat on a warmed serving platter and cut into slices.

2 ▲ Preheat the oven to 350°F. Heat the oil and butter in a large casserole. Add the vegetables, and cook over low heat until they soften, 8–10 minutes. Raise the heat, push the vegetables to one side and add the pork, browning it on all sides. Add the bay leaves and peppercorns, and season with salt.

~ VARIATION ~

This dish can also be made using a joint of veal. Substitute a piece of boneless veal and proceed as in the recipe. This dish is delicious served hot or cold.

Pork Fillet with Caper Sauce

Fettine di maiale con salsa di capperi

The caper sauce can be made in advance and reheated while the pork is sautéed.

Ingredients
1lb pork fillet, cut into thin slices
flour seasoned with freshly ground
  black pepper, for dredging
2 tbsp butter
2 tbsp olive oil
For the caper sauce
2 tbsp olive oil
$1/4$ cup butter
$1/2$ small onion, very finely chopped
1 anchovy fillet, rinsed and chopped
1 tbsp flour
2 tbsp capers, rinsed
1 tbsp finely chopped fresh parsley
4 tbsp wine vinegar
4 tbsp water
4 tbsp balsamic vinegar
serves 4–5

2 ▲ Stir in the flour and, when it
is well amalgamated, the capers and
parsley. Add the wine vinegar and
water, stirring constantly over low heat
to thicken the sauce. Just before serving
stir in another 2 tbsp of butter, and the
balsamic vinegar.

3 Meanwhile, flatten the pork fillets
with a meat pounder until thin.
Dredge lightly in the seasoned flour,
shaking off any excess.

4 ▲ Heat 2 tbsp of butter and the oil
in a large frying pan, and when hot add
some of the pork slices in one layer.
Brown the meat on both sides, cooking
it for a total of 5–6 minutes. Remove to
a heated serving dish, and repeat with
the remaining pork slices. Serve hot,
with the sauce.

1 Make the sauce by heating the oil
and 2 tbsp of the butter in a small
saucepan (not aluminum) and slowly
cooking the onion. When it is soft, add
the anchovy, mashing it into the onion
with a wooden spoon.

Pork Chops with Mushrooms

Costolette di maiale con funghi

The addition of dried porcini mushrooms gives fresh cultivated mushrooms a richer flavor.

Ingredients
3 tbsp dried porcini mushrooms
$1/3$ cup butter
2 garlic cloves, peeled and crushed
11oz fresh cultivated mushrooms,
  thinly sliced
salt and freshly ground black
  pepper
1 tbsp olive oil
4 pork chops, trimmed of excess fat
$1/2$ tsp fresh thyme leaves, or
  $1/4$ tsp dried
$1/2$ cup dry white wine
$1/3$ cup light cream
serves 4

1 Soak the porcini mushrooms in
1 cup warm water for 1 hour. Drain
and reserve the soaking water, first
filtering it through a layer of paper
towels.

2 Melt two-thirds of the butter in a
large frying pan. Add the garlic. When
the foam subsides, stir in all the
mushrooms. Season and cook over
moderate heat until the mushrooms
give up their liquid, 8–10 minutes.

3 Remove the mushrooms to a side
dish. Heat the oil and remaining butter
in the frying pan. Add the pork in one
layer and sprinkle with thyme. Cook
over moderate to high heat for about
3 minutes per side to seal. Reduce the
heat, and cook for 15–20 minutes
more. Remove to a warmed plate.

4 ▲ Spoon off any fat in the pan. Pour
in the wine and the mushroom water.
Cook over high heat until reduced
by about half, stirring to scrape up
the residues at the bottom. Add the
mushrooms and the cream, and cook
for 4–5 minutes more. Serve the chops
with the sauce.

Milanese Veal Chops

Costolette alla milanese

This famous dish depends on the chops being cooked carefully in butter.

Ingredients
2 veal chops or cutlets, on the bone
1 egg
salt and freshly ground black pepper
6–8 tbsp plain breadcrumbs
1/4 cup butter
1 tbsp vegetable oil
lemon wedges, to serve
serves 2

1 ▲ Trim any gristle or thick fat from the chops. Cut along the rib bone, if necessary, to free the meat on one side. Pound the meat slightly to flatten.

2 ▲ Beat the egg in a shallow bowl and season it with salt and pepper. Spread the breadcrumbs over a plate. Dip the chops into the egg, and then into the breadcrumbs. Pat the breadcrumbs to help them to stick.

> ~ COOK'S TIP ~
>
> Milanese cooks sometimes soak the chops in milk for about an hour to soften the meat.

3 ▲ Heat the butter with the oil in a heavy frying pan large enough to hold both chops side by side. Do not let it brown. Add the chops to the pan, and cook them slowly over low to moderate heat until the breadcrumbs are golden and the meat is cooked through. The timing will depend on the thickness of the chops. The important thing is not to overcook the breadcrumb coating while undercooking the meat. Serve hot with lemon wedges.

Veal Rolls with Sage and Ham

Saltimbocca

These rolls are so good that, as their Italian name implies, they "jump into your mouth".

Ingredients
8 small veal escalops
8 small slices prosciutto
8 leaves fresh sage
salt and freshly ground black pepper
3 tbsp butter
1/2 cup fresh or canned beef or chicken
    stock, warmed
makes 8 rolls

1 Gently pound the veal slices with a mallet until thin. Lay a piece of prosciutto over each slice. Top with a sage leaf, and season with salt and pepper. Roll the escalops around the filling and secure each roll with a wooden toothpick.

2 ▲ Heat half the butter in a frying pan just large enough to hold the rolls in one layer. When the butter is bubbling add the veal, turning the rolls to brown them on all sides. Cook for about 7–10 minutes, or until the veal is cooked. Remove to a warmed plate.

3 ▲ Add the remaining butter and the hot stock to the frying pan, and bring to a boil, scraping up the brown residue on the bottom of the pan with a wooden spoon. Pour the sauce over the veal rolls, and serve.

Veal Escalops with Marsala

Scaloppine di vitello con Marsala

This quick and delicious dish enlivens the mild flavor of veal with the sweetness of Marsala.

Ingredients
1lb veal escalops, preferably cut
across the grain, about $1/4$in thick
$1/2$ cup flour seasoned with salt
and freshly ground black pepper,
for dredging
$1/4$ cup butter
5 tbsp Marsala
5 tbsp stock or water
serves 4

1 Pound the escalops flat to a thickness of about $1/4$in. If they have not been cut across the grain or from one muscle, cut small notches around the edges to stop them curling during cooking.

2 ▲ Spread the flour out on a plate. Heat the butter in a large frying pan. Lightly dredge the veal slices in the flour, shaking off any excess. As soon as the foam from the butter subsides, put the veal into the pan in one layer, and brown the slices quickly on both sides, in two batches if necessary. Remove to a warmed serving plate.

3 ▲ Pour in the Marsala and the stock or water. Cook over moderate to high heat for 3–4 minutes, scraping up any meat residues from the bottom of the pan. Pour the sauce over the meat, and serve at once.

Ham and Cheese Veal Escalops

Scaloppine alla bolognese

This dish from Bologna can be made with Parmesan or Gruyère cheese.

Ingredients
8 veal escalops, about 1lb total,
preferably cut across the grain
$1/2$ cup flour seasoned with salt and
freshly ground black pepper, for
dredging
2 tbsp butter
2 tbsp olive oil
3 tbsp dry white wine
8 thin slices ham
$1/2$ cup freshly grated Parmesan,
or 8 thin slices Gruyère
serves 4

1 Preheat the oven to 400°F. Pound the escalops flat. If they have not been cut across the grain or from one muscle, cut small notches around the edges to prevent them from curling during cooking. Spread the seasoned flour over a plate.

2 ▲ Heat the butter with the oil in a large frying pan. Lightly dredge the veal slices in the flour, shaking off any excess. As soon as the foam from the butter subsides, put the veal into the pan in one layer, and brown the slices quickly on both sides. Remove to a shallow oven dish. Add the wine to the pan and cook for 1–2 minutes, scraping up the brown residue from the bottom of the pan with a wooden spoon. Pour over the escalops.

3 ▲ Place one slice of ham on top of each escalop. Sprinkle with one tablespoon of Parmesan, or top with one slice of Gruyère. Place in the oven and cook until the cheese melts, 5–7 minutes. Serve hot.

Cold Veal with Tuna Sauce

Vitello tonnato

This classic summer dish is best when prepared in advance and refrigerated for a few hours before serving. The dish can be kept for up to 3 days in the refrigerator.

Ingredients

1³/₄lb boneless roasting veal, in
   one piece
1 carrot, peeled
1 stalk celery
1 small onion, peeled and quartered
1 bay leaf
1 clove
1 tsp whole peppercorns
For the tuna sauce
14oz canned tuna, preferably in olive oil
4 anchovy fillets
2 tsp capers, rinsed and drained
3 tbsp fresh lemon juice
1¹/₄ cups mayonnaise
salt and freshly ground black pepper
capers and pickled cornichons,
   to garnish
serves 6–8

3 ▲ Scrape the tuna purée into a bowl. Fold in the mayonnaise. Check the seasoning and adjust as necessary.

4 Slice the veal as thinly as possible. Spread a little of the tuna sauce over the bottom of a serving platter.

5 ▲ Arrange a layer of the veal slices on top of the sauce. Cover with a thin layer of sauce. Make another layer or two of veal slices and sauce, ending with the sauce. Garnish with capers and cornichons. Cover with plastic wrap and refrigerate until needed.

1 ▲ Place the veal, vegetables and flavorings in a medium pan (not aluminum or copper). Cover with water. Bring to a boil and simmer for 50–60 minutes, until tender. Skim off any scum that rises to the surface. Do not overcook, or the veal will fall apart when sliced. Allow it to cool in its cooking liquid for several hours, or overnight.

2 Drain the tuna. Place it in a food processor or blender, and add the anchovies, capers and lemon juice. Process to a creamy paste. If it seems too thick, add 2–3 tbsp of the cool veal stock and process again.

Liver with Onions

Fegato alla veneziana

This classic Venetian dish is very good served with grilled polenta. Allow enough time for the
onions to cook very slowly, to produce a sweet flavor.

Ingredients
$^1/_3$ cup butter
3 tbsp olive oil
$1^1/_2$lb onions, very finely sliced
salt and freshly ground black pepper
$1^3/_4$lb calf's liver, sliced thinly
3 tbsp finely chopped fresh parsley,
   to garnish
grilled polenta wedges, to serve
   (optional)
serves 6

1 ▲ Heat two-thirds of the butter with
the oil in a large heavy frying pan. Add
the onions, and cook over low heat
until soft and tender, about 40–50
minutes, stirring often. Season with
salt and pepper. Remove to a side dish.

2 ▲ Heat the remaining butter in the
pan over moderate to high heat. When
it has stopped bubbling add the liver,
and brown it on both sides. Cook for
about 5 minutes, or until done.
Remove to a warmed side dish.

3 ▲ Return the onions to the pan.
Raise the heat slightly, and stir the
onions to mix them into the liver
cooking juices.

4 ▲ When the onions are hot, turn
them out onto a heated serving platter.
Arrange the liver on top, and sprinkle
with parsley. Serve with grilled
polenta wedges, if desired.

Veal Shanks with Tomatoes and White Wine

Osso buco

This famous Milanese dish is rich and hearty. It is traditionally served with risotto alla milanese, but plain boiled rice goes equally well. The lemony gremolata garnish helps to cut the richness of the dish, as does a crisp green salad—serve it after the osso buco and before the dessert, to refresh the palate.

Ingredients

2 tbsp flour
4 pieces of osso buco
2 small onions
2 tbsp olive oil
1 large celery stalk, finely chopped
1 medium carrot, finely chopped
2 garlic cloves, finely chopped
1 can (14 ounces) chopped tomatoes
1¼ cups dry white wine
1¼ cups chicken or veal stock
1 strip of thinly pared lemon rind
2 bay leaves, plus extra for
  garnishing (optional)
salt and freshly ground black pepper

For the gremolata

2 tbsp finely chopped fresh
  flat-leaf parsley
finely grated rind of 1 lemon
1 garlic clove, finely chopped
serves 4

1 ▲ Preheat the oven to 325°F. Season the flour with salt and pepper and spread it out in a shallow bowl. Add the pieces of veal and turn them in the flour until evenly coated. Shake off any excess flour.

2 ▲ Slice one of the onions and separate it into rings. Heat the oil in a large flameproof casserole, then add the veal, with the onion rings, and brown the veal on both sides over medium heat. Remove the veal shanks with tongs and set aside on paper towels to drain.

3 ▲ Chop the remaining onion and add it to the pan with the celery, carrot and garlic. Stir the bottom of the pan to incorporate the pan juices and sediment. Cook gently, stirring frequently, for about 5 minutes, until the vegetables soften slightly.

4 ▲ Add the chopped tomatoes, wine, stock, lemon rind and bay leaves, then season to taste with salt and pepper. Bring to a boil, stirring. Return the veal to the pan and coat with the sauce. Cover and cook in the oven for 2 hours or until the veal feels tender when pierced with a fork.

5 Meanwhile, make the gremolata. In a small bowl, combine the chopped parsley, lemon rind and chopped garlic. Remove the casserole from the oven and lift out and discard the strip of lemon rind and the bay leaves. Taste the sauce for seasoning. Serve the osso buco hot, sprinkled with the gremolata and garnished with extra bay leaves, if desired.

Cook's Tip
Osso buco is available at large supermarkets and good butchers. Choose pieces about ¾ in thick.

Calf's Liver with Balsamic Vinegar   *Fegato all'aceto balsamico*

This sweet-and-sour liver dish is a speciality of Venice. Serve it very simply, with green beans sprinkled with browned bread crumbs.

Ingredients
1 tbsp flour
1/2 tsp finely chopped fresh sage
4 thin slices of calf's liver, cut into
    serving pieces
3 tbsp olive oil
2 tbsp butter
2 small red onions, sliced and separated
    into rings
2/3 cup dry white wine
3 tbsp balsamic vinegar
pinch of sugar
salt and freshly ground black pepper
fresh sprigs of sage, to garnish
green beans sprinkled with browned
    bread crumbs, to serve
serves 2

Cook's Tip
Never overcook calf's liver, because
it quickly turns tough. Its delicate
flesh is at its most tender when it is
served slightly underdone and
pink—like a rare steak.

1 ▲ Spread out the flour in a shallow bowl. Season it with the sage and plenty of salt and pepper. Turn the liver in the flour until well coated.

2 Heat 2 tbsp of the oil with half of the butter in a wide heavy saucepan or frying pan until foaming. Add the onion rings and cook gently, stirring frequently, for about 5 minutes, until softened but not colored. Remove with a spatula and set aside.

3 ▲ Heat the remaining oil and butter in the pan until foaming, add the liver and cook over medium heat for 2–3 minutes on each side. Transfer to heated dinner plates and keep hot.

4 Add the wine and vinegar to the pan, then stir to mix with the pan juices and any sediment. Add the onions and sugar and heat through, stirring. Spoon the sauce over the liver, garnish with sage sprigs and serve immediately with the green beans.

Veal Cutlets with Lemon

Scaloppine al limone

Popular in Italian restaurants, this dish is very easy to make at home.

Ingredients

4 veal cutlets
2–3 tbsp flour
4 tbsp butter
¼ cup olive oil
¼ cup Italian dry white vermouth or dry
    white wine
3 tbsp lemon juice
salt and freshly ground black pepper
lemon wedges and fresh parsley, to garnish
green beans and peperonata, to serve
serves 4

1 ▲ Put each cutlet between two sheets of plastic wrap and pound until very thin.

2 Cut the pounded cutlets in halves or quarters, and coat in the flour, seasoned with salt and pepper.

3 ▲ Melt the butter with half the oil in a large, heavy frying pan until sizzling. Add as many cutlets as the pan will hold. Fry over medium to high heat for 1–2 minutes on each side, until lightly colored. Remove with a spatula and keep hot. Add the remaining oil and cook the remaining cutlets in the same way.

4 Remove the pan from the heat and add the vermouth and the lemon juice. Stir vigorously to mix with the pan juices, then return to the heat and return all the veal to the pan. Spoon the sauce over the veal. Shake the pan over medium heat until all of the cutlets are coated in the sauce and heated through.

5 Serve immediately, garnished with lemon wedges and parsley. Lightly cooked green beans and peperonata make a delicious accompaniment.

Variation

Use skinless boneless chicken breasts instead of the veal. If they are thick, cut them in half before pounding.

Chicken with Chianti

Pollo al chianti

Together the robust, full-flavored red wine and red pesto give this sauce a rich color and almost spicy flavor, while the grapes add a delicious sweetness. Serve the stew with grilled polenta or warm crusty bread, and accompany with piquant greens, such as arugula or watercress, tossed with a tasty dressing.

Ingredients
3 tbsp olive oil
4 part-boned chicken breasts, skinned
1 medium red onion
2 tbsp red pesto
1¼ cups Chianti
1¼ cups water
4 oz red grapes, halved lengthwise and
    seeded if necessary
salt and freshly ground black pepper
fresh basil leaves, to garnish
arugula salad, to serve
serves 4

1 ▲ Heat 2 tbsp of the oil in a large frying pan, add the chicken breasts and sauté over medium heat for about 5 minutes until they have changed color on all sides. Remove with a slotted spoon and drain on paper towels.

Cook's Tip
Use part-boned chicken breasts, if you can get them, in preference to boneless chicken for this dish, as they have a better flavor. Chicken thighs or drumsticks could also be cooked in this way.

2 Cut the onion in half, through the root. Trim off the root, then slice the onion halves lengthwise to create thin wedges.

3 ▲ Heat the remaining oil in the pan, add the onion wedges and red pesto and cook gently, stirring constantly, for about 3 minutes, until the onion is softened, but not browned.

4 ▲ Add the Chianti and water to the pan and bring to a boil, stirring, then return the chicken to the pan and add salt and pepper to taste.

5 Reduce the heat, then cover the pan and simmer gently for about 20 minutes or until the chicken is tender, stirring occasionally.

6 ▲ Add the grapes to the pan and cook over low to medium heat until heated through, then taste the sauce for seasoning. Serve the chicken hot, garnished with basil and accompanied by the arugula salad.

Variations
Use green pesto instead of red, and substitute a dry white wine such as pinot grigio for the Chianti, then finish with seedless green grapes. A few spoonfuls of mascarpone cheese can be added at the end if desired, to enrich the sauce.

Hunter's Chicken

Pollo alla cacciatora

This traditional dish sometimes has strips of green bell pepper in the sauce for extra color and flavor instead of the fresh mushrooms.

Ingredients

1 cup dried porcini mushrooms
2 tbsp olive oil
1 tbsp butter
4 chicken pieces, on the bone, skinned
1 large onion, thinly sliced
1 can (14 oz) chopped tomatoes
²/₃ cup red wine
1 garlic clove, crushed
leaves of 1 sprig of fresh rosemary,
    finely chopped
1³/₄ cups fresh field mushrooms, thinly
    sliced
salt and freshly ground black pepper
fresh rosemary sprigs, to garnish
serves 4

1 ▲ Put the porcini in a bowl, add 1 cup warm water and soak for 20–30 minutes. Remove from the liquid and squeeze the porcini over the bowl. Strain the liquid and reserve. Finely chop the porcini.

2 ▲ Heat the oil and butter in a large flameproof casserole until foaming. Add the chicken. Sauté over medium heat for 5 minutes or until golden. Remove and drain on paper towels.

3 ▲ Add the onion and chopped mushrooms to the pan. Cook gently, stirring frequently, for about 3 minutes, until the onion has softened but not browned. Stir in the chopped tomatoes, wine and reserved mushroom soaking liquid, then add the crushed garlic and chopped rosemary, with salt and pepper to taste. Bring to a boil, stirring all the time.

4 ▲ Return the chicken to the pan and coat with the sauce. Cover and simmer gently for 30 minutes.

5 Add the fresh mushrooms and stir well to mix into the sauce. Continue simmering gently for 10 minutes or until the chicken is tender. Taste for seasoning. Serve hot, with creamed potato or polenta, if desired. Garnish with rosemary.

Chicken with Tomatoes and Shrimp · · · · · · · · · · *Pollo alla marengo*

This Piedmontese dish was created especially for Napoleon after the battle of Marengo.

Versions of it appear in both Italian and French recipe books.

Ingredients

½ cup olive oil
8 chicken thighs on the bone, skinned
1 onion, finely chopped
1 celery stalk, finely chopped
1 garlic clove, crushed
12 oz ripe Italian plum tomatoes, peeled
    and roughly chopped
1 cup dry white wine
½ tsp finely chopped fresh rosemary
1 tbsp butter
8 small triangles of thinly sliced white
    bread, without crusts
20 large shrimp, shelled
salt and freshly ground black pepper
finely chopped flat-leaf parsley, to garnish
serves 4

1 ▲ Heat about 2 tbsp of the oil in a frying pan, add the chicken thighs and sauté over medium heat for about 5 minutes, until they have changed color on all sides. Transfer to a flameproof casserole.

2 ▲ Add the onion and celery to the frying pan and cook gently, stirring frequently, for about 3 minutes, until softened. Add the garlic, tomatoes, wine, rosemary and salt and pepper to taste. Bring to a boil, stirring.

3 Pour the tomato sauce over the chicken. Cover and cook gently for 40 minutes or until the chicken is tender when pierced.

4 ▲ About 10 minutes before serving, add the remaining oil and the butter to the frying pan and heat until hot but not smoking. Add the triangles of bread and shallow fry until crisp and golden on each side. Drain on paper towels.

5 ▲ Add the shrimp to the tomato sauce and heat until the shrimp are cooked. Taste the sauce for seasoning. Dip one of the tips of each fried bread triangle in parsley. Serve the dish hot, garnished with the bread triangles.

Variation

To make the dish look more like its original, authentic version, garnish it with a few large crayfish or shrimp in their shells.

Chicken with Prosciutto and Cheese   *Pollo alla valdostana*

The name Valdostana is derived from Val d'Aosta, home of the Fontina cheese used here.

Ingredients
2 thin slices of prosciutto
2 thin slices of Fontina cheese
4 part-boned chicken breasts
4 sprigs of basil
2 tbsp olive oil
1 tbsp butter
½ cup dry white wine
salt and freshly ground black pepper
tender young salad greens, to serve
serves 4

Cook's Tip
There is nothing quite like the
buttery texture and nutty flavor of
Fontina cheese, and it also has
superb melting qualities, but you
could use a Swiss or French
mountain cheese, such as Gruyère or
Emmental. Ask for the cheese to be
sliced thinly on the machine slicer, as
you will find it difficult to slice it
thinly yourself.

1 ▲ Preheat the oven to 400°F.
Lightly oil a baking dish. Cut the
prosciutto and Fontina slices in half
crosswise. Skin the chicken breasts,
open out the slit in the center of each
one, and fill each cavity with half a
ham slice and a basil sprig.

2 ▲ Heat the oil and butter in a wide
heavy frying pan until foaming. Cook
the chicken breasts over medium heat
for 1–2 minutes on each side, until they
change color. Transfer to the baking
dish. Add the wine to the pan juices, stir
until sizzling, then pour over the
chicken and season to taste.

3 Top each chicken breast with a
slice of Fontina. Bake for 20 minutes
or until the chicken is tender. Serve
hot, with tender young salad greens.

Deviled Chicken   *Pollo alla diavola*

You can tell this spicy, barbecued chicken dish comes from southern Italy because it has

dried red chilies in the marinade. Versions without the chilies are just as good.

Ingredients
½ cup olive oil
finely grated rind and juice of
    1 large lemon
2 garlic cloves, finely chopped
2 tsp finely chopped or crumbled dried
    red chilies
12 skinless, boneless chicken thighs,
    each cut into 3 or 4 pieces
salt and freshly ground black pepper
flat-leaf parsley leaves, to garnish
lemon wedges, to serve
serves 4

Cook's Tip
Thread the chicken pieces spiral-
fashion on the skewers so they do
not fall off during cooking.

1 ▲ Make a marinade by mixing the
oil, lemon rind and juice, garlic and
chilies in a large, shallow glass or
china dish. Add salt and pepper to
taste. Whisk well, then add the
chicken pieces, turning to coat with
the marinade. Cover and marinate in
the refrigerator for at least 4 hours
or, preferably, overnight.

2 ▲ When ready to cook, prepare the
barbecue or preheat the broiler and
thread the chicken pieces onto eight
oiled metal skewers. Cook on the
barbecue or under a hot broiler for
6–8 minutes, turning frequently,
until tender. Garnish with parsley
leaves and serve hot, with lemon
wedges.

Chicken with Peppers

Pollo con peperoni

This colorful dish comes from the south of Italy, where sweet peppers are plentiful.

Ingredients
3lb chicken, cut into serving pieces
3 large peppers, red, yellow, or green
6 tbsp olive oil
2 medium red onions, finely sliced
2 garlic cloves, finely chopped
small piece of dried chili, crumbled
   (optional)
$1/2$ cup white wine
salt and freshly ground black pepper
2 tomatoes, fresh or canned, peeled
   and chopped
3 tbsp chopped fresh parsley
serves 4

1 Trim any fat off the chicken, and remove all excess skin. Wash the peppers. Prepare by cutting them in half, scooping out the seeds, and cutting away the stem. Slice into strips.

2 ▲ Heat half the oil in a large heavy pan. Add the onions, and cook over low heat until soft. Remove to a side dish. Add the remaining oil to the pan, raise the heat to moderate, add the chicken and brown on all sides, 6–8 minutes. Return the onions to the pan, and add the garlic and dried chili, if using.

3 ▲ Pour in the wine, and cook until it has reduced by half. Stir in the peppers. Season. After 3–4 minutes, stir in the tomatoes. Lower the heat, cover the pan and cook, stirring occasionally, until the peppers are soft, and the chicken is cooked, about 25–30 minutes (the juices should run clear when the meat is pierced). Stir in the parsley and serve.

Chicken Breasts Cooked in Butter

Petti di pollo alla fiorentina

This simple and delicious way of cooking chicken brings out all of its delicacy.

Ingredients
4 small chicken breasts, skinned
   and boned
flour seasoned with salt and freshly
   ground black pepper, for dredging
$1/3$ cup butter
1 sprig fresh parsley, to garnish
serves 4

1 Separate the two fillets of each breast. They come apart very easily; one is large, the other small. Pound the large fillets lightly to flatten them. Dredge the chicken in the seasoned flour, shaking off any excess.

~ COOK'S TIP ~

This chicken dish should be accompanied by delicately flavored vegetables so that its subtle taste is not overpowered.

2 ▲ Heat the butter in a large heavy frying pan until it bubbles. Place all the chicken fillets in the pan, in one layer if possible. Cook over moderate to high heat for 3–4 minutes until they are golden brown.

3 ▲ Turn the chicken over. Reduce the heat to low to moderate, and continue cooking until the fillets are cooked through but still springy to the touch, about 9–12 minutes in all. If the chicken begins to brown too much, cover the pan for the final minutes of cooking. Serve immediately, garnished with a little parsley.

Roast Chicken with Fennel

Pollo con finocchio

In Italy this dish is prepared with wild fennel. Cultivated fennel bulb works just as well.

Ingredients
3¹/₂lb roasting chicken
salt and freshly ground black pepper
1 onion, quartered
¹/₂ cup olive oil
2 medium fennel bulbs
1 garlic clove, peeled
pinch of grated nutmeg
3–4 thin slices pancetta or bacon
¹/₂ cup dry white wine
serves 4–5

1 Preheat the oven to 350°F. Rinse the chicken in cold water. Pat it dry inside and out with paper towels. Sprinkle the cavity with salt and pepper. Place the onion quarters in the cavity. Rub the chicken with about 3 tbsp of the olive oil. Place in a roasting pan.

2 Cut the green fronds from the tops of the fennel bulbs. Chop the fronds with the garlic. Place in a small bowl and mix with the nutmeg. Season with salt and pepper.

3 ▲ Sprinkle the fennel mixture over the chicken, pressing it onto the oiled skin. Cover the breast with the slices of pancetta or bacon. Sprinkle with 2 tbsp of oil. Place in the oven and roast for 30 minutes.

4 Meanwhile, boil or steam the fennel bulbs until barely tender. Remove from the heat and cut into quarters or sixths lengthwise. After the chicken has been cooking for 30 minutes, remove the pan from the oven. Baste the chicken with any oils in the pan.

5 Arrange the fennel pieces around the chicken. Sprinkle the fennel with the remaining oil. Pour about half the wine over the chicken, and return the pan to the oven.

6 ▲ After 30 minutes more, baste the chicken again. Pour on the remaining wine. Cook for 15–20 minutes more. To test, prick the thigh with a fork. If the juices run clear, the chicken is cooked. Transfer the chicken to a serving platter, and arrange the fennel around it.

Chicken with Ham and Cheese

Petti di pollo alla bolognese

This tasty combination comes from Emilia-Romagna, where it is also prepared with veal.

Ingredients
4 small chicken breasts, skinned and
    boned
flour seasoned with salt and freshly
    ground black pepper, for dredging
¹/₄ cup butter
3–4 leaves fresh sage
4 thin slices prosciutto crudo, or
    cooked ham, cut in half
¹/₂ cup freshly grated Parmesan or
    Romano cheese
serves 4

1 Cut each chicken breast in half lengthwise to make two flat fillets of approximately the same thickness. Dredge the chicken in the seasoned flour, and shake off the excess.

2 ▲ Preheat the broiler. Heat the butter in a large heavy frying pan or skillet with the sage leaves. Add the chicken in one layer, and cook over low to moderate heat until golden brown on both sides, turning as necessary.

3 ▲ Remove the chicken from the heat, and arrange on a flameproof serving dish or broiling pan. Place one piece of ham on each chicken fillet, and top with the grated Parmesan or Romano. Broil for 3–4 minutes, or until the cheese has melted.

Mediterranean Turkey Skewers

Spiedini di tacchino

These skewers are delicious, and can be cooked under a broiler or on a charcoal barbecue.

Ingredients

6 tbsp olive oil
3 tbsp fresh lemon juice
1 garlic clove, finely chopped
2 tbsp chopped fresh basil
salt and freshly ground black pepper
2 medium zucchini
1 long thin eggplant
11oz boneless turkey, cut into
   2in cubes
12–16 pickled onions
1 pepper, red or yellow, cut into
   2in squares
serves 4

3 ▲ Prepare the skewers by alternating the turkey, onions, and pepper pieces. Lay the prepared skewers on a platter, and sprinkle with the flavored oil. Leave to marinate for at least 30 minutes. Preheat the broiler, or prepare a barbecue.

4 ▲ Broil for about 10 minutes, or until the vegetables are tender, turning the skewers occasionally. Serve hot.

1 ▲ In a small bowl mix the oil with the lemon juice, garlic and basil. Season with salt and pepper.

2 ▲ Slice the zucchini and eggplant lengthwise into strips ¼ inch thick. Cut them crosswise about two-thirds of the way along their length. Discard the shorter length. Wrap half the turkey pieces with the zucchini slices, and the other half with the eggplant slices.

Turkey Cutlets with Olives

Petto di tacchino con olive

This quick and tasty dish makes a good light main course.

Ingredients

6 tbsp olive oil
1 garlic clove, peeled and lightly crushed
1 dried chili, lightly crushed
1¼lb boneless turkey breast, cut into
 ¼in slices
salt and freshly ground black pepper
½ cup dry white wine
4 tomatoes, peeled and seeded, cut
 into thin strips
about 24 black olives
6–8 leaves fresh basil, torn
serves 4

1 ▲ Heat 4 tbsp of the olive oil in a large frying pan. Add the garlic and dried chili, and cook over low heat until the garlic is golden.

2 ▲ Raise the heat to moderate. Place the turkey slices in the pan, and brown them lightly on both sides. Season with salt and pepper. The turkey will be cooked after about 2 minutes. Remove the turkey to a heated dish.

3 ▲ Discard the garlic and chili. Add the wine, tomato strips and olives. Cook over moderate heat for 3–4 minutes, scraping up any meat residue from the bottom of the pan.

4 ▲ Return the turkey to the pan. Sprinkle with the basil. Heat for about 30 seconds, and serve.

Stuffed Turkey Breast with Lemon

Petto di tacchino ripieno

This elegant dish of rolled turkey breast makes an impressive but economical main course.

Ingredients

1¹/₂lb turkey breast, in one piece
1 carrot, cut into matchsticks
1 medium zucchini, cut into matchsticks
¹/₃ cup ham, cut into matchsticks
2 thick slices white bread, crusts
    removed, softened in a little milk
10 green olives, pitted and finely chopped
1 large garlic clove, finely chopped
4 tbsp chopped fresh parsley
4 tbsp finely chopped fresh basil
1 egg
¹/₈ tsp grated lemon zest
2 tbsp freshly grated Parmesan cheese
salt and freshly ground black pepper
4 tbsp olive oil
1 cup fresh or canned chicken stock,
    warmed
¹/₂ lemon, cut into thin wedges
2 tbsp butter
serves 4–5

1 ▲ Remove any bones, skin or fat from the turkey. Using a sharp knife, cut part of the way through the turkey breast and open the two halves out like a book.

~ VARIATION ~

Substitute 3 oz sliced mushrooms sautéed lightly in 3 tbsp butter for the ham in step 3. Omit the lemon wedges during cooking.

2 ▲ Pound the meat with a mallet to obtain one large piece of meat of as even a thickness as possible.

3 ▲ Preheat the oven to 400°F. Blanch the carrot and zucchini pieces in a small pan of boiling water for 2 minutes. Drain. Combine with the matchsticks of ham.

4 ▲ Squeeze the bread, and place in a mixing bowl, breaking it into small pieces with a fork. Stir in the olives, garlic and herbs, and the egg. Add the lemon zest and grated Parmesan. Season with salt and pepper.

5 ▲ Spread the bread mixture in one layer over the meat, leaving a small border all around. Cover with the ham and vegetable mixture. Roll the turkey up. Tie the roll in several places with string.

6 ▲ Heat the oil in a flameproof casserole. When the oil is hot, brown the meat on all sides. Remove from the heat, add the stock, and arrange the lemon wedges around the meat. Cover and place in the oven.

7 After 15 minutes, discard the lemon and baste the meat. Continue cooking, uncovered, for a further 25–30 minutes, basting occasionally, until the juices run clear when the meat is pierced. Allow the roll to stand for at least 10 minutes before slicing.

8 Strain the sauce. Stir in the butter and taste for seasoning. Serve the sliced roll warm with the sauce. If you wish to serve it cold, slice the roll just before serving and omit the sauce.

Turkey with Marsala Cream Sauce

Tacchino al marsala

Marsala makes a very rich and tasty sauce. The addition of lemon juice gives it a sharp edge, which helps to offset the richness.

Ingredients

6 turkey breasts
3 tbsp flour
2 tbsp olive oil
2 tbsp butter
¾ cup dry Marsala
¼ cup lemon juice
¾ cup heavy cream
salt and freshly ground black pepper
lemon wedges and chopped fresh
     parsley, to garnish
snow peas and green beans, to serve

serves 6

3 ▲ Heat the oil and butter in a wide heavy saucepan or frying pan until sizzling. Add as many pieces of turkey as the pan will hold and sauté over medium heat for about 3 minutes on each side, until crispy and tender. Transfer to a warmed serving dish with tongs and keep hot. Repeat with the remaining turkey.

4 ▲ Lower the heat. Mix the Marsala and lemon juice in a bowl, add to the pan and raise the heat. Bring to a boil, stirring in the sediment, then add the cream. Simmer, stirring constantly, until the sauce is reduced and glossy. Taste for seasoning. Spoon the sauce over the turkey, garnish with the lemon wedges and parsley and serve immediately with the snow peas and green beans.

1 ▲ Put each turkey breast between two sheets of plastic wrap and pound with a rolling pin to flatten and stretch. Cut each breast in half or into quarters, cutting away and discarding any sinew.

2 ▲ Spread out the flour in a shallow bowl. Season well and coat the meat.

Variation

Veal or pork cutlets or chicken breasts can be used instead of the turkey, and ¼ cup mascarpone cheese can be substituted for the heavy cream.

Duck with Chestnut Sauce

Petti di anatra con salsa di castagne

This autumnal dish makes use of the sweet chestnuts that are gathered in Italian woods.

Ingredients
1 sprig fresh rosemary
1 garlic clove, thinly sliced
2 tbsp olive oil
4 duck breasts, boned and fat removed
For the sauce
1lb chestnuts
1 tsp oil
1$\frac{1}{2}$ cups milk
1 small onion, finely chopped
1 carrot, finely chopped
1 small bay leaf
salt and freshly ground black pepper
2 tbsp cream, warmed
serves 4–5

1 ▲ Pull the leaves from the sprig of rosemary. Combine them with the garlic and oil in a shallow bowl. Pat the duck breasts dry with paper towels. Brush the duck breasts with the marinade. Allow to stand for at least 2 hours before cooking.

2 Preheat the oven to 350°F. Cut a cross in the flat side of each chestnut with a sharp knife.

~ COOK'S TIP ~

The chestnut sauce may be prepared in advance and kept in the refrigerator for up to 2 days, or it may be made when chestnuts are in season and frozen. Allow to thaw to room temperature before re-heating.

3 ▲ Place the chestnuts in a baking pan with the oil, and shake the pan until the nuts are coated with the oil. Bake for about 20 minutes, then peel.

4 Place the peeled chestnuts in a heavy pan with the milk, onion, carrot and bay leaf. Cook slowly for about 10–15 minutes until the chestnuts are very tender. Season with salt and pepper. Discard the bay leaf. Press the mixture through a strainer.

5 Return the sauce to the pan. Heat gently while the duck is cooking. Just before serving, stir in the cream. If the sauce is too thick, add a little more cream. Preheat the broiler, or prepare a barbecue.

6 ▲ Broil the duck breasts until medium rare, about 6–8 minutes. The meat should be pink when sliced. Slice into rounds and arrange on warm plates. Serve with the heated sauce.

Pan-Fried Marinated Poussin

Galletti marinati in padella

These small birds are full of flavor when marinated for several hours before cooking.

Ingredients
2 poussins, about 1lb each
5–6 leaves fresh mint, torn
1 leek, sliced into thin rings
1 garlic clove, finely chopped
salt and coarsely ground black pepper
4 tbsp olive oil
2 tbsp fresh lemon juice
1/4 cup dry white wine
mint leaves, to garnish
serves 3–4

1 Cut the poussins in half down the backbone, dividing the breast. Flatten the 4 halves with a mallet. Place them in a bowl with the mint, leek, garlic and pepper. Sprinkle with oil and half the lemon juice, cover, and allow to stand in a cool place for 6 hours.

2 ▲ Heat a large heavy frying pan or skillet. Place the poussins with their marinade in the pan. Cover and cook over moderate heat for about 45 minutes, turning occasionally, until the juices run clear when the meat is pierced. Season with salt during the cooking. Place on a warm serving dish.

3 ▲ Tilt the pan and spoon off any fat on the surface. Pour in the wine and remaining lemon juice, and cook until the sauce reduces. Strain the sauce, pressing the vegetables to extract all the juices. Place the poussins on individual dishes, and spoon over the sauce. Sprinkle with mint, and serve.

Quail with Grapes

Quaglie con uva

Small birds often feature in Italian recipes. Use the most flavorful grapes for this dish.

Ingredients
6–8 fresh quail, gutted
salt and freshly ground black pepper
4 tbsp olive oil
1/4 cup pancetta or bacon, cut into small
   dice
1 cup dry white wine
1 cup fresh or canned chicken stock,
   warmed
12 oz green grapes
serves 4

1 Wash the quail carefully inside and out with cold water. Pat dry with paper towels. Sprinkle salt and pepper into the cavities.

2 Heat the oil in a heavy sauté pan or flameproof casserole large enough to accommodate all the quail in one layer. Add the pancetta or bacon, and cook over low heat for 5 minutes.

3 ▲ Raise the heat to moderate to high, and place the quail in the pan. Brown them evenly on all sides. Pour in the wine, and cook over moderate heat until it reduces by about half. Turn the quail over. Cover the pan, and cook for about 10–15 minutes. Add the stock, turn the quail again, cover, and cook for 15–20 minutes more, or until the birds are tender. Remove to a warmed serving platter and keep warm while the sauce is being finished.

4 ▲ Meanwhile drop the grapes into a pan of boiling water, and blanch for about 3 minutes. Drain and reserve.

5 Strain the pan juices into a small cup. If bacon has been used, allow the fat to separate and rise to the top. Spoon off the fat and discard. Pour the strained gravy into a small saucepan. Add the grapes and warm them gently for 2–3 minutes. Spoon around the quail and serve.

Roast Pheasant with Juniper Berries

Fagiano arrosto

Sage and juniper are often used in Italian cooking to flavor pheasant and other game.

Ingredients

$2^{1}/_{2}$-3 lb pheasant with liver, finely
   chopped (optional)
3 tbsp olive oil
2 sprigs fresh sage
3 shallots, chopped
1 bay leaf
2 lemon quarters, plus 1 tsp juice
2 tbsp juniper berries, lightly crushed
salt and freshly ground black pepper
4 thin slices pancetta or bacon
6 tbsp dry white wine
1 cup fresh or canned chicken stock,
   heated
2 tbsp butter, at room temperature
2 tbsp flour
2 tbsp brandy
serves 3–4

1 ▲ Wash the pheasant under cool water. Drain well, and pat dry with paper towels. Rub with 1 tbsp of the olive oil. Place the remaining oil, sage leaves, shallots, and bay leaf in a shallow bowl. Add the lemon juice and juniper berries. Place the pheasant and lemon quarters in the bowl with the marinade, and spoon it over the bird. Allow to stand for several hours in a cool place, turning the pheasant occasionally. Remove the lemon.

2 Preheat the oven to 350°F. Place the pheasant in a roasting pan, reserving the marinade. Sprinkle the cavity with salt and pepper, and place the lemon quarters and bay leaf inside.

3 Arrange some of the sage leaves on the breast of the pheasant, and lay the pancetta or bacon over the top. Secure with string.

4 ▲ Spoon the remaining marinade on top of the pheasant, and roast until tender, about 30 minutes per 1 lb. Baste frequently with the pan juices and with the white wine. Transfer the pheasant to a warmed serving platter, discarding the string and pancetta.

5 Tilt the baking pan and skim off any surface fat. Pour in the stock. Stir over moderate heat, scraping up any meat residues from the bottom of the pan. Add the pheasant liver, if using. Bring to a boil and cook for 2-3 minutes Strain into a saucepan.

6 ▲ Blend the butter to a paste with the flour. Stir into the gravy a little at a time. Boil for 2-3 minutes, stirring to smooth out any lumps. Remove from the heat, stir in the brandy, and serve.

Rabbit with Tomatoes

Coniglio con pomodori

Rabbit is very popular in Italy, and is prepared in many ways. This is a hearty dish with strong and robust flavors.

Ingredients

1¹/₂lb boned rabbit, cut into chunks
2 garlic cloves, thinly sliced
¹/₂ cup thinly sliced pancetta or
   lean bacon
1¹/₂lb tomatoes, peeled, seeded and
   roughly chopped
3 tbsp chopped fresh basil
salt and freshly ground black pepper
4 tbsp olive oil
serves 4–5

3 ▲ Place the tomatoes in a layer in the bottom of a baking dish. Arrange the rabbit pieces on top of the tomatoes. Sprinkle with olive oil and place, uncovered, in the oven. Roast for 40–50 minutes.

4 ▲ Baste the rabbit occasionally with any fat in the dish. After the rabbit has cooked for about 25 minutes the dish may be covered with foil for the remaining time if the sauce seems to be too dry.

1 ▲ Preheat the oven to 400°F. Pat the rabbit pieces dry with paper towels. Place a thin slice of garlic on each piece. Wrap a slice of pancetta or bacon around it, making sure the garlic is held in place.

2 ▲ Place the tomatoes in a non-stick pan, and cook them for a few minutes until they give up some of their liquid and begin to dry out. Stir in the basil, and season with salt and pepper.

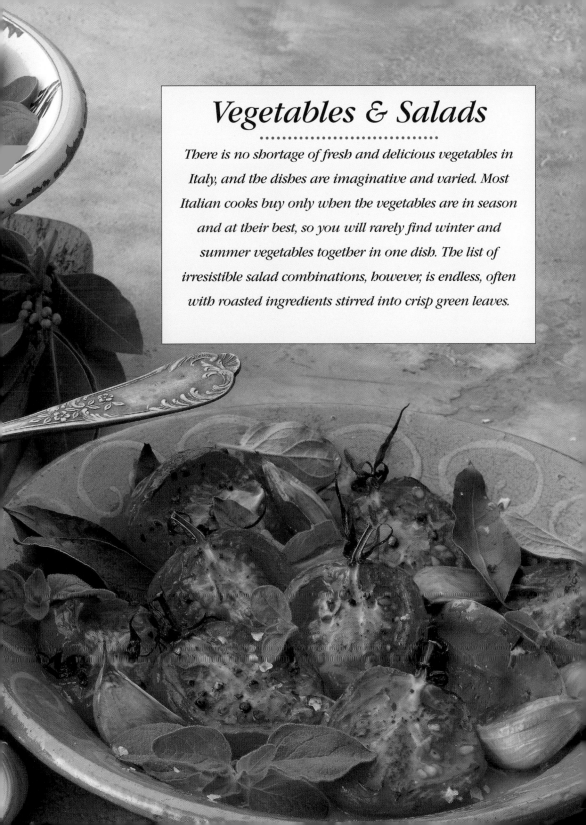

Vegetables & Salads

··

*There is no shortage of fresh and delicious vegetables in
Italy, and the dishes are imaginative and varied. Most
Italian cooks buy only when the vegetables are in season
and at their best, so you will rarely find winter and
summer vegetables together in one dish. The list of
irresistible salad combinations, however, is endless, often
with roasted ingredients stirred into crisp green leaves.*

Stuffed Artichokes

Carciofi ripieni

Artichokes grow almost wild in southern Italy and they are cooked in many different ways. In this recipe the artichokes are stuffed and baked whole.

Ingredients
1 lemon
6 large globe artichokes
For the stuffing
2 slices white bread, crusts removed
  (about 2oz)
3 anchovy fillets, finely chopped
2 garlic cloves, finely chopped
2 tbsp capers, rinsed and finely chopped
3 tbsp finely chopped fresh parsley
4 tbsp plain dry breadcrumbs
4 tbsp olive oil
salt and freshly ground black pepper
For baking
1 garlic clove, cut into 3 or 4 pieces
1 sprig fresh parsley
3 tbsp olive oil
serves 6

1 Prepare the stuffing. Soak the white bread in a little water for 5 minutes. Squeeze dry. Place in a bowl with the other stuffing ingredients and mix.

2 ▲ Squeeze the lemon, and put the juice and the squeezed halves in a large bowl of cold water. Wash the artichokes and prepare them one at a time. Cut off only the tip from the stem. Peel the stem with a small knife, pulling upwards towards the leaves. Pull off the small leaves around the stem, and continue snapping off the upper part of the dark outer leaves until you reach the taller inner leaves. Cut off the topmost part of these leaves with a sharp knife.

3 ▲ Open the artichoke slightly by spreading the leaves apart to get at the inner bristly "choke". Cut around it with the knife, and scrape it out with a small spoon. This forms a cavity inside the artichoke leaves. As soon as each artichoke has been prepared, place it in the bowl of acidulated water. This will prevent it from darkening. Preheat the oven to 375°F.

4 ▲ Place the garlic and the parsley leaves in a baking dish large enough to hold the artichokes upright in one layer. Pour in cold water to a depth of 1/2 inch. Remove the artichokes from the bowl, drain quickly, and fill the cavities with the stuffing. Place the artichokes upside down in the dish. Pour a little oil over each. Cover the dish tightly with foil. Bake for about 1 hour, or until tender.

Asparagus with Eggs

Asparagi alla milanese

The addition of fried eggs and grated Parmesan turns asparagus into something special.

Peeling enables the asparagus to cook evenly, and makes the whole spear edible.

Ingredients

1lb fresh asparagus
5 tbsp butter
4 eggs
4 tbsp freshly grated Parmesan cheese
salt and freshly ground black pepper
serves 4

4 ▲ As soon as the asparagus is cooked, remove it from the water with two slotted spoons. Place it on a cake rack covered with a clean dish towel to drain. Divide the spears between warmed individual serving plates. Place a fried egg on each, and sprinkle with the grated Parmesan.

5 ▲ Melt the remaining butter in the frying pan. As soon as it is bubbling pour it over the cheese and eggs on the asparagus. Serve at once with salt and pepper.

1 ▲ Cut off any woody ends from the asparagus. Peel the lower half of the asparagus spears by inserting a knife under the thick skin at the base, and pulling upwards towards the tip. Wash the asparagus in cold water.

2 Bring a large pan of water to a boil. Boil the asparagus until just tender when pierced with a knife.

3 ▲ While the asparagus is cooking, melt about a third of the butter in a frying pan. When it is bubbling, gently break in each egg, and cook until the whites have set but the yolks are still slightly soft.

Stewed Artichokes

Carciofi in umido

Artichokes are eaten in many ways in Italy, sometimes sliced paper-thin and eaten raw as a salad, sometimes cut up and stewed lightly with garlic, parsley and wine, as in this recipe.

Ingredients
1 lemon
4 large or 6 small globe artichokes
2 tbsp butter
4 tbsp olive oil
2 garlic cloves, finely chopped
4 tbsp chopped fresh parsley
salt and freshly ground black pepper
3 tbsp water
6 tbsp milk
6 tbsp white wine
serves 6

1 Squeeze the lemon, and put the juice and the squeezed halves in a large bowl of cold water. Wash the artichokes and prepare them one at a time. Cut off only the tip from the stem. Peel the stem with a small knife, pulling upwards towards the leaves. Pull off the small leaves around the stem, and continue snapping off the upper part of the dark outer leaves until you reach the taller inner leaves.

2 ▲ Slice the topmost part of the leaves off. Cut the artichoke into 4 or 6 segments.

3 Cut out the bristly "choke" from each segment. Place in the acidulated water to prevent the artichokes from darkening while you prepare the rest.

4 Blanch the artichokes in a large pan of rapidly boiling water for 4–5 minutes. Drain.

5 ▲ Heat the butter and olive oil in a large pan. Add the garlic and parsley, and cook for 2–3 minutes. Stir in the artichokes. Season with salt and pepper. Add the water and the milk, and cook for about 10 minutes, or until the liquid has evaporated. Stir in the wine, cover and cook until the artichokes are tender. Serve hot or at room temperature.

Green Beans with Tomatoes

Fagiolini verdi con pomodori

This dish is particularly good when fresh tomatoes are used.

Ingredients
1lb fresh green beans
3 tbsp olive oil
1 medium onion, preferably red, very
 finely sliced
12oz plum tomatoes, fresh or canned,
 peeled and finely chopped
$\frac{1}{2}$ cup water
salt and freshly ground black pepper
5–6 leaves of fresh basil torn into pieces
serves 4–6

1 Snap or cut the stem ends off the beans, and wash well in plenty of cold water. Drain.

2 ▲ Heat the oil in a large frying pan with a cover. Add the onion slices and cook until just soft, 5-6 minutes. Add the tomatoes and cook over moderate heat until they soften, about 6-8 minutes. Stir in the water. Season with salt and pepper, and add the basil.

3 ▲ Stir in the beans, turning them in the pan to coat with the sauce. Cover the pan, and cook over moderate heat until tender, about 15-20 minutes. Stir occasionally, and add a little more water if the sauce dries out too much. Serve hot or cold.

Eggplant Parmesan

Parmigiana di melanzane

This famous dish is a specialty of Italy's southern regions.

Ingredients
2lb eggplants
flour, for coating
oil, for frying
1/3 cup freshly grated Parmesan
2 cups mozzarella cheese, sliced
    very thinly
salt and freshly ground black pepper
For the tomato sauce
4 tbsp olive oil
1 medium onion, very finely chopped
1 garlic clove, finely chopped
1lb tomatoes, fresh or canned,
    chopped, with their juice
salt and freshly ground black pepper
a few leaves fresh basil or sprigs parsley
serves 4–6

1 Wash the eggplants. Cut into rounds about 1/2 inch wide, sprinkle with salt, and leave to drain for about 1 hour.

2 ▲ Meanwhile make the tomato sauce. Heat the olive oil in a medium pan. Add the chopped onion, and cook over moderate heat until it is translucent, 5–8 minutes. Stir in the chopped garlic and the tomatoes (add 3 tbsp water if you are using fresh tomatoes). Season with salt and pepper. Add the fresh basil or parsley. Cook for 20–30 minutes. Purée in a food mill or a food processor.

3 Rinse the eggplant and pat dry with paper towels. Coat lightly in flour. Heat a little oil in a large frying pan (preferably non-stick). Add one layer of eggplant, and cook over low to moderate heat with the pan covered until soft. Turn, and cook on the other side. Remove from the pan, and repeat with the remaining slices.

4 Preheat the oven to 350°F. Grease a wide shallow baking dish or pan. Spread a little tomato sauce in the bottom. Cover with a layer of eggplant. Sprinkle with a few teaspoons of Parmesan, season with salt and pepper, and cover with a layer of mozzarella. Spoon on some tomato sauce. Repeat until all the ingredients are used up, ending with a covering of tomato sauce and a sprinkling of Parmesan. Sprinkle with a little olive oil, and bake for about 45 minutes.

Sweet and Sour Eggplant

Caponata

This delicious Sicilian dish combines eggplant and celery in a piquant sauce.

Ingredients
1 1/2lb eggplants
2 tbsp olive oil
1 medium onion, finely sliced
1 garlic clove, finely chopped
8oz can plum tomatoes, peeled and
    finely chopped
1/2 cup white wine vinegar
2 tbsp sugar
salt and freshly ground black pepper
tender central stalks of a head of
    celery (about 6oz)
2 tbsp capers, rinsed
1/2 cup green olives, pitted
oil, for deep-frying
2 tbsp chopped fresh parsley
serves 4

1 Wash the eggplants and cut into small cubes. Sprinkle with salt, and leave to drain in a colander for 1 hour.

2 ▲ Heat the oil in a large pan. Stir in the onion, and cook until soft. Stir in the garlic and tomatoes, and fry over moderate heat for 10 minutes. Stir in the vinegar, sugar and pepper. Simmer until the sauce reduces, 10 minutes more. Blanch the celery stalks in boiling water until tender. Drain, and chop into 1 in pieces. Add to the sauce with the capers and olives.

3 ▲ Rinse the eggplant and pat dry with paper towels. Heat the oil to 360°F, and deep-fry the eggplant in batches until golden. Drain on paper towels.

4 Add the eggplant to the sauce. Stir gently and season. Stir in the parsley. Allow to stand for 30 minutes. Serve at room temperature.

Carrots with Marsala

Carote al Marsala

The sweet flavor of Marsala goes surprisingly well with carrots in this Sicilian dish.

Ingredients
4 tbsp butter
1lb carrots, cut into sticks
1 tsp sugar
$\frac{1}{2}$ tsp salt
$\frac{1}{4}$ cup Marsala
serves 4

1 Melt the butter in a medium pan, and add the carrots. Stir well to coat with the butter. Add the sugar and salt, and mix well.

2 ▲ Stir in the Marsala, and simmer for 4–5 minutes.

3 ▲ Pour in enough water to barely cover the carrots. Cover the pan, and cook over low to moderate heat until the carrots are tender. Remove the cover, and cook until the liquids reduce almost completely. Serve hot.

Broccoli with Oil and Garlic

Broccoletti saltati con aglio

This is a very simple way of transforming steamed or blanched broccoli into a succulent Mediterranean dish. Peeling the broccoli stalks is easy, and allows for even cooking.

Ingredients
2lb fresh broccoli
6 tbsp olive oil
2–3 garlic cloves, finely chopped
salt and freshly ground black pepper
serves 6

1 ▲ Wash the broccoli. Cut off any woody parts at the base of the stems. Use a small sharp knife to peel the broccoli stems. Cut any very long or wide stalks in half.

2 ▲ Boil water in the bottom of a pan equipped with a steamer, or bring a large pan of water to a boil. If steaming the broccoli, put it in the steamer and cover tightly. Cook for 8–12 minutes or until the stems are just tender when pierced with the point of a knife. Remove from the heat. If blanching, drop the broccoli into the pan of boiling water and blanch until just tender, 5-6 minutes. Drain.

3 ▲ In a frying pan large enough to hold all the broccoli pieces, gently heat the oil with the garlic. When the garlic is light golden (do not let it brown or it will be bitter) add the broccoli, and cook over moderate heat for 3-4 minutes, turning carefully to coat it with the hot oil. Season with salt and pepper. Serve hot or cold.

Meat-stuffed Cabbage Rolls
Involtini di verza ripieni di carne

Stuffed cabbage leaves are a good way of using up cooked meats. These rolls are quite substantial, and make a satisfying lunch dish.

Ingredients
1 head Savoy cabbage
$2/3$ cup white bread
milk, to soak bread
$1^1/_2$ cups cooked meat, very finely
    chopped, or fresh lean ground beef
1 egg
2 tbsp finely chopped fresh parsley
1 garlic clove, finely chopped
$1/_2$ cup freshly grated Parmesan cheese
pinch of grated nutmeg
salt and freshly ground black pepper
5 tbsp olive oil
1 medium onion, finely chopped
1 cup dry white wine
serves 4–5

2 ▲ Cut the crusts from the bread, and discard. Soak the bread in a little milk for about 5 minutes. Squeeze out the excess moisture with your hands.

1 ▲ Cut the leaves from the cabbage. Save the innermost part for soup. Blanch the leaves a few at a time in a large pan of boiling water for 4–5 minutes. Refresh under cold water. Spread the leaves out on clean dish towels to dry.

3 ▲ In a mixing bowl combine the chopped or minced meat with the egg and soaked bread. Stir in the parsley, garlic and Parmesan. Season with nutmeg, salt and pepper.

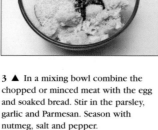

4 ▲ Divide any very large cabbage leaves in half, discarding the rib. Lay the leaves out on a flat surface. Form

little sausage-shaped mounds of stuffing, and place them at the edge of each leaf. Roll up the leaves, tucking the ends in as you roll. Squeeze each roll lightly in the palm of your hand to help the leaves to stick.

5 ▲ In a large, shallow, flameproof casserole or deep frying pan large enough to hold all the cabbage rolls in one layer, heat the olive oil. Add the onion, and cook gently until it softens. Raise the heat slightly, and add the cabbage rolls, turning them over carefully with a large spoon as they begin to cook.

6 ▲ Pour in half of the wine. Cook over low to moderate heat until the wine has evaporated. Add the rest of the wine, cover the pan, and cook for 10–15 minutes more. Remove the cover, and cook until all the liquid has evaporated. Remove from the heat, and allow to rest for about 5 minutes before serving.

~ VARIATION ~

Serve the rolls with a tomato sauce, spooned over just before serving.

Tuscan Baked Beans

Fagioli al forno alla toscana

Beans, both dried and fresh, are particularly popular in Tuscany, where they are cooked in many different ways. In this vegetarian dish the beans are flavored with fresh sage leaves.

Ingredients
1lb 6oz dried beans, such as cannellini
4 tbsp olive oil
2 garlic cloves, crushed
3 leaves fresh sage (if fresh sage is
    not available use 4 tbsp chopped
    fresh parsley)
1 leek, finely sliced
14oz can plum tomatoes, chopped,
    with their juice
salt and freshly ground black pepper
serves 6–8

3 ▲ In a large deep baking dish combine the beans with the leek and tomatoes. Stir in the oil with the garlic and sage. Add enough fresh water to cover the beans by 1 inch. Mix well. Cover the dish with a lid or foil, and place in the center of the preheated oven. Bake for 1³/₄ hours.

4 ▲ Remove the dish from the oven, stir the beans, and season with salt and pepper. Return the beans to the oven, uncovered, and cook for another 15 minutes, or until the beans are tender. Remove from the oven and allow to stand for 7–8 minutes before serving. Serve hot or at room temperature.

1 ▲ Carefully pick over the beans, discarding any stones or other particles. Place the beans in a large bowl and cover with water. Soak for at least 6 hours, or overnight. Drain.

2 ▲ Preheat the oven to 350°F. Heat the oil in a small pan and sauté the garlic cloves and sage leaves for 3–4 minutes until the garlic is tender but not brown. Remove from the heat.

Stewed Lentils

Lenticchie in umido

In Italy lentils are very often eaten as an accompaniment to duck and to zampone or cotechino sausages, but they are also good by themselves.

Ingredients

2 cups green or brown lentils
3 tbsp olive oil
$1/4$ cup pancetta or salt pork
1 medium onion, very finely chopped
1 stalk celery, very finely sliced
1 carrot, very finely chopped
1 garlic clove
1 bay leaf
3 tbsp chopped fresh parsley
salt and freshly ground black pepper
serves 6

1 ▲ Carefully pick over the lentils, removing any stones or other particles. Place them in a large bowl and cover with water. Soak for several hours. Drain.

2 ▲ Heat the oil in a large, heavy pan. Add the pancetta or salt pork and cook for 3 or 4 minutes. Stir in the onion, and cook over low heat until it is soft.

3 ▲ Add the celery and carrot and cook for 3-4 minutes more.

4 ▲ Add the lentils to the pan, stirring to coat them with the fat. Pour in enough boiling water just to cover the lentils. Stir well, adding the whole garlic clove, the bay leaf and the parsley. Cook over moderate heat until the lentils are tender, about 1 hour. Discard the garlic and bay leaf, and season with salt and pepper. Serve hot or at room temperature.

Fava Bean Purée with Ham

Purea di fave con prosciutto

Peeling fava beans leaves them tender and sweet. They go particularly well with the saltiness of prosciutto crudo in this Tuscan combination.

Ingredients
2lb fresh fava beans in their pods,
   or 14oz shelled fava beans,
   thawed if frozen
1 medium onion, finely chopped
2 small potatoes, peeled and diced
1/4 cup prosciutto crudo
3 tbsp extra-virgin olive oil
salt and freshly ground black pepper
serves 4

3 Chop the ham into very small dice. Heat the oil and sauté until the ham is just golden.

1 Place the shelled beans in a pan and cover with water. Bring to a boil and cook for 5 minutes. Drain thoroughly. When they are cool enough to handle, peel the beans.

2 ▲ Place the peeled beans in a pan with the onion and potatoes. Add enough water just to cover the vegetables. Bring to a boil. Lower the heat slightly, cover, and simmer until the vegetables are very soft, 15–20 minutes. Check occasionally that all the water has not evaporated. If necessary add a few tablespoons more.

4 ▲ Mash or purée the bean mixture. Return it to the pan. If it is very moist, cook it over moderate heat until it reduces slightly. Stir in the oil with the ham. Season and cook for 2 minutes.

Deep-fried Cauliflower

Cavolfiore fritto

Deep-frying is very popular in Italy, and everything from cheese to fruit may be fried. The cauliflower may be eaten as a side dish or as an antipasto.

Ingredients
1 large cauliflower
1 egg
salt and freshly ground black pepper
scant 1 cup flour
3/4 cup dry white wine
oil, for deep-frying
serves 4

1 Soak the cauliflower in a bowl of salted water. In a mixing bowl, beat the egg. Season and beat in the flour. The mixture will be very thick. Add the wine. If necessary add more to make a fairly runny batter. Cover, and allow to rest for 30 minutes.

2 Steam or boil the cauliflower until just tender – do not overcook. Cut it into small florets when cool.

3 ▲ Heat the oil until a small piece of bread sizzles as soon as it is dropped in (about 360°F). Dip each cauliflower piece into the batter before deep-frying it until golden.

4 ▲ Remove from the oil with a slotted spoon and drain on paper towels. Sprinkle lightly with salt and serve hot.

Baked Fennel with Parmesan Cheese
Finocchio gratinato

Fennel is widely eaten in Italy, both raw and cooked. It is delicious married with the sharpness of Parmesan cheese in this quick and simple dish.

Ingredients
2lb fennel bulbs, washed and cut in half
4 tbsp butter
1/3 cup freshly grated Parmesan cheese
serves 4–6

2 ▲ Cut the fennel bulbs lengthwise into 4 or 6 pieces. Place them in a buttered baking dish.

3 ▲ Dot with butter. Sprinkle with the grated Parmesan. Bake in the hot oven until the cheese is golden brown, about 20 minutes. Serve at once.

1 ▲ Cook the fennel in a large pan of boiling water until just tender and not at all mushy. Drain. Preheat the oven to 400°F.

~ VARIATION ~

For a more substantial version of this dish, sprinkle 3oz chopped ham over the fennel before topping with the cheese.

Roast Mushroom Caps
Funghi arrosti

Hunting for edible wild mushrooms is one of the Italians' great passions. The most prized are porcini which grow in forests, but are available here fresh in the markets in fall.

Ingredients
4 large mushroom caps, such as porcini
    or portobello
2 garlic cloves, chopped
3 tbsp chopped fresh parsley
salt and freshly ground black pepper
extra-virgin olive oil, for sprinkling
serves 4

1 Preheat the oven to 375°F. Carefully wipe the mushrooms clean with a damp cloth or paper towel. Cut off the stems. (Save them for soup if they are not too woody). Oil a baking dish large enough to hold the mushrooms in one layer.

2 ▲ Place the mushroom caps in the dish, smooth side down. Mix together the chopped garlic and parsley and sprinkle on the caps.

3 ▲ Season the mushrooms with salt and pepper. Sprinkle the parsley stuffing with oil. Bake for 20–25 minutes. Serve at once.

Roasted Plum Tomatoes and Garlic

Pomodori al forno

These are so simple to prepare, yet taste absolutely wonderful. Use a large, shallow

earthenware dish that will allow the tomatoes to sear and char in a hot oven.

Ingredients

8 plum tomatoes, halved
12 garlic cloves
¼ cup extra virgin olive oil
3 bay leaves
salt and freshly ground black pepper
3 tbsp fresh oregano leaves,
    to garnish

serves 4

Cook's Tip

Use ripe plum tomatoes for this recipe, as they keep their shape and do not fall apart when roasted at such a high temperature. Leave the stalks on, if possible.

1 ▲ Preheat the oven to 450°F. Select an ovenproof dish that will hold all the tomatoes snugly in a single layer. Place the tomatoes in the dish and push the whole, unpeeled garlic cloves between them.

2 ▲ Brush the tomatoes with the oil, add the bay leaves and sprinkle black pepper over the top. Bake for about 45 minutes, until the tomatoes have softened and are sizzling in the pan. They should be charred around the edges. Season with salt and a little more black pepper, if needed. Garnish with oregano and serve.

Marinated Baby Eggplants

Melanzane in agrodolce

Eggplants are especially popular in the south of Italy. This dish uses ingredients that have been included in recipes since Renaissance times. Make a day in advance, to allow the sour and sweet flavors to develop.

Ingredients

12 baby eggplants, halved lengthwise
1 cup extra virgin olive oil
juice of 1 lemon
2 tbsp balsamic vinegar
3 cloves
⅓ cup pine nuts
2 tbsp raisins
1 tbsp sugar
1 bay leaf
large pinch of dried red pepper flakes
salt and freshly ground black pepper
serves 4

1 Preheat the broiler to high. Place the eggplants, cut side up, in a broiler pan and brush with a little of the olive oil. Broil for 10 minutes, until slightly blackened, turning them over halfway through cooking.

2 ▲ To make the marinade, put the remaining olive oil, the lemon juice, vinegar, cloves, pine nuts, raisins, sugar and bay leaf in a small bowl or measuring cup. Add the red pepper flakes and salt and pepper and mix thoroughly.

3 ▲ Place the hot eggplants in an earthenware or glass bowl and pour the marinade over. Allow to cool, turning the eggplants once or twice. Serve cold.

Fennel Gratin

Finocchi gratinati

This is one of the best ways to eat fresh fennel. The fennel takes on a delicious, almost

creamy, flavor, which contrasts beautifully with the sharp, strong Gruyère.

Ingredients
2 fennel bulbs, about 1½ lb
    total weight
1¼ cups milk
1 tbsp butter, plus extra
    for greasing
1 tbsp flour
scant ½ cup dry white bread crumbs
3 oz Gruyère cheese, grated
salt and freshly ground black pepper
serves 4

Cook's Tip
Instead of the Gruyère, Parmesan,
Pecorino or any other strong cheese
would work perfectly.

1 ▲ Preheat the oven to 475°F.
Discard the stalks and root ends from
the fennel. Slice into quarters and
place in a large saucepan. Pour in the
milk and simmer for 10–15 minutes
until tender. Butter a baking dish.

2 Remove the fennel pieces with a
slotted spoon, reserving the milk, and
arrange the fennel pieces in the dish.

3 ▲ Melt the butter in a small
saucepan and add the flour, stir well,
then gradually whisk in the reserved
milk. Stir the sauce until thickened.

4 Pour the sauce over the fennel
pieces, and sprinkle with the bread
crumbs and grated Gruyère. Season
with salt and black pepper and bake
for about 20 minutes, until browned.

Sweet-and-Sour Onions

Cipolline in agrodolce

Onions are naturally sweet, and when they are cooked at a high temperature the sweetness

intensifies. Serve with roasts and meat dishes or as part of an antipasto.

Ingredients
4 tbsp butter
5 tbsp sugar
½ cup white wine vinegar
2 tbsp balsamic vinegar
1½ lb small pickling onions, peeled
salt and freshly ground black pepper
serves 4

Cook's Tips
This recipe also looks and tastes
delicious when made with either
yellow or red onions, which are cut
into either thin slices or chunks.
Cooking times will vary, depending
on the size of the onion pieces.

1 ▲ Heat the butter in a large
saucepan over low heat. Add the
sugar and heat until dissolved,
stirring constantly.

2 ▲ Add the vinegars to the pan
with the onions and combine well.
Season with salt and pepper and
cover and cook over medium heat
for 20–25 minutes, until the onions
are a golden color and soft when
pierced with a knife. Serve hot.

Zucchini with Sun-dried Tomatoes *Zucchini con pomodori*

One way to preserve tomatoes for winter is to dry them in the sun, as they do all over southern Italy. These tomatoes have a concentrated, sweet flavor that goes well with zucchini.

Ingredients

10 sun-dried tomatoes, dry or preserved
    in oil and drained
$^3/_4$ cup warm water
5 tbsp olive oil
1 large onion, finely sliced
2 garlic cloves, finely chopped
2lb zucchini, cut into thin strips
salt and freshly ground black pepper
serves 6

3 ▲ Stir in the garlic and the zucchini. Cook for about 5 minutes, continuing to stir the mixture.

4 ▲ Stir in the tomatoes and their soaking liquid. Season with salt and pepper. Raise the heat slightly and cook until the zucchini are just tender. Serve hot or cold.

1 ▲ Slice the tomatoes into thin strips. Place in a bowl with the warm water. Allow to stand for 20 minutes.

2 ▲ In a large, deep frying pan, heat the oil and stir in the onion. Cook over low to moderate heat until it softens but does not brown.

Stuffed Onions

Cipolle ripiene

These savory onions make a satisfying dish for a light lunch or supper. Small onions could be stuffed and served as an accompaniment to a meat dish.

Ingredients

6 large onions
scant ¹/₂ cup ham, cut into small dice
1 egg
¹/₂ cup dry breadcrumbs
3 tbsp finely chopped fresh parsley
1 garlic clove, finely chopped
pinch of grated nutmeg
³/₄ cup grated cheese, such as
    Parmesan or Romano
6 tbsp olive oil
salt and freshly ground black pepper
serves 6

1 Peel the onions without cutting through the base. Cook them in a large pan of boiling water for about 20 minutes. Drain, and refresh in plenty of cold water.

2 ▲ Using a small sharp knife, cut around and scoop out the central section. Remove about half the inside (save it for soup). Lightly salt the empty cavities, and leave the onions to drain upside down.

3 ▲ Preheat the oven to 400°F. In a small bowl, beat the ham into the egg. Stir in the breadcrumbs, parsley, garlic, nutmeg and all but 3 tbsp of the grated cheese. Add 3 tbsp of the oil, and season with salt and pepper.

4 Pat the insides of the onions dry with paper towels. Stuff them using a small spoon. Arrange the onions in one layer in an oiled baking dish.

5 ▲ Sprinkle the tops with the remaining cheese, and sprinkle with oil. Bake for 45 minutes, or until the onions are tender and golden on top.

~ VARIATION ~

For a vegetarian version, replace the ham with chopped olives.

Aromatic Stewed Mushrooms

Funghi trifolati

This dish from Piedmont combines both field and cultivated mushrooms, which give a balanced but not overwhelming flavor.

Ingredients
1½lb firm fresh mushrooms, field
    and cultivated
6 tbsp olive oil
2 garlic cloves, finely chopped
salt and freshly ground black pepper
3 tbsp chopped fresh parsley
serves 6

2 ▲ Cut off the woody tips of the stems and discard. Slice the stems and caps fairly thickly.

3 ▲ Heat the oil in a large frying pan. Stir in the garlic and, after about 1 minute, the mushrooms. Cook for 8–10 minutes, stirring occasionally. Season with salt and pepper, and stir in the parsley. Cook for 5 minutes more, and serve at once.

1 ▲ Clean the mushrooms carefully by wiping them with a damp cloth or paper towels.

Sautéed Peas with Ham

Piselli alla fiorentina

When fresh peas are in season, they can be stewed with a little ham and onion and served as a substantial side dish.

Ingredients
3 tbsp olive oil
½ cup pancetta or ham, finely diced
3 tbsp finely chopped onion
2lb whole peas (about 11oz shelled)
    or 10oz frozen petits pois, thawed
2–3 tbsp water
salt and freshly ground black pepper
a few leaves fresh mint or sprigs
    parsley
additional parsley or mint to garnish
    (optional)
serves 4

1 Heat the oil in a medium pan, and sauté the pancetta or ham and onion for 2–3 minutes.

2 ▲ Stir in the shelled fresh or thawed frozen peas. Add the water. Season with salt and pepper and mix well to coat with the oil.

3 ▲ Add the fresh herbs, cover, and cook over moderate heat until tender. This may take from 5 minutes for sweet fresh peas, to 15 for tougher, older peas. Serve as a side dish to meat dishes or frittate.

Roasted Potatoes with Red Onions
Patate al forno

These mouth-watering potatoes are a fine accompaniment to just about anything. The key is to use small firm potatoes; the smaller they are cut, the quicker they will cook.

Ingredients
1½ lb small firm potatoes
2 tbsp butter
2 tbsp olive oil
2 red onions, cut into chunks
8 garlic cloves, unpeeled
2 tbsp chopped fresh rosemary
salt and freshly ground black pepper
serves 4

Cook's Tip
To ensure that the potatoes are crisp, make sure they are completely dry before cooking. Resist the urge to turn the potatoes too often. Let them brown on one side before turning. Do not salt the potatoes until the end of cooking—salting beforehand encourages them to release their liquid, making them limp.

1 ▲ Preheat the oven to 450°F. Peel and quarter the potatoes, rinse them well and pat thoroughly dry with paper towels. Place the butter and oil in a roasting pan and place in the oven to heat.

2 ▲ When the butter has melted and is foaming, add the potatoes, red onions, garlic and rosemary. Toss well, then spread out in one layer.

3 Place the pan in the oven and roast for about 25 minutes, until the potatoes are golden and tender when tested with a fork. Shake the pan occasionally to redistribute the potatoes. When cooked, season with salt and pepper.

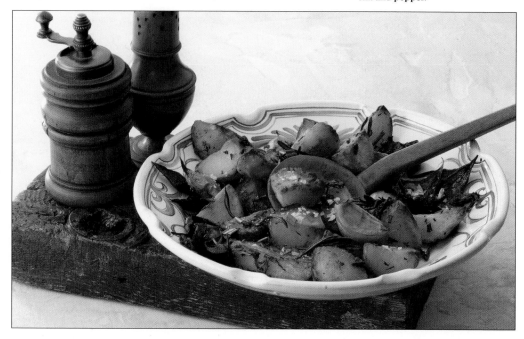

Radicchio and Chicory Gratin   *Radicchio e indivia gratinati*

Vegetables such as radicchio and chicory take on a different flavor when cooked in this way.

The creamy béchamel combines wonderfully with the bitter leaves.

Ingredients
2 heads radicchio, quartered lengthwise
2 heads chicory, quartered lengthwise
¹/₂ cup drained sun-dried tomatoes in oil,
    chopped roughly
2 tbsp butter
1 tbsp flour
1 cup milk
pinch grated nutmeg
¹/₂ cup grated Emmenthal cheese
salt and freshly ground black pepper
chopped fresh parsley, to garnish
serves 4

1 ▲ Preheat the oven to 350°F. Grease a 5-cup baking dish. Trim the radicchio and chicory and separate the leaves, discarding any that are damaged or wilted. Quarter them lengthwise and arrange in the baking dish. Scatter on the sun-dried tomatoes, and brush the leaves liberally with the oil from the jar. Sprinkle with salt and pepper and cover with foil. Bake for 15 minutes, then remove the foil and bake for another 10 minutes, until the vegetables are softened.

Cook's Tip
In Italy radicchio and chicory are often grilled outdoors on a barbecue. To do this, simply prepare the vegetables as above and brush with olive oil. Place cut-side down on the grill for 7–10 minutes until browned. Turn and grill until the other side is browned, about 5 minutes longer.

2 ▲ Make the sauce. Place the butter in a small saucepan and melt over medium heat. When the butter is foaming, add the flour and cook for 1 minute, stirring. Remove from the heat and gradually add the milk, whisking constantly. Return to the heat and bring to a boil, them simmer for 2–3 minutes to thicken. Season to taste and add the nutmeg.

3 ▲ Pour the sauce over the vegetables and sprinkle with the grated cheese. Bake for about 20 minutes, until golden. Serve immediately, garnished with parsley.

Potato and Pumpkin Pudding

Tortino di patate e zucca

Serve this savory pudding with any rich meat dish or simply with a mixed salad.

Ingredients
3 tbsp olive oil
1 garlic clove, sliced
large wedge (1½ lb) pumpkin, cut into
   ¾-inch chunks
12 oz potatoes, unpeeled
2 tbsp butter
scant ½ cup ricotta cheese
⅔ cup grated Parmesan cheese
pinch grated nutmeg
4 eggs, separated
salt and freshly ground black pepper
chopped fresh parsley, to garnish
serves 4

1 Preheat the oven to 400°F. Grease
an 8-cup, shallow, oval baking dish.

Cook's Tip
You may process the vegetables in a
food processor for a few seconds, but
be careful not to overprocess, as they
will become very gluey.

2 ▲ Heat the oil in a large frying pan,
add the garlic and pumpkin and cook,
stirring often to prevent sticking, for
15–20 minutes or until the pumpkin
is tender. Meanwhile, cook the
potatoes in boiling salted water for
20 minutes, until tender. Drain, leave
until cool enough to handle, then peel
off the skins. Place the potatoes and
pumpkin in a large bowl and mash
together well with the butter.

3 Mash the ricotta with a fork until
smooth and add to the potato and
pumpkin mixture, mixing well.

4 ▲ Stir the Parmesan, nutmeg and
plenty of seasoning into the ricotta
mixture—it should be smooth and
creamy.

5 Add the egg yolks one at a time
until mixed in thoroughly.

6 Whisk the egg whites with an
electric whisk until they form stiff
peaks, then fold gently into the
mixture. Spoon into the prepared
baking dish and bake for
30 minutes, until golden and firm.
Serve hot, garnished with parsley.

Fried Spring Greens

Cavolo fritto

*This dish can be served as a vegetable side dish, or it can be enjoyed simply on its own, with
some warm crusty bread.*

Ingredients
2 tbsp olive oil
2 tbsp butter
4 strips bacon, chopped
1 large onion, thinly sliced
1 cup dry white wine
2 garlic cloves, finely chopped
2 pounds spring greens, shredded
salt and freshly ground black pepper
serves 4

Cook's Tips
This dish would work just as well
using shredded red cabbage and
red wine. Let simmer for 10 minutes
longer, as red cabbage leaves are
slightly tougher than the spring
greens.

1 ▲ In a large frying pan, heat the oil
and butter and add the bacon. Fry for
2 minutes, then add the onions and
fry for another 3 minutes, until the
onion is beginning to soften.

2 Add the wine and simmer
vigorously for 2 minutes to reduce.

3 ▲ Reduce the heat and add the
garlic, spring greens and salt and
pepper. Cook over low heat for
about 15 minutes, until the greens
are tender. (Cover the pan so that
the greens retain their color.)
Serve hot.

Stuffed Peppers

Peperoni ripieni

Sweet peppers can be stuffed and baked with many different fillings, from leftover cooked vegetables to rice or pasta. Blanching the peppers first helps to make them tender.

Ingredients

6 medium to large peppers, any color
scant 1 cup rice
4 tbsp olive oil
1 large onion, finely chopped
3 anchovy fillets, chopped
2 garlic cloves, finely chopped
3 medium tomatoes, peeled and cut
    into small dice
4 tbsp white wine
3 tbsp finely chopped fresh parsley
$1/_2$ cup mozzarella cheese, cut into
    small dice
6 tbsp freshly grated Parmesan
    cheese
salt and freshly ground black pepper
Basic Tomato Sauce, to serve (optional)
serves 6

2 ▲ Boil the rice according to the instructions on the package, but drain and rinse it in cold water 3 minutes before the recommended cooking time has elapsed. Drain again.

1 ▲ Cut the tops off the peppers. Scoop out the seeds and fibrous insides. Blanch the peppers and their tops in a large pan of boiling water for 3–4 minutes. Remove, and stand upside down on racks to drain.

3 ▲ In a large frying pan, heat the oil and sauté the onion until soft. Stir in the anchovy pieces and the garlic, and mash them. Add the tomatoes, and the wine, and cook for 5 minutes.

4 ▲ Preheat the oven to 375°F. Remove the tomato mixture from the

heat. Stir in the rice, parsley, mozzarella and 4 tbsp of the Parmesan cheese. Season the mixture with salt and pepper.

5 ▲ Pat the insides of the peppers dry with paper towels. Sprinkle with salt and pepper. Stuff the peppers. Sprinkle the tops with the remaining Parmesan, and sprinkle with a little oil.

6 ▲ Arrange the peppers in a shallow baking dish. Pour in enough water to come $1/_2$ inch up the sides of the peppers. Bake for 25 minutes. Serve at once, with tomato sauce if desired. These peppers are also good served at room temperature.

~ COOK'S TIP ~

Choose peppers with sturdy, even bases, so they will stand on end unsupported. This will make them easier to cook and serve.

Stuffed Eggplants

Melanzane alla ligure

This typical Ligurian dish is spiked with paprika and allspice, a legacy from the days when spices from the East came into northern Italy via the port of Genoa.

Ingredients

2 eggplants, about 8 oz each, stalks removed
10 oz potatoes, peeled and diced
2 tbsp olive oil
1 small onion, finely chopped
1 garlic clove, finely chopped
good pinch of ground allspice and paprika
1 egg, beaten
½ cup grated Parmesan cheese
1 tbsp fresh white bread crumbs
salt and freshly ground black pepper
fresh mint sprigs, to garnish
salad greens, to serve
serves 4

1 Bring a large saucepan of lightly salted water to a boil. Add the whole eggplant and cook for 5 minutes, turning frequently. Remove with a slotted spoon and set aside. Add the potatoes to the pan and cook for 20 minutes until soft.

3 ▲ Heat the oil in a frying pan, add the onion and cook gently, stirring frequently, until softened. Add the chopped eggplant flesh and the garlic. Cook, stirring frequently, for 6–8 minutes. Pour into a bowl. Preheat the oven to 375°F.

4 Drain and mash the potatoes. Add the spices and beaten egg to the eggplant mixture. Set aside 1 tbsp of the Parmesan and add the rest to the eggplant mixture, stir in salt and pepper to taste.

5 ▲ Spoon the mixture into the eggplant shells. Mix the bread crumbs with the reserved Parmesan cheese and sprinkle the mixture onto the eggplants. Bake for 40–45 minutes, until the topping is crisp. Garnish with mint and serve with salad greens.

2 ▲ Meanwhile, cut the eggplants in half lengthwise and gently scoop out the flesh with a small sharp knife and a spoon, leaving ¼ in of the shell intact. Select a baking dish that will hold the eggplant shells snugly in a single layer. Brush it lightly with oil. Put the shells in the baking dish and chop the eggplant flesh roughly.

Cook's Tip
The eggplants can be filled in advance, then covered with foil and kept in the refrigerator. Add the crumb topping just before baking.

Bell Pepper Gratin

Peperoni gratinati

Serve this simple but delicious dish as an appetizer with a small mixed leaf or arugula salad and some good crusty bread to mop up the juices from the peppers.

Ingredients

2 red bell peppers
2 tbsp extra virgin olive oil
¼ cup fresh white bread crumbs
1 garlic clove, finely chopped
1 tsp drained bottled capers
8 pitted black olives, roughly chopped
1 tbsp chopped fresh oregano
1 tbsp chopped fresh flat-
    leaf parsley
salt and freshly ground black pepper
fresh herbs, to garnish
serves 4

1 ▲ Preheat the oven to 400ºF. Place the peppers under a hot broiler. Turn occasionally until they are blackened and blistered all over. Remove from the heat and place in a plastic bag. Seal and let cool.

2 ▲ When cool, peel the peppers. (Don't skin them under the tap, as the water would wash away some of the delicious smoky flavor.) Halve and remove the seeds, then cut the flesh into large strips.

3 ▲ Use a little of the olive oil to grease a small baking dish. Arrange the pepper strips in the dish.

4 ▲ Scatter the remaining ingredients on top, drizzle with the remaining olive oil and add salt and pepper to taste. Bake for about 20 minutes, until the bread crumbs have browned. Garnish with fresh herbs and serve immediately.

Stewed Peppers

Peperonata

This dish originated in the south of Italy, but has become a popular favorite everywhere. It can be eaten as a side dish or appetizer, and makes a delicious filling for a frittata.

Ingredients

4–5 very ripe peppers, preferably red
    or yellow, about 1$\frac{1}{2}$lb
4 tbsp olive oil
2 medium onions, thinly sliced
3 garlic cloves, finely chopped
12oz plum tomatoes, peeled,
    seeded and chopped
salt and freshly ground black pepper
a few fresh basil leaves
serves 6

1 Wash the peppers. Cut them into quarters, removing the stems and seeds. Slice them into thin strips.

2 ▲ In a large, heavy pan, heat the oil and sauté the onions until soft (covering the pan will prevent the onions from browning). Add the peppers, and cook for 5-8 minutes over moderate heat, stirring frequently.

3 ▲ Stir in the garlic and tomatoes. Cover the pan, and cook for about 25 minutes, stirring occasionally. The peppers should be soft, but should still hold their shape. Season, tear the basil leaves into pieces, and stir into the peppers. Serve hot or cold.

Broiled Radicchio and Zucchini

Verdure ai ferri

In Italy radicchio is often eaten broiled or barbecued. It is delicious and very easy to prepare.

Ingredients

2–3 firm heads of radicchio, round
    or long type
4 medium zucchini
6 tbsp olive oil
salt and freshly ground black pepper
serves 4

2 ▲ Cut the zucchini into $\frac{1}{2}$in diagonal slices.

3 ▲ When the broiler or barbecue is hot, brush the vegetables all over with the olive oil, and sprinkle with salt and pepper. Cook for 4-5 minutes on each side. Serve on their own or as an accompaniment to broiled fish or meat.

1 ▲ Preheat the broiler, or prepare a barbecue. Cut the radicchio in half through the root section or base. If necessary, wash in cold water. Drain.

Potatoes Baked with Tomatoes

Patate e pomodori al forno

This simple, hearty dish from the south of Italy is best when tomatoes are in season, but can also be made with canned plum tomatoes.

Ingredients

2 large red or yellow onions, thinly sliced
2lb potatoes, peeled and thinly sliced
1lb tomatoes, fresh or canned,
    sliced, with their juice
6 tbsp olive oil
1 cup freshly grated Parmesan or
    Romano
salt and freshly ground black pepper
a few leaves fresh basil
1/4 cup water
serves 6

1 Preheat the oven to 350°F. Brush a large baking dish generously with oil.

2 ▲ Arrange a layer of onions in the dish, followed by layers of potatoes and tomatoes. Pour on a little of the oil, and sprinkle with a little cheese. Season with salt and pepper.

layer of potatoes and tomatoes. Tear the basil leaves into pieces, and add them here and there among the vegetables. Sprinkle the top with cheese, and a little oil.

5 ▲ If the top begins to brown too much, place a sheet of foil or a flat cookie sheet on top of the dish. Serve hot.

3 ▲ Repeat until the vegetables are used up, ending with an overlapping

4 ▲ Pour on the water. Bake for 1 hour, or until tender.

Tomatoes with Pasta Stuffing
Pomodori ripieni di pasta

Tomatoes are one of Italy's staple foods, appearing in more than three-quarters of all Italian savory dishes. They can be baked with various stuffings. This one comes from the south.

Ingredients

8 large tomatoes, firm and ripe
1¹/₄ cups small soup pasta
8 black olives, pitted and finely
    chopped
3 tbsp finely chopped mixed fresh
    herbs, such as chives, parsley,
    basil and thyme
4 tbsp grated Parmesan cheese
4 tbsp olive oil
salt and freshly ground black pepper
serves 4

3 ▲ Preheat the oven to 375°F. Combine the pasta with the remaining ingredients in a bowl. Stir in the drained tomato pulp. Season with salt and pepper.

4 ▲ Stuff the tomatoes, and replace the tops. Arange them in one layer in a well-oiled baking dish. Bake for 15–20 minutes. Peel off the skins, if desired. Serve hot or at room temperature.

1 ▲ Wash the tomatoes. Slice off the tops, and scoop out the pulp into a strainer with a small spoon. Chop the pulp and turn the tomatoes upside down on a rack to drain.

2 ▲ Leave the pulp to drain. Meanwhile, boil the pasta in a pan of boiling salted water. Drain it 2 minutes before the recommended cooking time elapses.

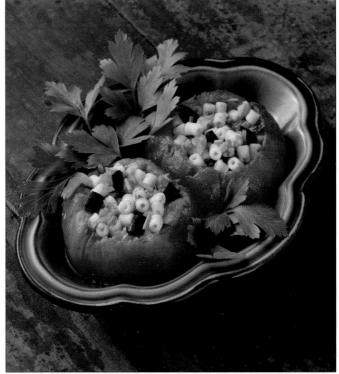

Tomato, Bell Pepper and Bread Salad   *Panzanella*

In this lively classic salad, a tangy blend of tomato juice, olive oil and red wine vinegar is

soaked up in a colorful mixture of roasted peppers, anchovies and toasted ciabatta.

Ingredients
8 oz ciabatta (about ⅔ loaf)
⅔ cup olive oil
3 red bell peppers
3 yellow bell peppers
2 oz can anchovy fillets
1½ lb ripe plum tomatoes
4 garlic cloves, crushed
4 tbsp red wine vinegar
2 oz capers
1 cup pitted black olives
salt and freshly ground black pepper
basil leaves, to garnish
serves 4–6

1 Preheat the oven to 400°F. Cut the ciabatta into ¾ in chunks and drizzle with ¼ cup of the oil. Broil the bread lightly until golden on both sides.

2 Put the peppers on a foil-lined baking sheet and bake for about 45 minutes until the skin begins to char. Remove from the oven, transfer to a large bowl, cover with a plate and leave until the peppers are cool enough to handle.

3 When the peppers are cool, peel off the skins, then cut the peppers into quarters, discarding the stalk ends and seeds. Drain, then coarsely chop the anchovies. Set aside.

4 To make the tomato dressing, peel and halve the tomatoes. Scoop the seeds into a strainer set over a bowl.

5 ▲ Press the tomato pulp in the strainer to extract the juice. Discard the pulp and add the remaining oil, the garlic, vinegar and seasoning to the juice. Layer the toasted bread, peppers, tomatoes, anchovies, capers and olives in a large bowl. Pour the dressing over and let stand for about 30 minutes, then serve garnished with plenty of basil leaves.

Radicchio and Artichoke Salad   *Insalata di radicchio e topinambur*

The distinctive, earthy taste of Jerusalem artichokes makes a lovely contrast to the sharp
freshness of radicchio and lemon. Serve warm or cold as an accompaniment to broiled
steak or barbecued meats.

Ingredients
1 large radicchio or 5 oz radicchio leaves
6 tbsp walnut pieces
3 tbsp walnut oil
1¼ lb Jerusalem artichokes
pared rind and juice of 1 lemon
coarse sea salt and freshly ground
    black pepper
flat leaf parsley, to garnish (optional)
serves 4

1 ▲ If using a whole radicchio, cut it into 8–10 wedges. Put the wedges or leaves in a shallow flameproof dish. Scatter the walnuts over the top, then pour over the oil and season. Broil for 2–3 minutes.

2 Peel the artichokes and cut up any large ones so the pieces are all roughly the same size. Add the artichokes to a pan of boiling salted water with half the lemon juice and cook for 5–7 minutes until tender. Drain. Preheat the broiler to high.

3 Toss the artichokes into the salad with the remaining lemon juice and the pared rind. Season with coarse sea salt and pepper. Broil until beginning to brown. Serve immediately, garnished with flat leaf parsley, if you like.

Bell Pepper and Tomato Salad *Peperoni arrostiti con pomodori*

This is one of those lovely recipes that brings together perfectly the colors, flavors and textures of southern Italian food. Eat this dish at room temperature with a green salad.

Ingredients
3 red bell peppers
6 large plum tomatoes
1/2 tsp dried red chili flakes
1 red onion, finely sliced
3 garlic cloves, finely chopped
grated rind and juice of 1 lemon
3 tbsp chopped fresh flat-
 leaf parsley
2 tbsp extra virgin olive oil
salt and freshly ground black pepper
black and green olives and extra
 chopped flat-leaf parsley,
 to garnish
serves 4

Cook's Tip
Peppers roasted this way will keep
for several weeks. After peeling off
the skins, place the pepper pieces in
a jar with a tight-fitting lid. Pour
enough olive oil over them to cover
completely. Store in the refrigerator.

1 ▲ Preheat the oven to 425°F.
Place the peppers on a baking sheet
and roast, turning occasionally, for
10 minutes or until the skins are
almost blackened. Add the tomatoes
to the baking sheet and bake for
5 more minutes.

2 Place the peppers in a plastic bag,
close the top loosely, trapping in
the steam, and then set them aside,
with the tomatoes, until they are cool
enough to handle.

3 ▲ Carefully pull off the skin from
the peppers. Remove the seeds, then
chop the peppers and tomatoes
roughly and place in a mixing bowl.

4 Add the chili flakes, onion, garlic,
lemon rind and juice. Sprinkle on the
parsley. Mix well, then transfer to a
serving dish. Sprinkle with a little
salt, drizzle on the olive oil and
scatter olives and extra parsley over
the top. Serve at room temperature.

Marinated Zucchini *Zucchini a scapece*

This is a simple vegetable dish that is prepared all over Italy using the best of the season's zucchini. It can be eaten hot or cold.

Ingredients
4 zucchini
1/4 cup extra virgin olive oil
2 tbsp chopped fresh mint, plus whole
 leaves, to garnish
2 tbsp white wine vinegar
salt and freshly ground black pepper
whole-wheat Italian bread and green
 olives, to serve
serves 4

Cook's Tip
Carrots, green beans, and onions can
also be prepared in this way.

1 ▲ Cut the zucchini into thin
slices. Heat 2 tbsp of the oil in a
wide heavy saucepan. Fry the
zucchini in batches, for 4–6 minutes,
until tender and brown around the
edges. Transfer the zucchini to a
bowl. Season well.

2 ▲ Heat the remaining oil in the
pan, then add the mint and vinegar
and let it bubble for a few seconds.
Pour the marinade over the zucchini.
Marinate for 1 hour, then serve
garnished with mint and
accompanied by bread and olives.

Tomato and Bread Salad

Panzanella

This salad is a traditional peasant dish from Tuscany which was created to use up bread that was several days old. It is best made with sun-ripened tomatoes.

Ingredients
3¹/₂ cups stale white or brown bread
    or rolls
4 large tomatoes
1 large red onion, or 6 scallions
a few leaves fresh basil, to garnish
For the dressing
4 tbsp extra-virgin olive oil
2 tbsp white wine vinegar
salt and freshly ground black pepper
serves 4

1 Cut the bread or rolls into thick slices. Place in a shallow bowl, and soak with cold water. Leave for at least 30 minutes.

2 ▲ Cut the tomatoes into chunks. Place in a serving bowl. Finely slice the onion or scallions, and add them to the tomatoes. Squeeze as much water out of the bread as possible, and add it to the vegetables.

3 ▲ Make a dressing with the oil and vinegar. Season with salt and pepper. Pour it over the salad and mix well. Decorate with the basil leaves. Allow to stand in a cool place for at least 2 hours before serving.

Broiled Pepper Salad

Insalata di peperoni

This colorful salad is a southern Italian creation: all the ingredients are sun-lovers which thrive in the hot, dry Mezzogiorno.

Ingredients
4 large peppers, red or yellow or a
    combination of both
2 tbsp capers in salt, vinegar, or brine,
    rinsed
18–20 black or green olives
For the dressing
6 tbsp extra-virgin olive oil
2 garlic cloves, finely chopped
2 tbsp balsamic or wine vinegar
salt and freshly ground black pepper
serves 6

1 Place the peppers under a hot broiler, and turn occasionally until they are black and blistered on all sides. Remove from the heat and place in a paper bag. Leave for 5 minutes.

2 ▲ Peel the peppers, then cut into quarters. Remove the stems and seeds.

3 Cut the peppers into strips, and arrange them in a serving dish. Distribute the capers and olives evenly over the peppers.

4 ▲ For the dressing, mix the oil and garlic together in a small bowl, crushing the garlic with a spoon to release as much flavor as possible. Mix in the vinegar, and season with salt and pepper. Pour over the dressing, mix well, and allow to stand for at least 30 minutes before serving.

Spinach and Roast Garlic Salad *Insalata di spinaci con aglio arrosto*

Don't worry about the amount of garlic in this salad. During roasting, the garlic becomes sweet and subtle and loses its pungent taste.

Ingredients

12 garlic cloves, unpeeled
¼ cup extra virgin olive oil
1 lb baby spinach leaves
½ cup pine nuts, lightly toasted
juice of ½ lemon
salt and freshly ground black pepper
serves 4

Cook's Tip
If spinach is to be served raw in a salad, the leaves need to be young and tender. Wash them well, drain and pat dry with paper towels.

1 ▲ Preheat the oven to 375°F. Place the garlic in a small roasting dish, toss in 2 tbsp of the olive oil and bake for about 15 minutes, until the garlic cloves are slightly charred around the edges.

2 ▲ While still warm, pour the garlic into a salad bowl. Add the spinach, pine nuts, lemon juice, remaining olive oil and a little salt. Toss well and add black pepper to taste. Serve immediately, inviting guests to squeeze the softened garlic purée out of the skin to eat.

Sweet-and-Sour Artichoke Salad

Carciofi in salsa agrodolce

Agrodolce is a sweet-and-sour sauce that works perfectly in this salad.

Ingredients

6 small artichokes
juice of 1 lemon
2 tbsp olive oil
2 medium onions, roughly chopped
1 cup fresh or frozen fava beans
1½ cups fresh or frozen peas (shelled)
salt and freshly ground black pepper
fresh mint leaves, to garnish

For the salsa agrodolce

½ cup white wine vinegar
1 tbsp superfine sugar
handful fresh mint leaves, roughly torn
serves 4

3 ▲ Add the peas, season with salt and pepper and cook for 5 more minutes, stirring occasionally, until the vegetables are tender. Strain through a sieve and place all the vegetables in a bowl, let cool, then cover and chill.

4 ▲ To make the salsa agrodolce, mix all the ingredients in a small pan. Heat gently for 2–3 minutes, until the sugar has dissolved. Simmer gently for about 5 minutes, stirring occasionally. Let cool. To serve, drizzle the salsa over the vegetables and garnish with mint leaves.

1 ▲ Peel the outer leaves from the artichokes and cut into quarters. Place the artichokes in a bowl of water with the lemon juice.

2 ▲ Heat the oil in a large saucepan and add the onions. Cook until the onions are golden. Add the beans and stir, then drain the artichokes and add to the pan. Pour in about 1¼ cups of water and cook, covered, for 10–15 minutes.

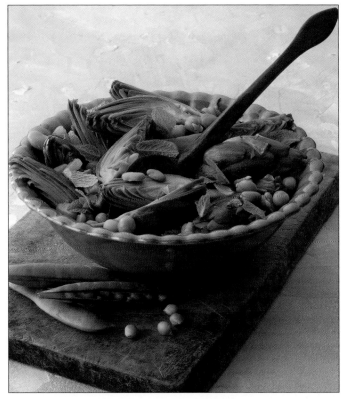

Fennel, Orange and Arugula Salad

Insalata di finocchio

This light and refreshing salad is ideal to serve with spicy or rich foods.

Ingredients
2 oranges
1 fennel bulb
4 oz arugula leaves
⅓ cup black olives

For the dressing
2 tbsp extra virgin olive oil
1 tbsp balsamic vinegar
1 small garlic clove, crushed
salt and freshly ground black pepper
serves 4

1 With a vegetable peeler, cut strips of rind from the oranges, leaving the pith behind, and cut into thin julienne strips. Cook in boiling water for a few minutes. Drain. Peel the oranges, removing all the white pith. Slice them into thin rounds and discard any seeds.

2 Cut the fennel bulb in half lengthwise and slice across the bulb as thinly as possible, preferably in a food processor fitted with a slicing disc or using a mandoline.

3 ▲ Combine the oranges and fennel in a serving bowl and toss with the arugula leaves.

4 ▲ Combine the oil, vinegar, garlic and seasoning and pour over the salad, toss together well and let stand for a few minutes. Sprinkle with the black olives and julienne strips of orange.

Eggplant, Lemon and Caper Salad

Caponata

This cooked vegetable relish is a classic Sicilian dish, which is delicious served as an

accompaniment to cold meats, with pasta or simply on its own with some good crusty bread.

Make sure the eggplant is well cooked until it is meltingly soft.

Ingredients
1 large eggplant, about 1½ lb
¼ cup olive oil
grated rind and juice of 1 lemon
2 tbsp capers, rinsed
12 pitted green olives
2 tbsp chopped fresh
    flat-leaf parsley
salt and freshly ground black pepper
serves 4

Cook's Tips
This will taste even better when made the day before. Serve at room temperature. It will keep, covered in the refrigerator, for up to 4 days. To enrich this dish to serve it on its own as a main course, add toasted pine nuts and shavings of Parmesan cheese. Serve with crusty bread.

1 ▲ Cut the eggplant into 1-in cubes. Heat the olive oil in a large frying pan and cook the eggplant cubes over medium heat for about 10 minutes, tossing regularly, until golden and softened. You may need to do this in two batches. Drain on paper towels and sprinkle with a little salt.

2 ▲ Place the eggplant cubes in a large serving bowl, toss with the lemon rind and juice, capers, olives and chopped parsley and season well with salt and pepper. Serve at room temperature.

Artichoke Salad with Eggs

Insalata di carciofi con uova

Artichoke bottoms are best when cut from fresh artichokes, but can also be bought frozen. This salad is easily assembled for a light lunch.

Ingredients

4 large artichokes, or 4 frozen
    artichoke bottoms, thawed
$1/2$ lemon
4 eggs, hard-boiled and shelled
For the mayonnaise
1 egg yolk
2 tsp Dijon mustard
1 tbsp white wine vinegar
salt and freshly ground black pepper
1 cup olive or vegetable oil
2 tbsp chopped fresh parsley
serves 4

1 ▲ If using fresh artichokes, wash them. Squeeze the lemon, and put the juice and the squeezed half in a bowl of cold water. Prepare the artichokes one at a time. Cut off only the tip from the stem. Peel the stem with a small knife, pulling upwards towards the leaves. Pull off the small leaves around the stem, and continue snapping off the upper part of the dark outer leaves until you reach the taller inner leaves. Cut the tops off the leaves with a sharp knife. Place in the acidulated water. Repeat with the other artichokes.

2 Boil or steam fresh artichokes until just tender (when a leaf comes away quite easily when pulled). Cook frozen artichoke bottoms according to the package instructions. Allow to cool.

3 ▲ Make the mayonnaise. Combine the egg yolk, mustard and vinegar in a mixing bowl. Add salt and pepper to taste. Add the oil in a thin stream while beating vigorously with a wire whisk. When the mixture is thick and smooth, stir in the parsley. Blend well. Cover and refrigerate until needed.

4 ▲ Pull the leaves off the fresh artichokes. Cut the stems off level with the base. Scrape the hairy "choke" off with a knife or spoon.

5 Assemble the salad by cutting the eggs and artichokes into wedges. Arrange on a serving plate, and serve garnished with the mayonnaise.

Fennel and Orange Salad

Insalata di finocchio con arancio

In seventeenth-century Italy fennel was often served at the end of the meal, sprinkled with salt. This refreshing salad originated in Sicily.

Ingredients
2 large fennel bulbs (about 1½ lb)
2 sweet oranges
2 scallions, to garnish
For the dressing
4 tbsp extra-virgin olive oil
2 tbsp fresh lemon juice
salt and freshly ground black pepper
serves 4

1 ▲ Wash the fennel bulbs and remove any brown or stringy outer leaves. Slice the bulbs and stems into thin pieces. Place in a shallow serving bowl.

2 ▲ Peel the oranges with a sharp knife, cutting away the white pith. Slice thinly. Cut each slice into thirds. Arrange over the fennel, adding any juice from the oranges.

3 ▲ For the dressing, mix the oil and lemon juice together. Season with salt and pepper. Pour the dressing over the salad. Mix well.

4 ▲ Slice the white and green sections of the scallions thinly. Sprinkle over the salad.

Potato Salad

Insalata di patate

This salad is dressed while the potatoes are still warm, so the flavors are fully absorbed. Use the best olive oil available.

Ingredients
2lb waxy potatoes
For the dressing
6 tbsp extra-virgin olive oil
juice of 1 lemon
1 garlic clove, very finely chopped
2 tbsp chopped fresh herbs, such as
      parsley, basil, thyme or oregano
salt and freshly ground black pepper
serves 6

1 Wash the potatoes, but do not peel them. Boil or steam them until tender. When they are cool enough to handle, peel them. Cut the potatoes into dice.

2 ▲ While the potatoes are cooking, mix together all the ingredients for the dressing.

3 ▲ Pour the dressing over the potatoes while they are still warm. Mix well. Serve at room temperature or cold.

Chickpea Salad

Ceci in insalata

This salad makes a good light meal, and is quickly assembled if canned chickpeas are used.

Ingredients
2 × 14oz cans chickpeas, or 2 cups
      cooked chickpeas
6 scallions, chopped
2 medium tomatoes, cut into cubes
1 small red onion, finely chopped
12 black olives, pitted and cut in half
1 tbsp capers, drained
2 tbsp finely chopped fresh parsley or
      mint leaves
4 hard-boiled eggs, cut into quarters,
      to garnish
For the dressing
5 tbsp olive oil
3 tbsp wine vinegar
salt and freshly ground black pepper
serves 4–6

1 Rinse the chickpeas under cold water. Drain. Place in a serving bowl.

2 ▲ Mix in the other vegetables with the olives, capers and parsley or mint.

4 ▲ Toss the salad. Pour the dressing over and mix well. Taste for seasoning. Allow to stand for at least 1 hour. Just before serving decorate the salad with the egg wedges.

3 ▲ Mix the dressing ingredients together in a small bowl.

~ VARIATION ~

Other types of canned cooked beans may be substituted in this salad, such as cannellini or borlotti.

Desserts

··

*An everyday Italian meal usually concludes with
fresh fruit. Desserts are reserved for special
occasions, and are often bought at the local
pasticceria or gelateria. This is not to say that
sweet things are unpopular, but they are usually
eaten with a cup of espresso coffee at other
times of the day.*

Coffee and Chocolate Bombe

Zuccotto

In Italy the commercial ice cream is so good that no one would dream of making their own ice cream for this dessert. Assembling the zuccotto is impressive enough in itself.

Ingredients
15–18 savoiardi (Italian ladyfingers)
about ¾ cup sweet Marsala
3 oz amaretti cookies
about 2 cups coffee ice cream, softened
about 2 cups vanilla ice cream, softened
2 oz bittersweet or plain
    chocolate, grated
chocolate curls and sifted cocoa powder
    or confectioners' sugar, to decorate
serves 6–8

3 ▲ Put the amaretti cookies in a large bowl and crush them with a rolling pin. Add the coffee ice cream and any remaining Marsala and beat until mixed. Spoon into the ladyfinger-lined dish.

4 Press the ice cream against the sponge to form an even layer with a hollow. Freeze for 2 hours.

5 Put the vanilla ice cream and grated chocolate in a bowl and beat together until evenly mixed. Spoon into the hollow in the center of the mold. Smooth the top, then cover with the overhanging muslin. Place in the freezer overnight.

6 To serve, run a spatula between the muslin and the basin, then unfold the top of the muslin. Invert a chilled serving plate on top of the zuccotto, then invert the two so that the zuccotto is upside down on the plate. Carefully peel off the muslin. Decorate the zuccotto with the chocolate curls, then sift cocoa powder or confectioners' sugar over. Serve immediately.

1 ▲ Line a 4-cup soufflé dish with a large piece of damp muslin, letting it hang over the top edge. Trim the ladyfingers to fit the basin, if necessary. Pour the Marsala into a shallow dish. Dip a ladyfinger in the Marsala, turning it quickly so that it becomes saturated but does not disintegrate. Stand it against the side of the basin, sugared-side out. Repeat with the remaining sponge fingers to line the basin fully.

2 Fill in the base and any gaps around the side with any trimmings and savoiardi cut to fit. Chill for about 30 minutes.

Cook's Tip
In Italy there are special dome-shaped molds for making this dessert, the name for which comes from the Italian word zucca, meaning pumpkin. The shape will not be quite the same when it is made in a soufflé dish.

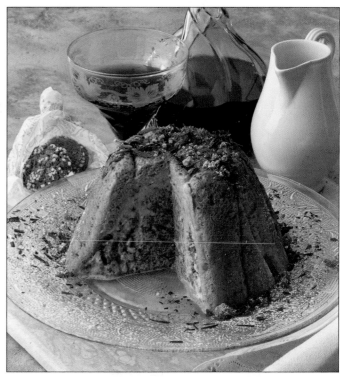

Apple Cake

Torta di mele

This moist cake is best served warm. It comes from Genoa, home of the whisked sponge.

When whipping the cream, add grated lemon rind—it tastes delicious.

Ingredients

1½ lb Golden Delicious apples
finely grated rind and juice of
    1 large lemon
4 eggs
¾ cup confectioners' sugar
1¼ cups flour
1 tsp baking powder
pinch of salt
8 tbsp butter, melted and cooled, plus
    extra for greasing
1 tbsp vanilla sugar, for sprinkling
very finely pared strips of citrus rind,
    to decorate
whipped cream, to serve
serves 6

1 ▲ Preheat the oven to 350°F.
Brush a 9-in springform pan with
melted butter and line the base with
parchment paper. Quarter, core and
peel the apples, then slice thinly. Put
the slices in a bowl and pour in the
lemon juice.

2 ▲ Put the eggs, sugar and lemon
rind in a bowl and whisk with a
hand-held electric mixer until the
mixture is thick and mousse-like.
The whisks should leave a trail.

3 ▲ Sift half the flour, all the baking
powder and the salt over the egg
mousse, then fold in gently with a
large metal spoon. Slowly drizzle in
the melted butter from the side of the
bowl and fold it in gently with the
spoon. Sift in the remaining flour,
fold it in gently, then add the apples
and fold these in equally gently.

4 ▲ Spoon into the prepared pan
and level the surface. Bake for
40 minutes or until a skewer comes
out clean. Let settle in the pan for
about 10 minutes, then invert on a
wire rack. Turn the cake the right way
up and sprinkle the vanilla sugar on
top. Decorate with the citrus rind.
Serve warm, with whipped cream.

Lemon Ricotta Cake

Torta di limone e ricotta

This lemony cake from Sardinia is quite different from a traditional cheesecake.

Ingredients
6 tbsp butter
3/4 cup granulated sugar
generous 1/3 cup ricotta
3 eggs, separated
1 1/2 cups flour
grated zest of 1 lemon
3 tbsp fresh lemon juice
1 1/2 tsp baking powder
confectioners' sugar, for dusting
serves 6–8

1 Grease a 9in round cake or springform pan. Line the bottom with parchment paper or waxed paper. Grease the paper. Dust with flour. Set aside. Preheat the oven to 350°F.

2 Cream the butter and sugar together until smooth. Beat in the ricotta.

3 Beat in the egg yolks, one at a time. Add 2 tbsp of the flour, and the lemon zest and juice. Sift the remaining flour with the baking powder and beat into the batter until just blended.

4 ▲ Beat the egg whites until they form stiff peaks. Fold them carefully into the batter.

5 ▲ Turn the mixture into the prepared pan. Bake for 45 minutes, or until a cake tester inserted in the center of the cake comes out clean. Allow the cake to cool for 10 minutes before turning it out onto a rack to cool. Dust the cake generously with confectioners' sugar before serving.

Peaches with Amaretti Stuffing

Pesche alla piemontese

Peaches are plentiful all over Italy. They are sometimes prepared hot, as in this classic dish.

Ingredients
4 ripe fresh peaches
juice of 1/2 lemon
2/3 cup crushed amaretti
2 tbsp Marsala, brandy or peach brandy
2 tbsp butter, at room temperature
1/2 tsp vanilla extract
2 tbsp granulated sugar
1 egg yolk
serves 4

1 Preheat the oven to 350°F. Wash the peaches. Cut them in half and remove the pits. Enlarge the hollow left by the pits by scooping out some of the peach with a small spoon. Sprinkle the peach halves with the lemon juice.

2 ▲ Soften the amaretti crumbs in the Marsala or brandy for a few minutes. Beat the butter until soft, and then stir in the amaretti mixture and all remaining ingredients.

3 ▲ Arrange the peach halves in a baking dish in one layer, hollow side upwards. Divide the amaretti mixture into 8 parts, and fill the hollows, mounding the stuffing up in the center. Bake for 35–40 minutes, until browned and bubbling. These peaches are delicious served hot or cold.

Chocolate Roll

Salame al cioccolato

This after-dinner treat resembles a salami in shape, hence its curious name. It is very rich and will serve a lot of people. Slice it very thinly and serve with espresso coffee and amaretto liqueur.

Ingredients
24 butter cookies, broken
12 oz bittersweet or plain chocolate,
   broken into squares
2 sticks unsalted butter, softened
1/4 cup amaretto liqueur
2 egg yolks
1/2 cup slivered almonds, lightly toasted
1/4 cup ground almonds
serves 8–12

1 ▲ Place the cookies in a food processor fitted with a metal blade and process until coarsely crushed.

2 Place the chocolate in a large heatproof bowl. Place the bowl over a saucepan of barely simmering water, add a small chunk of the butter and all the liqueur and heat until the chocolate melts, stirring occasionally.

Cook's Tip
Take care when melting chocolate that it does not overheat, or it will form a hard lump. The base of the bowl containing the chocolate must not touch the water, and the chocolate must be melted very slowly and gently. If you think the water is getting too hot, remove the pan from the heat.

3 ▲ Remove the bowl from the heat, let the chocolate cool for a minute or two, then stir in the egg yolks followed by the remaining butter, a little at a time. Pour in most of the crushed cookies, leaving behind a good handful, and stir well to mix. Stir in the almonds. Set aside the mixture in a cold place for about 1 hour, until it begins to stiffen.

4 ▲ Process the remaining crushed cookies in the food processor until they are very finely ground. Pour into a bowl and mix with the ground almonds. Cover and set aside until serving time.

5 ▲ Transfer the chocolate and cookie mixture to a sheet of lightly oiled waxed paper, then shape into a 14-in sausage with a spatula, tapering the ends slightly so that the roll looks like a salami. Wrap in the paper and freeze for at least 4 hours, until solid.

6 To serve, unwrap the "salami." Spread the ground cookies and almonds out on a clean sheet of waxed paper and roll the "salami" in them until **evenly** coated. Transfer to a board **and let st**and for about 1 hour before serving in slices.

Sicilian Ricotta Cake

Cassata siciliana

The word cassata is often used to describe a layered ice cream cake. In Sicily, however, it is a traditional cake made of layers of sponge, ricotta cheese and candied peel, imbibed with alcohol, and it looks and tastes truly delicious.

Ingredients
3 cups ricotta cheese
finely grated rind of 1 orange
2 tbsp vanilla sugar
5 tbsp orange-flavored liqueur
4 oz candied peel
8 trifle sponge cakes
¼ cup freshly squeezed orange juice
extra candied peel, to decorate
serves 8–10

1 ▲ Push the ricotta cheese through a sieve into a bowl, add the orange rind, vanilla sugar and 1 tbsp of the liqueur and beat well to mix. Transfer about one-third of the mixture to another bowl, cover and chill until serving time.

2 ▲ Finely chop the candied peel and beat into the remaining ricotta cheese mixture until evenly mixed. Set aside while you prepare the pan.

3 ▲ Line the base of a 5-cup loaf pan with non-stick baking paper. Cut the trifle sponges in half through their thickness. Arrange four pieces of sponge side by side in the bottom of the loaf pan and sprinkle with 1 tbsp each of liqueur and orange juice.

4 ▲ Put one-third of the ricotta and fruit mixture in the pan and spread it out evenly. Cover with four more pieces of sponge and sprinkle with another 1 tbsp each liqueur and orange juice as before.

5 Repeat the alternate layers of ricotta mixture and sponge until all the ingredients are used, soaking the sponge pieces with liqueur and orange juice each time, and ending with soaked sponge. Cover with a piece of parchment paper.

6 ▲ Cut a piece of cardboard to fit inside the pan, place on top of the parchment paper and weight down evenly. Chill for 24 hours.

7 Remove the weights, cardboard and paper and run a spatula between the sides of the cassata and the pan. Invert a serving plate on top of the cassata, then invert the two so that the cassata is upside down on the plate. Peel off the lining paper.

8 Spread the chilled ricotta mixture over the cassata to cover it completely, then decorate the top with candied peel, cut into fancy shapes. Serve chilled.

Cook's Tip
Don't worry if the cassata has pressed into an uneven shape when turned out. This will be disguised when the cake is covered in the chilled ricotta mixture.

Walnut and Ricotta Cake

Dolce di noci e ricotta

Soft, tangy ricotta cheese is widely used in Italian desserts. Here, it is included along with walnuts and orange to flavor a spongecake. Don't worry if it sinks slightly after baking – this gives it an authentic appearance.

Ingredients
1 cup walnut pieces
⅔ cup sweet butter, softened
⅔ cup sugar
5 eggs, separated
finely grated rind of 1 orange
⅔ cup ricotta cheese
6 tbsp flour

To finish
4 tbsp apricot jam
2 tbsp brandy
2 oz bittersweet or semisweet chocolate,
   coarsely grated
makes 10 slices

1 Preheat the oven to 375°F. Grease and line the base of a deep 9 in round, loose-based cake pan. Coarsely chop and then lightly toast the walnuts.

2 ▲ Cream together the butter and ½ cup of the sugar until light and fluffy. Add the egg yolks, orange rind, ricotta cheese, flour and walnuts and mix together.

Variation
Use toasted and chopped almonds in place of the walnuts.

3 ▲ Beat the egg whites in a large bowl until stiff. Gradually beat in the remaining sugar. Using a large metal spoon, fold a quarter of the beaten whites into the ricotta mixture. Carefully fold in the rest of the beaten whites.

4 Tip the mixture into the prepared pan and carefully level the surface. Bake for about 30 minutes, or until risen and firm. Allow the cake to cool in the pan.

5 ▲ Transfer the cake to a serving plate. Heat the apricot jam in a small saucepan with 1 tbsp water. Press through a strainer and stir in the brandy. Use to coat the top and sides of the cake. Scatter the cake generously with grated chocolate.

Chestnut Pudding

Budino di castagne

Sweet chestnuts are found in the mountainous regions of Italy in October and November.

Ingredients

1lb fresh sweet chestnuts
1¹/₄ cups milk
¹/₂ cup sugar
2 eggs, separated, at room temperature
¹/₄ cup unsweetened cocoa powder
¹/₂ tsp pure vanilla extract
¹/₃ cup confectioners' sugar, sifted
butter, for the mold(s)
fresh whipped cream, to garnish
marrons glacés, cut into small
    pieces, to garnish

serves 4–5

1 Cut a cross in the side of the chestnuts, and drop them into a pan of boiling water. Cook for 5-6 minutes. Remove with a slotted spoon, and peel while still warm.

2 ▲ Place the peeled chestnuts in a heavy or non-stick saucepan with the milk and half of the sugar. Cook over low heat, stirring occasionally, until soft. Remove from the heat and allow to cool. Press the contents of the pan through a strainer.

3 Preheat the oven to 350°F. Beat the egg yolks with the remaining sugar until the mixture is pale yellow and fluffy. Beat in the cocoa powder and the vanilla.

4 ▲ In a separate bowl, whisk the egg whites with a wire whisk or electric beater until they form soft peaks. Gradually beat in the sifted confectioners' sugar and continue beating until the mixture forms stiff peaks.

5 ▲ Fold the chestnut and egg yolk mixtures together. Fold in the egg whites. Turn the mixture into one large or several individual buttered pudding molds. Place on a cookie sheet, and bake in the oven until firm, 12-20 minutes depending on the size. Remove from the oven, and allow to cool for 10 minutes before unmolding. Serve garnished with whipped cream and marrons glacés.

Fruit Salad

Macedonia

A really good fruit salad is always refreshing, and in Italy it comes bathed in fresh orange and lemon juices. Use any mixture of fresh seasonal fruits.

Ingredients
juice of 3 large sweet oranges
juice of 1 lemon
1 banana
1–2 apples
1 ripe pear
2 peaches or nectarines
4–5 apricots or plums
²/₃ cup black or green grapes
²/₃ cup berries (strawberries,
   raspberries etc)
any other fruits in season
sugar, to taste (optional)
2–3 tbsp Kirsch, maraschino or
   other liqueur (optional)
serves 4–6

1 Place the fresh orange and lemon juices in a large serving bowl.

2 ▲ Prepare all the fruits by washing or peeling them as necessary. Cut them into bite-size pieces. Halve the grapes and remove any seeds. Core and slice the apples. Pit and slice soft fruits and leave small berries whole. As soon as each fruit is prepared, put it into the bowl with the juices.

3 ▲ Taste the salad, adding sugar if using. A few tablespoons of liqueur may also be added. Cover the bowl and refrigerate for at least 2 hours. Mix well before serving. In Italy, fruit salad is eaten alone, with vanilla ice cream or with zabaglione. It is not usually served with cream.

Baked Apples with Red Wine

Mele al forno

Italian baked apples include a delicious filling of golden raisins soaked in spiced red wine.

Ingredients
scant ¹/₂ cup golden raisins
1¹/₂ cups red wine
pinch of grated nutmeg
pinch of ground cinnamon
4 tbsp granulated sugar
pinch of grated lemon zest
6 cooking apples of even size
3 tbsp butter
serves 6

1 In a small bowl, combine the golden raisins with the wine. Stir in the spices, sugar and lemon zest. Allow to stand for 1 hour.

2 Preheat the oven to 375°F. Wash the apples. Use a corer or small, sharp knife to remove the central cores without cutting through to the bottom of the apples.

3 ▲ Divide the filling mixture between the 6 apples, spooning it into the hollow cores. Spoon in a little of the spiced wine.

4 ▲ Arrange the apples in a buttered baking dish. Pour the remaining wine around the apples. Top each core hole with a knob of butter. Bake for 40–50 minutes, or until the apples are soft but not mushy. Serve hot or at room temperature.

Zabaglione

Zabaglione

This sumptuous warm dessert is very quick and easy to make, but it does need to be served immediately. For a dinner party, assemble all the ingredients and equipment ahead of time so that all you have to do is quickly combine everything once the main course is over.

Ingredients
4 egg yolks
⅓ cup confectioners' sugar
½ cup dry Marsala
savoiardi (Italian ladyfingers), to serve
serves 6

Cook's Tip
When whisking the egg yolks, make sure that the bottom of the bowl does not touch the water or the egg yolks will scramble.

1 ▲ Half fill a pan with water and bring it to the simmering point. Put the egg yolks and sugar in a large heatproof bowl and beat with a hand-held electric mixer until pale and creamy.

2 ▲ Put the bowl over the pan and gradually pour in the Marsala, whisking the mixture until it is very thick and has increased in volume.

3 Remove the bowl from the water and pour the zabaglione into six heatproof, long-stemmed glasses. Serve immediately, with ladyfingers.

Lovers' Knots

Cenci

The literal translation of cenci is "rags and tatters," but they are often referred to by the more endearing term of lovers' knots. They are eaten at carnival time in February.

Ingredients
1¼ cups flour
½ tsp baking powder
pinch of salt
2 tbsp confectioners' sugar, plus extra
   for dusting
1 egg, beaten
about 1½ tbsp rum
vegetable oil, for deep-frying
makes 24

Cook's Tip
If you do not have a deep-fat fryer with a built-in thermostat, or a deep-fat thermometer, test the temperature of the oil before deep-frying by dropping in a scrap of the dough trimmings—it should turn crisp and golden in about 30 seconds.

1 ▲ Sift the flour, baking powder and salt into a bowl, then stir in the sugar. Add the egg. Stir with a fork until it is evenly mixed with the flour, then add the rum gradually and continue mixing until the dough draws together. Knead the dough on a lightly floured surface until it is smooth. Divide the dough into quarters.

2 ▲ Roll each piece out to a 6 x 3-in rectangle and trim to make them straight. Cut each rectangle lengthwise into six strips, ½ in wide, and tie into a simple knot.

3 Heat the oil in a deep-fat fryer to a temperature of 375°F. Deep-fry the knots in batches for 1–2 minutes, until crisp and golden. Transfer to paper towels with a slotted spoon. Serve warm, dusted with sugar.

Italian Trifle

Zuppa inglese

Known in Italy as "English Soup", this is a kind of trifle that has little to do with England!

Ingredients

2 cups milk
grated zest of $^1/_2$ lemon
4 egg yolks
$^1/_3$ cup superfine sugar
$^1/_2$ cup flour, sifted
1 tbsp rum or brandy
2 tbsp butter
7oz lady fingers or 11oz sponge
  cake, sliced into $^1/_2$in slices
$^1/_3$ cup Kirsch or cherry brandy
$^1/_3$ cup Strega liqueur
3 tbsp apricot jam
fresh whipped cream, to garnish
chopped toasted nuts, to garnish
serves 6–8

1 Heat the milk with the lemon zest in a small pan. Remove from the heat as soon as small bubbles form on the surface of the liquid.

2 ▲ Beat the egg yolks in a large bowl with a wire whisk. Gradually incorporate the sugar, and continue beating until pale yellow. Beat in the flour. Stir in the milk very gradually, pouring it in through a strainer to remove the lemon. When all the milk has been added, pour the mixture into a large, heavy pan. Bring to a boil stirring constantly with a whisk. Simmer for 5–6 minutes, stirring constantly. Remove from the heat and stir in the rum or brandy. Beat in the butter. Allow to cool to room temperature, stirring to prevent a skin from forming.

3 ▲ Brush the cookies or cake slices with the Kirsch or cherry brandy on one side, and the Strega liqueur on the other. Spread a thin layer of the custard over the bottom of a serving dish. Line the dish with a layer of cookies or cake slices. Cover with some of the custard. Add another layer of cookies which have been brushed with liqueur.

4 ▲ Heat the jam in a small saucepan with 2 tbsp water. When it is hot, pour or brush it evenly over the cookies. Continue with layers of custard and liqueur-brushed cookies until the ingredients have been used up. End with custard. Cover with plastic wrap or foil, and refrigerate for at least 2–3 hours. To serve, decorate the top of the trifle with whipped cream and garnish with chopped nuts.

Stuffed Peaches with Amaretto

Pesche ripiene

Together amaretti cookies and amaretto liqueur have an intense almond flavor, and they make a natural partner for peaches.

Ingredients
4 ripe but firm peaches
2 oz amaretti cookies
2 tbsp butter, softened
2 tbsp confectioners' sugar
1 egg yolk
1/4 cup amaretto liqueur
1 cup dry white wine
8 tiny sprigs of basil, to decorate
ice cream or heavy cream, to serve
serves 4

3 ▲ Cream the butter and sugar in a separate bowl until smooth. Stir in the reserved chopped peach flesh, the egg yolk and half the amaretto liqueur with the amaretti crumbs. Lightly butter a baking dish that is just large enough to hold the peach halves in a single layer.

4 ▲ Spoon the stuffing into the peaches, then stand them in the dish. Mix the remaining liqueur with the wine, pour over the peaches and bake for 25 minutes or until the peaches feel tender when tested with a skewer. Decorate with basil and serve immediately, with ice cream or cream.

1 ▲ Preheat the oven to 350°F. Following the natural indentation line on each peach, cut in half down to the central pit, then twist the halves in opposite directions to separate them. Remove the peach pits, then cut out a little of the central flesh to make a larger hole for the stuffing. Chop this flesh finely and set aside.

2 ▲ Put the amaretti cookies in a bowl and crush them finely with the end of a rolling pin.

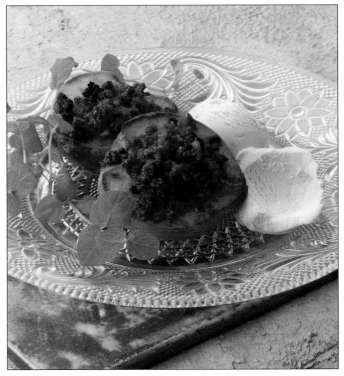

Tiramisù

The name of this popular dessert translates as "pick me up," which is said to derive from the fact that it is so good that it literally makes you swoon when you eat it. There are many, many versions, and the recipe can be adapted to suit your own taste—you can vary the amount of mascarpone, eggs, ladyfingers, coffee and liqueur.

Ingredients

3 eggs, separated
2 cups mascarpone cheese, at room temperature
1 tbsp vanilla sugar
³⁄₄ cup cold, very strong, black coffee
¹⁄₂ cup Kahlúa or other coffee-flavored liqueur
18 savoiardi (Italian ladyfingers)
sifted cocoa powder and grated bittersweet chocolate, to finish

serves 6–8

1 ▲ Put the egg whites in a grease-free bowl and whisk with an electric mixer until stiff and in peaks.

2 ▲ Mix the mascarpone, vanilla sugar and egg yolks in a separate large bowl and whisk with the electric mixer until evenly combined. Fold in the egg whites, then put a few spoonfuls of the mixture in the bottom of a large serving bowl and spread it out evenly.

3 ▲ Combine the coffee and liqueur in a shallow dish. Dip a ladyfinger in the mixture, turn it quickly so that it becomes saturated but does not disintegrate, and place it on top of the mascarpone in the bowl. Add five more dipped ladyfingers, placing them side by side.

4 ▲ Spoon in about one-third of the remaining mixture and spread it out. Make more layers in the same way, ending with mascarpone. Level the surface, then sift cocoa powder all over. Cover and chill overnight. Before serving, sprinkle with cocoa and grated chocolate.

Ricotta Pudding

Budino di ricotta

This creamy, rich dessert is very easy to make and, as it can be made up to 24 hours ahead, it is ideal for a dinner party. The combination of ricotta cheese and candied fruits is very popular in Sicily, where this recipe originated.

Ingredients

1 cup ricotta cheese
$\frac{1}{3}$ cup candied fruits
$\frac{1}{4}$ cup sweet Marsala
1 cup heavy cream
$\frac{1}{4}$ cup confectioners' sugar, plus extra
    to serve
finely grated rind of 1 orange
2 cups fresh raspberries
strips of thinly pared orange rind,
    to decorate

serves 4–6

Cook's Tip

Buy candied fruits in large pieces at a good gourmet food store—the chopped candied peel in tubs is too tough to eat raw, and should only be used in baking.

1 ▲ Press the ricotta through a sieve into a bowl. Finely chop the candied fruits and stir into the sieved ricotta with half of the Marsala. Put the cream, sugar and orange rind in another bowl and whip until the cream is standing in soft peaks.

2 ▲ Fold the whipped cream into the ricotta mixture. Spoon into individual glass serving bowls and top with the raspberries. Chill until serving time. Sprinkle with the remaining Marsala and dust the top of each bowl liberally with confectioners' sugar just before serving. Decorate with the orange rind.

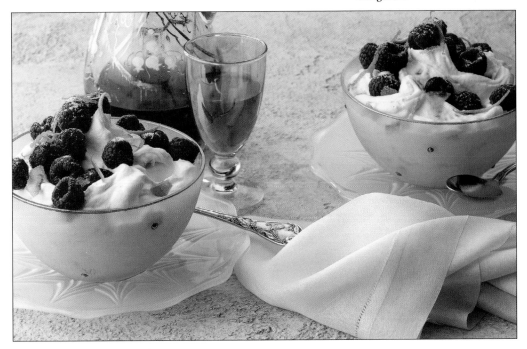

Coffee Granita

Granita di caffè

A granita is a cross between a frozen drink and a flavored ice. The consistency should be slushy, not solid. They can be made at home with the help of a food processor.

Ingredients
2 cups water
1/2 cup granulated sugar
1 cup very strong espresso
    coffee, cooled
whipped cream, to garnish (optional)
serves 4–5

2 ▲ Combine the coffee with the sugar syrup. Place in a shallow container or freezer tray, and freeze until solid. Plunge the bottom of the frozen container or tray in very hot water for a few seconds. Turn the frozen mixture out, and chop it into large chunks.

3 ▲ Place the mixture in a food processor fitted with metal blades, and process until it forms small crystals. Spoon into serving glasses and top with whipped cream, if desired. If you do not want to serve the granita immediately, pour the processed mixture back into a shallow container or ice tray and freeze until serving time. Allow to thaw for a few minutes before serving, or process again.

1 ▲ Heat the water and sugar together over low heat until the sugar dissolves. Bring to a boil. Remove from the heat and allow to cool.

Lemon Granita

Granita di limone

Nothing is more refreshing on a hot summer's day than a fresh lemon granita.

Ingredients
2 cups water
1/2 cup granulated sugar
grated zest of 1 lemon
juice of 2 large lemons
serves 4–5

1 Heat the water and sugar together over low heat until the sugar dissolves. Bring to a boil. Remove from the heat, and allow to cool.

2 Combine the lemon zest and juice with the sugar syrup. Place in a shallow container or freezer tray, and freeze until solid.

3 ▲ Plunge the bottom of the frozen container or tray in very hot water for a few seconds. Turn the frozen mixture out, and chop it into large chunks.

4 ▲ Place the mixture in a food processor fitted with metal blades, and process until it forms small crystals. Spoon into serving glasses.

Custard Ice Cream

Gelato di crema

Italian ice creams are soft in consistency, and should not be over-sweet.

Ingredients
3¹/₂ cups milk
¹/₂ tsp grated lemon zest
6 egg yolks
¹/₂ cup granulated sugar
makes about 3³/₄ cups

1 To make the custard, heat the milk with the lemon zest in a small pan. Remove from the heat as soon as small bubbles start to form on the surface. Do not let it boil.

2 Beat the egg yolks with a wire whisk or electric beater. Gradually incorporate the sugar, and continue beating for about 5 minutes until the mixture is pale yellow. Strain the milk. Slowly beat it into the egg mixture drop by drop.

3 ▲ When all the milk has been added, pour the mixture into the top of a double boiler, or into a bowl placed over a pan of simmering water. Stir over moderate heat until the water in the pan is boiling, and the custard thickens enough to lightly coat the back of a spoon. Remove from the heat and allow to cool.

4 Freeze in an ice cream maker, following the manufacturer's instructions. The ice cream is ready when it is firm but still soft.

5 ▲ If you do not have an ice cream maker, pour the mixture into a metal or plastic freezer container and freeze until set, about 3 hours. Remove from the container and chop roughly into 3in pieces. Place in the bowl of a food processor and process until smooth. Return to the freezer container, and freeze again until firm. Repeat the freezing-chopping process 2 or 3 times, until a smooth consistency is reached.

Chocolate Ice Cream

Gelato al cioccolato

Use good quality plain or cooking chocolate for the best flavor.

Ingredients
3¹/₂ cups milk
4in piece of vanilla bean
8oz cooking chocolate
4 egg yolks
¹/₂ cup granulated sugar
makes about 3³/₄ cups

1 Make the custard as in steps 1 and 2 of Custard Ice Cream, replacing the lemon with the vanilla. Meanwhile, melt the chocolate in a heatproof bowl over a pan of hot water.

2 ▲ Pour the custard into the bowl containing the melted chocolate. Stir over moderate heat until the custard thickens enough to lightly coat the back of a spoon. Remove from the heat and allow to cool.

3 ▲ Freeze in an ice cream maker, or follow step 5 of Custard Ice Cream, freezing and processing until a smooth consistency has been reached.

Hazelnut Ice Cream

Gelato di nocciola

This popular flavor goes very well with the chocolate and custard ice creams.

Ingredients
$^1/_2$ cup hazelnuts
2 cups milk
4in piece vanilla bean
4 egg yolks
6 tbsp granulated sugar
serves 4–6

1 Spread the hazelnuts out on a cookie sheet, and place under a broiler for about 5 minutes, shaking the pan frequently to turn the nuts over. Remove from the heat and allow to cool slightly. Place the nuts on a clean dish towel, and rub them with the cloth to remove their dark outer skin. Chop very finely, or grind in a food processor with 2 tbsp of the sugar.

2 Make the custard. Heat the milk with the vanilla bean in a small saucepan. Remove from the heat as soon as small bubbles start to form on the surface. Do not let it boil.

3 ▲ Beat the egg yolks with a wire whisk or electric beater. Gradually incorporate the sugar, and continue beating for about 5 minutes until the mixture is pale yellow. Beat in the milk very gradually, pouring it in through a strainer and discarding the vanilla bean. Stir constantly until all the milk has been added.

4 ▲ Pour the mixture into the top of a double boiler, or into a bowl placed over a pan of simmering water. Add the chopped or ground nuts. Stir over moderate heat until the water in the pan is boiling, and the custard thickens enough to lightly coat the back of a spoon. Remove from the heat and allow to cool.

5 ▲ Freeze in an ice cream maker, or follow step 5 of Custard Ice Cream, freezing and processing until a smooth consistency has been reached.

Fresh Orange Granita

Granita all'arancia

A granita is like a sorbet, but coarser and quite grainy in texture, hence its name. It makes a refreshing dessert after a rich main course, or a cooling treat on a hot summer's day.

Ingredients

4 large oranges
1 large lemon
³/₄ cup sugar
2 cups water
blanched pared strips of orange and
    lemon rind, to decorate
cookies, to serve

serves 6

1 ▲ Thinly pare the rind from the oranges and lemon, taking care to avoid the bitter white pith, and set aside for the decoration. Cut the fruit in half and squeeze the juice into a bowl. Set aside.

2 Heat the sugar and water in a heavy saucepan, stirring over low heat until the sugar dissolves. Bring to a boil, then boil without stirring for about 10 minutes, until a syrup forms.

3 ▲ Remove the syrup from the heat, add the pieces of orange and lemon rind and shake the pan. Cover and let cool.

4 ▲ Strain the sugar syrup into a shallow freezer container and add the fruit juice. Stir well to mix, then freeze, uncovered, for about 4 hours, until slushy.

Cook's Tip

To make the decoration, slice extra orange and lemon rind into thin strips. Blanch for 2 minutes, refresh under cold water and dry before use.

5 ▲ Remove the half-frozen mixture from the freezer and mix with a fork, then return to the freezer and freeze again for 4 more hours or until frozen hard. To serve, pour into a bowl and let soften for about 10 minutes, then break up with a fork again and pile into long-stemmed glasses. Decorate with the strips of orange and lemon rind and serve with cookies.

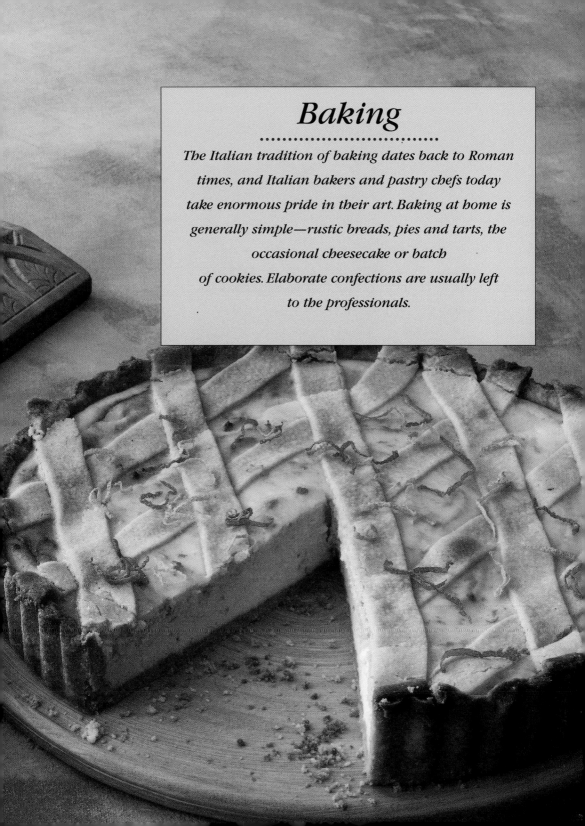

Baking

The Italian tradition of baking dates back to Roman times, and Italian bakers and pastry chefs today take enormous pride in their art. Baking at home is generally simple—rustic breads, pies and tarts, the occasional cheesecake or batch of cookies. Elaborate confections are usually left to the professionals.

Sun-dried Tomato Bread

Pane ai pomodori secchi

In the south of Italy, tomatoes are often dried off in the hot sun. They are then preserved in oil, or hung up in strings in the kitchen, to use in the winter. This recipe uses the former.

Ingredients

6 cups strong flour
2 tsp salt
2 tbsp sugar
1 oz fresh yeast
1⅔–2 cups warm milk
1 tbsp tomato paste
5 tbsp oil from the jar of
    sun-dried tomatoes
5 tbsp extra virgin olive oil
¾ cup drained sun-dried tomatoes in
    oil, chopped
1 large onion, chopped
makes 4 small loaves

1 ▲ Sift the flour, salt and sugar into a bowl, and make a well in the center. Crumble the yeast, mix with ⅔ cup of the warm milk and add to the flour.

2 ▲ Mix the tomato paste into the remaining milk until evenly blended, then add to the flour with the tomato oil and olive oil.

3 ▲ Gradually mix the flour into the liquid ingredients, until you have a dough. Turn out onto a floured surface, and knead for about 10 minutes, until smooth and elastic. Return to the clean bowl, cover with a cloth, and let rise in a warm place for about 2 hours.

4 ▲ Knock the dough back, and add the tomatoes and onion. Knead until evenly distributed through the dough. Shape into four balls and place on a greased baking sheet. Cover with a dish towel and let rise again for about 45 minutes.

5 Preheat the oven to 375°F. Bake the bread for about 45 minutes, or until the loaves sound hollow when you tap them underneath with your fingers. Allow to cool on a wire rack. Eat warm, or toasted with grated mozzarella cheese on top.

Cook's Tip
Use a pair of sharp kitchen scissors to cut up the sun-dried tomatoes.

Olive and Oregano Bread

Pane alle olive ed origano

This makes an excellent accompaniment to salads and soups and is particularly good served warm with a chunk of cheese.

Ingredients

1¼ cups warm water
1 tsp active dried yeast
pinch of sugar
1 tbsp olive oil
1 onion, chopped
4 cups strong flour
1 tsp salt
¼ tsp freshly ground black pepper
⅓ cup pitted black olives, coarsely
    chopped
1 tbsp black olive paste
1 tbsp chopped fresh oregano
1 tbsp chopped fresh parsley
serves 8–10

1 ▲ Put half of the warm water in a measuring cup. Sprinkle the yeast on top. Add the sugar, mix well and allow to stand for 10 minutes.

2 ▲ Heat the olive oil in a frying pan and fry the onion over medium heat until golden brown.

3 ▲ Sift the flour into a mixing bowl with the salt and pepper. Make a well in the center. Add the yeast mixture, the fried onion (with the oil), the olives, olive paste, herbs and the remaining water. Gradually incorporate the flour and mix to a soft dough, adding a litle extra water if necessary.

4 ▲ Turn out the dough onto a floured work surface and knead for 5 minutes until smooth and elastic. Place in a mixing bowl, cover with a damp dish towel and leave in a warm place to rise for about 2 hours until doubled in bulk. Lightly grease a baking sheet.

5 ▲ Turn out the dough onto a floured surface and knead again for a few minutes. Shape into an 8 in round and place on the prepared baking sheet. Using a sharp knife, make criss-cross cuts over the top. Cover and leave in a warm place for 30 minutes until well risen. Preheat the oven to 425°F.

6 ▲ Dust the loaf with a little flour. Bake for 10 minutes, then lower the oven temperature to 400°F. Bake for 20 minutes more, or until the loaf sounds hollow when it is tapped underneath. Transfer to a wire rack and allow to cool slightly before slicing and serving.

Focaccia

Focaccia

Focaccia is an antique form of flat bread which is oiled before baking. It is traditionally made on a large cookie sheet, and sold in bakeries cut into squares.

Ingredients
1 recipe Basic Pizza Dough, risen once
3 tbsp olive oil
coarse sea salt
serves 6–8 as a side dish

1 ▲ After punching the dough down, knead it for 3–4 minutes. Brush a large shallow baking pan with 1 tbsp of oil.

2 ▲ Place the dough in the pan, and use your fingers to press it into an even layer 1 in thick. Cover the dough with a cloth, and leave to rise in a warm place for 30 minutes. Preheat the oven to 400°F.

~ COOK'S TIP ~

To freeze, allow to cool to room temperature after baking. Wrap in foil and freeze. Thaw and place in a warm oven before serving.

3 ▲ Just before baking, use your fingers to press rows of light indentations into the surface of the focaccia dough.

4 ▲ Brush with the remaining oil, and sprinkle lightly with coarse salt. Bake for about 25 minutes, or until just golden. Cut into squares or wedges and serve as an accompaniment to a meal, or alone, warm or at room temperature.

Focaccia with Onions

Focaccia con cipolle

This appetizing flat bread has a topping of sautéed onions. It can be split and filled with prosciutto or cheese for an unusual sandwich.

Ingredients

1 recipe Basic Pizza Dough, risen once
5 tbsp olive oil
1 medium onion, sliced very thinly
    and cut into short lengths
¹/₂ tsp fresh thyme leaves
coarse sea salt
serves 6–8 as a side dish

3 ▲ Just before baking, use your fingers to press rows of light indentations into the surface of the focaccia. Brush with the remaining oil.

4 ▲ Spread the onions evenly over the top, and sprinkle lightly with coarse salt. Bake until just golden, about 25 minutes. Cut into squares or wedges and serve as an accompaniment to a meal, or alone, either warm or at room temperature.

1 ▲ After punching the dough down, knead it for 3–4 minutes. Brush a large shallow baking pan with 1 tbsp of the oil. Place the dough in the pan, and use your fingers to press it into an even layer 1 inch thick. Cover the dough with a cloth, and leave to rise in a warm place for 30 minutes. Preheat the oven to 400°F.

2 ▲ While the focaccia is rising, heat 3 tbsp of the oil in a medium frying pan. Add the onion, and cook over low heat until soft. Stir in the thyme.

Focaccia with Olives

Focaccia con olive

For this topping, pieces of pitted green olives are pressed onto the dough before baking.

Ingredients
1 recipe Basic Pizza Dough, risen once
3 tbsp olive oil
10–12 large green olives, pitted and
    cut in half lengthwise
coarse sea salt
serves 6–8 as a side dish

1 After punching the dough down, knead it for 3–4 minutes. Brush a large shallow baking pan with 1 tbsp of the oil. Place the dough in the pan, and use your fingers to press it into an even layer 1in thick. Cover the dough with a cloth, and leave to rise in a warm place for 30 minutes. Preheat the oven to 400°F.

2 ▲ Just before baking, use your fingers to press rows of light indentations into the surface of the focaccia. Brush with the remaining oil.

3 ▲ Dot the bread evenly with the olive pieces, and sprinkle with a little coarse salt. Bake for about 25 minutes, or until just golden. Cut into squares or wedges and serve alone or as an accompaniment to a meal, warm or at room temperature.

Focaccia with Rosemary

Focaccia con rosmarino

One of the most popular breads. If possible, use fresh rosemary for this recipe.

Ingredients
1 recipe Basic Pizza Dough, risen once
3 tbsp olive oil
2 medium sprigs fresh rosemary, coarse
    stalks removed
coarse sea salt

serves 6–8 as a side dish

1 ▲ After punching the dough down, knead it for 3–4 minutes. Brush a large shallow baking pan with 1 tbsp of the oil. Place the dough in the pan, and use your fingers to press it into an even layer 1 inch thick.

2 ▲ Sprinkle with the rosemary leaves. Cover the dough with a cloth, and leave to rise in a warm place for 30 minutes. Preheat the oven to 400°F.

3 ▲ Just before baking, use your fingers to press rows of light indentations into the surface of the focaccia. Brush with the remaining oil, and sprinkle lightly with coarse salt. Bake for about 25 minutes, or until just golden. Cut into squares or wedges and serve as an accompaniment to a meal, or alone, warm or at room temperature.

Italian Bread Sticks

Grissini

These typically Italian bread sticks are especially delicious when hand-made. They are still
sold loose in many bakeries in Turin and the north of Italy.

Ingredients
1 tbsp fresh bread yeast or $^1/_2$ tbsp
    active dried yeast
$^1/_2$ cup lukewarm water
pinch of sugar
2 tsp malt extract (optional)
1 tsp salt
$1^3/_4$–2 cups unbleached white
    bread flour
makes about 30

3 ▲ Sprinkle some of the remaining
flour onto a smooth work surface.
Remove all of the dough from the
bowl, and begin to knead it, working
in the remaining flour a little at a time.
Knead for 8–10 minutes. By the end
the dough should be elastic and
smooth. Form it into a ball.

5 ▲ Place one piece of dough on a
clean smooth work surface without
any flour on it. Roll the dough under
the spread-out fingers of both hands,
moving your hands backwards and
forwards to lengthen and thin the
dough into a long strand about $^3/_8$ inch
thick. Transfer to a very lightly greased
cookie sheet. Repeat with the
remaining dough pieces, taking care to
roll all the grissini to about the
same thickness.

1 ▲ Warm a medium mixing bowl
by swirling some hot water in it. Drain.
Place the yeast in the bowl, and pour
on the warm water. Stir in the sugar,
mix with a fork, and allow to stand
until the yeast has dispersed and starts
to foam, 5–10 minutes.

4 ▲ Tear a lump the size of a small
walnut from the ball of dough. Roll it
lightly between your hands into a
small sausage shape. Set it aside on a
lightly floured surface. Repeat until all
the dough is used up. There should be
about 30 pieces.

6 ▲ Preheat the oven to 400°F. Cover
the tray with a cloth, and place the
grissini in a warm place to rise for
10–15 minutes while the oven is
heating. Bake for about 8–10 minutes.
Remove from the oven. Turn the
grissini over, and return them to the
oven for 6–7 minutes more. Do not let
them brown. Allow to cool. Grissini
should be crisp when served. If they
lose their crispness on a damp day,
warm them in a moderate oven for a
few minutes before serving.

2 ▲ Use a wooden spoon to mix in
the malt extract, if using, the salt and
about one-third of the flour. Mix in
another third of the flour, stirring with
the spoon until the dough forms a
mass and begins to pull away from the
sides of the bowl.

~ VARIATION ~

Grissini are also good when rolled
lightly in poppy or sesame seeds
before being baked.

Bread with Grapes

Schiacciata con uva

This bread is made to celebrate the grape harvest in central Italy. Use small black grapes with or without seeds; in Italy wine grapes are used.

Ingredients
1$\frac{1}{2}$lb small black grapes
$\frac{1}{2}$ cup sugar
1 recipe Basic Pizza Dough, risen once
2 tbsp olive oil
serves 6–8

1 ▲ Remove the grapes from their stems. Wash them well, and pat dry with paper towels. Place in a bowl and sprinkle with the sugar. Set aside until they are needed.

2 ▲ Knead the dough lightly. Divide it into two halves. Roll out or press one half into a circle about $\frac{1}{2}$ inch thick. Place on a lightly oiled flat cookie sheet. Sprinkle with half of the sugared grapes.

3 ▲ Roll out or press the second half of the dough into a circle the same size as the first. Place it on top of the first.

4 ▲ Crimp the edges together. Sprinkle the top with the remaining grapes. Cover with a dish towel and leave in a warm place to rise for 30 minutes. Preheat the oven to 375°F. Sprinkle the bread with the oil, and bake for 50–60 minutes, until risen and golden. Allow to cool before cutting into wedges.

Spicy Fruit Cake from Siena

Panforte di Siena

This is a delicious flat cake with a wonderful spicy flavor. Panforte is very rich, so should be cut into small wedges—offer a glass of sparkling wine to go with it.

Ingredients

butter for greasing
1 cup hazelnuts, roughly chopped
$\frac{1}{2}$ cup whole almonds, roughly chopped
1$\frac{1}{3}$ cups mixed candied
   fruits, diced
$\frac{1}{4}$ tsp ground coriander
$\frac{3}{4}$ tsp ground cinnamon
$\frac{1}{4}$ tsp ground cloves
$\frac{1}{4}$ tsp grated nutmeg
$\frac{1}{2}$ cup flour
$\frac{1}{2}$ cup honey
generous 1 cup sugar
confectioners' sugar, for dusting
serves 12–14

1 Preheat the oven to 350°F. Grease an 8-in round cake pan with the butter. Line the base of the pan with parchment paper.

2 ▲ Spread the nuts on a baking tray and place in the oven for about 10 minutes, until lightly toasted. Remove and set aside. Lower the oven temperature to 300°F.

3 In a large mixing bowl combine the candied fruits, all the spices and the flour and stir together with a wooden spoon. Add the nuts and stir in thoroughly.

Cook's Tip

This will store in an airtight container for up to 2 weeks.

4 ▲ In a small heavy saucepan, stir together the honey and sugar and bring to a boil. Cook the mixture until it reaches 280°F on a sugar thermometer or when a small bit forms a hard ball when pressed between fingertips in ice water. Take care when doing this and use a spoon to remove a little mixture out of the pan for testing.

5 ▲ At this stage, immediately pour the sugar syrup into the dry ingredients and stir in well until evenly coated. Pour into the prepared pan. Dip a spoon into water and use the back of the spoon to press the mixture into the pan. Bake for 1 hour.

6 When ready, it will still feel quite soft but will harden as it cools. Cool completely in the pan and then turn out onto a serving plate. Dust with confectioners' sugar before serving.

Raisin and Walnut Bread

Pane di uva con noci

This bread is delicious with soup for a first course, or with salami, cheese and salad for lunch. It tastes good with jam and toasts extremely well when it is a day or two old.

Ingredients

2¾ cups flour
½ tsp salt
1 tbsp butter
1½ tsp active dry yeast
scant 1 cup golden raisins
½ cup walnuts, roughly chopped
melted butter, for brushing

makes 1 loaf

1 ▲ Sift the flour and salt into a bowl, cut in the butter with a knife, then stir in the yeast.

2 ▲ Gradually add ¾ cup tepid water to the flour mixture, stirring with a spoon at first, then gathering the dough together with your hands.

3 Turn the dough out onto a floured surface and knead for about 10 minutes, until smooth and elastic.

Cook's Tip

Active dried yeast is sold in envelopes at most supermarkets. It is a real boon for the busy cook because it eliminates the need to let the dough rise before shaping.

4 ▲ Knead the raisins and walnuts into the dough until they are evenly distributed. Shape into a rough oval, place on a lightly oiled baking sheet and cover with oiled plastic wrap. Let rise in a warm place for 1–2 hours, until doubled in bulk. Preheat the oven to 425°F.

5 Uncover the loaf and bake for 10 minutes, then reduce the oven temperature to 375°F and bake for 20–25 more minutes.

6 ▲ Transfer to a wire rack, brush with melted butter and cover with a dish towel. Cool before slicing.

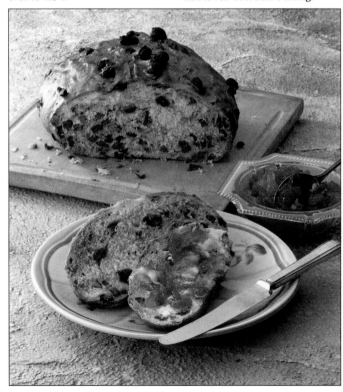

Chocolate Bread

Pane al cioccolato

In Italy it is the custom to serve this dessert bread as a snack with mascarpone or Gorgonzola cheese and a glass of red wine. Although this combination may sound unusual, it is really delicious. Chocolate bread also tastes good spread with butter, and is excellent toasted the next day for breakfast and served with butter and jam.

Ingredients

4 cups flour
½ tsp salt
2 tbsp butter
2 tbsp confectioners' sugar
2 tsp active dry yeast
2 tbsp cocoa powder
½ cup chocolate chips
melted butter, for brushing

makes 2 loaves

1 ▲ Sift the flour and salt into a bowl, cut in the butter with a knife, then stir in the sugar, yeast and cocoa powder.

2 Gradually add 1¼ cups of tepid water to the flour mixture, stirring with a spoon at first, then gathering the dough together with your hands.

3 ▲ Turn the dough out onto a floured surface and knead for about 10 minutes, until smooth and elastic.

4 ▲ Cut the dough in half and knead half the chocolate chips into each piece of dough until they are evenly distributed. Shape into rounds, place on lightly oiled baking sheets and cover with oiled plastic wrap. Let rise in a warm place for 1–2 hours, until the dough has doubled in bulk.

5 Preheat the oven to 425°F. Uncover the loaves and bake for 10 minutes, then reduce the oven temperature to 375°F and bake for 15–20 more minutes.

6 ▲ Place the loaves on a wire rack and brush liberally with butter. Cover with a dish towel and let cool.

Ricotta Cheesecake

Crostata di ricotta

Low-fat ricotta cheese is excellent for cheesecake fillings because it has a good, firm texture.

Here it is enriched with eggs and cream and enlivened with tangy orange and lemon rind to

make a Sicilian-style dessert.

Ingredients

2 cups low-fat ricotta cheese
$^1/_2$ cup heavy cream
2 eggs
1 egg yolk
$^1/_3$ cup confectioners' sugar
finely grated rind of 1 orange
finely grated rind of 1 lemon

For the pastry

1$^1/_2$ cups flour
3 tbsp sugar
pinch of salt
8 tbsp chilled butter, diced
1 egg yolk
serves 8

1 ▲ Make the pastry. Sift the flour, sugar and salt onto a cold work surface. Make a well in the center and put in the diced butter and egg yolk. Gradually work the flour into the diced butter and egg yolk, using your fingertips.

Variations

Add $^1/_3$–$^2/_3$ cup finely chopped candied peel to the filling in step 3 (or use $^1/_3$ cup chocolate chips). For a really rich dessert, you can add both candied peel and some grated plain chocolate.

2 ▲ Gather the dough together, reserve about a quarter for the lattice, then press the rest into a 9-in fluted tart pan with a removable base. Chill the pastry shell for 30 minutes.

3 ▲ Meanwhile, preheat the oven to 375°F and make the filling. Put all the ricotta, cream, eggs, egg yolk, sugar and orange and lemon rinds in a large bowl and beat until evenly mixed.

4 ▲ Prick the bottom of the pastry shell, then line with foil and fill with baking beans. Bake blind for 15 minutes, then transfer to a wire rack, remove the foil and beans and allow the tart shell to cool in the pan.

5 ▲ Spoon the cheese and cream filling into the pastry case and level the surface. Roll out the reserved dough and cut into strips. Arrange the strips on the top of the filling in a lattice pattern, sticking them in place with water.

6 Bake for 30–35 minutes, until golden and set. Transfer to a wire rack and let cool, then carefully remove the side of the pan, leaving the cheesecake on the pan base.

Jam Tart

Crostata di marmellata di frutta

Jam tarts are popular in northern Italy, traditionally decorated with pastry strips.

Ingredients

1³/₄ cups flour
pinch of salt
¹/₄ cup granulated sugar
¹/₂ cup butter or margarine, chilled
1 egg
¹/₄ tsp grated lemon zest
1¹/₄ cups fruit jam, such as
  raspberry, apricot or strawberry
1 egg, lightly beaten with 2 tbsp
  whipping cream, for glazing
serves 6–8

1 ▲ Make the pastry by placing the flour, salt and sugar in a mixing bowl. Using a pastry blender or two knives, cut the butter or margarine into the dry ingredients as quickly as possible until the mixture resembles coarse meal. Beat the egg with the lemon zest in a cup, and pour it over the flour mixture. Combine with a fork until the dough holds together. If it is too crumbly, mix in 1–2 tbsp of water.

2 Gather the dough into 2 balls, one slightly larger than the other, and flatten into discs. Wrap in parchment or waxed paper, and refrigerate for at least 40 minutes.

3 Lightly grease a shallow 9 in tart or pie pan, preferably with a removable bottom. Roll out the larger disc of pastry on a lightly floured surface to a thickness of about ¹/₈ inch.

4 Roll the pastry around the rolling pin and transfer to the prepared pan. Trim the edges evenly with a small knife. Prick the bottom with a fork. Refrigerate for at least 30 minutes.

5 ▲ Preheat the oven to 375°F. Spread the jam evenly over the base of the pastry. Roll out the remaining pastry.

6 ▲ Cut the pastry into strips about ¹/₂ inch wide using a ruler as a guide. Arrange them over the jam in a lattice pattern. Trim the edges of the strips even with the edge of the pan, pressing them lightly onto the pastry shell. Brush the pastry with the egg and cream glaze. Bake for about 35 minutes, or until the crust is golden brown. Allow to cool before serving.

Chocolate Nut Tart

Crostata di cioccolata con nocciole

This is a luxurious relative of the simple tart in the previous recipe.

Ingredients
1³/₄ cups flour
pinch of salt
¹/₄ cup granulated sugar
¹/₂ cup butter or margarine, chilled
1 egg
1 tbsp Marsala
¹/₄ tsp grated lemon zest
For the filling
1³/₄ cups amaretti
³/₄ cup blanched almonds
¹/₂ cup blanched hazelnuts
3 tbsp sugar
7 oz plain cooking chocolate
3 tbsp milk
¹/₄ cup butter
3 tbsp liqueur, such as amaretto,
  or brandy
2 tbsp light cream
serves 6–8

3 Grind the amaretti to crumbs in a food processor. Remove to a mixing bowl. Set 8 whole almonds aside, and place the rest in the food processor bowl with the hazelnuts and sugar. Grind to a medium texture. Add the nuts to the amaretti, and mix well.

4 ▲ Preheat the oven to 375°F. In a bowl set over a pan of simmering water, melt the chocolate with the milk and butter. Stir until smooth.

5 Pour the chocolate mixture into the ground amaretti and nuts, and mix well. Add the liqueur and cream.

6 ▲ Spread the chocolate and nut filling evenly in the pastry shell. Bake for about 35 minutes, or until the crust is golden brown and the filling has puffed up and is beginning to darken. Allow to cool to room temperature. Split the remaining almonds in half, and use them to decorate the tart.

1 ▲ Make the pastry as for the Jam Tart, beating the Marsala with the egg and lemon zest, and mixing into the dry ingredients.

2 Lightly grease a shallow 9 inch tart or pie pan, preferably with a removable bottom. Roll out the pastry on a lightly floured surface to a thickness of about ¹/₈ inch. Roll the pastry around the rolling pin and transfer to the prepared pan. Trim the edges evenly with a small knife. Prick the bottom with a fork. Refrigerate for at least 30 minutes.

Pine Nut Tart

Pinolata

Strange though it may seem, this traditional tart is an Italian version of the rustic Bakewell tart from Derbyshire in England.

Ingredients
8 tbsp butter, softened
generous ¹/₂ cup confectioners' sugar
1 egg
2 egg yolks
1¹/₄ cups ground almonds
1 cup pine nuts
¹/₄ cup seedless raspberry jam
confectioners' sugar, for dusting
whipped cream, to serve (optional)

For the pastry
1¹/₂ cups flour
¹/₃ cup confectioners' sugar
¹/₄ tsp baking powder
pinch of salt
8 tbsp chilled butter, diced
1 egg yolk
serves 8

1 ▲ Make the pastry. Sift the flour, sugar, baking powder and salt onto a cold work surface. Make a well in the center and put in the diced butter and egg yolk. Gradually work the flour into the butter and egg yolk, using your fingertips.

2 ▲ Gather the dough together, then press it into a 9-in fluted tart pan with a removable base. Chill for 30 minutes.

3 ▲ Meanwhile, make the filling. Cream the butter and sugar with an electric mixer until light and fluffy, then beat in the egg and egg yolks a little at a time, alternating them with the ground almonds. Beat in the pine nuts.

Cook's Tip
This pastry is too sticky to roll out, so simply mold it into the bottom and sides of the pan with your fingertips.

4 ▲ Preheat the oven to 325°F. Spread the jam over the pastry shell, then spoon in the filling. Bake for 30–35 minutes or until a skewer inserted in the center of the tart comes out clean.

5 Transfer to a wire rack and let cool, then carefully remove the side of the pan, leaving the tart on the pan base. Dust with confectioners' sugar and serve with whipped cream, if desired.

Baked Sweet Ravioli

Ravioli dolci al forno

These delicious sweet ravioli are made with a rich pastry flavored with lemon and filled

with the traditional ingredients used in Sicilian cassata.

Ingredients
2 cups flour
1/3 cup superfine sugar
8 tbsp butter
1 egg
1 tsp finely grated lemon rind
confectioners' sugar and grated
    chocolate, for sprinkling

For the filling
3/4 cup ricotta cheese
1/4 cup confectioners' sugar
3/4 tsp vanilla extract
1 medium egg yolk
1 tbsp mixed candied fruits or mixed
    citrus peel
1 oz dark chocolate, finely chopped or
    grated
1 small egg, beaten

serves 4

1 Put the flour and sugar into a food processor and, working on full speed, add the butter in pieces until fully worked into the mixture. With the food processor still running, add the egg and lemon rind. The mixture should form a dough that just holds together. Scrape the dough onto a sheet of plastic wrap, cover with another sheet, flatten and chill until needed.

2 ▲ To make the filling, push the ricotta through a sieve into a bowl. Stir in the sugar, vanilla extract, egg yolk, peel and chocolate until combined.

3 ▲ Remove the pastry from the refrigerator and let it come to room temperature. Divide the pastry in half and roll each half between sheets of plastic wrap to make strips, measuring 6 x 22 in. Preheat the oven to 350°F.

4 Arrange heaping spoonfuls of the filling in two rows along one of the pastry strips, ensuring there is at least 1 in clear space around each spoonful. Brush the pastry between the dollops of filling with beaten egg. Place the second strip of pastry on top and press down between each mound of filling to seal.

5 Using a 2¹/₂-in plain cookie cutter, cut around each mound of filling to make circular ravioli. Lift each one and, with your fingertips, seal the edges. Place the ravioli on a greased baking sheet and bake for 15 minutes, until golden brown. Serve warm sprinkled with confectioners' sugar and grated chocolate.

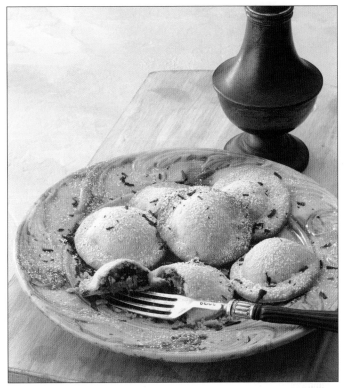

Chocolate Almond Cookies

Amaretti al cioccolato

This delicious variation on the classic Italian cookies includes cocoa powder, as well as the traditional almond flavoring.

Ingredients
1 cup blanched almonds
½ cup sugar
1 tbsp cocoa powder
2 tbsp confectioners' sugar
2 egg whites
pinch of cream of tartar
1 tsp almond extract
sliced almonds, to decorate
makes about 24

1 Preheat the oven to 350°F. Spread out the blanched almonds on a baking sheet and bake for 10–12 minutes, stirring occasionally until the almonds are golden brown. Remove the almonds from the oven and allow to cool.

2 Reduce the oven temperature to 325°F. Line one large or two small baking sheets with baking parchment.

Cook's Tip
If you prefer, you can toast the blanched almonds under a hot broiler. Spread them out in the broiler pan and cook for a few minutes, stirring them frequently so that they brown evenly. Make sure that the almonds are completely cold before processing them with the sugar.

3 ▲ Process the toasted almonds in a food processor with ¼ cup of the sugar until the almonds are finely ground, but not oily. Transfer to a mixing bowl, sift in the cocoa powder and confectioners' sugar, stir to blend and set aside.

4 ▲ In a large mixing bowl, beat the egg whites and cream of tartar until stiff peaks form. Sprinkle in the remaining sugar, a tablespoon at a time, beating well after each addition. Continue beating until the whites are glossy and stiff. Beat in the almond extract.

5 ▲ Sprinkle the almond sugar mixture over the top and gently fold into the beaten egg whites until just blended. Spoon the mixture into a large icing bag fitted with a plain ½ in nozzle. Pipe 1½ in rounds about 1 in apart on the prepared baking sheet. Press a sliced almond into the center of each.

6 ▲ Bake the cookies for about 12–15 minutes or until they appear crisp. Remove from the baking sheet using a spatula and transfer to a wire rack to cool completely. When cold, store in an airtight container.

Choux Pastries with Two Custards

Bigné alle due creme

Italian pastry shops are filled with displays of sweetly scented pastries such as these.

Ingredients
scant 1 cup water
$^1/_2$ cup butter
1in piece vanilla bean
pinch of salt
$1^1/_4$ cups flour
5 eggs
For the custard fillings
2oz semisweet chocolate
$1^1/_4$ cups milk
4 egg yolks
scant $^1/_3$ cup granulated sugar
generous $^1/_3$ cup flour
1 tsp pure vanilla extract
$1^1/_4$ cups whipping cream
unsweetened cocoa powder and
    confectioners' sugar, to garnish
makes about 48

1 ▲ Preheat the oven to 375°F. Heat the water with the butter, vanilla and salt. When the butter has melted, beat in the flour. Cook over low heat, stirring constantly, for about 8 minutes. Remove from the heat.

2 ▲ Mix in the eggs one at a time. Remove the vanilla bean.

3 ▲ Butter a flat cookie sheet. Using a pastry bag fitted with a round nozzle, squeeze the mixture out onto the tray in balls the size of small walnuts, leaving space between the rows. Bake for 20–25 minutes, or until the pastries are golden brown. Remove from the oven and allow to cool before filling.

4 ▲ Meanwhile, prepare the custard fillings. Melt the chocolate in the top half of a double boiler, or in a bowl set over a pan of simmering water. Heat the milk in a small saucepan, taking care not to let it boil.

~ VARIATION ~

The choux pastries may be filled with fresh whipped cream flavored with 1 tsp vanilla extract or 2–3 tbsp spirit such as brandy or rum. Mix well, spoon the cream into a pastry bag and proceed as in Step 6.

5 ▲ Beat the egg yolks with a wire whisk or electric beater. Gradually incorporate the sugar, and continue beating until the mixture is pale yellow. Beat in the flour. Beat in the hot milk very gradually, pouring it in through a strainer. When all the milk has been added, pour the mixture into a heavy medium pan, and bring to a boil. Simmer for 5–6 minutes, stirring constantly. Remove from the heat and divide the custard between two bowls. Add the melted chocolate to one, and stir the vanilla extract into the other. Allow to cool completely.

6 ▲ Whip the cream. Fold half of it carefully into each of the custards. Fill two pastry bags fitted with round nozzles with the custards. Fill half of the choux pastries with the chocolate custard, and the rest with the vanilla custard, making a little hole and piping the filling in through the side of each pastry. Dust the tops of the chocolate-filled pastries with cocoa powder, and the rest with confectioners' sugar. Serve immediately after filling.

Italian Almond Cookies

Biscotti

These lovely Italian cookies are partially baked, sliced to reveal a feast of mixed nuts, then baked again until crisp and golden. Traditionally they're served dipped in vin santo, a sweet dessert wine – perfect for rounding off an Italian meal.

Ingredients

¼ cup sweet butter,
  softened
½ cup sugar
1½ cups self-rising flour
¼ tsp salt
2 tsp baking powder
1 tsp ground coriander
finely grated rind of 1 lemon
½ cup polenta
1 egg, lightly beaten
2 tsp brandy or orange-flavored liqueur
½ cup unblanched almonds
½ cup shelled pistachio nuts

makes 24

1 Preheat the oven to 325ºF. Lightly grease a baking sheet. Cream together the butter and sugar using a wooden spoon until smooth.

2 ▲ Sift together the flour, salt, baking powder and ground coriander into the bowl with the creamed mixture. Add the lemon rind, polenta, egg and brandy or liqueur and mix together to make a soft dough.

Cook's Tip

Use a sharp, serrated knife to slice the cooled cookies, otherwise they will crumble.

3 ▲ Stir in the nuts until evenly combined. Halve the mixture. Shape each half into a flat sausage about 9 in long and 2½ in wide. Bake for about 30 minutes until risen and just firm. Remove from the oven.

4 ▲ When cool, cut each sausage diagonally into 12 thin slices. Return to the baking sheet and cook for another 10 minutes until crisp.

5 Transfer to a wire rack to cool completely. Store in an airtight tin for up to 1 week.

Hazelnut Bites
Nocciolini

Serve these sweet little nut cookies as petits fours with after-dinner coffee.

Ingredients

8 tbsp butter, softened
³/₄ cup confectioners' sugar, sifted
1 cup flour
³/₄ cup ground hazelnuts
1 egg yolk
blanched whole hazelnuts, to decorate
confectioners' sugar, to finish
makes about 26

1 ▲ Preheat the oven to 350°F. Line 3–4 baking sheets with parchment paper. Cream the butter and sugar with an electric mixer until light and fluffy.

2 ▲ Beat in the flour, ground hazelnuts and egg yolk until evenly mixed.

Cook's Tip

Don't worry that the cookies are still soft at the end of the baking time— they will harden as they cool.

3 ▲ Take a teaspoonful of the mixture at a time and shape it into a round with your fingers. Place the rounds well apart on the baking paper and press a whole hazelnut into the center of each one.

4 ▲ Bake the cookies, one tray at a time, for about 10 minutes or until golden brown, then transfer to a wire rack and sift over confectioners' sugar over them to cover. Let cool.

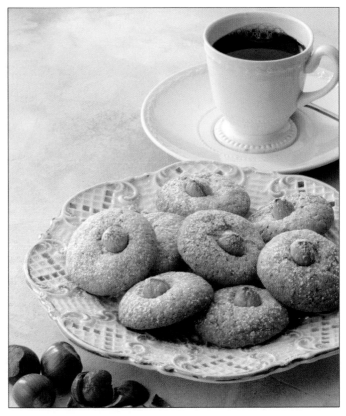

Golden Raisin Cornmeal Cookies   *Gialletti*

These little yellow cookies come from the Veneto region.

Ingredients
1/2 cup golden raisins
3/4 cup finely ground yellow cornmeal
1 1/2 cups plain flour
1 1/2 tsp baking powder
pinch of salt
1 cup butter
1 cup granulated sugar
2 eggs
1 tbsp Marsala or 1 tsp vanilla extract
makes about 48

1 Soak the golden raisins in a small bowl of warm water for 15 minutes. Drain. Preheat the oven to 350°F.

2 Sift the cornmeal and flour, the baking powder and the salt together into a bowl.

3 Cream the butter and sugar together until light and fluffy. Beat in the eggs, one at a time. Beat in the Marsala or vanilla extract.

4 ▲ Add the dry ingredients to the batter, beating until well blended. Stir in the golden raisins.

5 ▲ Drop heaped teaspoons of batter onto a greased cookie sheet in rows about 2 in apart. Bake for 7–8 minutes, or until the cookies are golden brown at the edges. Remove to a rack to cool.

Amaretti   *Amaretti*

These crisp almond cookies are often served with fruit-based or creamy desserts.

Ingredients
1 3/4 cups almonds
1 cup sugar
2 egg whites
1/2 tsp almond extract or 1 tsp vanilla extract
confectioners' sugar, for dusting
makes about 36

1 Preheat the oven to 325°F. Peel the almonds by dropping them into a pan of boiling water for 1–2 minutes. Drain. Rub the almonds in a cloth to remove the skins.

2 Place the almonds on a cookie sheet and let them dry out in the oven for 10–15 minutes without browning. Remove from the oven and allow to cool. Turn the oven off.

3 Finely grind the almonds with half of the sugar in a food processor.

4 ▲ Use an electric beater or wire whisk to beat the egg whites until they form soft peaks. Sprinkle half of the remaining sugar over them and continue beating until stiff peaks are formed. Gently fold in the remaining sugar, the vanilla and the almonds.

5 Spoon the almond mixture into a pastry bag with a smooth nozzle. Line a flat cookie sheet with baking parchment paper. Dust this with flour.

6 ▲ Pipe out the mixture in rounds the size of a walnut. Sprinkle lightly with the confectioners' sugar, and allow to stand for 2 hours. Near the end of this time, turn the oven on again and preheat to 350°F.

7 Bake the amaretti for 15 minutes, or until light golden. Remove from the oven and cool on a rack. When completely cool, the cookies may be stored in an airtight container.

Ladies' Kisses

Baci di dama

These old-fashioned Piedmontese cookies make pretty petits fours.

Ingredients
10 tbsp butter, softened
¹/₂ cup confectioners' sugar
1 egg yolk
¹/₂ tsp almond extract
1 cup ground almonds
1¹/₂ cups flour
2 ounces chocolate
makes 20

1 Cream the butter and sugar with an electric mixer until light and fluffy, then beat in the egg yolk, almond extract, ground almonds and flour until evenly mixed. Chill until firm, about 2 hours.

2 Preheat the oven to 325°F. Line 3–4 baking sheets with parchment paper.

3 ▲ Break off small pieces of dough and roll into balls with your hands, making 40 altogether. Place the balls on the baking sheets, spacing them out, as they will spread in the oven.

Cook's Tip
These cookies look extra dainty served in frilly petit four cases.

4 Bake the cookies for 20 minutes or until golden. Remove the baking sheets from the oven, lift off the paper with the cookies on, then place on wire racks. Let the cookies cool on the paper. Repeat with the remaining mixture.

5 ▲ When the cookies are cold, lift them off the paper. Melt the chocolate in a bowl over a pan of hot water. Sandwich the cookies in pairs, with the melted chocolate. Let cool and set before serving.

Tea Cookies

Pastine da the

These cookies are very quick and easy to make. If you don't want to pipe the mixture, simply spoon it onto the baking paper and press it down with a fork.

Ingredients
10 tbsp butter, softened
³/₄ cup confectioners' sugar, sifted
1 egg, beaten
a few drops of almond extract
2 cups flour
2–3 large pieces of candied peel
makes 20

Variation
Use 10 candied cherries instead of the candied peel. Cut them in half and press one half, cut-side down, into the center of each cookie.

1 Preheat the oven to 450°F. Line two baking sheets with non-stick baking paper.

2 Cream the butter and sugar with an electric mixer until light and fluffy, then beat in the egg, almond extract and flour until evenly mixed.

3 ▲ Spoon the mixture into a piping bag fitted with a star nozzle and pipe 10 rosette shapes on each of the baking sheets.

4 ▲ Cut the candied peel into small diamond shapes and press one diamond into the center of each cookie, to decorate. Bake for 5 minutes or until golden. Transfer the cookies on the baking paper to a wire rack and let cool. Lift the cookies off the paper when cool.

Index

Index

Index

Index

Index

Index

Index

Index

Index

Acknowledgements

Photographs are by William Adams-Lingwood, Amanda Heywood and Janine Hosegood (cut-outs) except the pictures on pages 6–9, which are by John Heseltine.